MW01012585

PRAISE FOR *THE RIGHT TO MAIM*

"Jasbir K. Puar's must-read book *The Right to Maim* revolutionizes the study of twenty-first-century war and biomedicine, offering a searingly impressive reconceptualization of disability, trans, and queer politics. Bringing together Middle East studies and American studies, global political economy and gendered conflict studies, this book's exciting power is its revelation of the incipient hegemony of maiming regimes. Puar's shattering conclusions draw upon rigorous and systematic empirical analysis, ultimately offering an enthralling vision for how to disarticulate disability politics from this maiming regime's dark power."
—PAUL AMAR, author of *The Security Archipelago: Human-Security States, Sexuality Politics, and the End of Neoliberalism*

"In signature style, Jasbir K. Puar takes readers across multiple social and textual terrains in order to demonstrate the paradoxical embrace of the politics of disability in liberal biopolitics. Puar argues that even as liberalism expands its care for the disabled, it increasingly debilitates workers, subalterns, and others who find themselves at the wrong end of neoliberalism. Rather than simply celebrating the progressive politics of disability, trans identity, and gay youth health movements, *The Right to Maim* shows how each is a complex interchange of the volatile politics of precarity in contemporary biopower."
—ELIZABETH A. POVINELLI, author of *Geontologies: A Requiem to Late Liberalism*

The Right to Maim

ANIMA

A SERIES EDITED BY MEL Y. CHEN AND JASBIR K. PUAR

The Right to Maim

Debility, Capacity, Disability

JASBIR K. PUAR

Duke University Press   Durham and London   2017

© 2017 Duke University Press. All rights reserved
Printed in the United States of America on acid-free paper ∞
Interior design by Courtney Leigh Baker
Cover design by Matthew Tauch
Typeset in Whitman and Gill Sans by Westchester Publishing Services

Cataloging-in-Publication Data is available from the Library of Congress.

ISBN 978-0-8223-6892-2 (hardcover : alk. paper)
ISBN 978-0-8223-6918-9 (pbk. : alk. paper)
ISBN 978-0-8223-7253-0 (ebook)

Cover art: Wangechi Mutu, *Howl,* 2006. Archival pigment print with
silkscreen on archival paper, 40 × 28 in. Courtesy of the artist.

CONTENTS

PREFACE: HANDS UP, DON'T SHOOT!

The intensification of the writing of this book, and the formulation of "the right to maim," its most urgent political theoretical contribution, began the summer of 2014. This was the summer police shot Michael Brown in Ferguson, Missouri, and the summer of Operation Protective Edge, the fifty-one-day Israeli siege of Gaza. Organizers protesting these seemingly disparate events began drawing connections, tracing the material relationships between the Israeli occupation of Palestine and the militarization of police in Ferguson, from the training of U.S. law enforcement by the Israeli state to the tweeting of advice from Palestinians on how to alleviate tear gas exposure. Descriptions of the militarized containment of civilians in Ferguson echoed those of the settler colonial occupation of Palestine. It was not long before the "Ferguson to Gaza" frame starting taking hold as an organizing rubric. Ferguson-to-Gaza forums sought to correlate the production of settler space, the vulnerability and degradation of black and brown bodies, the demands for justice through transnational solidarities, and the entangled workings of settler colonialism in the United States and Israel. The comparisons, linkages, and affective resonances between Ferguson and Gaza were not perfectly aligned, and they did not always yield immediate alliances. But these efforts were convivial in their mutual resistance to the violent control of populations via targeted bodily assaults, and reflected desires for reciprocating, intersectional, and co-constituted assemblages of solidarity.

One striking aspect of the connective tissue between Ferguson and Gaza involved security practices mining the relationship between disability and death. Police brutality in the United States toward black men and women in particular showed a definitive tendency to aim for death, often shooting numerous bullets into an unarmed, subjugated, and yet supposedly threatening body—overkill, some might call it. Why were there seemingly so few attempts to minimize the loss of life? The U.S. security state enacted powerful sovereign entitlements even as it simultaneously claimed tremendous vulnerability. The police were merely "doing their job," a dangerous, life-threatening one. This calculation of risk is the founding rationalization for the impunity of "the right to kill" wielded by U.S. law enforcement.

The might of Israel's military—one of the most powerful in the world—is built upon the claim of an unchanging ontological vulnerability and precarity, driven by history, geopolitics, and geography. Alongside the "right to kill," I noted a complementary logic long present in Israeli tactical calculations of settler colonial rule—that of creating injury and maintaining Palestinian populations as perpetually debilitated, and yet alive, in order to control them. The Israeli Defense Forces (IDF) have shown a demonstrable pattern over decades of sparing life, of shooting to maim rather than to kill. This is ostensibly a humanitarian practice, leaving many civilians "permanently disabled" in an occupied territory of destroyed hospitals, rationed medical supplies, and scarce resources. This pattern appeared again during Operation Protective Edge; the number of civilian casualties was reported daily and justified through the logic of collateral damage, while the number of injuries was rarely commented upon and never included in reflections of the daily toll of the siege.

Shooting to maim in order not to kill might appear as minor relief given the proclivity to shoot to kill. Why indeed were so many unarmed black victims of police brutality riddled with scores of bullets? But oscillations between the right to kill and the right to maim are hardly haphazard or arbitrary. The purportedly humanitarian practice of sparing death by shooting to maim has its biopolitical stakes not through the right to life, or even letting live, but rather through the logic of "will not let die." Both are part of the deliberate debilitation of a population—whether through the sovereign right to kill or its covert attendant, the right to maim—and are key elements in the racializing biopolitical logic of security. Both are mobilized to make power visible on the body. Slated for death or slated for debilitation—both are forms of the racialization of individuals and populations that liberal (disability) rights frameworks, advocating for social accommodation, access, acceptance, pride, and empowerment, are unable to account for, much less disrupt.

Fast-forward to the summer of 2016. July 10, 2016, was the fourth day of Black Lives Matter protests going on in New York City, as well as in many other locations across the United States. During the previous week, the police shootings of Philando Castile in St. Paul, Minnesota, and Alton Sterling in Baton Rouge, Louisiana, had galvanized protests all around the country. The shooting and killing of five police officers during a Black Lives Matter rally in Dallas had only amplified the lines of battle between civilians and law enforcement. The June 12 shooting in an Orlando queer club magnified a homonationalist discourse that posits Muslim homophobes as the primary danger to queer liberals of all colors, resulting in increased policing of LGBTQ pride events during the summer. Bombings by ISIS in the previous month had targeted Nice, Istanbul, and Dhaka. Protesters started gathering at Standing Rock to fight the Dakota Access Pipeline. There were more shootings of black bodies to come.

On this particular day, the main Black Lives Matter protest in New York City was happening in Times Square. Not far from this location, the Second Annual Disability Pride parade, marketed as a festival and celebration, was marching on Broadway from Union Square to Madison Square Park. International in scope, the parade included veterans and actors involved in the development of the United Nations Convention on the Rights of Persons with Disabilities. I was in a part of Manhattan equidistant from both activities, one being an action and the other being an event. The relationship between the two confounded me. I recalled that on June 24, Black Lives Matter withdrew from the San Francisco Pride Parade, citing fear of increased police presence in the parade post-Orlando. On July 3, Black Lives Matter, selected as the Toronto Pride Parade's Honored Group, brought the parade to a complete halt in order to demand a series of conditions, including banning police from marching in the parade. I was struck by the discord between an increasingly visible disability empowerment discourse in human rights platforms, cultural productions, and public discourse, and the divestment of Black Lives Matter from narratives of pride, with dominant messaging at Black Lives Matter actions including: "Hands up, don't shoot!" and "I can't breathe!" I remained in the middle, perplexed. This is not an either/or situation, but neither is it resolved by the commonsense logic of both/and. Disability empowerment and pride are part of rights discourses even as expressions of maiming, debilitation, and disabling are central to economies and vocabularies of violence and exploitation.

What kinds of biopolitical fissures produce a spectacle of disability empowerment and pride mere blocks from a movement protesting the targeted debilitation of an entire racialized population, contesting the production

FIG. PREF.1. Peoples Power Assemblies providing powerful counternarratives at the NYC Disability Pride March, July 10, 2016.

of disability that is central to state securitization practices? The New York City branch of the Peoples Power Assemblies (PPA), a part of the Movement for Black Lives, organizes a presence yearly at the Disability Pride March. Participants carry Black Disabled Lives Matter banners, signs that say "Stop the War on Black America" and "Support the Black Lives Matter Movement," and placards noting that more than 50 percent of police shootings of black bodies involve individuals with disabilities. It is a direct action rather than a pride celebration, one demanding attention to both targeting of the disabled and targeting to disable, with distinctly different terms from empowerment and pride rhetorics. As PPA member Colin Ashley put it, "Those on the sidelines either get it automatically and really cheer, or seem completely mystified as to why we would be in the march. We feel it is necessary to go in order to disrupt the normative messaging."[1] For its part, Black Lives Matter has been clear that people with disabilities are both survivors of injustice and also part of their assembly. Alicia Garcia writes that "Black Lives Matter affirms the lives of Black queer and trans folks, disabled folks, Black-undocumented folks, folks with records, women, and all Black lives along the gender spectrum. It centers those that have been marginalized within Black liberation movements. It is a tactic to (re)build

FIG. PREF.2. The location where Jamar Clark was killed by Minneapolis police on November 15, 2015, following the March 29, 2016, decision by Hennepin County attorney Mike Freeman not to charge the officers involved in the shooting. Photo by Tony Webster.

the Black liberation movement."[2] And yet, the Movement for Black Lives received important feedback, specifically from the Harriet Tubman Collective, "A Collective of Black Deaf & Black Disabled organizers, community builders, activists, dreamers, lovers striving for radical inclusion and collective liberation," about the absence of any acknowledgment of or discussion about the impact of disability in black communities in their six-point platform released in August 2016.[3] The intervention from the Harriet Tubman Collective not only highlights ableist frameworks of resistance; it also raises questions about how, in this time of political upheaval and dissent, meetings, protests, and actions could become more accessible to people with varying debilities, capacities, and disabilities.

Today the solidarity pathways between Black Lives Matter and Free Palestine are rhizomatic and bountiful.[4] Pro-Palestinian antiwar activists will join PPA next year, protesting both the targeting of disabled Palestinians by the IDF and the targeting to debilitate, part of a biopolitics not of disability alone but a biopolitics of debilitation. I contend that the term "debilitation" is distinct from the term "disablement" because it foregrounds the slow wearing down of populations instead of the event of becoming disabled. While the latter concept creates and hinges on a narrative of before and after for individuals who will eventually be identified as disabled, the former comprehends those bodies that are sustained in a perpetual state of debilitation precisely through foreclosing the social, cultural, and political translation to disability. It is this tension, the tension between *targeting the disabled* and *targeting to debilitate*, the tension between being and becoming, this is the understated alliance that I push in this project. The first presumes a legitimate identification with disability that is manifest through state, market, and institutional recognition, if not subjective position: I call myself disabled. But this cannot be the end of the story, because what counts as a disability is already overdetermined by "white fragility" on one side and the racialization of bodies that are expected to endure pain, suffering, and injury on the other.[5] As such, the latter is an understanding of biopolitical risk: to extrapolate a bit from Claudia Rankine's prose: "I am in death's position."[6] And to expand: I am in debility's position.

The biopolitics of debilitation is not intended to advocate a facile democratization of disability, as if to rehash the familiar cant that tells us we will all be disabled if we live long enough. In fact, depending on where we live, what resources we have, what traumas we have endured, what color our skin is, what access we have to clean water, air, and decent food, what type of health care we have, what kind of work we do . . . we will not all be disabled. Some of us will simply not live long enough, embedded in a distribution of risk already factored into the calculus of debilitation. Death's position. Others, at risk because of seeming risky, may encounter disability in ways that compound the debilitating effects of biopolitics.

DEBILITY, CAPACITY, DISABILITY

Disability is not a fixed state or attribute but exists in relation to assemblages of capacity and debility, modulated across historical time, geopolitical space, institutional mandates, and discursive regimes. The globalization of disability as an identity through human rights discourses contributes to a standardization of bodily usefulness and uselessness that discounts not only the specificity of location but also the ways bodies exceed or defy identities and subjects. The non-disabled/disabled binary traverses social, geographic, and political spaces. The distinctions or parameters between disabled and non-disabled bodies shift historically, as designations between productivity, vagrancy, deviancy, illness, and labor market relations have undergone transformations from subsistence work to waged labor to hypercapitalist modes of surplus accumulation and neoliberal subject formation. They shift geographically, as varied cultural, regional, and national conceptualizations of bodily habitations and metaphysics inhabit corporeal relations differently and sometimes irreconcilably, and issues of environmental racism are prominent. They shift infrastructurally, as a wheelchair-accessible elevator becomes a completely altered vehicle of mobility, one that masks various capacities to climb stairs, in many parts of the world where power outages are a daily, if not hourly, occurrence. They shift legally, administratively, and legislatively, as rights-bearing subjects are formed and dismantled in response to health care and insurance regimes, human rights discourses, economic opportunism, and the uneven distribution of resources, medical supplies, and basic care. They shift scientifically, as prosthetic technologies of capacity, from wheelchairs to cell phones to DNA testing to steroids, script and rescript what a body can, could, or should do. And they shift representationally, as discourses of multicultural diversity and plurality absorb "difference" into regimes of visibility that then reorganize sites of marginalization into subjects of privilege, indeed privileged disabled subjects.

In *The Right to Maim: Debility, Capacity, Disability*, I think through how and why bodies are perceived as debilitated, capacitated, or often simultaneously both. I mobilize the term "debility" as a needed disruption (but also expose it as a collaborator) of the category of disability and as a triangulation of the ability/disability binary, noting that while some bodies may not be recognized as or identify as disabled, they may well be debilitated, in part by being foreclosed access to legibility and resources as disabled. Relatedly, some bodies may well be disabled but also capacitated. I want to be clear here: I am not diluting or diffusing the identity rubrics of disability by suggesting all bodies are disabled to some extent or another, or by smoothing disability into a continuum of debility and capacity. Quite the opposite; I am arguing that the three vectors, capacity, debility, and disability, exist in a mutually reinforcing constellation, are often overlapping or coexistent, and that debilitation is a necessary component that both exposes and sutures the non-disabled/disabled binary. As Christina Crosby rightly points out, "The challenge is to represent the ways in which disability is articulated with debility, without having one disappear into the other."[7] I would add that the biopolitical management of disability entails that the visibility and social acceptance of disability rely on and engender the obfuscation and in fact deeper proliferation of debility.

In her work on bodily impaired miners in Botswana who do not necessarily articulate their plight in relation to disability, Julie Livingston uses the term "debility," defined broadly to encompass "experiences of chronic illness and senescence, as well as disability per se."[8] She demonstrates that historically many bodily infirmities "were not regarded as disabilities: indeed they were 'normal' and in some cases even expected impairments."[9] I take up Livingston's intervention with an important refinement: debility in my usage is not meant to encompass disability. Rather, I mobilize debility as a connective tissue to illuminate the possibilities and limits of disability imaginaries and economies. Debilitation as a normal consequence of laboring, as an "expected impairment," is not a flattening of disability; rather, this framing exposes the violence of what constitutes "a normal consequence." The category of disability is instrumentalized by state discourses of inclusion not only to obscure forms of debility but also to actually produce debility and sustain its proliferation. In a literal sense, caretakers of people with disabilities often come from chronically disenfranchised populations that endure debilities themselves. Conceptually, state, medical, and other forms of recognition of disability may shroud debilities and forms of slow death while also effacing the quotidian modalities of wide-scale debilitation so prevalent due to capitalist exploitation and imperialist expansion. In my usage, debility signals precisely the temporospatial frame eclipsed by toggling between exceptionalizing disability and exceptional disability: the endemic. Relational forms of capitalism, care, and racialization inform an assemblage of disability to a constellation of debilities and capacities. If, in one definition, disability becomes a privileged category by virtue of state recognition,[10] another definition of disability may well be that body or that subject that can aspire both economically and emotionally to wellness, empowerment, and pride through the exceptionalized status it accrues while embedded within unexceptional and, in fact endemic, debility. The compounding of disability and poverty as a field of debilitation is certainly happening in the era of Donald Trump, whose efforts to completely eliminate any whiff of socialized medicine are only really remarkable because they definitively expose the actual scale of disregard for human life, having blown so far open so quickly. Access to health care may well become the defining factor in one's relationship to the non-disabled/disabled dichotomy.

Debility is thus a crucial complication of the neoliberal transit of disability rights. Debility addresses injury and bodily exclusion that are endemic rather than epidemic or exceptional, and reflects a need for rethinking overarching structures of working, schooling, and living rather than relying on rights frames to provide accommodationist solutions. Challenging liberal disability rights frames, debility not only elucidates what is left out of disability imaginaries and rights politics; it also illuminates the constitutive absences necessary for capacitating discourses of disability empowerment, pride, visibility, and inclusion to take shape. Thus, I argue, disability and debility are not at odds with each other. Rather, they are necessary supplements in an economy of injury that claims and promotes disability empowerment at the same time that it maintains the precarity of certain bodies and populations precisely through making them available for maiming.

In a context whereby four-fifths of the world's people with disabilities are located in what was once hailed as the "global south," liberal interventions are invariably infused with certitude that disability should be reclaimed as a valuable difference—the difference of the Other—through rights, visibility, and empowerment discourses—rather than addressing how much debilitation is caused by global injustice and the war machines of colonialism, occupation, and U.S. imperialism. Assemblages of disability, capacity, and debility are elements of the biopolitical control of populations that foreground risk, prognosis, life chances, settler colonialism, war impairment, and capitalist exploitation. My analysis centralizes disability rights as a capacitating frame that recognizes some disabilities at the expense of other disabilities that do not fit the respectability and empowerment models of disability progress—what David Mitchell and Sharon Snyder term the "biopolitics of disability."[11] But the normalization of disability as an empowered status purportedly recognized by the state is not contradicted by, but rather is produced through, the creation and sustaining of debilitation on a mass scale. Debilitation is not a by-product of the operation of biopolitics but an intended result, functioning both as a disruption of the non-disabled/disabled binary—as an in-between space—and as a supplement to disability, that which shadows and often overlaps with disability. I therefore do not offer debility as an identity; it is instead a form of massification. My alternative conceptualization of the biopolitics of debilitation not only refers to the remaindering of what the liberal inclusion of disability fails to fully embrace, but also points to the forms of violent debilitation of those whose inevitable injuring is assumed by racial capitalism. I therefore seek to connect disability, usually routed through a conceptual frame of identification, and debilitation, a practice of rendering populations available for statistically likely injury.

WHY BIOPOLITICS?

The Right to Maim situates disability as a register of biopolitical population control, one that modulates which bodies are hailed by institutions to represent the professed progress made by liberal rights–bearing subjects. As with *Terrorist Assemblages*, this book is largely about what happens after certain liberal rights are bestowed, certain thresholds or parameters of success are claimed to have been reached: What happens when "we" get what "we" want? In other words, how is it that we have come to this historical juncture where we can or must talk about "(white) privilege," and "disability" together? But my argument also makes a critical intervention into the literatures of and scholarship on biopolitics, which have been less likely to take up issues of disability and debility. Michel Foucault's foundational formulation hinges on all the population measures that enable some forms of living and inhibit others: birthrates, fertility, longevity, disease, impairment, toxicity, productivity. In other words, these irreducible metrics of biopolitics are also metrics of debility and capacity. Biopolitics deployed through its neoliberal guises is a capacitation machine; biopolitics seeks capacitation for some as a liberal rationale (in some cases) or foil for the debilitation of many others. It is, in sum, an ableist mechanism that debilitates.

Biopolitics as a conceptual paradigm can thus be read as a theory of debility and capacity. Addressing disability directly forces a new, discrete component into the living/dying pendulum that forms most discussions of biopolitics: the living dead, death worlds, necropolitics, slow death, life itself. These frames presume death to be the ultimate assault, transgression, or goal, and the biopolitical end point or opposite of life. I am arguing that debilitation and the production of disability are in fact biopolitical ends unto themselves, with moving neither toward life nor toward death as the aim. This is what I call "the right to maim": a right expressive of sovereign power that is linked to, but not the same as, "the right to kill." Maiming is a source of value extraction from populations that would otherwise be disposable. The right to maim exemplifies the most intensive practice of the biopolitics of debilitation, where maiming is a sanctioned tactic of settler colonial rule, justified in protectionist terms and soliciting disability rights solutions that, while absolutely crucial to aiding some individuals, unfortunately lead to further perpetuation of debilitation.

In *The Right to Maim*, I focus less on an important project of disability rights and disability studies, which is to refute disability as lack, as inherently undesirable, and as the sign, evidence, or fetish of injustice and victimhood. I am not sidestepping this issue. Rather, I centralize the quest for justice to situate what material conditions of possibility are necessary for such positive reenvisionings of disability to flourish, and what happens when those conditions are not available. My goal here is to examine how disability is *produced*, how certain bodies and populations come into biopolitical being through having greater risk to become disabled than others. The difference between disability and debility that I schematize is not derived from expounding upon and contrasting phenomenological experiences of corporeality, but from evaluating the violences of biopolitical risk and metrics of health, fertility, longevity, education, and geography.

Disability studies scholars such as Nirmala Erevelles and Christopher Bell have insistently pointed out the need in disability studies for intersectional analyses in order to disrupt the normative (white, male, middleclass, physically impaired) subjects that have historically dominated the field.[12] The epistemic whiteness of the field is no dirty secret.[13] Part of how white centrality is maintained is through the policing of disability itself: what it is, who or what is responsible for it, how one lives it, whether it melds into an overarching condition of precarity of a population or is significant as an exceptional attribute of an otherwise fortunate life. These normative subjects cohere not only in terms of racial, class, and gendered privilege; they also tend toward impairments that are thought to be discernible, rather than cognitive and intellectual disabilities, chronic pain conditions like fibromyalgia or migraines, and depression.

The (largely unmarked) Euro-American bias of disability studies has had to confront itself, as the production of most of the world's disability happens through colonial violence, developmentalism, war, occupation, and the disparity of resources—indeed, through U.S. settler colonial and imperial occupations, as a sign of the global reach of empire.[14] In 2006, Livingston noted that "while four-fifths of the world's disabled persons live in developing countries, there is a relative dearth of humanities and social science scholarship exploring disability in non-Western contexts."[15] The same cannot be said ten years later. Crucial work now exists in southern disability studies; the relation of disability to U.S. incarceration, settler colonialism, and imperialism; and a systemic critique of the military-industrial complex and its debilitating global expanse.[16] The reproduction of this violence through neoliberal biomedical circuits of capital ensures that human rights regimes impose definitions about what disability is, creating evaluations and judgments, and distributes resources unevenly with effects that reorganize and/or reiterate orderings and hierarchies.[17]

Further to this project of unmooring disability from its hegemonic referents, critical ethnic studies, indigenous studies, and postcolonial studies have long been elaborating the debilitating effects of racism, colonialism, exploitative industrial growth, and environmental toxicities. Yet these literatures, because they may not engage the identity rubric of the subject position of the disabled person, are not often read as scholarship on disability.[18] As such, I seek here to connect critical race theory and transnational and postcolonial theory to disability studies scholarship. From the vantage of these interdisciplinary fields, disability is everywhere and yet, for all sorts of important reasons, not claimed as such. Many bodies might not be hailed as disabled but certainly are not awash in the privileges of being able-bodied either. This project is thus less interested in what disability is (or is not), less interested in adding to the registers of disability—for example, including people of color with disabilities—and more driven by the question: what does disability as a concept do? The stigmatization of bodily difference, racialized bodily difference, often understood as bodily defect, is already at the core of how populations come to be in the first place. My project refuses to reify racialization as defect but rather asks what other conceptual alternatives are available besides being relegated to defect or its dichotomous counterpart, embracing pride.

The Right to Maim is absorbed with excavating the chunkiness of power more so than the subtleties of navigating it. That is to say that assemblages can get stuck, blocked, frozen, and instrumentalized. Stories of dividuality are stories of control societies. Rather than assuming a corrective stance, I am interested in contributing to and expanding the critical lexicon, vocabulary, and conceptual apparatuses of biopolitical inquiry on disability, especially for bodies and populations that may fall into neither disability nor ability, but challenge and upturn these distinctions altogether. Throughout the text, multiple relationships of disciplinary, control, and sovereign power are central to my analyses. Detailing the interface of technologies of discipline and control makes the case for multiplying the relations of the two beyond teleological or geographic deterministic mappings. While the rise of digital forms gives control an anchoring periodization and geospatial rationale, a reliance on this narrative obscures the ongoingness of discipline and the brutal exercise of sovereign power, often cloaked in humanitarian, democratic, or life preservationist terms.

Traversing a number of contemporary political and social issues, my elaboration of debilitation as potentiating capacitation is expounded throughout the book: an examination of the spate of "queer suicides" and the "It Gets Better" response that occurred in the fall of 2010, foregrounding queer (theory) as a capacitation machine; the coalitional potential of trans people and people with disabilities, examining the array of access, delimitation, and foreclosure that trans bodies have in relation to discourses and alliances with disability, the medical-industrial complex, and the recapacitation of whiteness that strategic manipulations of embodiment might afford; Israel's complex program of rehabilitation through the debilitation of Palestinian life and land; the "rehabilitation" of the Israeli state as part of a biopolitical assemblage of control that instrumentalizes a spectrum of capacities and debilities for the use of the occupation of Palestine; the role of targeted debilitation whereby Israel manifests an implicit claim to the right to maim and debilitate Palestinian bodies and environments as a form of biopolitical control and as central to a scientifically authorized humanitarian economy. The framing of the right to maim haunts the book throughout, until it reaches its climactic and most forceful articulation in the final chapter on debilitation as a biopolitical end point unto itself. Observations from time spent in occupied East Jerusalem and the West Bank in January 2016 underscore the effects of the collision between disability rights practices and discourses, largely generated by international nongovernmental organizations, and the reality of the occupation as the primary producer of debility.

WHEN WE BREATHE

In a series in the *New York Times* on "people living with disabilities," feminist disability studies scholar Rosemarie Garland-Thomson wonders why pride movements for people with disabilities "have not gained the same sort of traction in the American consciousness" as the pride movements of "women, gay people, racial minorities, and other groups." Mentioning

FIG. PREF.3. ADAPT activists demonstrating for accessible transportation in Atlanta, Georgia, October 1990. Photo courtesy of Tom Olin.

Black Lives Matter and the LGBTQ rights movement as examples of this traction, she responds to her musings: "One answer is that we have a much clearer collective notion of what it means to be a woman or an African American, gay or transgender person than we do of what it means to be disabled."[19] There is perhaps misrecognition of Black Lives Matter as a "pride" movement, not to mention that at an earlier moment in history, the disability rights movement often marked itself as both intertwined with and following in the path of the black civil rights movement.[20] Analogies between disability and race, gender, and sexuality tend to obfuscate biopolitical realities, as Garland-Thomson's clunky list of identifications attests. Movements need to be intersectional, says Angela Davis, and the rapid uptake of this seasoned observation is invigorating and hopeful.[21] This invocation of intersectional movements should not leave us intact with ally models but rather create new assemblages of accountability, conspiratorial lines of flight, and seams of affinity.

In the midst of the Movement for Black Lives, the fight against the Dakota Access Pipeline, the struggle for socialized health care in the United States, the demand to end U.S. imperial power in the Middle East (Israel,

FIG. PREF.4. The Palestine contingent at the Millions March, New York City, December 2014. The ends of the banner display the pattern of the Palestinian keffiyeh. The Washington Square Arch is visible in the background. Photo courtesy of Direct Action Front for Palestine. Reprinted with artist's permission.

Afghanistan, Iraq, Syria, Yemen), what constitutes the able body is ever evolving, and its apparent referents are ever shrinking. What is an able body in this context? What is a non-disabled body, and is it the same as an able body? Layers of precarity and vulnerability to police brutality, reckless maiming and killing, deprivation, and destruction of resources that are daily features of living for some populations must not be smoothed over by hailing these bodies as able-bodied if they do not have or claim to be a person(s) with a disability. In the wise words of disability studies scholar and prison abolitionist Liat Ben-Moshe, "It does not matter if people identify as disabled or not."[22] "Hands up, don't shoot!" is not a catchy slogan that emerges from or announces able-bodied populations. Rather, this common Black Lives Matter chant is a revolutionary call for redressing the debilitating logics of racial capitalism. It is a compact sketch of the frozen black body, rendered immobile by systemic racism and the punishment doled out for not transcending it. It is the story of a Palestinian resister shot dead for wielding a knife (if that) against an IDF solider who has the full backing of the world's military might. "I can't breathe!" captures the suffocation of chokeholds on movement in Gaza and the West Bank as it does the violent forces of restraint meted out through police brutality. "Hands up, don't shoot!" and "I can't breathe!" are, in fact, disability justice rally cries.

The Right to Maim therefore does not seek to answer the question, where is our disability pride movement? Instead, it hopes to change the conversation to one that challenges the presumption that the distinction between who is disabled and who is not should fuel a pride movement. I explore if and how this binary effaces the biopolitical production of precarity and (un)livability that runs across these identities. The project, then, is not just one that hopes to contribute to intersectional movement building, though let me insist that this is crucial from the outset. That is to say, Black Lives Matter and the struggle to end the Israeli occupation of Palestine are not only movements "allied" with disability rights, nor are they only distinct disability justice issues. Rather, I am motivated to think of these fierce organizing practices collectively *as a disability justice movement itself*, as a movement that is demanding an end to so many conditions of precaritization that debilitate many populations. At our current political conjuncture, Black Lives Matter, the Palestinian solidarity movement, the protest against the Dakota Access Pipeline to protect sacred grounds and access to water: these are some of the movements that are leading the way to demand livable lives for all. These movements may not represent the most appealing or desired versions of disability pride. But they are movements anchored, in fact, in the lived experiences of debilitation, implicitly contesting the right to maim, and imagining multiple futures where bodily capacities and debilities are embraced rather than weaponized.

ACKNOWLEDGMENTS

This is a book first and foremost about biopolitics. It is a continuation of thinking about many of the issues raised in *Terrorist Assemblages*, a text that was fortunate enough to garner several unexpected readerships. Noted disability studies scholars Robert McRuer and David Mitchell offered expansive re-readings of the "upright" homonationalist citizen, elegantly wedding conceptions of "ablenationalism" and "crip nationalism" to homonationalism and expanding its frame considerably. The other major readership that invited me into new directions was that of scholars of Middle Eastern studies. I welcomed the solicitation of *Terrorist Assemblages* into these conversations and worked diligently to foster the kinds of inter- and transdisciplinary connections that I believe are the payoff of the risks that such frames allow. As such, this scholarship is active, insofar as I have attempted to grapple with reception, responses, and events as they have emerged. For quite some time I thought I was writing two distinct books, one on racism as chronic debilitation that posed a challenge to non-disabled/disabled binaries, the other on settler colonial occupation and sexuality in Palestine. Where and how these two projects became one is evident, I believe, in the manner in which this book unfolds and in the productive tensions between abstraction and location, intellectual analysis and political commitment (should those even be fantasized as separable). The effort herein to bring together conceptual impulses typically rendered distinct, dichotomous even, signals the main political import of this work. Moreover it seemed necessary to write a book marking the limits of Euro-American framings of disability while also providing concepts to spatialize the relationality of absence to presence and actually attending in some small way to alleviating the absence itself. Through this process, it is now hard to imagine ever conceiving of this book as two stand-alone projects. This fusion or juxtapositioning or assemblage here—call it what you will—is one effort to think through coexisting scales of loss and privilege, of loss as privilege, and of the unevenness of slow death across different populations and for different bodies. For the sake of brevity, I have kept my thank-yous short, for it would be impossible to acknowledge all of the many people whose paths I crossed during the eight years of writing this book. Words big and small, some piercing, some grazing—all of them have had impact.

I owe tremendous thanks to chosen kin for buoying me through the year of 2016 and what became a truly transformative, heart-altering experience: my fellow fierce Jersey girl Jennifer Doyle; patient advocate and interlocutor extraordinaire Julie Livingston; a true life companion Patricia Clough; coauthor and partner in crime Maya Mikdashi; HN Lukes, funniest accomplice in convivial thought; my Palestine GF Roya Rastegar; Paul Amar, a four-continent comrade; my gateway drug to Lebanon, Rasha Moumneh; the brilliant and politically spot-on Sherene Seikaly; longtime collaborator and dance partner Amit Rai; fellow Chelsea girl Amber Musser; my dearest graduate school friend and fantastic flamenco dancer Marisa Belausteguigoitia; Catherine Zimmer, whose wit and hilarity make everything better; longtime New York City confidante Christina Hanhardt; Chase Joynt, who is equal parts brilliant, funny, and fearless; and Chucho, my quirky little furry interspecies life partner.

My special love always to Rebecca Coleman; we continue to grow together in surprising and delightful ways, and I am very glad to be in life with you.

Huge gratitude goes to my incredible sister, Kimpreet K. Puar. I am so lucky that she is a steady presence in life, time after time, handling major events with aplomb and smart humor. And thanks also to my parents, whose political pragmatism and dry, jaded, nonplussed responses to explosive global events ("what did you expect?"; "yes he is a fascist") keep me grounded (and astounded).

I thank my colleagues in the Department of Women's and Gender Studies; the Social Text Collective; the American University of Beirut, where I was fortunate to hold the Edward Said Chair for one year; and Cornell University, where I had a fellowship at the Society for the Humanities. I am grateful as well to be part of several spaces that enrich my life well outside of academia: the Audre Lorde Project, Decolonize This Place, and Palestine solidarity organizing networks in New York City and nationally.

Many helped at various stages of conceiving and writing this book, and/or hosted me to present material from it (I know there are people, probably many, whom I have not remembered to acknowledge, and for this I ask your forgiveness): Aeyal Gross, Aimee Bahng, Anjali Arondekar (huge pyaar), Ann Pellegrini, Camille Robcis, Colin Ashley, Dana Luciano, David Eng, David Leonard, David Mitchell, Ed Cohen, El Glasberg, Geeta Patel, Gil Hochberg, Hentyle Yapp, J. Kehaulani Kauanui, Jack Halberstam, Jody Dean, John Andrews, Jordy Rosenberg, the late José Esteban Muñoz, Judith Butler, Kara Keeling, Karen Tongson, Kateřina Kolářová, Kyla Schuller, Lauren Berlant, Lisa Hajjar, Lezlie Frye, Margaret Shildrick, Martin Manalansan, Neel Ahuja, Nirmala Erevelles, Omar Dewachi, Paola Bacchetta, Pete Coviello, Sandy Sufian, Sarah Schulman, Rahul Rao, Robert McRuer, Ros Petchesky, Sara Ahmed, Sarah Franklin, Sima Shakhsari, Susan Stryker, Tavia Nyong'o.

Liat Ben-Moshe read the manuscript in its entirety and offered vital feedback and great conversation; I am excited about collaborating on future ventures. I owe huge thanks to my fantastic research assistants, who are also, or were, our fantastic graduate students in Women's and Gender Studies at Rutgers University: Stephen Seely, Max Hantel, Carolina Alonso Bejarano, Jacky Rossiter, and Rasha Moumneh. A very special debt of gratitude goes to Arev Pivazyan, who valiantly guided the book (and me) through the final stages of copyediting and production. Ken Wissoker has not only been an amazingly supportive editor throughout the years; he also has a keen sense of current intellectual debates and necessary interventions. Thank you also to Courtney Berger for her faith in our series and to the inimitable Mel Chen for being a feral co-conspirator in thought.

There are many places—too many to list—where I was fortunate enough to meet engaged audiences who were so generous with feedback and constructive critique. Every interaction sits with me and finds its way into words, and I thank the many audiences who invited me to their campuses over the past ten years.

My deepest thanks go to friends and comrades in Palestine: Ghadir Al-Shafie, Habshe Yossef, Baraah Awad Owdeh, Nadera Shalhoub-Kevorkian, Haneen Maikey, Rita Giacaman, the many families we visited in refugee camps, the centers that hosted us, and all the workers and community members who took time to share their experiences with us. Amin Husain and Nitasha Dhillon are inspirational organizers and cultural producers, and I admire deeply their commitment to the communities they draw together through the crucial work they do.

This book is dedicated to the fortitude of the Palestinian people, the imminent liberation of Palestine, and whatever new worlds and struggles that may bring.

INTRODUCTION: THE COST OF GETTING BETTER

Many things are lost in the naming of a death as a "gay youth suicide."[1] In what follows, I offer a preliminary analysis of the prolific media attention to gay youth suicides that began in the fall of 2010.[2] I am interested in how the hailing of this event recalls affective attachments to neoliberalism that index a privileged geopolitics of finance capitalism. These tragic deaths were memorialized in numerous public statements, vigils, and public displays of mourning. I have been struck by how the discourses surrounding gay youth suicide partake in a spurious binarization of an interdependent relationship between bodily capacity and bodily debility. These discourses reproduce neoliberalism's heightened demands for bodily capacity, even as this same neoliberalism marks out populations for what Lauren Berlant has described as "slow death"—the debilitating ongoingness of structural inequality and suffering.[3] In the United States, where personal debt incurred through medical expenses is the number one reason for filing for bankruptcy, the centrality of what is termed the medical-industrial complex to the profitability of slow death cannot be overstated.[4] My intervention here is an attempt to go beyond the critique of the queer neoliberalism and homonormativity—indeed, homonationalism—embedded in the tendentious mythologizing that "It Gets Better" by confronting not only the debilitating aspects of neoliberalism but, more trenchantly, the economics of debility. If the knitting of finance capitalism and the medical-industrial complex means that debility pays, and pays well, how can a politics of disability move beyond the conventional narratives of resistance to neoliberalism? What are the vectors for a politics of disability if debility marks the convergence of capitalism and slow death via its enfolding into neoliberalism?

Disability and debility can be thought of as two concepts describing similar phenomena under late capitalism with strikingly different effects and entangled political limitations and possibilities. I argue, first, for a critical deployment of the concepts of debility and capacity to rethink disability through, against, and across the disabled/non-disabled binary. I situate disability in relation to concepts such as neoliberal and affective capacitation, debilitation, and slow death; "slow death" is in some sense a mode of neoliberal and affective capacitation or debilitation as mediated by different technological assemblages. Second, I want to explore the potential of affective tendencies to inform these assemblages of debility, capacity, and disability, noting that capacity is a key word of affective theorizing that can be generative when situated within the political economies of control societies. Affect amalgamates nonhuman entities, objects, and technologies. Technological platforms—new media, prosthetic technologies, biomedical enhancements—mediate bodily comportments, affects, and what is recognized as bodily capacity and bodily debility. Technology acts both as a machine of debility and capacity and as portals of affective openings and closures. I engage technology and slow death as they modulate debility and capacity without relying on conventional and straightforward political cants of a rational public sphere, autonomous political actors, and the binary of resistance/passivity.

LIFELOGGING AND ECOLOGIES OF SENSATION

What kinds of cultural assumptions are reflected within and produced through the "event" of queer suicide? Tyler Clementi was a Rutgers University undergraduate who joined a growing list of young gay men who took their own lives in the fall of 2010. Two students, Dharun Ravi and Molly Wei, were involved in several instances of sex surveillance of Clementi's dating during the time leading up to the suicide. All three were living on Busch campus in Piscataway, already codified as the science or premed "geek" campus (some might say "sissies"). At Rutgers, where I teach, Busch is also informally racially demarcated as the "Asian" campus, an identity often converging with that of "geek" at U.S. colleges. Clementi's suicide predictably occasioned a vicious anti-Asian backlash replete with overdetermined notions of "Asian homophobia" and calls to "go back to where you came from" (Ravi and Wei are from New Jersey).[5] Commenting on the biases of the criminal justice system against those of non-normative race, ethnicity, and citizenship, a press release from a Rutgers organization called Queering the Air remarked that Garden State Equality (a New Jersey LGBT advocacy group) and Campus Pride (a national group for LGBTQ students) demanded the most severe consequences for Ravi and Wei, prosecution for hate crimes, maximum jail time, and expulsion without disciplinary hearing, noting that "18,000 people endorse an online group seeking even more serious charges—manslaughter."[6] Discussions quickly turned to antibullying legislation and other forms of state intervention, as well as the need for more LGBTQ centers and organizations in schools and on campuses.[7] Blame was accorded to the perpetrators of the bullying, the schools where these environments are sustained, the apparent lack of legal redress, conservative opposition to antibullying legislation, gay marriage bans, Don't Ask Don't Tell (DADT), and society at large.

The implications of two "model minority" students from New Jersey suburbs targeting an effete young queer white man might be considered beyond convenient cultural narratives of the so-called inherent homophobia within racialized immigrant communities. The war on terror did much to suture a homonational rendering of the sexual other as white and the racial other as straight, and this binary unsurprisingly informed much discourse implicitly, if not explicitly. In the trial that ensued and its aftermath, several things came into relief. First of all, the consolidation of Ravi's "homophobia"—whether a reasonable assessment or not of Ravi's affective comportment—produced a powerful mechanism to deflect from manifold vectors of homophobia, in particular the upset of Clementi's mother to his recent "coming out."[8] Ravi's own complex masculinity seems to involve model minority immigrant conditioning that both made him vulnerable to taunts to "go back to where he came from" (even though he migrated from India to the United States at age five) and the threat of deportation and also parsed him out from a "person of color" identification or positioning, distinct from blacks or Latinos, who are more likely to face incarceration.[9] Thus, while the contestation of the mistreatment of Ravi largely revolved around the racial biases of the U.S. criminal justice system, Ravi was scapegoated in part not only because he was vulnerable to racism but because he was perceived as having had eclipsed and excelled past such structures of race. In other words, Ravi was punished not because he is the target population of biopolitical incarceration but rather for supposedly daring to escape this target population. The disciplinary apparatus at work here, then, which is not only about reinforcing the criminality of certain always-already criminals but also about creating docile subjects among those who just barely manage to escape the projection of criminality, has thus little to do with whether Ravi is sentenced to jail time. The use of the charge of "homophobia" to discipline and domesticate racialized minorities is by now a well-worn tactic in the biopolitical management of populations folded into life but "not quite/not white" or "almost the same but not quite."[10] No doubt this charge has had effects on the comportment of students of color across the Rutgers campuses if not far beyond.[11]

Is it possible to see all three students involved as more alike—all geeks, in fact—than different? Instead of rehashing that old "gaybashers are secretly closet cases" canard, perhaps there is a reason to destabilize the alignments of "alikeness" and "difference" away from a singular, predictable axis pivoting on a discrete and knowable "sexuality." A letter circulated by Queering the Air claims that Clementi's death was the second suicide by an LGBTQ student since March and that four of the last seven suicides at Rutgers were related to sexuality.[12] What, then, is meant here by "related to sexuality"? I am prompted by Amit Rai's reformulation of sexuality as "ecologies of sensation"—as affect instead of identity—that transcends the designations of straight and gay and can further help to disaggregate these binary positions from their racialized histories.[13]

Accusations of "homophobia," "gay bullying," and even "cyberbullying" do not do justice to the complex uptake of digital "lifelogging" technologies in this story. Lifelogging refers to forms of emergent technologies, loosely grouped together, that seek to ensure that every event in (your) life is logged. These include surveillance technologies—technologies of pleasure, fun, amusement, and capacity enhancement that wind up surveilling as their by-product—as well as technologies that deliberately surveil for capacity production as their primary task. All are part of a milieu of apparatuses that appear, through various methods, to document, record, translate, and qualify the everydayness of living.[14] Missing from the debate about Clementi's suicide is a discussion about the proclivities of young people to see the "choice" of Internet surveillance as a regulatory part of their subject formations while also capacitating bodily habits and affective tendencies. Note that the designation of the "digital native" carries largely negative associations, with this term linked to the perceived loss of normative "face-to-face" sociality. For these youth (but not only for youth) "cyberstalking" is an integral part of what it means to become a neoliberal (sexual) subject. Think of the ubiquity of sexting, applications like Grindr, Tinder, Manhunt, DIY porn, and mass cell phone circulation of images, technologies that create simultaneous sensations of exposure (the whole world is watching) and alienation (no one understands).

These cyborgian practices proliferate new relations between public and private, with speed, so much so that we are often dealing with the effect of such repatterning before we comprehend the force of it. "Invasion of privacy" remains uncharted territory for jurisprudence in relation to the Internet. More significantly, these technologies impel the affective tendencies of bodies, altering forms of attention, distraction, practice, and repetition.[15] The presumed differences between "gay" and "straight" could otherwise be thought more generously through the quotidian and banal activities of sexual self-elaboration via social media—emergent habituations, corporeal comportment, and an array of diverse switchpoints of bodily capacity.[16] In this broadcast environment, Clementi's participation in the testimonial spaces of the chat room to detail his roommate's invasion into his "privacy" and his use of Facebook for the explanatory "suicide note" reflect precisely the shared continuities with his perpetrators through ecologies of sensation.

The multimodality of connective media involved in the "event" (text, Facebook, Internet, IM, Skype, video camera, Twitter) also impacts and potentially changes what "narrative" is and how it is constructed and excavated. Implicit in lifelogging is the rescaled and temporized notion of what constitutes an "event," which now coheres through the act of logging/recording and the placement of a time stamp.[17] One such instance of rescaling occurred in Ravi's trial, where it became unclear whether erasing one's texts automatically insinuated an erasing of evidence. Events are thus data-driven, informational as well as experiential, the digitalizing of information rotating in the loop between memory and archive. Facebook, Twitter, and numerous other documentation technologies that seduce the securitization of memory can no longer be constituted as simply extracurricular activities.[18] Rather, they have been incorporated and normativized into quotidian rhythms of communication, information dissemination and retention, and the affective tendencies and habituations of bodies.[19]

Exhortations of protest regarding the encroachment of privacy abound, even as the offering up of one's privacy becomes the very currency of proven competency and proficiency of the usage of these technologies, not to mention of modern-day storytelling of the self. This contradiction of the neoliberal subject—of wanting one's privacy while being increasing impelled into circuits that might seemingly reward for revealing what that privacy shields—is not only bred of the sense of orchestrating how, when, and where such intimate privates are crafted and rejected. Rather, the neo/liberal "right to privacy" seems to coexist—because of rather than despite these contradictions—with desires for intimacies, intimacies that cannot be determined or defined alone by relations of proximity or experiences of intrusion. The seemingly contradictory unfolding of Clementi's suicide, involving both the violation of privacy through the video-camming of sexual activity and his announcement of his suicidal intentions in a chat room and on Facebook, are actually co-constitutive elements of this modern paradox of privacy and intrusion. Action-at-a-distance technologies create forms of touching—whether through "subtle coercion or explicit duress."[20] These touchings mediate intimacy as a relation of proximity, reorganizing the scale and temporal mandates of intimate connection. Clementi's suicide, then, could be thought of as an "action-at-a-distance" mediated event, one that unfolded by increasing zones of contact between bodies rather than participating in traditional notions of proximity/distance, public/private divides, and experiences of violation, intrusion, and exposure.

DOES IT GET BETTER?

Because the idea of the enviable life has now replaced the idea of the good life, it may be difficult to hear, or listen to, the parts of our patients or students that are not interested in success. There are, as we know, people around for whom being successful has not been a success. . . . Our ambitions—our ideals and success stories that lure us into the future—can too easily become ways of not living in the present, or of not being present at the event, a blackmail of distraction; ways, that is, of disowning, or demeaning, the actual disorder of experience. Believing in the future can be a great deadener. Perhaps we have been too successful at success and failure, and should now start doing something else. —ADAM PHILLIPS, On Flirtation

Narrations of the relationship between Clementi and Ravi utterly foreclosed queer-on-queer cyberstalking as a possibility. Not once were the sexual orientations of the Asian American students even speculated upon; mainstream discourses automatically defaulted to the assumption that they were both heterosexual. This pernicious binary, the sexual other is white, the racial other is straight, is also in full display in a video produced by gay journalist Dan Savage in response to Tyler Clementi's and other suicides of young, mostly white gay men, titled "It Gets Better." As noted by cultural critic Tavia Nyong'o, Savage's sanctimonious "It Gets Better" video is a mandate to fold into urban, neoliberal gay enclaves, a form of liberal handholding and upward mobility that discordantly echoes the now discredited "pull yourself up by the bootstraps" immigrant motto.[21] Savage embodies the spirit of a secular neoliberal coming-of-age success story. He is monied, confident, well traveled, and suitably partnered; he betrays no trace of abjection or shame. His message translates to: come out, move to the city, travel to Paris, adopt a kid, pay your taxes, demand representation, save yourself; that's how it's done. In this video, Savage is basically a representative of "your" future, of how "you" should model it, universalizing a neoliberal politics of exceptional responsibilization. The focus on the future normalizes the present tense of teen bullying and evacuates the politics of the now from culpability, letting contemporary conditions, along with any politics attempting to redress it, off the hook. In terms of genre, it parallels what disability studies scholar Stella Young called "inspiration porn."[22] While Savage explains that he left behind his small town and his Catholic school–educated past, his story nonetheless evokes the religious genre of spiritual salvation, Savage having survived and thus earned his homosexual stripes.[23] There is uncanny resonance with the religious exhortation "I was saved"—albeit not by a divine force, but by himself. Who or what is the agent in the exhortation "It Gets Better"? The genre of religious conversion is relevant here; Savage is proselytizing. In concert with this proselytizing ethos, "It Gets Better" has become a veritable campaign, inaugurating spin-offs in multiple genres, languages, and programming platforms.[24] It has also become the mantra for Google's own advertising of its media platforms (Chrome and YouTube in particular) and the power of social media as a force harnessed for social change.[25]

How useful is it to imagine troubled gay youth might master their injury and turn blame and guilt into transgression, triumph, and all-American success? Savage's "retro-homo-reprofuturism," a term coined by Dana Luciano to describe "the projection of one's own past self onto the youth of today in order to revise one's own ordinary life into exceptional progress narrative," functions to misread the impasse of the present as an inability to imagine the future.[26] In his closing imperative statement—"You have to live"—Savage capitalizes on a neoliberal sentiment that detaches individual well-being from any collective, social responsibility. During the U.S.

▦ It Gets Better Project.mov

ogress: ▬▬▬▬▬▬▬▬▬▬▬▬▬▬▬▬▬▬ **100%**

'review:

Eht New York Times

WORLD   U.S.   N.Y. / REGION   BUSINESS   TECHNOLOGY   SCIENCE   HEALTH   SPORTS   OPINIC

The Suicides of Gay Teenagers

Published: October 11, 2010

"Several Recent Suicides Put Light on Pressures Facin
Teenagers" (news article, Oct. 4) underscores how bul'
cyberbullying and depression can lead to suicide. Thes

FIGS. INTRO.1 AND INTRO.2. Screenshots from Google Chrome's "It Gets Better" video, featuring Dan Savage.

AIDS crisis, the charge of ACT UP activists was "You are killing us!," the "you" being the state, understood as responsible for addressing the crisis and providing care to its citizens (and noncitizens). The "you" is also the social and the political, the broader social and political contexts within which homosexual bodies could be sacrificed to such indifference and neglect. By contrast, Savage does not direct his message to the endemic social and political forces that continue to manifest homophobic hatred. Instead, his "you" is the individual, to whom and only to whom he credits the survival of gay bullying. In this regard, "It Gets Better" presumes the end, the aftermath of the AIDS crisis, rather than any homage to its ongoing deleterious effects or current situation. The move from AIDS as death to homosexual life also mirrors moves from sex and public sexuality to kinship and its privatized familial forms and from the state as the site of redress to the market as the site of the actualization and realization of the queer self. Queer failure is braided into this story of success.

Although it has been lauded by gay liberals for having "done something" to address the recent spate of queer youth suicides, critics note that queers of color, trans, genderqueer, and gender-nonconforming youth, and lesbians have not been inspirationally hailed by IGB.[27] Diana Cage of Velvetpark: Dyke Culture in Bloom contends: "We all know it gets better a lot sooner if you are white, cisgendered, and middle class."[28] Several writers ask what is forgotten in the push to imagine "gay youth" as exceptionally susceptible to bullying and more likely to commit suicide than their straight peers.[29] Laurel Dykstra worries about seeming unsympathetic by questioning this oft-cited empirical "fact," pointing out that Aboriginal youth in Canada and the United States might in fact have a higher suicide rate than queer youth.[30] Finally, racial and sexual harassment, rape, and other forms of sexual policing of girls remain unaddressed through the use of a reified notion of "homophobia." In "It Doesn't Get Better," Alec Webley writes, "The problem is not homophobia. The problem is bullying." Webley argues that teenage bullying is a widespread phenomenon that affects youth of many persuasions who are "different" and "don't fit in"; he also highlights the wide prevalence of workplace bullying.[31]

The momentum from "It Gets Better" has generated a fairly predictable array of U.S. liberal gay movement anger toward conservative opposition to antibullying legislation, even as the apparently "sudden" spate of queer suicides appears irreconcilable with the purported progress of the gay and lesbian rights movement.[32] The symbolism of Clementi's transit from central New Jersey to the George Washington Bridge that connects northern New Jersey to upper Manhattan is painfully apparent. Part of the outrage generated by these deaths is based precisely in a belief that things are indeed (supposed to be) better, especially for a particular class of white gay men, and especially as compared with other parts of the "less civilized" world. From this vantage, IGB reflects a desire for the reinstatement of (white) racial privilege that was lost by being gay, one that is achievable through equality rights agendas like gay marriage and participation in neoliberal consumer culture. In other words, IGB is based on an expectation that it was supposed to be better. And thus IGB might turn out to mean, you get more normal. Such affirmations—and, indeed, mandates—of life may well work to actually inhibit other kinds of lives. Thus, "It Gets Better" circulates as a projection of bodily capacity that ultimately partakes in slow death, even as it reforms the valence of debility—homosexual identity—through a white/liberal/male assemblage: a recapacitation machine.

Despite this critique, the "It Gets Better" project should hardly be dismissed out of hand; its virality is in itself interesting.[33] It is no doubt crucial that IGB opened space for the expression of public anguish and collective mourning. But ultimately, the best part of the viral explosion of Savage's project is that so many have chimed in to explain how and why it doesn't just get better. The very technological media platform of the phenomenon allows for immanent critique. The universalizing force of IGB is undercut by the rapid accumulation of community promoted by the Google Chrome advertisement using the "It Gets Better" campaign. The commercial marshals IGB to exhibit the utility of Google Chrome, specifically, and to demonstrate the community-building capacity of the Internet more generally. In this brilliant example of the monetization of affect, the advertisement assembles varied expressions of IGB—varied in terms of bodies, comportments, languages. Unlike the proselytizing tone of IGB, the advertisement draws on a different affect, that of religious ecstasy and rapture. Life is already better, life is fantastic, and the numbers are flying around. Further, Google Chrome manages to transact a savvy linkage to political activism without doing anything but more of what it does, devoid of political substance. As such, the "It Gets Better" campaign now shimmers on the Internet as an ironic testament to how it actually may not get better.

Savage has also mastered, if we follow S. Lochlann Jain on the "politics of sympathy," the technique of converting his injury into cultural capital not only through rhetorics of blame, guilt, and suffering but also through those of triumph, transgression, and success.[34] The subject of redress and grievance thus functions here as a recapacitation of a debilitated body. The preceding sections recast the white queer/immigrant homophobe binary by distilling the event of queer suicide through ecologies of sensation, technics, and affect. Here I want to further shift the registers of this conversation from one about the pathologization versus normativization of sexual identity, to questions of bodily debility, capacity, disability. This is not at all to dismiss these queer suicides as privileged forms of death. I want to emphasize this: I am not making a critique about relative intersectional privilege.

Rather, I am probing what kinds of slow deaths have been ongoing that a suicide might represent an escape from. In order to "slow down" the act of suicide—to offer a concomitant yet different temporality of relating to living and dying—one must slow down the speed of encounter, as speed itself might be understood as debilitating. These temporalities of speed and slowness are thus convivial, not antagonistic. Berlant's piece on slow death discusses the most prevalent health problem in the United States, that of obesity.[35] I cannot do her formulation of temporality and living adequate justice here, but I would like to highlight the following aspects of her argument that I find compatible to—indeed generative for—my own thinking. Berlant moves us away from the event of trauma or catastrophe, proposing that "slow death occupies the temporalities of the endemic."[36] This echoes the transformation of the epidemic into the endemic whereby, for Michel Foucault, writing in *Security, Territory, Population*, "death becomes durational."[37] Displacing military encounters, genocides, and other discrete time frames of traumatic events (though later in this book I contest the formulation of these happenings as discrete), slow death occurs not within the time scale of the crisis, not of the event of the suicide or the epidemic, but in "a zone of temporality . . . of ongoingness, getting by, and living on, where the structural inequalities are dispersed, the pacing of their experience intermittent, often in phenomena not prone to capture by a consciousness organized by archives of memorable impact."[38] In this nonlinear temporality, for it starts and stops, redoubles and leaps ahead, Berlant is not "defining a group of individuals merely afflicted with the same ailment, [rather] slow death describes populations marked out for wearing out."[39] That is to say, slow death is not about an orientation toward the death drive, nor is it morbid; rather, it is about the maintenance of living, the "ordinary work of living on."[40] Slow death is, quite simply, "a condition of being worn out by the activity of reproducing life."[41] As Berlant notes, this puts living and dying into a specific zone of proximity and precarity: "While death is usually deemed an event in contrast to life's 'extensivity,' in this domain dying and the ordinary reproduction of life are coextensive."[42]

Queer suicide, in the context of slow death mediated by technocultural ecologies of sensation, reorganizes what is thought of as the event, distills the experience of trauma, and requires a turn to debility, capacity, and disability, concepts that give us alternative temporal frames for imagining the body in processes of de- and regeneration. David Mitchell's moving invocation of disability "not as exception, but the basis upon which a decent and just social order is founded," hinges upon a society that acknowledges, accepts, and even anticipates disability.[43] This anticipatory disability has been the dominant temporal frame of disability rights activism—"you're only able-bodied until you're disabled," or "temporarily able-bodied." This statement is mobilized to defuse ableist fantasies of endless capacity, to challenge the presentation of life as an unlimited resource, and to collectivize a rights-based politics of disability. Disability is posited as the most common identity category because "we" will all belong to it "someday, if we live long enough." Despite this purportedly inevitable communal fate, David Mitchell and Sharon Snyder argue that disability is "reified as the true site of insufficiency."[44] But Berlant's formulation of slow death implies that we might not (only) be haunted by the disability to come, but also disavowing the debility that is already here. More trenchantly, some are living the disability that does not get codified or recognized as such, not only as a true site of insufficiency but as a mark or remainder or reminder of that which is already constituted as insufficient. There are two different progressive forms of temporality that are upended here. One, slow death neutralizes the descriptor "better" in "It Gets Better," proposing that the pathways to getting better are limned with precarity. Two, "We will all be disabled one day, if we live long enough"—the disability to come—is already built on an entitled hope and expectation for a certain longevity.

Berlant argues that "health itself can then be seen as a side effect of successful normativity."[45] Therefore, in order to honor the complexity of these suicides, they must be placed within the broader context of neoliberal demands for bodily capacity (what are often constituted as neoliberal "opportunities" or "choices" for the body) as well as the profitability of debility, both functioning as central routes through which finance capital seeks to sustain itself. Capacity and debility are, on the one hand, seeming opposites generated by increasingly demanding neoliberal formulations of health, agency, and choice—what I call a liberal eugenics of lifestyle programming—that produce, along with biotechnologies and bioinformatics, population aggregates. Those "folded" into life are seen as more capacious or on the side of capacity, while those targeted for premature or slow death are figured as on the side of debility. Such an analysis reposes the question: Which bodies are made to pay for "progress"? Which debilitated bodies can be reinvigorated for neoliberalism, available and valuable enough for rehabilitation, and which cannot be?

In this regard, Savage's project refigures queers, along with other bodies heretofore construed as excessive and/or erroneous, as capacity-laden, demanding that queerness operates as a machine of capacity.[46] Even though poststructuralist queer theory critically deploys registers of negativity (and increasingly negative affect) in reading practices primarily deconstructive in their orientation, such a figuration of queer theory has emerged from a homeostatic framework: queer theory is already also a machine of capacity in and after the cybernetic turn. (This is important because what is being hailed as the antisocial turn in queer theory and its opposite, a focus on hope, optimism, and utopia, are rebounding within a dialectic that misses the implication of the capacity machine that is queer theory).[47] Furthermore, bioinformatic frames—in which bodies figure not as identities or subjects but as data—entail that there is no such thing as nonproductive excess but only emergent forms of new information.[48] This revaluing of excess is potent because, simply put, debility is profitable for capitalism. In neoliberal, biomedical, and biotechnological terms, the body is always debilitated in relation to its ever-expanding potentiality. This is precisely what Foucault presciently outlined in his 1978–79 lectures, now translated into English as *The Birth of Biopolitics*. Foucault writes that the "theory of human capital"[49]—a breakdown of labor into capital and income that builds on the Marxian conception of labor power—is one of "capital ability" where "the worker himself appears as a sort of enterprise for himself."[50] This formulation of human capital Foucault calls an "abilities machine": "being for himself, his own capital, being for himself his own producer, being for himself, the source of (his) earnings."[51] He continues: "The wage is nothing other than the remuneration, the income allowed to a certain capital, a capital we will call human capital inasmuch as the ability-machine of which it is the income cannot be separated from the human individual who is its bearer."[52] What composes the assemblage of the abilities machine? With a brief nod to hereditary differences, Foucault turns to educational investments, quality of parenting, affective attention, mobility, migration, health care, public hygiene, and any number of related elements that create a "whole environmental analysis."[53] Here in Foucault are the eerie echoes of Dan Savage's exhortations to live in "It Gets Better." The body as an ability-machine takes its place among other forms of for-profit capital.

One might wonder, given Foucault's formulation, what body is not an ability-machine? Or, more succinctly, what body is not striving toward becoming an ability-machine? Margrit Shildrick writes, "The binary of disabled and non-disabled undoubtedly lingers . . . but it is increasingly destabilized by the intimation that all forms of embodiment are subject to reconstruction, extension, and transformation, regardless of the conventionally identified vectors of change and decay."[54] Even as the demands of able-body-ism weigh heavily and have been challenged by disability scholars and activists, attachments to the difference of disabled bodies may reify an (human) exceptionalism that only certain privileged disabled bodies can occupy.[55] Efforts to "diversify" and multiply the subjects of study of disability have led to an impasse as the notion of the subject itself is already revealed to be a disciplinary construct of ableism, especially in the realm of cognition, agency, and "voice"—all challenges to any political platform that is fueled predominantly through representational mandates. Nicole Markotic and Robert McRuer caution against what they term "disability culturalism"—a dominant focus on representational politics—along with variants of "barbarism" and "crip nationalism" that reinscribe the centrality of prevailing discourses on race, national identity, gender, and region, producing privileged disabled bodies in distinction to various "others." In sum, the particular binary categorization of dis/abled subjectivity is one that has many parallels to as well as intersects with other kinds of binary categorizations propagated—in fact, demanded—by neoliberal constructions of failed and capacitated bodies. Therefore, we cannot see this binary production as specific only to the distinction of disabled versus non-disabled subjects—all bodies are being evaluated in relation to their success or failure in terms of health, wealth, progressive productivity, upward mobility, enhanced capacity. And, there is no such thing as an "adequately abled" body anymore.

How does the study of capacity and debility complicate the terms of disability rights paradigms? While the disability rights movement in large part understands disability as a form of nonnormativity that deserves to be depathologized, disability justice activists seek to move beyond access issues foregrounded by the Americans with Disabilities Act as well as global human rights frames that standardize definitions of disability and the terms of their legal redress across national locations. Rights discourses produce human beings in order to give them rights; they discriminate which bodies are vested with futurity, or more accurately, they cultivate (some/certain) bodies that can be vested with futurity. Critiquing the disability rights movement, disability justice activist Mia Mingus, who identifies as a "queer, physically disabled Korean woman transracial and transnational adoptee," writes: "Most access right now is about inclusion and equality: how do we bring disabled people to our table? How do we make sure disabled people have access to what we have? How do we get disabled people access to the current system? Rather than thinking that the entire 'table' or 'system' might need to change or working to embrace difference. Justice does not have to equal sameness or assimilation; and justice and equality are not the same thing."[56]

Mingus highlights populations (institutionalized, incarcerated, racialized) for whom claiming the term and identity of disability is difficult given many are already stigmatized as nonnormative, and deemed in need of fixing, by the medical-industrial complex. Claiming that the "disabled people who identify as '(politically) disabled' are often white disabled people," Mingus continues: "Over and over I meet disabled women of color who do not identify as disabled, even though they have the lived reality of being disabled. And this is for many complicated reasons around race, ability, gender, access. . . . It can be very dangerous to identify as disabled when your survival depends on you denying it."[57]

Her analysis suggests that access to the identity of disability in this regard is a function, result, and reclamation of white privilege. The further fact of the duress under which racially marked communities labor means, as Mingus writes, "the bodies of our communities are under siege by forces that leverage violence and ableism at every turn."[58] In working poor and working-class communities of color, disabilities and debilities are not non-normative, even if the capacitizing use of the category disabled may be tenuous and the reign of ableism is a constitutive facet. The goal of these activist efforts does not remain at the restitution of the disabled subject—soliciting tolerance, acceptance, and empowerment—but rather directs attention to the debilitating conditions of the medical-industrial complex itself. To this end, Mingus avows: "As organizers, we need to think of access with an understanding of disability justice, moving away from an equality-based model of sameness and 'we are just like you' to a model of disability that embraces difference, confronts privilege and challenges what is considered 'normal' on every front. We don't want to simply join the ranks of the privileged; we want to dismantle those ranks and the systems that maintain them."[59]

Thus a political agenda that disavows pathology is intertwined with a critique of the embedded structures of liberal eugenics propagated by the medical-industrial complex and its attendant forms of administrative surveillance—those structures that issue forth the distinctions between (racial) pathologization and normality in the first instance.[60] Such work suggests that an increasingly demanding ableism (and, I would add, an increasingly demanding disableism inherent in normative forms of disability as exceptionalism) is producing nonnormativity not only through the sexual and racial pathologization of certain "unproductive bodies" but more expansively through the (in)ability to register within neoliberal capacity.

What is implicit (if not often explicit) in disability justice critiques is the constitutive slow death of debility in terms of precarity and populations. The term "debility" can attach to the global south but can also be deployed in disenfranchised communities within global north locales to suggest debility as endemic, perhaps even normative, to disenfranchised communities: not nonnormative, not exceptional, not that which is to come or can be avoided, but a banal feature of quotidian existence that is already definitive of the precarity of that existence. The conditions that make disability endemic as opposed to exceptional are already ones of entrenched economic, racial, political, and social disenfranchisement. Attending to this banality might involve "engag[ing] in the actuarial

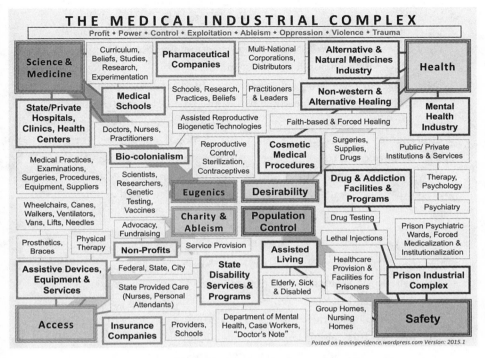

FIG. INTRO.3. The medical-industrial complex diagram. Created by disability justice activist Mia Mingus.

imaginary of biopolitics," says Berlant, "to turn ordinary life into crisis ordinariness."[61]

If debility is endemic to disenfranchised communities, it is doubly so because the forms of financialization that accompany neoliberal economics and the privatization of services also produce debt as debility. This relationship between debt and debility can be described as a kind of "financial expropriation": "The profit made by financial institutions out of the personal income of workers is a form of financial expropriation, seen as additional profit generated in the realm of circulation."[62] Further, as Berlant expounds, medicalization as privatization is a "rerouting of the relations of governmental, corporate, and personal responsibility rather than, as it often seems to be, the ejection of the state from oversight of the public good in deference to corporations."[63] Debt peonage, in the context of Foucault's theory of human capital, is an updated version of Marx's critique of "choice" under capitalism. Debt as enclosure, as immobility, is what Gilles Deleuze writes of in his description of control societies: "Man is no longer man enclosed, but man in debt."[64] This is especially true, as mentioned earlier, in the United States, where health care expenses are the number one cause of personal bankruptcy, a capacitation of slow death through debt undertaken to support one's health. This theory of human capital entails that when one falls short of proper investment in the enterprise of oneself, one is, as Geeta Patel points out, paying for one's own slow death, through insurial and debt structures predicated on risk and insecurity, and essentially forced into agreeing to one's own debilitation.[65]

FROM EPISTEMOLOGICAL CORRECTIVE
TO ONTOLOGICAL IRREDUCIBILITY

The Right to Maim inhabits the intersections of disability studies, critical race studies, and the affective turn, all fields of inquiry that put duress on the privileging of the subject as a primary site of bodily interpellation. The affective turn, alongside the critical deployment of affect as a rubric of analysis and inquiry, more potently signals the contestation over the dominant terms of critical theory itself and the limits of poststructuralist interpretive practices that focus solely on language, signification, and representation. The sites of struggle and their targets include social constructionism (reinvigorated interrogation of biological matter that challenges both biological determinism and also performativity); epistemology (supplemented with ontology and ontogenesis); psychoanalysis (trauma rethought as the intensification of the body's relation to itself); humanism (the capacities of nonhuman animals as well as the durational capacities of inorganic matter are highlighted by scholarship on object-oriented ontology, critical animal studies, and posthumanism); and agency (linked to cognition, perception, emotion, and feeling: an anthropocentric framing of movement challenged by affect, force, intensity, and theories of sensation).[66] These undulating trajectories are arguably more significant than what affect is or what it means. They open a reinvigorated interrogation of biological matter that still challenges biological determinism and the "ontological realism" of matter through displacing the role of language, signification, representation, and the linguistic essentialism of the human.[67] What exactly language is and the place of language itself are being resignified and multiplied.[68] Part of this reenvisioning is forecasted by Mel Chen's understanding that language is not opposed to matter; rather, language is matter.[69]

Thus the affective turn goes far beyond the consolidation and dispersal of affect as an analytic. The modulation and surveillance of affect operates as a form of sociality that regulates good and bad subjects, possible and impossible bodily capacities. Affect is at once an exchange or interchange between bodies and also an object of control. Why the destabilization of the subject and a turn to affect matters is because affect—as a bodily matter—makes identity both possible and yet impossible. And if affect makes identity cohere and dissolve—identity as the habituation of affect—it more forcefully marks the limits of identity itself. Affect impels not only dissolution of the subject but, more significantly, a dissolution of the organic body (the contours of which should never be assumed to be stable, disability studies reminds us) as forces of energy are transmitted, shared, and circulated. The body, as Brian Massumi argues, "passes from one state of capacitation to a diminished or augmented state of capacitation," always bound up in the lived past of the body but always in passage to a changed future.[70] Affect is precisely the body's hopeful opening, a speculative opening not wedded to the dialectic of hope and hopelessness but rather a porous affirmation of what could or might be. It is thus not an opening toward or against or in relation to a teleological notion of time, prognosis time, or forces that simply resist or disrupt progressive time. Affect moves us away from terms such as "past," "present," and "future" to reorient us around what Manuel DeLanda calls "non-metric time": speed, pace, duration, timing, rhythms, frequency. Time becomes less an epistemological unit of organization and instead thought of as ontologically irreducible, constitutive to becoming, a speculative opening—indeed, time in affective terms is becoming itself.

One supposition of affective analysis is that there is no pure debility or pure capacity. Debility and capacity are not properties or attributes of one discrete body or a representational grid certain bodies are placed into. Debility may well simultaneously appropriate bodily capacities closing off, perhaps to give rise to a new set of bodily capacities. Capacity is not discretely of the body. It is shaped by and bound to interface with prevailing notions of chance, risk, accident, luck, and probability, as well as with bodily limits/incapacity, disability, and debility. This deployment of the term "capacity" is an amendment to affect studies, which posits affect as the endless capacitation of the individuated body, even as it might always see that body as relational. In reading affect through and with populations along with bodies, dividuals beside individuals, and societies of control working through forms of discipline, I want to provide a necessary corrective to studies of affect that take the integrity of the human form for granted.

The political mandate behind such conceptualizations of disability—not what disability is but what it does and how it is used to simultaneously capacitate and debilitate—is to put the disabled/non-disabled binary in dialogue with assemblages of disability, capacity, and debility. Inviting a deconstruction of what able-bodiedness and capacity mean (they are not equivalent to each other), affectively and otherwise, entails schematizing the biopolitics of debility, one that destabilizes the seamless production of able bodies in relation to disability and also suggests the capacitation of disabled bodies through circuits of (white) racial and economic privilege, citizenship status, and legal, medical, and social accommodations. Access is theorized not only in terms of infrastructure, work, social services, and public space but also in terms of access to health itself. While providing a much-needed intersectional critique that destabilizes the white, Euro-American, economically privileged subjects that are most likely to be interpellated as "a person with disabilities," I am also building off of solidly argued critiques of identity to highlight constantly shifting assemblages of power.

Recent theorizations of affect argue for a destabilization of humanist notions of the body and of the politics of voice and visibility. Mel Chen, for example, interrogates a liberal yet brutal humanism that accords liveliness and sentience—animacies—to human animals, nonhuman animals, and matter through a biopolitics of race, sex, and bodily ability. These are not a priori categories but rather are constructed with and through the epistemic projects that have functionalized their coherence. I seek to intersectionally pressure the assumed subjects of disability and also to address the constant *ontological* assembling of power and its effects. My intervention is less wedded to the elaboration of subjects and identities—and attempting to determine what their contents or attributes are—than to the elaboration of bodies and their affective modalities as they are modulated in control societies. Far from being postrace or postintersectional, this methodological demand is about redressing the epistemological bifurcation that has occurred around intersectional theorizing that has let white feminists, especially those working on technoscience and (new) materialisms, off the hook and has, quite frankly, burdened women of color theorists and activists, most directly black feminist theorists, with the responsibility of adjudicating and defending the perceived successes or failures of intersectional scholarship.

DISCIPLINE AND CONTROL

Capacity and debility entail theorizing not only specific disciplinary sites but also broader techniques of social control, marking a shift in terms from the regulation of normativity (the internalization of self/other subject formation) to what Foucault calls the regularization of bodies, or what has been hailed "the age of biological control."[71] This is akin to what Giorgio Agamben perceives as the difference between regulating to produce order (discipline) and regulating disorder (security).[72] While Deleuze's techno-optimism leads him to proclaim rapid and complete transitions from discipline to control, Foucault is very clear about their braided and enmeshed historical and spatial modalities.[73] The oscillation between disciplinary societies and control societies, following Foucault's "apparatuses of security," both refracts and projects numerous tensions.[74] In control societies, Patricia Clough argues, bodies will not be captured or set free by re/presentation, but rather through affect and attention.[75] There is thus an affective differential, whereby the body is curated not only through disciplinary drilling but also through a composite of statistics, from normal/abnormal to variegation, fluctuation, modulation, and tweaking. Discrete and discontinuous sites of punishment—the prison, the mental hospital, the school—are extended spatially and temporally through continuous regimes of securitization driven by calculated risks and averages. While disciplinary power works to distinguish those who should be included from those who must be excluded or eliminated, security apparatuses have the "constant tendency to expand . . . new elements are constantly being integrated . . . allowing the development of ever-wider circuits" through the management of circulation determining not whether to include, but how.[76] Discipline is centripetal while apparatuses of security are centrifugal. Intense oscillation occurs between the following: subject/object construction and microstates of differentiation; difference between and difference within; the policing of profile and the patrolling of affect; will and capacity; agency and affect;

subject and body. And finally and, I believe, most important, between Althusserian interpellation (hey, you!) and an array of diverse switchpoints of the activation of the body, where bodies are positioned through openings and closings in order to ground practices of exploitation, extraction, dispossession, and expulsion commensurate with flexible modes of work and sociality.

How does disability function in control societies? Because there are gradations of capacity and debility in control societies—rather than the self-other production of being/not being—the distinction between disabled and non-disabled becomes fuzzier and blurrier. Disciplinary normalization, otherwise termed "normation" by Foucault, "goes from the norm to the final division between the normal and the abnormal" through "positing a model, an optimal model that is constructed in terms of a certain result"— the power of normalization versus normalization of power.[77] In security apparatuses, instead of distinguishing the normal from the abnormal, there are "different curves of normality . . . establishing an interplay between these different distributions of normality . . . acting to bring the most unfavorable in line with the more favorable. . . . The norm is an interplay of differential normalities."[78] Biopolitical apparatuses of control are invested in modulating a prolific range of affective bodily capacities and debilities— "differential normalities"—that invariably render rights-based interventions unable to fully apprehend the scenes of power. Disability identity is already part and parcel of a system of governing inclusion and exclusion, creating forms of what Robert McRuer calls "disability nationalism in crip times": liberal state and national recognition of people with disabilities that solicits the incorporation of certain disabilities into neoliberal economic circuits.[79] This conditional invitation latches onto and propagates celebratory claims of successful integration in order to continue to deplete resources from other, less acceptable bodies with disabilities. That is to say, the promoting and lauding of certain people with disabilities as markers of acceptance and progress ultimately serves to further marginalize and exclude most people with disabilities and serves also to sustain and create networks of debilitation in relation to these privileged disabled bodies. This is also what David Mitchell and Sharon Snyder analyze in *The Biopolitics of Disability*, in which they refer to the paradoxical means by which some disabled people gain entrance into late capitalist culture as "ablenationalism."[80]

This biopolitics of disability, I would further argue, is most efficient not just in the way it deploys some identities against others.[81] Rather, biopolitical control operates most perniciously and efficiently through reifying intersectional identity frames—these are frames that still hinge on discrete notions of inclusion and exclusion—as the most pertinent ones for political intervention, thus obfuscating forms of control that insidiously include in order to exclude, and exclude in order to include. Mitchell and Snyder state: "Control of the coordinates of bare biological life among citizens in market capitalism has been fashioned on the basis of systems of total oversight specific to disability and others occupying peripheral embodiments. . . . Disability is foundational to the development of cultural strategies in neoliberalism to 'seize hold of life in order to suppress it.' These strategies of seizure are the essence of bio-politics."[82]

The extraction and exploitation of body capacities and habituations pivot not only on the individual but more insidiously on the dividual. Foucault states that "discipline is a mode of individualization of multiplicities rather than something that constructs an edifice of multiple elements on the basis of individuals who are worked on as, first of all, individuals."[83] The individual is less a collection of multiplicities that form a whole than a stripping down or segregating of multiplicities, of "organizing a multiplicity, of fixing its points of implantation." Writing on vectors of control, Deleuze says of the hospital: "The new medicine 'without doctor or patient' . . . singles out potential sick people and subjects at risk, which in no way attests to individuation—as they say—but substitutes . . . the code of a dividual material to be controlled."[84] The code of dividual material, says Foucault, is generated by "security mechanisms [that] have to be installed around the random element inherent in a population of living beings so as to optimize a state of life."[85] Foucault explains that while discipline and control both work to maximize bodily extraction, unlike discipline, control does not work at "the level of the body itself: It is therefore not a matter of taking the individual at the level of individuality but, on the contrary, of using overall mechanisms and acting in such a way as to achieve overall states of equilibrium or regularity . . . a matter of taking control of life and the biological processes of man-as-species and of enduring that they are not disciplined, but regularized."[86]

The debate about discipline and control marks a shift in terms from the regulation of normativity (the internalization of self/other subject formation) to the regularization of bodies. Many relations between discipline (exclusion and inclusion) and control (modulation, tweaking) have been proffered. As various overlapping yet progressive stages of market capitalism and governmentality, the telos of discipline to control might function as a recasting of neoliberal modernity. Certain bodies are more subject to persisting disciplinary institutions (prisons, mental hospitals, military service, torture, factory work), relegating disciplinary sites as part of the primitive in a modernist telos.[87] Deleuze as well proclaims that hacking is replacing strikes, but are strikes being relegated to the "global south"?[88] Two suppositions can be inferred here: one, the distinction between bodies subjected to discipline and those "incorporated" into control economies is in itself a racializing technology; two, the intersections between discipline and control, and their techniques of power, on various bodies is precisely the mechanism that funnels populations into being. Helpfully, Foucault's own formulations are more porous: as coexisting models and exercises of power; control as the epitome of a disciplinary society par excellence, in that disciplinary forms of power exceed their sites to reproduce everywhere; and finally, discipline as a form of control and as a response to the proliferation of control. Ilana Feldman, in her work on governmentality in Gaza, argues that what Foucault seeks to "identify is a shift in emphasis, where different epochs display greater reliance on certain of these technologies."[89] These shifts themselves, I would argue, suggest the supplementary and entwined configurations of power that are adaptable across spatial and temporal variations.

And, in fact, control societies operate covertly by deploying disciplinary power to keep or deflect our attention around the subjection of the subject, thus allowing control to manifest unhindered. I suggest therefore that disciplinary apparatuses function in part as foils for control mechanisms and not in teleological or developmentalist progressions. Here I am following the lead of Seb Franklin's theorization of control as episteme with operational logics, rather than a system of power wedded solely to specific periodizations and geographies. Franklin's analysis demonstrates that the *logic* of control—as a partitioning, measuring, computational technology—permeates predigital schemas of power as well as non-computer-based realms of the social.[90]

Modulation of affect is a critical technology of control. One prominent example of the medicalization of affect may well be that of depression. Nikolas Rose maintains that depression will become the number one disability in the United States and the United Kingdom by 2020.[91] While it may well be the case, as Allan V. Horwitz and Jerome C. Wakefield have argued in *The Loss of Sadness: How Psychiatry Transformed Normal Sorrow into Depressive Disorder*, that the third and fourth editions of the *Diagnostic and Statistical Manual of Mental Disorders* (DSM-III and DSM-IV) have caused major depressive disorder to be overdiagnosed because of "insufficiently restrictive definitions," this expansion of depressed populations, or depressives, will not occur only through a widespread increase of depression, or an increase of its dispensation as a diagnosis, but also through the finessing of gradation of populations. In other words, it will not occur through the hailing and interpellation of depressed subjects—and a distinction between who is depressed and who is not—but rather through the evaluation and accommodation of degrees: To what degree is one depressed?[92] One is already instructed by television advertisements for psychotropic drugs such as Abilify, claiming that "two out of three people on anti-depressants still have symptoms" and offering a top-off medication to add to a daily med regime. Through this form of medical administration bodies are (1) drawn into a modulation of subindividual capacities (this would be the diverse switchpoints); (2) surveilled not on identity positions alone (though the recent work of Dorothy Roberts and Jonathan Metzl elaborates how this remains a trenchant issue) but through affective tendencies, informational body-as-data, and statistical probabilities—through populations, risk, and prognosis; and (3) further stratified across registers of the medical-industrial complex: medical debt, health insurance, state benefits, among other feedback loops into the profitability of debility.[93] How the disaggregation of depressed subjects into various states, intensities, and tendencies will change the dimensionality of disability remains an open prospect, but at the very least, it forces recognition of the limits of disability as a category. The disability at stake is an affective tendency of sorts as well as a mental state, and as such challenges the basis upon which disability rights frames have routed their representational (visibility) politics.

POSTHUMAN SUBALTERNS

In *The Right to Maim* I also foreground an intervention into the fields of posthumanism, object-oriented ontology, and new materialisms, insisting on an analysis of the subhuman or not quite human along with the cyborgian and the posthuman. I believe it is utterly crucial not to leave these fields alone to play in their unraced genealogies. Critics of these fields have interrogated the relation between objects and objectification and how and why certain objects get to be subjects while others remain objectified and/or commodified, for example, Fred Moten on the para-ontology of the commodity in contrast to the flat ontology centered by object-oriented ontologists, where everything is leveled.[94] Mel Chen's work emphasizes the pros and cons of investing in notions of vibrant matter without concomitant attention to the material conditions of the production of that matter, not to mention deracinated and desexualized notions of vibrancy and agency. Disability theories and theorists in general have much fodder for challenging object-oriented ontologies, rarely having had the privilege of taking objects and human relations to them for granted. Eunjung Kim writes: "Instead of defending the fraught definition of 'human' as the basis of a 'moral' and caring world in order to valorize disabled existence, I suggest recognizing the intercorporeal ontology of objects, with the aim not of conferring inherent rights on them but, rather, of undermining efforts to deny a being humanness on the basis of object-like status."[95] Bodies understood as disabled, in particular cognitively disabled, have often been cast as inert passive objects rather than human subjects through a projection of "degraded objecthood" elevated over "qualified personhood."[96] Thus the mere status of objecthood itself cannot revitalize our relations to objects: our attitudes toward objects need to be reevaluated. In other words: *objects are vaunted unless they are humans who are considered objects (slaves, "vegetables").*[97]

This recognition, in turn, has challenged the status of rational, agential, survivor-oriented politics based on the privileging of language capacity to make rights claims. Why? Because the inability to "communicate" functions as a significant determinant of mental or cognitive impairment (thereby regulating the human/animal distinction, as well as a distinction between humans and objects), thus destabilizing the centrality of the human capacity for thought and cognition. Language is multiple—for example, math and computation are considered to be languages, and nonhuman animals certainly have forms of communication that could be considered linguistic.[98] And yet "language" has been reduced to a singularly human capacity, though we might want to make distinctions between linguistic domains, the province of many nonhuman animals, unlike "language proper."[99] Not only is language the primary or even defining attribute that separates humans from animals at this current historical juncture—and it is worth noting, following Jacques Derrida, that the distinction is differently articulated in different eras and areas of knowledge, variously as one of sentience, of capacity to feel pain, and of subjective capacity. As Mel Chen writes, the "linguistic criteria are established prominently and immutably in humans' terms, establishing human preeminence before the debates about the linguistic placement of humans' animal subordinates even begin."[100] So humans decide, based on the linguistic capacities defined by human language, that "language" forever appears as human language, and this language by definition creates humans as superior to nonhuman animals. There are thus two interventions needed: first, the understanding of language as running across species rather than articulating a human/nonhuman animal divide; and second, destabilizing what is often called the "primacy of language," interrogating the place of language itself. In doing so, language can enter multiplicity, and it can also be resituated as one intensification of a bodily capacity, one manner of many that the body can articulate itself, one platform out of many through which politics can enunciate, and finally one kind of matter. Language is not opposed to matter, but rather is matter—among many matters. If, according to posthumanist thinkers such as Manuel DeLanda and Karen Barad, language has been granted too much power, non-anthropomorphic conceptions of humans—that is, conceptions of humans that do not anthropomorphize themselves—are necessary to resituate language as one of many captures of the intensities of bodily capacities, an event of bodily assemblages rather than a performative act of signification.[101]

In an effort to open up capacity as a source of generative affective politics rather than only a closure around neoliberal demands, I would briefly like to return to Gayatri Spivak's "Can the Subaltern Speak?," perhaps unfashionably so.[102] In the context of debility, capacity, and disability, "Can the subaltern speak?" becomes not only a mandate for epistemological correctives. This haunting query also points to ontological and bodily capacity, as granting "voice" to the subaltern comes into tension with the need, in the case of the human/nonhuman animal distinction, to destabilize privileged modes of communication, representation, and language altogether. For Spivak, "subaltern consciousness" is a theoretical fiction. "Representation"—darstellen (portrait) and vetreten (proxy)—is an anthropocentric demand, and a philosophical and political privilege of the human—an overrepresentation, in

Sylvia Wynter's sense. Spivak's own ambivalence toward representation as an anthropocentric demand and as the philosophical privilege of the human surfaces momentarily, most significantly in the section discussing Sigmund Freud's seminal essay "A Child Is Being Beaten." Here I discern two realms where the dominance of language as a distinctly and exceptional human attribute remains yet to be established. The first, further drawing on psychoanalysis, is the prelinguistic realm of the child, where the analyst has to speak for the child, giving voice for and to the child. There is a paradox in Freud's statement of the speaker who cannot speak; or, the child is not yet a speaking subject, and therefore not a subject. Spivak grafts onto the "dangers run by Freud's discourse" another sentence that fumbles "our efforts to give the subaltern a voice in history": "White men are saving brown women from brown men." The second realm is where Spivak's impulse to push back against humanism appears, in a reference to the "archaic past," part of a history of repression of "a preoriginary space where human and animal were not yet differentiated."[103] The first instance is a triangulation that positions the hapless child/woman in need of rescue from two figures interchangeably rotating from savior to perpetrator. The second harks the prelinguistic or the semiotic and references the becoming of the subject in both psychic and historical terms.

It remains unclear to me whether for Spivak the problem is the epistemic enclosure in which the subaltern is stuck, or if representation itself is the problem, in which case she might ultimately be more aligned with Deleuze's (and Foucault's) project than (she) originally thought. Is she really so interested in saving the subject? Or is she already diagnosing the political impasse of representation, in that "speech," a normative function of humanist politics, is seemingly foreclosed for Spivak? The lexicon of debility and capacity saturates this text. In relation to the normative function of speech, for example, the subaltern is "mute."[104] The invocation of conditions of disability is crucial here, as Spivak in effect is making an argument about the debilitating (for many) and capacitating (for few) conditions of contemporary political, intellectual, and epistemological knowledge production practices. Undoing these knots between representation and language has led me to question why the subaltern is usually assumed to be necessarily human. If subalternity is by definition a relation of the un/non/subhuman that are excluded from dominant systems of circulation, deemed unfit for recognition or unable to be recognized, the subaltern, then, could be generously rethought as a nonhuman or inhuman configuration. In Spivak's schema, "woman" as a potential subaltern cannot simply be added to the list of pious items slated for rescue, remedied through an epistemological corrective; by extension, neither can "species" or nonhuman animals, or even "people with disabilities." In my torquing of this field-defying essay, the subaltern cannot speak because of the human/nonhuman animal divide that dictates that speech always shows up in an anthropocentric, and thus ableist, form; the subaltern cannot speak nor be heard within (phallo)logocentric, and thus anthropocentric, frames of legibility. To challenge geopolitically uninflected theorizations of post/humanism, I follow Wynter's formulation of the human as representationally overdetermined by one *genre* of human, through the ongoing restoration of humanism via the individual despite the force of biopolitical population construction. For Wynter, the project of a radical humanism has yet to be begun, much less left behind for posthumanist waters. Her project is not one of demanding inclusion into the Overrepresentation of Man as human, and therefore does not reassert the frames of temporality, progression, or priority. Rather, she insists on the multiplicity of humans and human forms that have yet to be known, a revolutionary humanism with deep commitments to those entities that are instrumentally denied humanity in order for it to be sustained.[105] The Overrepresentation of Man as human is thus the closed system that can only project onto/ as the subaltern what Spivak calls the "itinerary of Man." Reading Spivak and Wynter together reveals the speaking subject of politics and history is a genre of the human that the subaltern defies, populated by nonhuman entities as well as humans produced as objects, as property, as animals, as subhumans unworthy of political consideration.

Therefore, disability studies, posthumanism, and critical animal studies may perhaps articulate a common interest in a nonanthropocentric, interspecies vision of affective politics. While disability studies has diligently refuted the negative slurs referencing animality unleashed against those with cognitive and physical disabilities, it has, at times, unwittingly reinforced a privileging of the human in doing so.[106] Noting that disability activists argue for rights for those disabled who are "lacking certain highly valued abilities like rationality and physical independence," Sunaura Taylor asks, "How can disability studies legitimately exclude animals for these reasons without contradiction? I argue that disability studies has accidentally created a framework of justice that can no longer exclude other species."[107] The burgeoning field of critical animal studies is thus also a part of the endeavor to situate human capacities within a range of capacities of species as opposed to reifying their singularity. Following Taylor's critique, it is also necessarily a site where a persistent examination of the entwinement of race and animality cannot be elided. Critical posthumanist or inhumanist theorizing questions the boundaries between human and nonhuman, matter and discourse, technology and body, and interrogates the practices through which these boundaries are constituted, stabilized, and destabilized. It, however, can also be the case that "the posthuman," as Alexander Weheliye notes, "frequently appears as little more than the white liberal subject in techno-informational guise."[108] Provocatively suggesting that "perhaps the 'post'human is not a temporal location but a geographic one," Zakiyyah Iman Jackson asks: "Might there be a (post)humanism that does not privilege European Man and its idiom? . . . Is it possible that the very subjects central to posthumanist inquiry—the binarisms of human/animal, nature/culture, animate/inanimate, organic/inorganic—find their relief outside of the epistemological locus of the West?"[109] Dan Goodley, Rebecca Lawthom, and Katherine Runswick Cole, however, call for a "posthuman disability studies," arguing that disabled bodies epitomize the ethical reaches of posthumanist discourses that challenge the stability and centrality of the human form.[110] So, even as scholars rightly challenge romanticized versions of posthumanism, these challenges betray an assumption that the posthuman always refers to an idealized humanness.

TO WHATEVER EXTENT LIVING IS, can be, has been, or continues to be a maximal output of energy and capacity with a minimal set of resources, many populations are engaged at some moment, if not continuously, with their slow deaths. It might be too obvious to state that things simply "do not get better." More perniciously, one could suggest, as does Geeta Patel, that finance capital enforces repeated mandatory investments in our own slow deaths, continually reproducing the conditions of possibility that enable the sustained emergence and proliferation of debility, capacity, and disability. Furthermore, the proliferation of these modalities happens not only via neoliberal subjects but also through affective tendencies and inhuman economies of temporality, spatiality, and corporeality. The chapters that follow offer analyses of trans becoming in relation to affect and the matter of race; U.S. imperialism and the effect of belated and disavowed debilitation on populations produced as "elsewhere"; Israel's project of rehabilitation through the spatial, affective, and corporeal debilitation of Palestine; and the sovereign right to maim wielded by Israel in relation to the right to kill.

[1]

Bodies with New Organs

Becoming Trans, Becoming Disabled

"Transgender rights are the civil rights issue of our time." So stated Vice President Joe Biden just one week before the November 2012 election. Months earlier, President Barack Obama had publicly declared his support for gay marriage, sending mainstream LGBT organizations and queer liberals into a tizzy.[1] It was an unexpected comment for an election season, and nearly inaudibly rendered during a conversation with a concerned mother of Miss Trans New England. Yet Biden's remark, encoded in the rhetoric of recognition, seemed logical from a well-established civil rights era teleology: first the folks of color, then the homosexuals, now the trans folk.[2] Biden's proclamation could be one genesis of the "transgender tipping point," a term coined by *Time* magazine in June 2014 to delineate a plethora of (positive) media representation of transgender people. Indeed, a slew of antidiscrimination laws were passed under Obama's presidency; a national debate emerged about women's colleges and the presence of trans students; accessibility to gender-neutral bathrooms was lauded and also abhorred; *Orange Is the New Black* brought Laverne Cox and other trans actors to widespread public attention; and Bruce Jenner came out as Caitlyn.

There were also unprecedented numbers of trans women of color, mainly black trans women, murdered during this same tipping point periodization.

The narrative of the tipping point feeds into the post–civil rights era story about the linear progression of the bestowal of rights. What happens to conventional understandings of "women's rights" in this telos? The "transgender question" puts into crisis the framing of women's rights as human rights by pushing further the relationships between gender normativity and access to rights and citizenship. I could note, as many have, that failing an intersectional analysis of these movements, we are indeed left with a very partial portrait of who benefits and how from this according of rights, not to mention their tactical invocation within this period of liberalism whereby, as Elizabeth Povinelli argues, "potentiality has been domesticated."[3] As Jin Haritaworn and C. Riley Snorton argue, "It is necessary to interrogate how the uneven institutionalization of women's, gay, and trans politics produces a transnormative subject, whose universal trajectory of coming out/transition, visibility, recognition, protection, and self-actualization largely remains uninterrogated in its complicities and convergences with biomedical, neoliberal, racist, and imperialist projects."[4] In relation to this uneven institutionalization, Haritaworn and Snorton remark that trans of color positions are "barely conceivable." The conundrum here, as elsewhere, involves measuring the political efficacy of arguing for inclusion within and for the same terms of recognition that rely on such elisions. Desires for trans of color positions to become conceivable necessarily deploy their bare inconceivability to critique and upend that which seems conceivable.[5]

Biden's remarks foreshadow the steep cost of the intelligibility of transgender identity within national discourses and legal frames of recognition. Does his acknowledgment of transgender rights signal the uptake of a new variant of homonationalism—a "trans(homo)nationalism"? Or is transgender identity a variation of processes of citizenship and nationalism through disciplinary normativization rather than a variation of homonationalism? In either instance, such hailings, I argue, generate new figures of citizenship through which the successes of rights discourses will produce new biopolitical failures—trans of color, for one instance. Susan Stryker and Aren Z. Aizura call the "production of transgender whiteness" a "process of value extraction from bodies of color" that occurs both nationally and transnationally.[6] Thinking of this racial dynamic as a process of value extraction highlights the impossibility of a rights platform that incorporates trans of color positions, since their inconceivability is a precondition to the emergence of the rights project, not to mention central to its deployment and successful integration into national legibility. Adding biopolitical capacity to the portrait, Aizura writes that this trans citizenship entails "fading into the population . . . but also the imperative to be 'proper' in the eyes of the state: to reproduce, to find proper employment; to reorient one's 'different' body into the flow of the nationalized aspiration for possessions, property [and] wealth."[7] This trans(homo)nationalism is therefore capacitated, even driven, not only by the abjection of bodies unable to meet these proprietary racial and gendered mandates of bodily comportment, but also by the concomitant marking of those abjected bodies as debilitated. The debilitating and abjecting are co-substancing processes.

In light of this new but not entirely surprising assimilation of gender difference through nationalism, I want to complicate the possibilities of accomplishing such trans normativization by foregrounding a different historical trajectory: one not hailed or celebrated by national LGBT groups or the media, nor explicitly theorized in most queer or trans theory. This is the move from the 1990 Americans with Disabilities Act (ADA) to the present moment of trans hailing by the U.S. state.[8] Historically and contemporaneously, the nexus of disability and trans has been fraught, especially for trans bodies that may resist alliances with people with disabilities in no small part because of long struggles against stigmatization and pathologization that may be reinvoked through such an affiliation. But stigmatization is only part of the reason for this thwarted connection. Neoliberal mandates regarding productive, capacitated bodies entrain trans bodies to re-create an able body not only in terms of gender and sexuality but also in terms of economic productivity and the development of national economy.[9] Thus, trans relation to disability is not simply one of phobic avoidance of stigma; it is also about trans bodies being recruited, in tandem with many other bodies, for a more generalized transformation of capacitated bodies into viable neoliberal subjects.

Many trans bodies are reliant on medical care, costly pharmacological and technological interventions, legal protections, and public accommodations from the very same institutions and apparatuses that functionalize gender normativities and create systemic exclusions. How do people who rely on accessing significant resources within a political economic context, where the possessive individual is the basis for rights claims—including the right to medical care—disrupt the very models on which they depend?

This dependence is required in order to make the claims that, in the case of trans people, enable trans people to realize themselves as trans in the first place. I explore this conundrum for trans bodies through the ambivalent and vexed relationship to disability in three respects: (1) the legal apparatus of the ADA, which sets the scene for a contradictory status to disability and the maintenance of gender normativity as a requisite for disabled status, one organized through hierarchies of race; (2) the fields of disability studies and trans studies, which both pivot on certain exceptionalized figures that may delimit their entanglements; and (3) political organizing priorities and strategies that partake in transnormative forms not only of passing but also of what I call "piecing," a recruitment into neoliberal forms of fragmentation of the body for capitalist profit.[10] Finally, I offer a speculative imagined affiliation between disability and trans, "becoming trans," which seeks to link disability, trans, racial, and interspecies discourses to acknowledge porous boundaries constitutive of the overwhelming force of ontological multiplicity, attuned to the perpetual differentiation of variation and the multiplicity of affirmative becomings.[11] What kinds of assemblages appear that might refuse to isolate trans as one kind of specific or singular variant of disability and disability as one kind of singular variant of trans?[12] What kind of political and scholarly alliances might potentiate when each takes up and acknowledges the inhabitations and the more generalized conditions of the other, creating genealogies that read both as implicated within the same assemblages of power? The focus here is not on epistemological correctives but on ontological irreducibilities that transform the fantasy of discreteness of categories not through their disruption but, rather, through their dissolution via multiplicity. Rather than produce conceptual interventions that map onto the political or produce a differently political rendering of its conceptual moorings, reflected in the debate regarding transnormativity and trans of color conceivability, I wish to offer a generative, speculative reimagining of what can be signaled by the political.

DISABILITY LAW AND TRANS DISCRIMINATION

The legal history that follows matters because it both reflects and enshrines the contradictory relationship that trans bodies may have to resisting pathological medicalization yet needing to access benefits through the medical-industrial complex. The explicit linkages to the trans body as a body rendered disabled and/or rehabilitated from disability have been predominantly routed through debates about gender identity disorder (GID). Arriving in the third edition of the American Psychiatric Association's *Diagnostic and Statistical Manual of Mental Disorders* (DSM-III, published in 1980), on the heels of the DSM-II depathologization of homosexuality in 1974, GID was eliminated in the DSM-5, released in May 2013, and replaced with the diagnosis gender dysphoria.[13] These complex debates have focused largely on a series of explicit inclusions and exclusions of GID in relation to the DSM and the ADA. The inclusion of GID in 1980 and its focus on childhood behavior were largely understood as a compensatory maneuver for the deletion of homosexuality, thus instating surveillance mechanisms that would perhaps prevent homosexuality.[14] In contrast, a notable passage in the ADA specified the exclusion of "gender identity disorders not resulting from physical impairments" as a disability—couched in an exclusionary clause that included "transvestitism, transsexualism, pedophilia, exhibitionism, voyeurism, . . . 'other sexual disorders,'" and completely arbitrary "conditions" such as compulsive gambling, kleptomania, pyromania, and substance use disorders involving illegal drugs.[15] This clause was largely understood (unlike the specific exclusion of homosexuality) as an entrenchment of the pathologization of GID. This deliberate inclusion of the terms of exclusion is a crucial piece of the story, in part because to date the ADA is "the most extensive civil rights law to address bodily norms."[16]

Given the ADA's hodgepodge of excluded conditions, many of which carry great social stigma and/or are perceived as criminal activity, most commentators concur with L. Camille Herbert's sentiment that "while one might argue for the exclusion of certain conditions from the definition of disability as justified by not wanting to pathologize certain individuals and conditions, this does not appear to have been the motivation of Congress."[17] The process by which Congress arrived at these exclusions was marred by moral panic discourses about diseased and debilitated bodies, discourses that the ADA was produced in part to ameliorate. Former senator Jesse Helms (R-NC), writes R. Nick Gorton, "raised the specter that the law would provide disability protections to numerous politically unpopular groups," concluding that most people who are HIV-positive are drug addicts, homosexuals, bisexuals, pedophiles, or kleptomaniacs, among others, and that the exclusion was enacted "as a direct result of Helms's efforts."[18] Noting that the ADA "unequivocally" endorses the use of the DSM in recognizing conditions of disability, Kari Hong argues that "understanding why a dozen conditions were removed becomes an important task," as the exclusion not only disqualifies certain conditions from consideration as a disability but also "isolate[s] particular conditions from medical authority." Hong also points out that Helms's "bifurcation of disability into 'good' (wheelchairs) and 'bad' (transvestitism) categories echoes a disturbing misuse of medicine."[19] Ultimately, Congress capitulated and sacrificed these excluded groups in exchange for holding onto the protection of another vilified "minority" group: individuals with HIV.[20] This move of course insists on problematic bifurcations, perhaps strategically so, between individuals diagnosed with GID and individuals diagnosed with HIV.

Thus, Kevin Barry argues, "The ADA is a moral code, and people with GID its moral castaways." He adds that GID "sits at the uneasy crossroads of pathology and difference,"[21] an uneasy crossroads that continues to manifest (especially now as GID has been eliminated in the DSM-5).[22] Adrienne L. Hiegel elaborates this point at length, with particular emphasis on how this exclusion recodes the labor capacities of the transsexual body. In segmenting off "sexual behavior disorders" and "gender identity disorders" from the ADA's definition of disability, the "Act carves out a new class of untouchables. . . . By leaving open a space of permissive employer discrimination, the Act identifies the sexual 'deviant' as the new pariah, using the legal machinery of the state to mark as outsiders those whose noncompliant body renders them unfit for full integration into a working community."[23]

From this perspective, the ADA does less to change the ethical and symbolic weight of nonnormative corporeality and disability itself; instead, it reifies standards of bodily capacity and debility through the reproduction of gender normativity as integral to the productive potential of the disabled body. Further, the disaggregation, and thus the potential deflation, of political and social alliances between homosexuality, transsexuality, and individuals with HIV is necessary to the solidification of this gender normativity, solicited in exchange for the conversion of disability from a socially maligned and excluded status to a version of liberal acknowledgment, inclusion, and incorporation. The modern seeds of what Nicole Markotic and Robert McRuer call "crip nationalism"—the hailing of some disabilities as socially productive for national economies and ideologies that then further marginalize other disabilities—are evident here. The tolerance of the "difference" of disability is negotiated through the disciplining of the body along other normative registers of sameness.[24] And further, what Sharon Snyder and David Mitchell term "ablenationalism"—that is, the ableist contours of national inclusion and registers of productivity— ironically underwrites the ADA even as the ADA serves as groundbreaking legislation to challenge it. Snyder and Mitchell describe ablenationalism as the "implicit assumption that minimum levels of corporeal, intellectual, and sensory capacity, in conjunction with subjective aspects of aesthetic appearance, are required of citizens seeking to access the 'full benefits' of citizenship."[25] In reorganizing the terms of disability, ablenationalism redirects the pathos and stigma of disability onto different registers of bodily deviance and defectiveness, in this particular instance that of gender nonnormativity. In that sense, crip nationalism goes hand in hand with ablenationalism; indeed, ablenationalism is its progenitor.

The specific details of the exclusionary clause might gesture toward the multifaceted reasons that, as Snyder and Mitchell observe, "queer, transsexual, and intersexed peoples . . . exist at the margins of disability discourse."[26] It is also worth remembering, pace Hortense Spillers, that gender normativity coagulates through biopolitical control of reproduction, civilizational discourses, and racial hierarchies.[27] Therefore, whiteness is not a by-product of this cohesion, but rather constitutive of the consolidation of gender-normative yet disabled difference. Spillers argues that debilitation of slavery involved not only mutilation and dismemberment but also the denial of the gendering constitutive of legitimate kinship, whereby "one is neither female, nor male, as both subjects are taken into 'account' as quantities."[28] She continues:

> In the historic outline of dominance, the respective subject-positioning of "male" and "female" adhere to no symbolic integrity. At a time when current critical discourses appear to compel us more and more decidedly toward gender "undecidability," it would appear reactionary, if not dumb, to insist on the integrity of female/male gender. But undressing these conflations of meaning, as they appear under the rule of dominance, would restore, as figurative possibility, not only Power to the Female (for Maternity), but also Power to the Male (for Paternity). We would gain, in short, the *potential* for gender differentiation as it might express itself along a range of stress points, including human biology in its intersection with the project of culture.[29]

The potential for gender differentiation *in the first instance* is already the potential—indeed the capacitation—of whiteness; the capacity to lean into gender "undecidability," the province of that same whiteness.

It is not simply that the ADA excludes GID and, by extension, trans from recognition as potentially disabling. Rather, transsexuality—and likely those versions of transsexuality that are deemed also improperly raced and classed—is understood as "too disabled" to be rehabilitated into citizenship, or not properly disabled enough to be recoded for labor productivity. Further, the ADA arbitrates the distinctions between homosexuality and transsexuality along precisely these pathologized lines. Contrary to what Hiegel claims, the sexual "deviant" is hardly the "new pariah." Rather, there is a new sexual deviant in town, demarcated from an earlier one. Indeed, the enthusiastic embracing of the ADA by some gay and lesbian activists and policy makers for the exclusion of homosexuality as a "sexual behavior disorder" did not go unnoticed by trans activists who felt differently about the ADA.[30] Proclivities toward queer ableism are therefore predicated on the ADA's parsing homosexuality from other "sexual disorders," as well as in the histories of political organizing. Zach Strassburger describes the process of homonationalism by noting that "as the gay and lesbian rights movement gained steam, the transgender movement grew more inclusive to cover those left behind by the gay and lesbian movement's focus on its most mainstream members and politically promising plaintiffs."[31] Given the political history of parsing trans from queer through the maintenance of gender normativity, can disability function proactively and productively, as a conversion or translation of the stigma through which trans can demarcate its distance from aspects of LGBT organizing that are increasingly normative?[32]

I offer this brief historical overview to lay out the stakes for the debate between demedicalizing trans bodies (favoring the use of gender discrimination law to adjudicate equality claims) and successfully using disability law to access crucial medical care. What is evident from these discussions is that vociferous debates about the utility of the medical model in trans jurisprudence persist. Strassburger, who argues for an "expanded vision of disability" based on the social model that could be applied for trans rights, notes nonetheless that the medical model of trans has often been more successful than sex and gender discrimination and sexual orientation protection. He contends that in its emphasis on demedicalization, the transgender rights movement, despite reluctantly admitting the success of medical strategy, ignores the pragmatic aspects of litigation. Strassburger also notes that "demedicalization would mirror the gay rights movement's very successful efforts to frame gayness as good rather than a disease."[33]

For others, the debate between medicalization and demedicalization forestalls a broader conversation about access to proper medical care, one that has been foregrounded by feminist struggles over reproductive rights, for example.[34] Proponents of the use of disability law further argue that difficult access to medical care is not a complete given for all disenfranchised populations. For example, Alvin Lee argues that the "unique aspects of incarceration and prison health care justify and indeed compel the use of the medical model when advocating for trans prisoners' right to sex reassignment surgery."[35] Lee notes that the usual bias against lower-income populations in the use of the medical model does not apply to the "right-to-care" prison context, where medical evidence is the best way to demonstrate serious and necessary rather than elective health care, given the "general principle that individual liberties should be restricted in prison."[36] Other legal practitioners such as Jeannie J. Chung and Dean Spade are curious about the success of social models of disability in transgender litigation. Spade, for example, has carefully elaborated his ambivalence about the use of disability law and the medical model in relation to his firm social justice commitment to the demedicalization of trans, arguing for a "multi-strategy approach."[37]

TRANS EXCEPTIONALISM: PASSING AND PIECING

In addition to the robust debates about jurisprudence on trans and disability, transgender studies and disability studies are often thought of as coming into being in the early 1990s in the U.S. academy, a periodization that reflects a shift in practices of recognition, economic utility, and social visibility that obscures prior scholarship. In terms of trans, for example, Stryker and Aizura note that "to assert the emergence of transgender studies as a field only in the 1990s rests on a set of assumptions that permit a differentiation between one kind of work on 'transgender phenomena' and another, for there had of course been a great deal of academic, scholarly, and scientific work on various forms of gender variance long before the 1990s." Among the various historical changes they list as significant to this emergence are "new political alliances forged during the AIDS crisis, which brought sexual and gender identity politics into a different sort of engagement with the biomedical and pharmaceutical establishments."[38]

This emergence of disability and trans identity as intersectional coordinates required exceptionalizing both the trans body and the disabled body to convert the debility of a nonnormative body into a form of social and cultural capacity, whether located in state recognition, identity politics, market economies, the medical-industrial complex, academic knowledge production, subject positioning, or all of these. As a result, both fields of study—trans studies and disability studies—suffer from a domination of whiteness and contend with the normativization of the acceptable and recognizable subject. The disabled subject is often a body with a physical "impairment." In trans identity, the more recently emergent trajectory of female-to-male (FTM) enlivened by access to hormones, surgical procedures, and prosthetics has centralized a white trans man subject. While the disabled subject has needed to reclaim forms of debility to exceptionalize the transgression and survivorship of that disability, the transnormative subject views the body as endlessly available for hormonal and surgical manipulation and becoming, a body producing toward ableist norms. Further, transgender does not easily signal within "conventional notions of disability" because it is not a "motor, sensory, psychiatric, or cognitive impairment" or a chronic illness.[39]

Eli Clare, a trans man with cerebral palsy, has generated perhaps the most material on the specific epistemological predicaments of the disabled trans subject or the trans disabled subject, providing much-needed intersectional analysis. Clare writes of the ubiquity of this sentiment: "I often hear trans people—most frequently folks who are using, or want to use medical technology to reshape their bodies—name their trans-ness a disability, a birth defect."[40] Here Clare emphasizes the trans interest in a cure for the defect, a formulation that has been politically problematized in disability rights platforms, reinforces ableist norms, and alienates potential convivialities: "To claim our bodies as defective, and to pair defect with cure . . . disregards the experiences of many disabled people."[41] Disability here is not only the "narrative prosthesis" through which the trans body will overcome and thus resolve its debility, but also the "raw material out of which other socially disempowered communities make themselves visible."[42] Seen through this mechanism of resource extraction, disability is the disavowed materiality of a trans embodiment that abstracts and thus effaces this materiality from its self-production.

Toby Beauchamp adds to the conversation about cure the notion of concealment via legal (identity documents) and medical intervention, stating: "Concealing gender deviance is about much more than simply erasing transgender status. It also necessitates altering one's gender presentation to conform to white, middle-class, able-bodied, heterosexual understandings of normative gender."[43] The cure, then, revolves around rehabilitation to multiple social norms. Beauchamp further notes that the process of diagnosis and treatment inevitably reinforces this rehabilitation: "Medical surveillance focuses first on individuals' legibility *as* transgender, and then, following medical interventions, on their ability to *conceal* any trans status or deviance."[44] While access to adequate and sensitive health care for trans people can be a daunting if not foreclosed process, emergent conversations on "transgender health" can also function to reassert neoliberal norms of bodily capacity and debility.[45] The transnormative subject might categorically reject the potential identification and alliance with disability, despite the two sharing an intensive relation to medicalization, and perhaps because of the desire for rehabilitation and an attendant indebtedness to medicalization. Clare avers that while the "disability rights movement fiercely resists the medicalization of bodies" to refuse the collapsing of the body "into mere medical condition," in his estimation "we haven't questioned the fundamental relationship between trans people and the very idea of diagnosis. Many of us are still invested in the ways we're medicalized."[46]

Even in politically progressive narrations of transgender embodiment, for example, an unwitting ableism and the specter of disability as intrinsic disenfranchisement often linger as by-products of the enchantment with the transformative capacities of bodies. For example, Eva Hayward's take on the "Cripple" toggles a very tenuous line between the "Cripple" as a metaphor of regeneration and the crippling effects of amputation.[47] Likewise, Bailey Kier, describing an instance of fishes' ability to transsex in response to toxic endocrine-disrupting chemicals (EDCs), wonders if such transformations are a "technology beyond our grasp," disregarding the uneven biopolitical distribution of such toxins that render his desires for a global "embracing [of] our shared transsex" violently idealistic: "EDCs are part of the food, productive and re/productive chain of non-human and human life and we will need to devise ways, just like fish, to adapt to their influence."[48]

Emerging identifications with "transability" also have a vexed relationship to disability: seemingly positive on the outset, potentially violently idealizing and appropriative upon closer examination. Transabled individuals, linked to the diagnosis of bodily integrity identity disorder, are those who desire amputation, paralysis, blindness, deafness, and use of wheelchairs, superglue, cotton stuffed in ears, personal alarms, ototoxic drugs, surgeries to sever the auditory nerve, leg braces, blindfolds, and other forms of body modification and alteration to simulate certain conditions of disability.[49] According to both Bethany Stevens and Anne Lawrence, the analogy of transability to transgender is made largely because of the alignments of desires for surgical modification and reconciliation of internal identity and external embodiment, and early childhood onset of a sense of being "trapped in the wrong body."[50] Nikki Sullivan's work excavates the (ultimately unhelpful) taxonomic work entailed in producing the "wannabee" as a devotee who mistakes the object of desire for the desiring self/subject. Such conclusions that the wannabee or the transablist mistakes desire for a disabled other as a desire for disabling the self have been deduced in large part due to comparisons with the understanding of transsexuality as a sexual disorder where one is aroused by seeing oneself as the opposite gender.[51]

Saturated within the resonant discourses of "being in the wrong body," "wanting to feel whole," and "transitioning" into being disabled, transablists seek bodily modification that is considered pathological because of its purported decapacitation of the body. Transabled individuals claim that it is not disability per se that is desired but the reconciliation of body image with the body. The sources of what is otherwise constituted as a disability are perceived as enhancing, capacitating, and enlivening bodily attributes. The "disability," then, is located in the able body, a debilitation due to the incongruence of the "whole" body in relation to the desired body that is missing a limb or that cannot walk, hear, or see. "Pretending" in this context—the act of passing as disabled—is not simply about a transition from "being able-bodied" to "being disabled." It is about radically recapacitating the body through means otherwise considered to be profoundly debilitating.[52] Given the overlaps between transgender and transableism, the ableist (positive) terms with which some trans body modification is hailed seem to then render transabled desires for body modification to be cast in negative terms. What transability might engender is a body that not only scrambles hierarchies of organ ordering, divesting from normative attachments of capacity to various organs, but also refuses the capacitation of the able-oriented model altogether.

In her research on transability, Stevens notes that generally, only physical impairments are desired, reifying a hierarchy of disability.[53] Sometimes called parasites by people with disabilities, transablists raise questions about what the boundaries of disability are, how (a "real") disability is defined, and whether probing about the authenticity of disability is an ethical and fair endeavor. Stevens conjectures that transablists may well be dealing with a mental health issue, which then "makes them a part of the disability community but perhaps not in the way that they want." She is, however, ultimately not persuaded by the plight of transablists: "The proximity to a devotee-type fetishization of disability, however, makes the acceptance of transability as even a mental health issue a bit too muddled."[54] This assessment, however, does not detract from a certain form of capacitation claimed by the process and desire of becoming disabled.

There is a third element here that produces disability as the disavowed material co-substance of trans bodies. While there are understandable desires to avoid stigma and, as the ADA demonstrates, a demand for bodies with disabilities to integrate into a capitalist economy as productive bodies, the third factor involves aspirational forms of trans exceptionalism, one version of which seeks rehabilitation, cure, and concealment. However, this exceptionalism is not only about passing as gender normative; it is also about inhabiting an exceptional trans body—which is a different kind of trans exceptionalism. A new transnormative citizen is predicated not on passing but on "piecing," galvanized through mobility, transformation, regeneration, flexibility, and the creative concocting of the body. Trans piecing performs medicalization as strategic embodiment. Regarding piecing as an elemental aspect of neoliberal biomedical approaches to bodies with disabilities, now globalized to all bodies, Mitchell and Snyder argue that the body has become "a multi-sectional market" distinct from Fordist regimes that divided workers from each other: "We are now perpetual members of an audience encouraged to experience our bodies in pieces. . . . Whereas disabled people were trained to recognize their disabled parts as definitely inferior, late capitalism trains everyone to separate their good from bad—a form of alienation that feeds the market's penchant for 'treating' our parts separately. The body becomes a terrain of definable localities, each colonized by its particular pathologies dictated by the medicalized marketplace."[55] While this partitioning of the body is not a recent emergence—there is a long history of bodily compartmentalization as a prerequisite for capitalist production—this piecing is not only about enhancing productive capacities but also about extending the body experientially and extracting value not just from bodies, but also from body parts and particles.[56]

In this economy of alienated parts, piecing becomes a prized capacity, a mark of manifesting "the body as entrepreneurial enterprise," to paraphrase Foucault.[57] Jack Halberstam observes that "the transgender body has emerged as futurity itself, a kind of heroic fulfillment of post-modern promises of gender flexibility."[58] Halberstam is cautious about overinvesting in gender fluidity as transgressive capacity, noting that market economies already capitalize on "flexibility" as the hallmark of neoliberal economic productivity. But which transgender body (bodies?) is actually understood as "futurity itself"? This suturing of trans to exceptional futurity and the potential that the future offers is the new transnormative body. Again, this is not the transnormative body that passes but the transnormative body that "pieces," the commodification not of wholeness or of rehabilitation but of plasticity, crafting parts from wholes, bodies without and with new organs. Piecing thus appears transgressive when in fact it is constitutive not only of transnormativity but also of aspects of neoliberal market economies.

To situate this trans body that is "futurity itself," it might be helpful to turn to trans organizing. Importantly, strategic interfaces between disability law and trans discrimination are also mirrored in growing political organizing and alliances between the two groups. One example includes a coalition of trans and persons with disabilities organized at the University of California, Santa Barbara, to jointly address the gendered and ableist expectations governing access, space, and surveillance in public restrooms called People in Search of Safe and Accessible Restrooms (pissar).[59] As another example, the Transgender Law Center in San Francisco has issued an activist handbook titled *Peeing in Peace* that uses disability-informed arguments for gender-neutral public toilets.

Along with a distinction between the disability rights movement and disability justice organizing maintained by activists such as Mia Mingus (discussed in the introduction), one should also retain a distinction between the transgender rights movement and trans justice organizing. TransJustice, one of the two major initiatives of the Audre Lorde Project in New York City, is a political group created by and for trans and gender-nonconforming people of color. TransJustice works to mobilize its communities and allies into action on the pressing political issues that trans of color folks face, including better access to jobs, housing, and education; the

FIG. 1.1. A blue gender-neutral bathroom sign at the University of California, Irvine, September 2014. Source: Reuters.

need for trans-sensitive health care, HIV-related services, and employment training programs; and resisting police, government, and anti-immigrant violence. The members of TransJustice tend to be African American and Latino working-class youth, and most are male-to-female (MTF). The convergence of racial identity and MTF seems significant and hardly incidental. Everything available on economic indicators, transgender health, incarceration, employment, street violence, and education amply demonstrates that trans women of color, especially black trans women, are massively disenfranchised in relation to other trans bodies and that the gulf between them and (white) FTMs is vast. Data are sparse but stark: "In 2003, 14 murders of transpeople were reported in the U.S., and 38 worldwide. Most were MTF and most were people of color."[60] The major concerns of TransJustice members cluster around access to school, employment, welfare provisions, and uncontaminated and inexpensive drugs and treatments—hormones, fillers, and surgeries. Many articulate their awareness of trans identity occurring simultaneously with a realization that they were attracted to the "wrong" sex (so not only or necessarily that they were in the "wrong" body). They desire to pass as beautiful, feminine, sexy. While a trans politics might render such forms of passing either a validation of a radical identity or a version of assimilation, misrecognition, or "selling out," for these members it is often entwined with, albeit obliquely, avoiding police harassment, community stigmatization, and familial rejection. Their engagement with the medical-industrial complex and with desires for transformative embodiment is not necessarily or only victorious, empowered by choice, or ultimately capacity building. Medicalization can be experienced as transformative, capacitating, debilitating, or all of the above, not to mention exclusionary.[61] They do not embody "futurity itself"; rather, their bodies can be read as sites of intensive struggle (medical, educational, employment, legal, social) over who indeed does get to embody—and experience—futurity, and who as a result will be cast off as the collateral damage of such strivings to capture the essence of the future.

Kris Hayashi, former director of the Audre Lorde Project, elaborates the emphases of trans organizing in New York City in general and TransJustice specifically:

> In New York City, TGNC [trans and gender-nonconforming] youth of color and low-income youth in the West Village neighborhood face ongoing violence and harassment at the hands of the police, as well as from residents who are primarily White and middle class to upper class. As a result, FIERCE!, an organization led and run primarily by TGNC low-income and homeless youth of color, prioritizes issues of police brutality and violence, as well as gentrification. TransJustice, a project of ALP [the Audre Lorde Project] that is led and run by TGNC people of color, has prioritized issues of unemployment and education access due to high rates of unemployment (60%–70%) facing TGNC people of color. Also in New York, a coalition of organizations and groups including TransJustice, Welfare Warriors, and the LGBT Community Center's Gender Identity Project have prioritized efforts to end the regular harassment and discrimination faced by TGNC people seeking to gain access to public assistance. Finally, many TGNC groups led primarily by people of color and low-income communities have also prioritized ending the U.S. war on terrorism, both in the United States and abroad.[62]

The work of TransJustice situates the vexed relations to futurity that its trans constituency must mediate in terms of quotidian survival.[63] In doing so, TransJustice activists expose how transnormativity functions through the privilege of whiteness, foregrounding a critical approach to the racializing technologies of trans identity. Further, the link that TransJustice makes to domestic and transnational manifestations of the war on terror rests upon two premises: one, the intrinsic imbrication of the global war on terror and racial capitalism in the United States (gentrification, unemployment, access to education, public assistance); two, the production of trans identity, activism, and politics that is not only sensitive to but intertwined with a transnational register accountable for and working against a U.S.-centric trans-homonationalism. Their analyses centralize who is *able to be* hailed/recognized as disabled and is *able to be* hailed/recognized as transgender as a function of state and legal recognition that is often elusive for their bodies, demonstrating that capacity—not only to pass but to piece—rather than primarily debility, deviance, victimhood, ostracization, or nonnormativity is at the center of these projects. The trans normative body that pieces, then, also passes, not as gender-normative male or female, but as trans. Susan Stryker and Nikki Sullivan, elaborating on this capacitation through piecing, write: "Our research . . . leads us toward a new understanding of bodily integration, one predicated not on the organic integrity of the human organism, but rather on the body's suitability for integration, its ability to be integrated as a biopolitical resource into a larger sociotechnical field, or into an apparatus such as the State."[64] In other words, they suggest a critique of the rehabilitation model as intrinsically a return to wholeness. Integration through piecing, rather than wholeness through passing, becomes a valued asset in control societies. Stryker and Sullivan continue: "The integrity of the body—that is, the ability of the body to be *integrated*—is thus, paradoxically, dependent on its enfleshment as always already torn, rent, incomplete, and unwhole."[65] This capacity to "integrate" oneself—not to pass but to piece—thus mediates the production as well as the lived experiences of molar categories such as race, class, and gender. What I am arguing here is that capacitation around health and attendant registers of bodily prowess, not necessarily identity as trans or disabled or abled or queer or not-trans, ultimately serves as the dividing social practice in biopolitical terms.[66] The debates about the disabled self and the non-disabled other reflect wider discourses of how those selves are materially constructed through the discourses that abound on abject and successful bodies.

While the capacity to piece (in order to pass as not passing) can produce new forms of transnormativity, Stryker and Sullivan rightly point out that bodily comportments that do not strive to manifest wholeness or an investment in the self as coherent do not have to reproduce liberal norms of being: "It is this aspect of bodily being that the liberal discourse of property rights in oneself does not, and cannot, account for; it is this aspect of bodily being that we seek to highlight when suggesting that individual demands for bodily alteration are also, necessarily, demands for new social bodies—new somatechnologies that ethically refigure the relationship between individual corporealities and aggregate assemblages of bodies."[67] This formulation, then, of new somatechnologies that refuse the individualizing mandate of neoliberal paradigms of bodily capacity and debility in favor of articulating greater connectivities between "aggregate assemblages of bodies" precisely flags the challenge of crafting convivial political praxes. And yet, it is also the case that such political praxes must never occlude the stratifications inherent in the quest to access such somatechnologies. The transnormative body of futurity that reflects neoliberal celebrations of flexibility and piecing remains an elusive reality for many. The distinctions between passing and piecing are thus fluid and shifting, given the kinds of piecing together of medical access and legal accommodations that many, perhaps most, trans of color bodies are forced to seek in any efforts to pass.

BECOMING TRANS? A GEOPOLITICS OF RACIAL ONTOLOGY

Molecular lines of flight trace out little modifications, they make detours, they sketch out rises and falls, but they are no less precise for all this, they even direct irreversible processes. . . . Many things happen on this second kind of line—becomings, micro-becomings, which don't even have the same rhythm as history. This is why family histories, registrations, commemorations, are so unpleasant, whilst our true changes take place elsewhere—another politics, another time, another individuation. —GILLES DELEUZE, Dialogues II

Thus far I have surveyed how biopolitical recognition of disability has installed a version of gender normativity, in this case specifically through the political apparatus of the ADA. I have then outlined forms of bodily exceptionalism that may produce transableist discourses. I turn now from the focus on subject construction—the trans subject(s) and the disabled subject(s) that are hailed and/or denied by legal legitimation, state recognition, public accommodation, and resource distribution—to offer a reconceptualization of corporeal assemblages that foregrounds ontological constellations. It is an approach that highlights how bodies are malleable as composites of parts, affects, compartmentalized capacities and debilities, and as data points and informational substrates. Continuous oscillation between identity, rights-based claims of the subject seeking recognition and biopolitical control operating largely though securing the sub- and paraindividual capacities of bodies for privatized (in the United States) regimes for pay is presumed. These "poles" of individuation and dividuation, as Gilles Deleuze and Félix Guattari note, are never without each other: "These two poles are inseparable; they entertain perpetual relations of transformation, conversion, jumping, falling, and rising."[68] The battle against the extraction and exploitation of bodily capacities and habituations is not going to happen through the terrain of intersectional politics alone. Biopolitical control societies work insidiously by using disciplinary power to keep or deflect our attention around the subjection of the subject, thus allowing control to manifest unhindered. As noted earlier, I argue that another interpretation of disciplinary apparatuses is that in part they function as foils for control mechanisms.

Enacting this oscillation moves between questions such as what disability is and what trans is toward what disability does and what trans does. James Overboe develops the Deleuzian notion of the impersonal life—one without a self—to cut through a disability politics of identity that centralizes the self-reflexive individual. He generates this intervention in order to "affirm disabled lives that are simply expressed without cognition, intent, or agency." Overboe writes: "The vitalism of an impersonal life is often considered noise that will be filtered out, in the name of clarity, in order to facilitate the real business of social change and so-called emancipation. This reestablishes and reinscribes the dominant language or communication style associated with being a person or individual with agency."[69] There is a refusal here of the medical impairment versus social construction impasse.[70] This has occurred in part because Deleuzian theory embraces biomateriality, foregrounding vitalism and potentiality of impairment rather than seeking its recontextualization in the social.[71] Overboe also reminds us that the construct of the subject itself—even the disabled subject—is already discursively able-bodied.

One could also point to efforts articulating trans as an ontological force that impels indeterminate movement rather than an identity, or movement between identities, that demands epistemological accountability. Paisley Currah, Lisa Jean Moore, and Susan Stryker explicate the "trans-" (trans-hyphen) in the sociopolitical.[72] Jami Weinstein develops the notion of transgenre.[73] Mel Chen argues that the "simultaneous limitation and promise" of a Body without Organs (BwO) is "precisely that the genitals (or non-genitals) matter, but are not necessarily constrained by normative gender and sexuality."[74] Chen is pointing to trans as a reordering of what organs signify which genders, or if any organs need to signify genders at all.[75]

Deleuze and Guattari's use of the term "transsexuality" encourages a fluid spectrum of possibility: trans as a motion, as a continuum of intensity that may or may not inform identity.[76] Deleuze and Guattari propose a three-step agenda to destabilize the sign from signification into "significance": one, to locate the sign within its normative frame of interpretation; two, to deconstruct the sign via its deployment through inverse or obverse chains of signification; three, to "try to create new, as yet unknown statements for that proposition, even if the result were a patois of sensual delights, physical and semiotic systems in shreds, asubjective affects, signs without signifiance [sic] where syntax, semantics, and logics are in collapse."[77] The third step, then, is a wrenching of the logic of enunciation from expression, from coherence and order. Deleuze diagrams these three steps through the terms "heterosexuality," "homosexuality," and "transsexuality," mapping how on the first two levels "the sexes themselves, however, remained statistical, aggregate or 'molar' . . . (since each individual belongs to either one series or the other at any given time)."[78] As such, Deleuze and Guattari's invocation of "real transsexualities" gestures toward an entity that does not simply hybridize or add to the designations of male and female sex through a third configuration—trans—but actually transcends sex itself, that is, goes beyond the demarcations that make up sex, and more crucially dissembles sex as a master sign, as a taxonomic chain of signifiers.

While earlier I highlighted the troubling discourse of shared transsex in relation to unmarked and uneven biopolitics of toxicity distribution, I return to Kier's formulation of transgender as all-encompassing category—"everyone on the planet is now encompassed within the category of transgender." This claim is suggestive to me not of the desire to retain the category of transgender but, rather, of its imbrication in an unfolding interspecies biopolitical vision. Kier proclaims that "we might be better off responding to this rearrangement, not through fear of the eco-catastrophic assumptions transsex invokes, but by embracing our shared interdependent transsex."[79] Weinstein also mobilizes the notion of becoming as a dismantling of the "very speciation and biopolitical identity construction" that Foucault elaborates.[80] In a critique of species taxonomy, Julie Livingston and I use the term "biopolitical anthropomorphism" or, reworded more appropriately, "biopolitical anthropocentrism" to "highlight the biopolitical processes that cohere the centrality of the human, and of certain humans; and, the tendency of biopolitical analyses to reinscribe this centrality by taking human species as the primary population upon which cleavages of race and sex occur."[81] Biopolitics, as Foucault describes, is the process by which humans become a species (and in fact specimens) to join all other biological species. This becoming is also the process by which anthropomorphic frames of the human thus take force and are consolidated. Foucault explains in *Security, Territory, Population* that "the dimension in which the population is immersed amongst the other living beings appears and is sanctioned when, for the first time, men are no longer called 'mankind' (*le genre humaine*)" and begin to be called "the human species (*l'espece humaine*)."[82] A paradox occurs: the animalism of humans—"the life of the body and the life of the species"—is taken up as a project of population construction, and humans join species.[83] The (androcentric) human is thus rearticulated as an exceptional form of animality within an anthropomorphized category: humanity. Therefore, although Foucault's own work does not explore the implications of this in terms of interspecies relating, his theory of biopolitics understands anthropocentrism as a defining facet of modernity.

Transgender studies has taken on the question of speciation through a posthumanist or nonhumanist turn. This meeting of transgender studies, animal studies, and posthumanist studies is fantastically rich, considerably complicating humanist presumptions of sex dimorphism and conceptualizing sex as a reaction norm in dynamic emergence with the environment and as an effect of genes and (hormonal) environments interfacing.[84] Myra Hird's work defuses the nature/culture distinction by unpacking the human exceptionalism embedded in continually evoking the trans human body as transgressive of nature. Given its plentitude in nonhuman forms, Hird argues that trans is not a cultural artifact of technological means, or gloriously perverse in that it is unnatural, but is in fact constitutive of nature itself. Hird deploys trans not just beyond or across sex but across "traditional species classifications." Taking a cue from the complexity of intersex and transsex and the nonapplicability of gender and sexual dimorphism to most nonhuman life, Hird argues against a nature/culture binary where the human trans body is understood as a technological invention alone. The upshot of Hird's argument is that trans is not transgressive but, rather and in fact, natural.[85] In concert with Vicky Kirby's proposition that nature is writing and re-presenting itself, and that perhaps culture has been nature all along, Hird quotes Margulis and Dorion to argue that technology must be understood through its interspecies dimensions: "The use of technology to distinguish between nature and culture obscures the very real and energetic invention and use of technology by nonhuman living organisms . . . as well as the extent to which so-called human technologies actually mimic technology already invented by other species."[86] Hird's argument, which complicates if not refuses the nature/culture bifurcation, has vast implications regarding the biomedical versus social model of disability. Within the context of transgender jurisprudence and activist debates regarding the use of the medical model in legislative battles for health care and attendant provisions, her analysis suggests a strategic deployment of the model might defuse pathological conceptualizations when posited as a manipulation of the terms of technology and what constitutes the natural.

But despite challenging the foregrounding of the human and its centrality to defining the parameters of sex, gender, and sexual reproduction, the deepening conversations between transgender studies, animal studies, and posthumanism have not spurred an enthusiastic engagement with disability studies, a field always in conversation with arrangements of the human, especially as it relates to cognitive, mental, and intellectual disabilities. This occlusion is further notable in light of a rich, emerging dialogue between disability studies and animal studies.[87] Further, the growing partnership between transgender studies and animal studies has been less attentive to discussions of racial difference and biopolitical anthropocentrism, foregrounding instead the category species, as if species were not also a forum for understanding cleavages of racial difference.[88] One effort to redress these elisions is Chen's articulation of the "prefixal trans-"—a materialism of grammar—as a "way to explore that complexity of gender definition that lies between human gender systems and the gendering of animals."[89] In attending to the relationship between human animals and nonhuman animals as a racializing technology of biopolitics, Chen's analysis articulates trans not just as "mutilating gender," as the rescrambling and reorganizing of gender, but trans as mutilating, or perhaps better stated, as mutating race as well.[90] In some cases, this mutating is a reterritorialization and enhanced capacitation of racial privilege and the projection of racial coherence through rearranging gender. Bobby Jean Noble, for example, describes his process of regeneration from a working-class butch woman to a trans man as one of moving from "formerly off-white [to a] now White person" in a landscape wherein "the 'self' is the hottest and most insidious capitalist commodity."[91] The confusing designation of "off-white" notwithstanding, Noble describes this capacitation of race—a revival of the privileges of whiteness now afforded through masculinity—as a by-product of trans body modification. If one queries this derivative formulation, however, the possibility that mutilating gender might not be so easily cleaved from (desires for?) racial recuperation or from constructs of ableism needs to be considered. What kinds of attempted recuperation of one sort or another subtend or even preface these rearrangements of gender?

Recall that for Foucault racism is not derivative of biopower but, rather, a prerequisite for how biopolitics works; that is to say, Foucault wrenches racism out of notions of cultural tolerance by stating that the caesura in the biological spectrum that is accorded to race is necessary for licensing the four coordinates of biopolitical will: making live, making die, letting live, letting die. This formulation of racism as a "caesura in the biological domain" can be mobilized as a preemptive critique of a posthumanism that does not acknowledge race as a critical threshold of demarcation.[92] Given the centrality of racial demarcatedness to biopolitics, I read Foucault's expounding of apparatuses of security, later recapitulated and torqued in Deleuze's theorization of control societies, as in fact the *geopolitics of racial ontology*.

Resuturing the foundational function of race within biopolitics to the production of ontologically irreducible entities in control societies, the geopolitics of racial ontology marks the manifestation of different spatializing regimes of the body, and its particles, such that the biological caesura that demarcates the cut of or for racism is now not just a question of visible racial difference or of the taxonomic and eugenic science of phrenology and the scientific racism of the eighteenth century through the early twentieth century. It is also driven by biotechnologies of genetic engineering, assisted reproductive technologies, human genome sequencing, and phenotypical variation—which intersect with and appear as gendered transformations. The "cut" of racism is not made only through disciplinary categories of race but, more perniciously, through biopolitical control aggregates of population.[93] This geopolitics of racial ontology destabilizes the relentless focus on epistemological correctives that tend to dominate political interventions. But, more trenchantly, the emphasis on geopolitics amends what might otherwise be a locationless notion of ontology. The unmarked locational investment of recent work on ontology thus discounts the productive force of geopolitics within its scholarly purview as well as disavows the geopolitical forces that enable theorizing.

In the oscillation between discipline and control, which is less about the end of disciplining and more about the constellation of relations between discipline and control, the question, are you trans? morphs to, how trans are you? Both discipline and control pivot on the fantasy of a body that is concretely and distinctly a real trans body—the (transnormative?) body that pieces—manifest in opposition to the body that is most certainly cisgender. Similarly, the question, are you disabled? morphs to, how abled are you? and how disabled are you? In the context of an array of medical procedures that change in terms of access, signification, cultural capital, and socialization, the moves around these questions are not signaling merely degree. The end goal—to pass? to piece?—is impossible and always shifting: there is no trans. Trans becoming masquerades as a teleological movement, as if one could actually become trans. Trans is often mistaken as the horizon of trans and, as such, is mistaken for becoming trans as linear telos, as a prognosis that becomes the body's contemporary diagnosis and domesticates the trans body into the regulatory norms of permanence.[94]

Becoming trans, then, as opposed to trans becoming, must highlight this impossibility of linearity, permanence, and end points. In Deleuzian terms, becoming is the "I" cascading into the impersonal, the stripping of all registers of signification that make each body succumb to subjectification over "significance." Becoming, as Weinstein contends, is a "wholesale deterritorialization of the human" and a "becoming imperceptible"—a divestment of codes, of signification, of identity and a process of taking on the register of the impersonal.[95] Becoming is not about trying to make the body more capacitated but about allowing and reading more multiplicity, multiplicities of the impersonal and of the imperceptible. Importantly, becomings have no static referent of start point, end point, or climax; they have no narrative. Becoming is awash in pure immanence, never coincident with itself, marked only by degrees of intensity and duration.[96] But none of this is to obscure the fact that becoming has become a zone for profit for contemporary capitalism, for neoliberal piecing and profiteering, a mode through which profit is being aggressively produced. And, as such, all theorizations of becoming are generated through and within the geopolitics of racial ontology that it inhabits.

As trans transition is increasingly theorized as the mobilization, modulation, and modification of bodily matter rather than a retroactive cutting and severing from being in the wrong body, control societies must be understood as deeply sympathetic to if not partially productive of this reframing. Control mines gradations of surface and depth, tension and attention, penetration and withdrawal, finding multiple uses for the diversification of vestments and investments. Once again, however, we can de-exceptionalize trans bodies, as they are neither exceptionally susceptible to control and its forms of continuous surveillance (given the continuities between rhinoplasty and trans surgical procedures, for example, and body modification in general), nor exceptionally capable of modulation, flexibility, and attunement.[97]

Biopolitical control foregrounds the subindividual capacities, the non-human capacities, the prosthetic capacities, the molecular capacities, the hormonal capacities, manipulating the telos of degree granting driven by the medical-industrial complex. Paul Preciado develops a formulation of the "pharmaco-pornographic" to describe the proliferation of bodily modulations in control societies, forms of "soft technologies" that "enter the body to form part of it: they dissolve in the body; they become the body": "Here the body no longer inhabits disciplinary spaces, but is inhabited by them. The bio-molecular and organic structure of the body is a last resort for these control systems."[98] The disciplinary spaces Preciado writes of—encompassing the molar categories of race, gender, sex—proliferate from bodily habitations of identity to inhabitations of the body. This inhabitation is perhaps one of the most pernicious modalities of power that control can manifest—control as discipline par excellence, in that discipline reproduces itself continuously throughout time and space. These "micro-prosthetics" of control, which Preciado claims impel "a process of miniaturization," "take the form of the body; they control by transforming into 'body,' until they become inseparable and indistinguishable from it."[99] Thus, the term "body modification" becomes a redundancy: the body is (endless) modification. This body, however, is not only the contoured organic body with a race and a sex; it is composites of information that splay the body across registers of disciplinary space and time. The target is data, not only identity or the subject or its representation. Communities of belonging—traditionally understood through disciplinary categories of identity, spatiality, coherence—are reorganized through statistical populations, stratified through aggregates of biopolitical life chances in the nexus where state, market, scientific, and geopolitical realms meet.

While I find Preciado's description of control economies of bodily inhabitation very persuasive, they optimistically describe the molecular as the "paradoxical condition of contemporary resistance and revolt": "We are molecularly equipped to remain complicit with dominant repressive formations. But the contemporary pharmaco-pornographic body . . . is *not* docile. This body is not simply an effect of the pharmaco-pornographic systems of control; it is first and above all the materialization of . . . 'power of life' that aspires to transfer to all and to every body. This is the paradoxical condition of contemporary resistance and revolt: pharmaco-pornographic subjectivity is at the same time the effect of biopolitical technologies of control and the ultimate site of resistance to them."[100]

We might want to pause at the formulation of the molecular and the non-docile body within which it resides as "the ultimate site of resistance." This statement assumes an ontologizing of the molecular as a thriving site of resistance by virtue of its mere presence and flexible relation to biomedical control economies (indeed, part of the transnormative body that pieces, thus driving the reterritorialization of whiteness). The geopolitics of racial ontology condition any possibilities for becoming, for a wholesale deterritorialization of the human. Given that all coordinates of the medical model, the social model, access to subject recognition, and the medical-industrial complex revolve around not just gender and sexual alterity, but also racial alterity and disenfranchisement through racial difference, I propose that *becoming trans* is a capacitation of race, of racial ontologies, that informs the functioning of geo- and biopolitical control. Becoming trans is a process that not only courts the transformation of bodies in terms of gender but also solicits the capacity of race to reinvent its terms. Race here is understood not only as a function or synonym of color/identity/social construction but also, and perhaps more perniciously, as speciation. Becoming trans is distinct from trans being, or trans normativity that revels in the futurity of the body that pieces, because it specifically and deliberately acknowledges a political commitment to thinking through the forms of racial capacitation and reterritorialization that subtend and inform trans movements.

We could see becoming trans, then, as the dissolution of this category of signification through manifesting the intensive multiplicity of race, outpacing the forces of signification that seek to contain and compartmentalize what is raced, what is not raced. Insofar as *race* continues to be defined in relation to the White Man who sets its parameters, what Amit Rai calls "race racing" proliferates racial ontologies that are irreducible and unto themselves, in relation through infinite variation rather than difference from (the White Man). The impetus for race racing stems, for Rai, from the context of antiracist organizing in Britain, where he laments the continual reiteration of the centrality and normativity of white subjects and bodies in even the most progressive antiracist political forums. On thinking race not representationally but intensively, what he calls race racing, Rai writes:

> If one is to consistently think race racing as an intensive process, the multiplicity of race lacks any resemblance to itself; race racing multiplicities give form to processes, not to this or that final product (a race, a name . . .). Indeed, the end results of processes realizing the same multiplicity may be highly dissimilar from each other, like the spherical soap bubble and the cubic salt crystal, or like Jazz music and the narrative novel, "which not only do not resemble one another, but bear no similarity to the topological point guiding their production." The multiplicity of race racing is of an obscure yet distinct nature quite different from the clear and distinct identity of rationalistic essences.[101]

Race racing, as Rai elaborates, tracks the insistent becoming of race, the way race—"lack[ing] any resemblance to itself"—is always mutilating and mutating (to invoke the language from mutilating gender) its form in order to resituate and revive its capacitation within biopolitical fields. Race racing, then, allows a reading of racial capacitation—deterritorialization, reterritorialization—in becoming trans. Becoming trans is of course just one potentiality of race racing. But if we are serious, to invoke Chen and others who think of trans as a movement not tethered to modulations and modifications solely of gender and sexuality but also of species, race racing changes trans becoming insofar as it potentially changes what race is, proliferates its intensive, singular forms, reorganizes its registers of significance and signification, and reterritorializes and multiplies its capacitation, its presence, its mutability. But becoming trans also carries through and out a process of racialization as much as it also marks an intensive race racing, a moment of race-becoming futurity. There is no doubt that the reterritorialization of whiteness, in particular of white masculinities, might occur through the reassembling of gender and sexuality into versions of transnormativity. But becoming trans as a practice and a politics takes on a deterritorializing force not only in relation to gender and sex but also in relation to race and speciation. The question, then, is not, does gender and sex nonnormativity lead to racial nonnormativity? but, rather, what are the creative lines of flight that mutate and distort and swerve in Lucretian fashion? Not swerve from, just swerve, creating intensive rather than qualified difference. Thinking of becoming trans as a form of race racing illuminates the relations of white transnormative (FTM) bodies of futurity—the ones that pass by exemplifying piecing—to the TransJustice (MTF) bodies of color, those that struggle to piece (in order to perhaps pass), by seeing all these bodies as implicated in the redistribution of capacitations and reterritorializations of race in their intensive differences. The multiplicity, not the either/or of normativity or nonnormativity, of racial and gender difference is foregrounded. Thus, passing and piecing would be destabilized from their discrete sexual and racial referents and understood, rather, as produced through interfacing assemblages of de- and reterritorialization, of proliferating not only genders but also races and, indeed, species.

A deconstructive model of race insistently repositions the white male subject as determinant of what race is, of making sense or different sense of a representational format or forum; language dominates the political realm here.[102] But theorists such as Arun Saldanha and Amit Rai are arguing for a political and theoretical methodology that intensifies and proliferates race rather than deconstructs it. This proliferation, rather than hoping to dissolve binaries, makes them fade through the overwhelming force of ontological multiplicity, attuned to the perpetual differentiation of variation to variation, of difference within rather than between, and the multiplicity of affirmative becomings: the becoming otherwise of difference, whereby language is resituated as just one potential platform of the political. It is attuned to soliciting sense, rather than making sense (of) or inciting discourse. Seeking the creation of potentialities of emergence, this methodology is less invested in a reinvestment of form and more attuned to the perpetual differentiation of becomings.[103] If race is a technology of regeneration, in that race is insistently reinventing itself in manners both "obscure" and "distinct," as Rai avers, this methodology doggedly pursues the inventive movements of race itself. Writing that "race is a whole event," Saldanha exhorts: "Every time phenotype makes another machinic connection, there is a stutter. Every time bodies are further entrenched in segregation, however brutal, there needs to be an affective investment of some sort. This is the ruptural moment in which to intervene. Race should not be eliminated, but *proliferated*, its many energies directed at multiplying racial differences so as to render them joyfully cacophonic."[104]

This joyful cacophony resonates with what Rai understands as "an experimentation on race itself," one that would "continuously mutate, never resembling itself, changing the metric of its own measure through a resonance that moves beyond its terms."[105] Unlike Preciado, for whom resistance is simply a priori installed in the molecular as the "ultimate site of resistance" and utterly unbeholden to any collective—an ontologizing and individuating politics at best, as Jord/ana Rosenberg so deftly demonstrates—Rai calls for social and political practices of experimentation, a deeply pragmatic manipulation of the partitioning capacities of bodies.[106] I suggest this "[move] beyond its terms" is one way of working through and also against how biopolitical control seeks to modulate sub- and paraindividual capacities of the body. Control seeks to modulate the impersonal, the becoming, all while promoting an individual recourse to subject identification. Becoming trans, as suggested by race racing, would be a politics of manifesting beyond what control can control, a molecular line of flight, a moment of intensification in the process of becoming that is characteristic of race racing. As with all becomings, lines of flight are immanent. As such their availability for reterritorialization and capacity to newly territorialize is imminent. The revolution is not molecular; rather, movement resides in the interstitial shuttling—"the ruptural moment in which to intervene"— between intensive multiplicity and its most likely recapture.

[2]

Crip Nationalism

From Narrative Prosthesis
to Disaster Capitalism

WORKING AND WARRING

Once again, who could say which is better and which is worse? It is true that war kills, and hideously mutilates. But it is especially true after the State has appropriated the war machine. Above all, the State apparatus makes the mutilation, and even death, come first. It needs them preaccomplished, for people to be born that way, crippled and zombielike. The myth of the zombie, of the living dead, is a work myth and not a war myth. Mutilation is a consequence of war, but it is a necessary condition, a presupposition of the State apparatus and the organization of work (hence the native infirmity not only of the worker but also of the man of State himself, whether of the One-Eyed or the One-Armed type): "The brutal exhibition of severed flesh shocked me. . . . Wasn't it an integral part of technical perfection and the intoxication of it . . . ? Mankind has waged wars since the world began, but I can't remember one single example in the *Iliad* where the loss of an arm or a leg is reported. Mythology reserved mutilation for monsters, for human beasts of the race of Tantalus or Procrustes. . . . It is an optical illusion to attribute these mutilations to accidents. Actually, accidents are the result of mutilations that took place long ago in the embryo of our world; and the increase in amputations is one of the symptoms bearing witness to the triumph of the morality of the scalpel. The loss occurred long before it was visibly taken into account" [Jünger, *The Glass Bees*, 112]. The State apparatus needs, at its summit as at its base, predisabled people, preexisting amputees, the still-born, the congenitally infirm, the one-eyed and one-armed. — GILLES DELEUZE AND FÉLIX GUATTARI, *A Thousand Plateaus*

In their brutal diagnostic of the relations between state apparatuses, war machines, debilitation, and labor, Gilles Deleuze and Félix Guattari direct our attention to the genealogy of the accident. The accident is no accident: "It is an optical illusion to attribute these mutilations to accidents . . . accidents are the result of mutilations that took place long ago."[1] The accident functions as an alibi for the constitutive relations of force necessary to bring about something, an event that is in retrospect deemed an accident. What does the "accident" of wartime mutilation mask? Indebted to what structure does the accident labor? Deleuze and Guattari upend the teleological assumption of the statements "war kills" and "war hideously mutilates" by showing us that the war machine of the state predisposes those who are to be mutilated, and those who are to be killed. Linking mutilation as "a presupposition of the State apparatus" of the war machine to the "organization of work," they refuse the mythology of the work zombie, articulating instead the linkage between work and war. The zombie as work myth, in fact, aids the elision of mutilation and crippling in war mythology. Fusing these two together—the work myth and the war myth—Deleuze and Guattari insist on the utility of what they call "predisabled people" to the braided operations of capitalism and the war machine of the state. Mutilation and amputation are thus no accident but are part of the biopolitical scripting of populations available for injury, whether through laboring or through warring or both: laboring in the service of war that mutilates both national bodies and foreign entities denoted as enemies; or laboring as an inverted form of warfare against a disposable population ensnared as laborers-consigned-to-having-an-accident.

The twinning of working and warring predicates the emergence of the modern subject of disability. The aftermath of World War II gives rise to forms of activism, visibility, and collective consciousness about the plight of injured veterans.[2] Work and war as debilitating activities foreground U.S. imperialism, global injustice, exploitative labor conditions, the industry of incarceration, and environmental toxicity.[3] These are situations where the accident is not even invoked as unfortunate because it is constituted as "part of the job" and thus quite the intended accident. Here, the façade of the accident is easily unpeeled. And yet Deleuze and Guattari also warn that "accidents are the result of mutilations that took place long ago in the embryo of our world."[4] The embryo is the site where the biopolitics of debilitation come together to weaponize genetics: environmental toxicity, generational trauma, the structural and psychic impacts of racism, imperialism, and capitalism.

The work machine and the war machine both need bodies that are preordained for injury and maiming, often targeted maiming. Capitalism, war, forced migration, settler colonial occupation, and, in the case of this chapter, U.S. capitalist imperialism are the generators of much of the world's disability, yet contribute unruly source material for rights discourses that propagate visibility, empowerment, identification, and pride. Much of this debilitation is caused by the exploitative capital and imperial structures of the global north. Claiming an empowered disability identity as a site of creative embodiment and resistance—what David Mitchell and Sharon Snyder call "peripheral embodiment"—is perhaps more tenable when disability is perceived or felt as the result of an unfortunate accident, or a misfortune, as an exceptional circumstance for which the body impacted is in no way to blame.[5] Far from suggesting that there is by any means a "fortunate" accident, I am gesturing to bodily experiences that can be capacitated through a reorganization of resources, of white privilege and class and economic mobility. For others, disability is a product—not a by-product, but a deliberate product—of exploitative labor conditions, racist incarceration and policing practices, militarization, and other modes of community disenfranchisement. Lived as the ongoing marking of an already defective body, this body, Alison Kafer writes, is one whose "disablement [is] a foregone conclusion."[6]

Disability in these cases does not present any possibility of the reorganization of privilege; rather, it reinforces the stigma of lack of privilege. Often perceived as the result of aberrant or destructive individual lifestyle "choices," the inevitability of debility should more accurately be comprehended as wedded to biopolitical population metrics. Kafer points out that the responsibilization narrative of disability scrutinizes how it has occurred and how it is lived, placing the failure or success of "overcoming" disability on the individual, either as the fault or as the virtuousness of the body in question.[7] The responsibility for disability works inversely as well, in that certain bodies are seen as the bearers of disability—responsible for the very fact of their disability because of markers of race, class, religion, and region. Other bodies, unmarked by other markers of defect, in other words, not already an Other, are projected as unfortunately maligned in a system that should have protected them. In other words, their disability is not an inherent property of the body.

When disability becomes fodder for life, when it is seen as not the fault of the body living that disability or of the population to which that body belongs, there is (limited) availability of a recapacitation of disability within the biopolitical vector of make live. When disability is instrumentalized necropolitically, when, as Nirmala Erevelles points out, "human variation (e.g. race) is itself deployed in the construction of disabled identities for purely oppressive purposes (e.g. slavery, colonialism, immigration law, etc.)" combined with the deliberate deprivation and dearth of avenues of support and recapacitation, disability then becomes a commodity that functions for what Rey Chow calls "the ascendency of whiteness."[8] That is not to claim that all uses of the category of disability are a capacitation of (not always literal) whiteness, but rather to note the explicit instances in which disability is biopolitically mobilized in the service of white supremacy, liberal racism, and nationalist projects of modernity. These Möbius strip–like enfoldings and divisions are modulated through global north/south and developed/developing demarcations, whereby the global north holds the key to the liberalization of disability while the global south bears the brunt of its weaponization. They are also temporally demarcated through positing a eugenics-oriented past against a contemporary biopolitical incorporative mechanism of inclusion, which then creates a temporal drag of racialization between discipline and control. These divisions can be blurry, shifting, and unstable; they are folds, folding in and out, of the mechanism of biopolitical population racism.

The biopolitical distribution between disability as an exceptional accident or misfortune, and the proliferation of debilitation as war, as imperialism, as durational death, is largely maintained through disability rights frameworks. The liberalization of injury entails that disability created through imperial war is further depoliticized through frameworks that "include" disability "in other locations," usually national locations, a problem already foregrounded by many critiques of disability models of inclusion.[9] Efforts to diversify disability studies have resulted not only in welcoming people of color with disabilities into the field but also in theorizing racialization as a process of debilitation, of the mark of a defective body, of bodies that do not easily fall into either the non-disabled or the disabled body as the binary currently functions.[10] How one comes to disability, whether it be through the exceptional accident—the loss of able-bodied whiteness, for example, the single-axis identity formation, the one thing that makes one different—or living racialization, and in fact racism as debilitation, profoundly shapes what disability is and what it can become. In turn, these distinctions drive political projects that are often divergent and in contradiction to one another.

Phenomenological elaborations of the multiplicity of material embodiment of bodies with disabilities and the political stakes in the liberatory facets of bodily difference notwithstanding, I join a growing chorus of scholars and activists who urge greater attention not only to how disabled bodies are maintained in difference and hierarchy but also to how disabled bodies are solicited and manufactured. This is a crucial facet of disability that complicates the exceptionalism of certain kinds of disabilities and disabled bodies with attention to debilitation as a primary activity of capitalist global expansion. Theorizing these two together—the biopolitics of disability and the biopolitics of debilitation—demands nothing less than the crafting of a scholarly platform that seeks to address and attempts to eliminate the local and global conditions of inequality that give rise to the incidence of much—if not most—of the world's disability. A disability justice approach, as many have argued, is unequivocally antiwar, pro-labor, antiracist, prison abolitionist, and anti-imperialist. This approach is resolutely vigilant about critiquing U.S. imperialism both within the United States—as a settler colonial state—and internationally, as the director of the war on terror, an occupier of Afghanistan and Iraq, and as the main entity legitimating and funding Israel's settler colonial occupation of Palestine. There cannot be a focus on growing disability culture alone, for indeed this growth happens within the context of these imperial projects, is informed by them, and cannot be separated from them.[11] Any flourishing of cultures of disability and disability pride must be evaluated in the context of these fissures in order to ask who is able to participate in empowerment discourses and practices and why.

Among the most urgent critiques are those from disability studies scholars working in or on the global south. Calling disability studies "a form of scholarly colonialism," Helen Meekosha argues that the field needs to be "rethought taking full account of the 400 million disabled people living in the global South."[12] This statistic is perhaps already a problem because it may reflect a brutal empirical standardization of vastly different bodily impairments and comportment that still epistemologically circulate through, and thus validate, the global north. And yet, only by ignoring the vastly uneven geopolitical distribution of disability, and our (U.S.) complicity in producing debilitation elsewhere, can leading disability studies scholar Rosemarie Garland-Thomson profess that "disability is a resource, rather than a restriction," promoting a highly privileged conversation about Western philosophical bioethics that remains uninterrogated in terms of distinctions between

FIG. 2.1. "Disability justice means resisting together from solitary cells to open-air prisons." Micah Bazant and Sins Invalid, *To Exist Is to Resist*, 2014. An original drawing. Sins Invalid is a performance project that celebrates artists with disabilities, centralizing artists of color and queer and gender-variant artists. Reprinted with the artist's permission.

disability and debilitation. While resignifying the category of disability may aid in addressing what Bryan S. Turner (quoted by Garland-Thomson) calls "ontological contingency" by deconstructing the presumed, taken-for-granted capacities-enabled status of able-bodies, such ontological contingencies should not sublimate the sociopolitical contexts within which they occur, nor be thought of by any means as "the truth of our body's vulnerability to the randomness of fate."[13] Garland-Thomson continues: "Each one of us ineluctably acquires one or more disabilities—naming them variably as illness, disease, injury, old age, failure, dysfunction, or dependence. This inconvenient truth nudges most of us who think of ourselves as able-bodied toward imagining disability as an uncommon visitation that mostly happens to someone else, as a fate somehow elective rather than inevitable."[14]

This statement by Garland-Thomson does not take into account the politics of debilitation that render some populations as definitively unworthy of health and targeted for injury. Neither accidental nor necessarily cast as unfortunate, debilitation is not a by-product of social injustice and inequity. More trenchantly, it is constitutive of the very mechanisms that enable certain populations to occupy the "make live" vector, to experience "ontological contingency" as an ultimate reserve of the body abstracted from sociality, and to imagine disability as something that one acquires inevitably rather than something that is unevenly endemic to the quotidian realities of poverty, permanent war, racism, imperialism, and colonialism. Debilitation is required because the debilitation of bodies is, in part, how these populations come to be populations as such in the first place.

As Heather Lukes points out, the concept of disability has recently come under such critique and duress that its adequacy and relevance within broader social phenomena are questionable.[15] Prominent disability studies scholar Nirmala Erevelles also convincingly argues that "the very category of 'disability' operates as a commodity fetish that occludes the violence of the socio-economic system."[16] The conditions of possibility that enable the simultaneous mass production of debilitation and the emergence of disability as a biopolitical state category are indebted to the biopolitical "ascendancy of whiteness."[17] Noting that the "violence of imperialism is instrumental not only in the creation of disability but also in the absence of public recognition of the impact of disability in the third world," Erevelles seeks deeper engagement with U.S. imperialism in Euro-American disability studies.[18] Implicitly included in her statement is also settler colonialism as ongoing debilitation and settler subjectivity as the production of ableist whiteness. Further, including within a diversity model the difference of disability from "other" countries, through the national frame and often through rights and identity formations, may also stratify the production of debilitation "elsewhere" that works in part to promote the protection of disability "here." Proposing a "southern theory of disability," Meekosha writes: "The prevention of impairments as social products on a global scale as a result of, for example, war and environmental pollution, calls for a global perspective by disability scholars that specifically incorporates the role of the global North in 'disabling' the global South."[19] Meekosha draws on postcolonial theory to suggest the concept of "social suffering" might be more appropriate, backending personal tragedy to prioritize the politics of endemic debilitation of disenfranchised populations.[20] As a rebuttal to Garland-Thomson's hailing the "randomness of fate," then, Meekosha's framing is a necessary reminder that much social suffering is neither random nor arbitrary.

There is a productive tension, then, between embracing disability as a universal and inevitable condition, and combating the production of disability acquired under duress of oppressive structures of social injustice. While the former became necessary to push back against the exceptionalizing view of disability as a singular misfortune and a private tragedy, disability should not then be conceptualized as a universal problem affecting everyone.[21] Without attending to the unevenness of that universal affectation in geopolitical and biopolitical terms, this necessary rejoinder to exceptionalizing tendencies invites a problematic liberalizing democratization; universalizing in order to counter exceptionalizing leaves the binary operative. Naturalizing socially produced disability as "ontological contingency" provides fodder for rights-based platforms offering modes of accommodation and the façade of cultural rehabilitation to obscure the production of debilitation as an active practice of exploitation. These platforms further delimit the imaginary of interventions to rights-based agendas at the expense of social justice approaches, putting a cosmetic fix on a systemic issue and drawing political, social, and economic capital both toward responsibilization and also toward celebrating disability pride rather than preventing the weaponization of debilitation.[22] They privilege the individual and often exceptional experiences of disability over the quotidian forms of debilitation experienced by much of the world, blaming the individuals and populations who cannot survive and lauding the success of the ones who do, rather than seeing the supplementary relation of the two. These tendencies accumulate and work collectively in the service of disability rights discourses that function as a foil for U.S. settler colonialism and imperialism and its debilitating machinery.

Crip nationalism, as Nicole Markotic and Robert McRuer argue, functions as a version of national recognition that proffers conditional, tentative forms of citizenship within human rights regimes, international forums of hyperpatriotism (such as the Paralympics), and transnational activist networks.[23] As I discuss later, the Americans with Disabilities Act of 1990, for example, has arguably done less to incorporate people with disabilities into labor pools and more to cultivate a privileged class of disabled citizens; this would be one variant of crip nationalism.[24] Crip nationalism draws attention to how some forms of disability now might possibly be read as "privileged" within internal national hierarchies and within transnational liberal rights frames. In networks of globalization, examples of crip nationalism abound. Neoliberal human rights and biomedical rights regimes may

FIG. 2.2. ADAPT action protesting the American health care system, Las Vegas, 1994. Photo by Tom Olin. Reprinted with artist's permission.

unwittingly impose definitions, evaluation, and judgments about what disability is across geopolitical difference.[25] In tandem with the brutal liberalism of such frameworks, resources are distributed, missionary-style and often unevenly, with effects that reorganize as well as reiterate hierarchies of bodily debility and capacity. Disenfranchised populations are with increasing frequency recruited for projects involving biomedical, genomic, and reproductive technologies that enable forms of capacitation for few.[26] Crip nationalism functions both by marking investments in nationalism and national location and more perniciously by relying on the specific circumstances of a location that is unmarked, unaccounted for, and deployed as transparent universalism.

Crip nationalism is thus a constitutive function of what Mitchell and Snyder call the biopolitics of disability. I follow their definition of the biopolitics of disability as the lauded though partial and unfinished incorporation of disabilities at the expense of other less recognized forms of disability—that is to say, a critique of the neoliberal politics of exclusion that manifest racial, classed, gendered, and national terms of disability exceptionalism.[27] The transnational deployment of this exceptionalism renders the United States an advanced and progressive nation of disability awareness, accommodation, and incorporation while projecting backward-ness and incapacity of modernity onto those Others elsewhere. Less ex-amined, however, is how this transnational deployment of exceptionalism works not only as a process of Othering to retain copyright as the progeni-tor and arbiter of ableist modernity, but more trenchantly as camouflage of what I am calling the biopolitics of debilitation.

The oscillation between the biopolitics of disability and the biopolitics of debilitation is between those who are disabled who are excluded from the dominant mechanisms and imaginaries of disability inclusion and those made available and targeted for injury: those for whom identifying as dis-abled is practically an insult to a future-injured, available-for-injury body, for whom long-term bodily health and integrity is already statistically unlikely. These are often, but not always, overlapping populations. Foregrounding a direct critique of the debilitating tactics of capitalism and imperialism, this toggling relation between disability and debilitation thus extends crip nationalism as a feature of U.S. imperialism, from its national ideological iterations to its imbrication in practices of injuring and maiming. While the biopolitics of disability still hinges on frames of inclusion within liberal models of disability, noting who is excluded and why from the frames, the biopolitics of debilitation reveals that the propagation of such frames not only excludes those who cannot perform exceptional cultural rehabilitation or exceptional relations to disability but also works to obscure the explicit injuring and debilitation of populations, highlighting at whose expense—whose slow deaths—these frames hinge. While the distinctions between disability and debilitation may not always be clear-cut, insisting on clarify-ing their potential differences is important in understanding the fissures between different political projects, constituencies, and geopolitical spaces.

To encapsulate, the biopolitics of debilitation is an analytic that allows us to see the assemblage relations of disability, debility, and capacity, noting that Euro-American rights frames, often centralizing individuals extracted from populations, operates through forms of capacitation in relation to that which it must sublimate: the material conditions of deliberate population debilitation. This assemblage thus not only deindividualizes disability, a move that many disability scholars have pushed for. It also shifts from positing disability as a collective experience (of aging, of inevitable frailty and illness) to nuancing that observation through attention to populations and their differential and uneven precarity. Rethinking disability through the precarity of populations not only acknowledges that there is more disability within disenfranchised and precarious populations, but also insists that debilitation is a tactical practice deployed in order to create and precaritize populations and maintain them as such. The biopolitics of debilitation thus situates disability within formulations of risk, calculation, prognosis, and statistical probability, whereby disability is understood not as phenomenological essence, identity, or a personal attribute, but as risk coding, as an embedded aspect of biopolitical population management.[28] Public health practitioners, for example, understand racism as a risk factor. Race is "a marker of risk for racism-related exposures. Race is useful in that it enables the identification of persons at risk for exposures that vary by racial category (e.g., discrimination)."[29] Thus the biopolitics of debilitation informs the biopolitics of disability with the understanding that the frame of inclusion and exclusion is already infused with economies of risk. Such frames are therefore foundational to the regulation of the categories of disability and ability that delimit an acknowledgment of debilitation as a distribution of risk. Debility is thus understood as a process rather than an identity or attribute, a verb and a doing rather than a happening or happening to or done to. It complicates the notion of a workplace injury or accident by understanding the statistical likelihood by which certain populations are expected to yield themselves to bodily debilitation, deterioration, and outright harm.

Relevant considerations that Meekosha centralizes in a southern theory of disability bracket momentarily the adherence to the binary production of the non-disabled versus the disabled body, so often used to determine and evaluate who is "actually disabled." Addressed immediately is the social justice question of what is access to health? What does it mean to have access to health, or to access health, and to access health care? This formulation centralizes the connections between poverty, debt, and disability.[30] Poverty itself may well be thought of as a form of debilitation; debt and austerity are increasingly linked to the collapse of health care systems and the inability to access medical care. Tropes of disability are used to describe the past as well as the future of capitalism, such that debt functions as debility. The concept of "crippling debt," for example, reveals the ways in which fiscal "health" is a form of capacitation or capacity. Theorizing debt as bodily vulnerability recognizes the historical and structural relationships between poverty and disability—engendered by colonization, occupation, environmental degradation, war, biomedicine, and labor exploitation. It also highlights that disability can be negotiated through access to medical care only for the very few. More important, within the context of the financial expropriation endemic to the lack of socialized health care in the United States, and given the high rates of bankruptcy due to medical bills, theorizing debt as debility entails mapping out a system of profit for capital that mines and multiplies debilitated bodies.

If one is against the neoliberal normativizing and micromanaging of health as a forever impossible ideal to reach, if one is indeed "against health," to use a framing from Jonathan Metzl and Anna Kirkland, how are populations who have little access to health situated in this formulation?[31] The social model of disability, elaborated at length, states that it is not the body that is impaired but the social that maintains ableist structures. Warfare, exploitative laboring conditions, occupations, incarceration count as a large component of these structures, part of an inaccessible ableist social, as much as buildings, curbs, ramps, elevators, service animals, cognitive normativity, and chemical sensitivities. When one asks, "Is it accessible?" the social model asks, "Accessible to what? What does an accessible health care infrastructure look like, and for whom?" Maintaining a construction of the social that revolves around built infrastructure and obstacles to them, rather than a social that includes work and warring as debilitating processes, is a function of racial, class, and locational privilege. Is a young black man without a diagnosed disability living in the United States who is statistically much more likely than most to be imprisoned, shot at by police, or killed by the time of adulthood actually a referent for what it means to be able-bodied?[32] What I am arguing *would not diminish the specificity of disabled embodiment, nor necessarily expand what the term "disability" encompasses.* Rather, this approach connects disability to those who are debilitated, to those whose bodily experiences challenge a disaggregation of an us/them binary in terms of who is seen as able-bodied, and acknowledges the now-regulatory functions of the category of disability.

FROM MODERNIST EXCEPTION TO POSTMODERNIST
EXCEPTIONALISM

One potential relation between the biopolitics of disability and the biopolitics of debilitation is that, ironically, the sublimation of debilitation underpins the emergence of the modern rights-bearing subject of disability.[33] How does this elision of warring and working through the conjuncture of disability take hold? While this assessment is by no means definitive, the passage of the Americans with Disabilities Act (ADA) of 1990 is part of the modulation of disability and debility. It is beyond the purview of this chapter to delve into the history of activist organizing and political struggle that led to the passage of the landmark legislation, much of it driven by post–World War II veterans and the plight of war debilitation.[34] Nevertheless, it is important to state that this legislation represents the most wide-sweeping civil rights platform in the United States for people with disabilities and has been replicated as a blueprint in many national locations and in more recent United Nations human rights declarations.[35] The ADA was tasked with three major goals: "elimination of arbitrary barriers faced by disabled persons; an end to the inequality of opportunity; and a reduction in unnecessary dependency and unrealized productivity."[36] A prime desired outcome, as signaled by the third goal, was the reduction of the unemployment of people with disabilities.

As many have noted, however, the ADA failed in this regard, with no major shift in the widespread incorporation of people with disabilities into multiple vectors of the U.S. workforce.[37] For example, Marta Russell and Jean Stewart claimed that in 2000, ten years after the passage of the ADA, the unemployment rate of people with disabilities had not changed from 65–71 percent: "This appalling figure remains steadfast despite a growing U.S. economy, a low aggregate national official unemployment rate (4.2 percent), advances in technology which have expanded the range of jobs disabled workers can perform, and a poll showing that over 70 percent of working-age disabled persons say they would prefer to have a job."[38]

In the more than twenty-five years since the passage and implementation of the ADA, it has become evident that one of its shortcomings is that it uses capitalist logic to solve a problem largely created by capitalism. It mistakes the demands for greater incorporation into economic circuits of productivity as a tacit acceptance of current structures of laboring and workplace conditions, and transposes and thus dilutes a systemic critique of structures of employment into a liberal identity politics focused on inclusion and recognition. It ironically desires assimilation of people with disabilities into some of the very structures that debilitated them initially: potentially hazardous working conditions, not the least of which includes work in the military.[39] The ADA does not so much challenge prevalent constructions of the organization of labor that might be debilitating as it minoritizes the otherwise inadequate labor contributions of bodies deemed disabled by insisting on their incorporation into work spaces that are modified especially for them. The changes are to access to workplaces but not to workplaces in general, treating disability as another hindrance to social mobility that must be resolved, rather than a facet of life that might tell us something about failures of how time and labor and space are organized. Further, it should be noted that the ADA does not address the practices of debilitation manifested by U.S. policy elsewhere. The convergence of the passage of the ADA and the beginning of the first Gulf War in 1991 surely merits deeper consideration.[40] The ADA is in part the victory of the long-term activist efforts of war-injured veterans, only to be followed by more warring activities that debilitate populations of the U.S. military as well as civilians in Iraq.

Countering accommodationist models, Marta Russell and Ravi Malhotra argue for an understanding of disability grounded in anticapitalist critique rather than in liberal models of recognition, rights, tolerance, and acceptance. Noting that the "'minority' model of disability . . . views it as the product of a disabling social and architectural environment," they write: "In contrast, we take the view that disability is a socially-created category derived from labour relations, a product of the exploitative economic structure of capitalist society: one which creates (and then oppresses) the so-called 'disabled' body as one of the conditions that allow the capitalist class to accumulate wealth. Seen in this light, disability is an aspect of the central contradiction of capitalism."[41]

In the view of Russell and Malhotra, then, centralizing people with disabilities demands a radical reenvisioning of laboring, a transformation in the temporal pulse and spatial determinations of capitalism.[42] Bodies deemed disabled bear the burden of displaying what is exploitative about the organization of labor, staking a claim in the "end of capitalism."[43] Forms of "peripheral embodiment," they imply, are neither exceptional nor peripheral; they do not defy or challenge the norm. Rather, the periphery exposes the perceived norm as a fantasy of the social.[44] In fact, the debilitated laboring body is a constitutive and endemic facet of the normative functioning of capitalist exploitation.

Neoliberal investments in the body as portfolio, as site of entrepreneurship, entail transition of *some* disabled bodies from the disciplinary institutions of containment, quarantine, and expulsion into forms of incorporative biopolitical control. David Mitchell and Sharon Snyder argue that "disabled people have shifted from modernity's *exception* (a line of defect to be isolated and eradicated) to postmodernist [neoliberal] *exceptionality* (failing bodies resuscitated by an increasingly medicalized state). In this latter state, the ontology of disability retrieves a formerly fallen object and makes it newly available for *cultural rehabilitation*," a euphemism for producing cultural docility.[45] Mitchell and Snyder track this shift of people with disabilities located from "a former era of economic burden" of paternalistic, institutional, and welfare regimes when disabled people were "social pariahs," to what they term "objects of care" that impel the investment of service economies and neoliberal strategies of intervention and rehabilitation—"a 'hot' ticket item for potential research and funding schemes."[46]

Mitchell and Snyder's claim situates the disabled body as the site of extreme productivity—and thus, profitability—precisely through its lack of conventional productive laboring value. Once excluded from the labor system because of their "unproductivity," disabled bodies have become the "sites for the exercise of the primitive accumulation that fuels capitalism."[47] This productivity is thus not "measured by his or her ability to produce goods and services that satisfy social/human needs," as Erevelles points out, but rather "based solely on capitalist exploitative demands for increasing profit."[48]

And yet, despite this profitability, Mitchell and Snyder argue that the disabled non/laborer is also a resistant non-capacitated body, implicitly challenging the incomplete liberal project of docility by refusing to assimilate into a laboring capacity. In echoing Russell and Malhotra's conviction that disability reveals a central contradiction, a paradox even, of capitalism, Mitchell and Snyder laud Michael Hardt and Antonio Negri's rerouting from the worker as the paradigmatic resistant subject in Marxist theory to "living labor" or "non-productive bodies," as the nascent site of dissent. No longer able to locate a single site of resistance to capitalism in a "simple, agonistic division of labor," Mitchell and Snyder ask, "Where does resistance manifest itself once a concept of the workers' revolution no longer seems tenable and how will this resistance govern itself without the institution of new hierarchies of inequality?"[49] In other words, the undermining of capitalism will come from those who cannot or will not work, from those whose "capacities make them 'unfit' for labor."[50] This unfitness, they argue, proves "imminently productive" because these bodies inhabit and generate alternative biopolitical scripts of consumption, family, and nation.[51] They evidence this assertion by averring that "the disabled people that we know are some of the worst consumers on the planet because they have neither the means, the interest, nor the gullibility of mistaking meaning with market . . . disabled artists in the U.S. live some of the most sparingly non-consumptive lives and, yet, this is what we admire about them the most."[52]

I will leave aside for a moment the geopolitical inflections fueling certitude regarding the passé potential of organized resistance at the point of production. The claim about the inherent resistant capacity of the non-productive disabled laborer bears a complex relation to Mitchell and Snyder's earlier conviction that disabled bodies have now transitioned into objects of care that represent a unique site for the capture of every element for capitalist profit.[53] Do the individual consumption practices of disabled people (artists) mitigate, even remotely, the profitability of the sites of primitive accumulation that objects of care generate? Further, the resistance of non-consumptive lives pales in a global economic context where, as Gayatri Spivak reminds us, humanistic training in consumerism is foreclosed for populations whose labor creates consumer opportunities for others.[54] The (individual) capacity to consume—or to refuse to consume—is already predicated on the privileged position of the consumer-citizen. Mitchell and Snyder lionize the non-laboring debilitated body as the new threshold of resistance—a crypto-capacity—via their positions as improper producers as well as consumers. But this formulation, as much as it would seem empowering to embrace, actually relies on the occlusion of the centrality of debilitation to the workings of capitalism. It effaces the unflinching need for "social pariahs" available for injury, excluded from the economies that hail certain bodies worthy of being objects of care, however compromised this inclusion may be. There are surely individuals with disabilities who perhaps neither labor nor consume "properly," but any resistance this may signal is not an a priori feature of being disabled. Further, populations that are not roped into an economy of rehabilitative objects of care are sites of profit precisely for their availability for injury, their inability to labor, their exclusion from adequate health care, and their ideological production as lazy, criminal, and burdensome. While these populations may well enact various forms of resistance to capitalism, they do not escape the violent processes of primitive accumulation that extract profit from the disposability that threatens these exact populations.

Mitchell and Snyder further vacillate between the figures of the resistant non-productive unfit non/worker and that very same worker as incorporated into capitalist sites of profit. They argue that "we are increasingly approaching a time when all that formerly passed as the undesirability of life in a disabled body proves increasingly 'advantageous' from the standpoint of an immaterial labor market."[55] The immaterial labor market is a reference to technologies that allow for productivity to be redefined against the grain of the "laboring body"—for example, fostering virtual participation in workplaces for mobility-impaired individuals. However, these very same technologies, driven by the conventional laboring body, produce vastly debilitated populations across the globe, from Chinese laborers in Apple factories who commit suicide, to wheelchair technology that enhances mobility developed in Israel 48 on the backs of Palestinian oppression and immobility, to the mountains of e-waste hand-sanded by the working poor in India, to the neocolonial extraction of minerals and natural substances from resource-rich areas for the purposes of manufacturing hardware.

Is it possible that the figure of the non-productive disabled body becomes something of a fetish in Mitchell and Snyder's text, recoding resistance as a form of automatic capacitation, an onto-crypto-capacity? This body occludes, to some extent, populations that are neither positioned as resistant to capitalism nor promoted as objects of care. Rather these populations are constructed as objects of imminent disposability, continually subjected to paternalistic austerity regimes, violent institutionalization, and debilitation that is *not* in any way redeemable through cultural rehabilitation. (Cultural rehabilitation as an avenue to normalization can be eschewed only if in fact it is an available possibility to turn away from.) Their debilitation functions as a form of value extraction for otherwise disposable bodies. Lauding the inherent resistance to capitalism of disabled bodies as well as the advantages of the immaterial labor market for people with disabilities both depend on three factors: first, the assumption or invocation of the identity or grouping of disabled people as an a priori given; which then, secondly, entails the substantial occlusion of the *manufacturing* of disability, that is, capitalist exploitation as an ongoing process of debilitation; which then, thirdly, submerges the supplemental relation between objects of care and social pariahs or objects of disposability— disability as a potential site of cultural incorporation and debilitation of populations made available and/or targeted for injury—in a neoliberal economy that profits from both. The burden-to-care periodization is one that therefore racializes as well as temporospatializes: between eugenics as it has been and the biopolitics of inclusion of the now (described as "post-imperialist"), a split that largely speaks to liberal spaces of privilege; and between the progress of the West/developed nations and the disarray of the rest/developing nations.

"Objects of care" thus function as alibis for deeper entrenchment of inequality. The transformations in the valuation and incorporation of disabled bodies are indebted to uneven development (pace David Harvey), the craggy geopolitical terrain of biopolitical control that has hardly abandoned disciplinary structures of containment. In other words, disciplinary apparatuses of containment and incorporative forms of biopolitical control are more accurately produced through and in relation to each other, rather than as a wholesale transition, thus requiring careful attention to the economic material conditions of uneven development. Service economies, for example, are impelled into the production of these objects of care; new social pariahs and forms of "economic burden" emerge from these service economies. These economies include (but are hardly limited to) care workers, diagnostic testing industries, surrogates, organ donors, and clinical trial workers/subjects. How do workers in service economies produce toward objects of care when they are often left without the resources to care for themselves and fall into the categorization of objects of disposability?[56] How do such objects of care resonate with patterns of accumulation of wealth from the global north to the global south, reproducing the standardization of what disability is in human rights regimes, the distribution of disabilities and abilities in biomedical circuits, and the debilitating mechanisms of war machines?[57]

These burden-to-care relations do not only grip the international division of labor or an increasingly fuzzy global north/south divide. In the United States, the most salient example of the failure to achieve such a totalizing transition is the "onset of deinstitutionalization and the nearly simultaneous rise of 'law and order' politics."[58] An estimated 70 percent of incarcerated populations in the United States have a developmental or physical disability.[59] The growth of the prison-industrial complex depends on the school-to-prison pipeline that fuels it.[60] The disciplinary containment and isolation of prison and the supposed economic burden of prisoners are sustained by the profitability of the regulation of bodies modulated as "objects of care"—potential criminals—from school to prison. The historical downsizing of welfare provisions and disability provisions coincides with the rise of the prison-industrial complex and the expansion of populations deemed criminal.[61]

The prison-industrial complex is thus a proliferating site of the institutionalization of disability, albeit not just any body with disabilities.[62] Critical prison studies amply evidences that the institutionalization of disability intensifies at points where incarceration and race (as criminality), specifically blackness, meet.[63] Black bodies have carried the mark of the institutionalization of disability from slavery to Jim Crow to the prison-industrial complex, with incarceration, as Michelle Alexander argues, forming a "racial caste system."[64] Nirmala Erevelles writes of the enclosure of blackness in the circuitry of signification and production of disability.[65] Extending the discussion of flesh in Hortense Spillers's seminal essay "Mama's Baby, Papa's Maybe," she argues that the inferiority of black flesh is literally inscribed by the master's whip, thus suturing the constructed association of blackness with defect to the physical attribution of disability: "It is precisely the historical moment when one class of human beings was transformed into cargo that black bodies become disabled and disabled bodies become black."[66] Racialization here is a form of impairment unto itself (black flesh as disabled flesh), as well as an invitation and solicitation to visibilize debilitation as a marking of this symbolic relationship (disabled flesh as black flesh). Erevelles's analysis not only emphasizes the necessity of an intersectional frame. (An intersectional approach need not mobilize the term "disability" itself, rather exposes the term for the racial elisions it relies upon.) She demonstrates the constitutive facets of racialization to the functioning of the identity positioning of disability itself, rendering the intersections between disability and race to be already a reduction of the multiplicity inherent to the social construction of the black body as inferior.[67] Disability is for Erevelles the "ideological lynchpin utilized to (re)constitute social difference" along identity axes.[68] Disability thus coheres a long-standing avenue for policing, surveilling, and securitizing deviant bodies from slavery through the prison-industrial complex. These differing yet contiguous forms of enclosure are processes of debilitation in the most literal and stark terms.[69]

Debilitation is therefore not just an unfortunate by-product of the exploitative workings of capitalism; it is required for and constitutive of the expansion of profit. Certain bodies are employed in production processes precisely because they are deemed available for injury—they are, in other words, objects of disposability, bodies whose debilitation is required in order to sustain capitalist narratives of progress.[70] Participation in the labor market may also entail extraction of biological information as a source of value.[71] Bioinformatic economies—DNA encoding and species preservation, stem cell research, digitization, biometrics, surveillance technologies, regenerative medical sciences—increase the contact zones and points of interface between subindividual bodily capacities while facilitating the constant amassing of information. They rely on and reassert extractive economies. Kaushik Sunder Rajan details the life trajectory of the "experimental subject," one increasingly displaced from conventional forms of agricultural and manual labor (often from the global south) to biocapital regimes where information is extracted from bodily material.[72] In another example, Raewyn Connell writes, "Both the tissue economy and the redefinition of bodies have effects on disability: the former by literally manufacturing impaired bodies in the global periphery (the 'donors'), the latter by circulating fantasies of the perfect body and inciting desire among the global rich to buy perfection. Both produce, as the dark side of the pursuit of health and desirability, a category of rubbish people (to use an Australian indigenous expression) who can be seen as contemptible and expendable."[73] It is the "rubbish people"—literally described as objects of disposability—whose exclusion from the imaginaries and practices of biopolitical incorporation are necessary, whose debilitation upholds the terms of cultural rehabilitation.

The curation of objects of care is linked to the purchasing of prognostic power: in other words, the capacity to attempt to outpace the variables of calculated risk attached to biopolitical populations through the mobilization of biomedical, economic, and social resources. The purchase of prognostic power is tethered to what Sunder Rajan calls the patient-in-waiting.[74] This patient is inevitably hailed as a consumer-in-waiting, enabled, literally and conceptually, by the experimental subject. The neoliberal consumer subject of health—an object of care—assumes the right not to be injured in the usage of products, even as accidents that derive from product design can be predicted with statistical precision, mapping the bodies that are likely to be implicated in these dynamics. As Catherine Waldby and Robert Mitchell write, "The wealthy can purchase the fantasy of a regenerative body at the expense of the health of other, less valuable bodies."[75] Snyder and Mitchell offer the figure of Oscar Pistorius as an indication of "a new era of disabled athleticism—buffed, muscular, yet technologically supplemented bodies—promising all of the transcendent capacity a hyper-medicalized culture could offer."[76] These bodies Snyder and Mitchell demarcate the "able-disabled."

Neoliberal regimes of biocapital produce the body as never healthy enough, and thus always in a debilitated state in relation to what one's bodily capacity is imagined to be. As such, the democratization of disability as an inevitable state that will interpellate everyone, discussed earlier, is itself a repetition of this neoliberal framework, which produces profit from precisely this logic. Aging itself is seen as debilitation, as some populations

FIG. 2.3. The abled-disabled: "So . . . What's Your Excuse Again? Beyond Ordinary."
Workowt! Magazine, 2012.

live longer but also live with more chronic illness. Regenerative medicine produces the experience of "double biological time": as the body ages, the (unrealistic) possibility of restoring its various parts to at least an "earlier" state proliferates, and a certain promised return to capacity accompanies the experience of aging through debility.[77] Being "better than well" emerges as the alibi for the translation of sensation and affect into symptom and thus the rationale for all types of medical intervention, manufacturing the "continual enlargement of the domain of the therapeutic."[78] One example of enhancing capacitation is the historical emergence of shyness as a social anxiety disorder, whereby psychotropic drugs become "personality optimizers."[79] Another example is the burgeoning field of "cosmetic neurology," a term used to "describe the practice of using drugs developed for recognized medical conditions to strengthen ordinary cognition," such as the growing use of Ritalin and Adderall among college students and marathon poker players.[80] A third example is yet the idea that we always die prematurely or should not be subjected to chance at all. Suggested in the legal notion of "lost chance," the loss of chance itself can be injurious such that one should be compensated for not being given every last opportunity to prevent death.

In these many examples we see the entwinement of the biopolitics of disability and the biopolitics of debilitation, as bodies that are hailed into a liberal politics of disability, and biopolitically incorporated as objects of care are folded in as part of the exploitation and disavowal of debilitated bodies. Such a division, therefore, between "economic burden" (i.e., social pariahs) and "objects of care" rests on an erasure of how capitalism has always created and sustained debilitation. Per Russell and Malhotra's argument that disability is an aspect of the central contradiction of capitalism, bodies that hinge or are the conduits between economic burden/social pariahs and objects of care are mediated through race, class, gender, region, and causes of disability. Further, Connell argues, the divisions between social pariahs and objects of care get newly recharged and redefined—sometimes, depending on context, obversely—through neoliberalism: "Under workfare regimes that claim to end paternalistic care and dependence—in fact re-regulating the relation between welfare and the labour market—some disabled bodies are defined as work-able, others as deserving of welfare. . . . To enforce this view of disability, rising levels of surveillance are required. The globalization of neoliberal capitalism has extended this logic of disability around the world."[81] As such, we might want to be wary of claims that generalize any major historical shift, claims that unwittingly also betray a telling geographic locatedness and schema, in relation to capitalist exploitation of bodies that generate profit through disabled bodies versus bodies that need to be debilitated in order to be productive. What I want to suggest now, and elaborate later, is that in the leap from exception to exceptionality, or disability exceptionalism, the temporality of the endemic has been obfuscated.

NARRATIVE PROSTHESIS

In one of their earliest contributions to the then-nascent field of Euro-American disability studies, Snyder and Mitchell convincingly argue that the trope of disability has long functioned as a "narrative prosthesis," a habituated emplotment for overcoming tragedy and lack in order to re-consolidate the able body. As their rich scholarship demonstrates, in novel after film after short story, the body that no longer functions properly, whether physically, emotionally, or sexually, drives narrativization through a cause-and-effect relation to rehabilitation and resolution, highlighting the normativity of able bodies and leading to the climax of the story. As they write, "The able body cannot solidify its own abilities in the absence of its binary Other."[82] In this brilliant analysis they complicate the representational politics of disability by making a formalist argument about the ableist underpinnings of a certain narrative structure itself. Thus, what it means to represent disability is already superseded by the logic of narrative that pivots on the exceptional accident and triumphant rehabilitation from it. The prosthesis of disability allows a story to chug along. Their conceptualization also mirrors the tensions between ablenationalism—whereby the debilitated body is quarantined, banished, or rehabilitated—and the reformulation of the narrative prosthesis in relation to those bodies able to purchase prognostic power. Reflective of the ambivalent deployment of narrative prostheses are the forms of temporal rehabilitation and debilitation implied in the following two statements: "It Gets Better" and "Everyone will be disabled if they live long enough" (or "You're only able-bodied until you're disabled"). While "It Gets Better" refers specifically to a now global campaign addressing gay suicide, it mirrors "inspiration porn": narratives of overcoming disability or championing exceptional disability that are rife with fantasies of what McRuer and Mollow call "rehabilitated futurism."[83]

Compare these narratives of overcoming disability that signal able-nationalism or crip nationalism with other articulations of temporality and social death that work through the unevenness of how populations live and get to live time, risk, prognosis, and probability. Michael Ralph argues that artistic creativity is roused by "surplus time" for hip-hop artists—time "freed up" by virtue of a prognosis that says you don't have much time to live, a euphoric release of freedom occasioned by exceeding the dismal prognosis that you will die at an early age.[84] Andrea Smith and Scott Morgensen insistently alert us to the (queer) settler colonial mentality implicit in any invocation of futurity; indigenous populations in settler colonial states represent the vanishing point of national time, a futural gesture that is driven by a presumptive origin manufactured through the genocide of native peoples. Inclusion in (national) invocations of collective futurity is thus consent to genocide.[85] Afro-pessimists have argued that blackness remains ontologically incongruent with emphases on futurity.[86] Disability studies scholars such as Alison Kafer have critically interrogated the debilitating fantasy of immortality but at the same time queried both Lee Edelman's and Jack Halberstam's rejections of the future and of longevity.[87] Ruth Wilson Gilmore frames the temporal through a carceral racism that produces premature death.[88] Gilmore defines racism as "the state-sanctioned and/or extralegal production and exploitation of group-differentiated vulnerability to premature death."[89] Gilmore's definition implies that "health for all cannot be achieved if structural racism persists. Eliminating racism, therefore, is part and parcel to achieving the objectives of public health."[90] Premature death counters the notion that everyone will be disabled if they live long enough, foregrounding enduring associations of disability with racial difference. Much if not most racial difference continues to be perceived as defect, despite all efforts to challenge such associations and redress the structural injustices that suture them.

In these formulations of temporal life span, the capacity to inhabit futurity is already a privilege of ableism. This capacity is not simply affective or phenomenological but also structural, biopolitical, and ensnared in economies of risk, calculation, and survival. The future is already here, but it is unevenly distributed, in bits and pieces in time and space, as extremes and also as banalities. The disability to come is thus due not to aging or the exceptional accident but to the racialized body as available for injury, what Deleuze and Guattari denote as the "pre-disabled." Furthermore, durational death is not something that is overcome or resolved; rather, it is constitutively and foundationally installed. The body that is seen as consigned to death is the body that is already debilitated in biopolitical terms. These framings are situated within an endemic rather than epidemic or exceptional relation to debilitation. What these multivalent narratives about the endemic, even constitutive, nature of debilitation might suggest is that the narrative prosthesis actually functions as a prosthetic to the operations of capitalism. To extend Mitchell and Snyder's formulation, then, this model of narrative that climaxes with the resolution of the disabled body as banished or functionally restored works to proffer imminent rehabilitation for disability in one sense while masking the maintenance of debilitation as an endemic state on the other. The crisis, then, of disability is no longer marked by temporal transitoriness concluded through the climax of the narrative but rather extends and expands into the normalization of, to use the economic language of everyday crisis, "the swindle" or "the scandal."

These refigured narratives of both bodies and capital suggest that the narrative structures that solicit or posit resolution to disability—whether through rehabilitation or through elimination—are actually foils for a neoliberal economic structure that does not need to overcome disability and debility (or swindles and scandals). As Naomi Klein details in *The Shock Doctrine*, capitalism thrives on the shocks to the system and profits from sustaining crisis as a normative state, both bodily and economically.[91] The narrative prosthesis, then, may give us the cultural artifacts for the fantasy of resolution while economic structures manifest the proliferation of debilitation, using aspirational tropes for cover. The narrative prosthesis, then, not only fuels ableist and crip nationalist fantasies of the triumphant resolve of the human body but simultaneously sutures debilitation as an integral feature of what Klein calls "disaster capitalism."[92] What disaster capitalism does, and Klein unearths this, is assert disaster as the temporality of crisis to avert attention from the normalization of crisis, such that crisis is everywhere and yet unnoticed, or only noticed through the event of disaster. The difference between disaster capitalism and capitalism could thus be said to be nonexistent.

Robert McRuer's recent work demonstrates that austerity measures throughout North America, Europe, and Brazil are mounting sustained attacks on disabled populations, as the rollback of welfare provisions, social services, and health care infrastructures implicitly if not explicitly targets these communities. Disability, he argues, is a central yet undertheorized aspect of global austerity measures.[93] But, more perniciously, capitalism is also invested in producing and sustaining disability and debility. That disability creates more disability and relies on, if not engenders, a deeper entrenchment of debility in disenfranchised sectors of society, of the globe, is indeed one of the most insidious facets of a capitalism that normalizes "shock" rather than overcoming it, in order to sustain disaster capitalism. That is quite simply to say that disability, and creating and maintaining these patterns of disabilities to debilities, is good—meaning, profitable— for neoliberal capitalism. Beyond interrogating for whom identity politics benefit and for whom are they detrimental, this mapping gestures to how identity- and rights-based frames sustain the relation of perpetual, normalized crisis in relation to debility. Disaster capitalism becomes the norm that promotes the maintenance of the "disaster" of disability as debility—endemic, durational, and profitable.

THE DISABILITY THAT IS ALREADY HERE/ELSEWHERE

Even while I am eager to celebrate these instances where outlaw subjectivities flout the ineffectual disciplinary practices of compulsory able-bodiedness . . . , I hesitate, afraid to rain on this parade of possibility by foregrounding the historical and the material constraints of the social. Conscious that I may be blunting the transgressive edges where a feisty discursive aesthetic . . . meets a resourceful non-compliant theoretic, my own commitment to a transnational feminist class politics makes it difficult for me to locate these conditions of possibility outside the political and economic structures and social relations emerging from the historical conditions of an exploitative transnational capitalism. Here, there is no respite from the harsh living conditions of poverty nor from the exploitative social relations of production and consumption or from the historical continuities of (neo) colonial wars and a (neo)imperialist political economy—all of which produce, propagate, and proliferate disability while simultaneously rendering disabled people completely invisible. Will the field of disability studies look away from these borders that limit the conditions of endless possibility? And what will be the implications if it does?

In posing these last set of questions, I do not mean to imply that re-imagining transgressive possibilities is necessarily disconnected from the historical and the material constraints of the social. Nor do I want to suggest that scholarship that enables such imaginings is incompatible with historical materialist analyses. Rather, I highlight the potential tensions that can arise when disability studies scholarship is confronted by *relational analyses where the emancipation of some bodies is related to the disposability of other bodies within historical contexts that nurture such disjunctions.* —NIRMALA EREVELLES, "Thinking with Disability Studies" (emphasis added)

In her careful diagnosis, Nirmala Erevelles suggests that affirming the ontological paths of outlaw bodies for the purpose of affirming disability cultures and the imperative to halt the production of disability are not at odds with each other but, rather, are productively in tension. Helen Meekosha similarly writes that there "exists an intellectual and political tension between pride, celebration and prevention."[94] However, these mostly distinct theoretical, scholarly, and political trajectories, I suggest, not only are in tension but also lead to and capacitate very different political projects. Further, the tension, I would suggest, is not one of different needs and agendas rubbing up against each other, creating friction, but rather indicative of them being relational supplements to each other, one proliferating through the production of the other. Suggestive of this supplementary relation, Meekosha forcefully writes: "Maybe it is too confronting to deal with the continuing disabling of people in the global South because in trying to claim the positives of a disability identity it becomes difficult to acknowledge the overwhelming suffering that results from colonisation, war, famine, and poverty."[95] Thus, the analysis of "southern disability" is not simply "left out" of disability studies; it is, rather, a constitutive and capacitating absence. Further, the paradigms of disability justice do not choose one over the other but indeed address the latter in order to embrace the former. As Laura Jordan Jaffee succinctly writes: "Realizing desirable crip futures . . . , wherein disability is no longer constructed as a deficit but instead understood as a possibility, necessitates attending to and rejecting the ways in which disabling is presently employed as a mechanism for oppression in global contexts."[96]

It is especially within the global circuitry of the U.S. war machine that one can clearly discern how debility can get translated into a form of capacity, how disability functions as a state alibi, how debility is the shadow of that which state and neoliberal recognition mark as disability, and how the narrative prosthesis operates as a foil for debilitation. The disavowal of disability, onto the "elsewhere" of U.S. imperial occupations, involves the rationalization of the production of debilitation "over there" to enable wartime interests.[97] This disavowal of disability elsewhere is engendered through rights discourses in the imperial metropole that celebrate the difference of disability without sufficient attention to the debilitation actively propagated through U.S. military occupations. Via this circuitry, disability— or, rather, debility and debilitation—is an exported product of imperial aggression. This exportation not only is disavowed but is done so through the belated arrival of such disability. Insofar as the debilitating effects of toxicity and other wartime remnants may well surface in generations to come, after the perpetration of imperial violence, it remains unknown and ever unfolding "what future forms of state-produced disability lie before us."[98] The U.S. military, for example, encompassing more than seven hundred bases globally, is the world's greatest polluting entity.[99] Mel Chen's theorization of toxicity in relation to multiple chemical sensitivity (MCS) challenges the temporal distancing from disability implicit in the understanding that "we will all be disabled some day if we live long enough," and also "we are all able-bodied until we are disabled"—familiar aphorisms that organize life span time in disability rights organizing. Instead, Chen notes that the debilitation of toxicity is already here, envisioning the "disability to come" as the debility that is "already a truth of nearly every body."[100] Toxicity forces us to "[embrace], rather than [refuse] in advance, heretofore unknown reflexes of raciality, gender, sexuality, dis/ability" in ways that "intervene into the binary between the segregated fields of 'life' and 'death,' vitality and morbidity."[101] Undermining distinctions of before and after, presence and absence ("both are here," writes Chen), inside and outside, domestic and foreign, toxicity forces "interabsorption over corporeal exceptionalism," in Chen's words.[102]

And yet, the recognition of the disability that is already here requires attention to the debilitation that is relegated elsewhere, to the "there." It is easier to confront the notion of toxicity as already here when it is linked to consumer culture rather than to the U.S. imperial war machinery, in particular the U.S.-initiated and U.S.-led war on terror. The two most obvious contemporary cases of disavowed, belated disability in relation to the United States are Afghanistan and Iraq. While there has been a gradual uptick in concern about the high rates of post-traumatic stress disorder and suicide among war veterans returning to the United States from Afghanistan and Iraq, there is tepid public discourse in the United States on the deeply entrenched forms of belated disability caused by U.S. imperial occupations.[103] When the United States invaded Afghanistan on October 7, 2001, using the name Operation Enduring Freedom, the country was already "one of the least healthy places in the world to live, with a legacy of landmines, drought, and malnutrition."[104] Afghanistan also had the world's largest amputee population, "so large that almost every shoe shop in Kabul has a section selling half-pairs only."[105] There is a plentitude of noteworthy empirical research on Afghanistan; behold just a snippet: "Since the start of the war in Afghanistan in 2001, about 26,270 civilians have been killed by direct war-related violence and more than 29,900 civilians have been injured. The health care system remains burdened by war and stressed due to the destruction of Afghan infrastructure and the inability to rebuild in some regions. . . . Humanitarian workers still face attacks from militants and a generally unsafe environment. The total for all categories of direct war violence in the Afghanistan war approaches 92,000 people."[106] The 2005 National Disability Survey in Afghanistan found at that time that 17 percent of all disabilities in Afghanistan were war related.[107] Ten years later, Abdul Khaliq Zazai, executive director of Accessibility Organization for Afghan Disabled, stated that "nearly four decades of war have left an estimated 3 million people disabled," amounting to 10 percent of the population, including mental and physical disabilities among both civilians and security forces.[108]

The situation is very grim in Iraq as well: "Iraq has also suffered 15 years of war, economic sanctions, and now the US invasion and ongoing occupation of Iraq. A new study by the United Nations Development Program (UNDP) contains the following indices of what they term the 'social misery' in Iraq: Nearly a quarter of Iraq's children suffer from chronic malnutrition. The probability of dying before 40 of Iraqi children born between 2000 and 2004 is approximately three times the level in neighboring countries. . . . More than 200,000 Iraqis have 'chronic' disabilities caused by war."[109] Further, the toxic aftereffects of the two Gulf Wars have belatedly appeared through significant increases in the number of congenital birth defects, part of what medical anthropologist Omar Dewachi calls the "toxicity of everyday survival." Dewachi notes that "Operation Desert Storm, fought in 1991, was the first time in military history that depleted uranium (DU)—a nuclear waste by-product—was systematically employed against both military and civilian targets. US forces used DU on a much larger scale during the war and occupation that started in 2003."[110] In this usage of DU we can see the new yet underacknowledged version of nuclear warfare, and the Middle East has been the experimental ground on which nuclear-driven armaments are normalized. Recent analysis on Fallujah claims that dramatic increases in infant mortality, cancer, and leukemia are occurring at rates that exceed those reported by survivors of Hiroshima and Nagasaki.[111] Since 2005, doctors have been overwhelmed by increasingly debilitated infants born with severe congenital anomalies, a four-times increase in cancer, and a twelve-times increase in cancer in children under age fourteen, much higher than the regional norms in Egypt, Jordan, and Kuwait.[112] Unlike Afghanistan, Iraq had a "robust health care system" that was systematically eroded by the targeting of electricity grids, water sanitation, and communication networks in 1991, followed by an "unprecedented regime of international sanctions" that reduced medical supplies. Dewachi concludes: "The effects of more than twenty years of direct military engagement in Iraq has both overwhelmed and incapacitated the country's health care system and doctors' ability to preserve life."[113]

Arguing that the lines between health care and warfare are increasingly blurred, Dewachi notes that health infrastructure has become a normalized target of warfare, effectively ignoring 150 years of the adherence to the ethics of medical neutrality as set forth by international humanitarian law. Medical neutrality prohibits the targeting of medical infrastructural and medical person personnel, defined as noncombatants.[114] His analysis, which also examines drone casualties in Pakistan, suggests that the normalization of the disintegration of the doctrine of medical neutrality is happening in and through the greater Middle East.[115] Evidence for this assault on medical neutrality surfaced again when U.S. drone airstrikes hit a Doctors Without Borders hospital in Afghanistan.[116] Erevelles explains that "by foregrounding disability as an imperialist ideology that equates certain racialized, gendered, sexual, and class differences as 'defect,' it is possible to also foreground the eugenic impulses articulated via the 'War on Terror' . . . the sheer scope of this violence should be difficult to ignore and yet it is ignored, its invisibility justified by the imperialist/neocolonial state through its claims of regulating and controlling differences that are seen as disruptive to the 'natural' order of global civil society."[117] The targets of the war on terror are not civilians but rather are deemed terrorists, further justifying their debilitation. The import of Erevelles's observation: racialization—in this case, as terrorist, as insurgent—is a licensing to disable, a projection of the simultaneous understanding that the racialized body is in a constant state of becoming disabled. Dewachi agrees, arguing that the blurring between combatant and noncombatant through the designation of "terrorist" in opposition to civilian is a "Eurocentric system of checks and balances" and a contemporary echo of colonial wars that works to legitimate ignoring medical neutrality protocol.[118]

When disability is perceived as the result of the exceptional accident or when its cause is unknown, reclaiming disability as a valuable, empowering difference may be more possible than when debilitation is caused by practices of global domination and social injustice. The apparatus of belated and disavowed disability can be constituted very crassly as such: the United States displaces its production of debilitation through incarceration and racialization practices both "here" and in the "elsewhere," temporally as well as spatially, creating objects of un-care—social pariahs. This then allows the foregrounding of and sustaining—capacitating, even—the proliferation of crip nationalism (the objects of care) in both literal and figurative senses. By reproducing this story about the capitalist transition from economic burden to object of care, the split between the disabled subject as valuable difference and the debilitated body as degraded object is sustained. What is revealed is that there has been hardly any such complete transition at all but instead a shuffling of the bodies that are deemed economically burdensome, as well as deepening entrenchment of their institutionalization and debilitation. Some versions of disability studies in the United States thus manifest a complex elision of their own imbrication in the production of debilitation through an absent critique of U.S. imperialism. The end result, I would argue, is that crip nationalism ironically emanates quite forcefully from the site that is actually most responsible for its critique.

Disabled Diaspora, Rehabilitating State

The Queer Politics of Reproduction
in Palestine/Israel

PINKWASHING AND ITS DISCONTENTS

The advertisement opens with the tantalizing twangs of exotic music, setting the scene for a double date; two cisgender men and two cisgender women face each other at an intimate dinner table. While three of the party members might potentially be read as white, one is definitely not. A black woman is notably distinct from her companions, the rest of whom, despite having somewhat varied features, pass as familiar bodies of the Levantine region. As the languorous tune unfolds, the black woman slips off one of her shoes with her other foot and boldly reaches her toes out to the feet of the pretty woman sitting across from her, who promptly lurches, spilling her glass of wine on herself. The bearded man sitting next to her gives her a confused look, until he feels the advance of toes on his crotch from underneath the table. After catching a quick wink from his counterpart, he bursts into the laughter of recognition: all are welcome here. As the laughter infects the scene, the video, directed to Canadians specifically and North Americans and Europeans more generally, in bold caption announces, "In Israel, Love Has No Boundaries." This shameless conviction, blatantly challenging all conventional understanding of the territorial apparatus of the occupation and its perfection of the proliferation and instrumentalization of boundaries, is then followed by the written phrases "Tel Aviv Is the Host to One of the World's Largest Gay Pride Parades" and, shortly after, "Israel, Small Country, Big Pride."[1]

This piece of advertising, created by the pro-Israel organization Size Doesn't Matter as part of an ad campaign focused on promoting the virtues of Israel to Canadians, can be hailed as an example of "pinkwashing," a piece of propaganda highlighting the LGBT rights record of Israel as a function of obscuring or legitimating its occupation of Palestine.[2] Repurposed in 2009 from campaigns to critique facile medical corporate support of breast cancer research, pinkwashing has been redefined as the Israeli state's use of its admittedly stellar LGBT rights record to deflect attention from, and in some instances to justify or legitimate, its occupation of Palestine. Resonating within a receptive field of globalized Islamophobia significantly amplified since September 11, 2001, this messaging is reliant on a civilizational narrative about the modernity of the Israelis juxtaposed against the backward homophobia of the Palestinians. As such, pinkwashing has become a commonly used tag for the cynical promotion of LGBT bodies as representative of Israeli democracy. More generally, it is the erasure of hierarchies of power through the favoring of the "gay-friendly nation" imagery. It is a discourse about civilizational superiority that relies on a transparent and uninterrogated construction of "Palestinian homophobia" contingent upon the foreclosure of any questioning about "Israeli homophobia." Besides making Zionism more appealing to (Euro-American) gays, part of the mechanism at work that benefits Israel is a disciplining of Palestinian queers into legible subjects. At the same time, as Haneen Maikey has noted, the most relevant and damning effect of pinkwashing is its contribution to the processes of internal colonization: the naturalization of Israeli superiority by Palestinians themselves. The most important targets of pinkwashing therefore are not actually Euro-American gay tourists but (queer and gay) Palestinians themselves.[3] As such, I would argue that it functions dually, as a form of discursive preemptive securitization that marshals neo-orientalist fears of Palestinians as backward, sexually repressed terrorists, and as an intense mode of subjugation of Palestinians under settler colonial rule.

For whom is pinkwashing legible and persuasive as a political discourse, and why? First of all, a neoliberal accommodationist economic structure engenders the niche marketing of various ethnic and minoritized groups and has normalized the production of a gay and lesbian tourism industry built on the discursive distinction between gay-friendly and not-gay-friendly destinations.[4] The claims of pinkwashing are often seen as plausible when rendered through an LGBT rights discourse that resonates within North America and Europe as a dominant measurement of teleological progress.[5] These claims make far less sense in the "Middle East," for example, where there is a healthy skepticism about the universalizing of LGBT rights discourses and where knowledge of the complexities of sexualities in the region is far more nuanced. Additionally, in some senses Israel is a pioneer of homonationalism, as its particular position at the crosshairs of settler colonialism, occupation, and neoliberalist accommodationism creates the perfect storm for the normalization of homosexuality through national belonging. The homonationalist history of Israel illuminates a burgeoning of LGBT rights and increased mobility for gays and lesbians during the concomitant increased segregation and decreased mobility of Palestinian populations, especially post-Oslo. I have detailed this point at greater length elsewhere, but to quickly summarize: the advent of gay rights in Israel begins around the same time as the first intifada, with the 1990s known as Israel's "gay decade" brought on by the legalization of homosexuality in the Israeli Defense Forces, workplace antidiscrimination provisions, and numerous other legislative changes.[6] The IDF becomes a notable site of homonationalist distinction in relation to other countries in the "Middle East," as "Only in Israel" can "Gay Officers Serve Their Country."

The financial, military, affective, and ideological entwinement of U.S. and Israeli settler colonialisms, and the role of the United States more generally, should also not be minimized when evaluating why pinkwashing appears to be an effective discursive strategy.[7] The United States and Israel are the greatest beneficiaries of homonationalism in the current global geopolitical order, as homonationalism operates to manage difference on the scalar registers of the internal, territorial, and global. Moreover, pinkwashing is an ideological and economic solicitation directed to the United States—Israel's greatest financial supporter internationally—and to Euro-American gays who have the political capital and financial resources to invest in Israel. Thus, pinkwashing's unconscious appeal to U.S. gays is produced through the erasure of U.S. settler colonialism enacted in the tacit endorsement of Israel's occupation of Palestine.[8]

FIG. 3.1. "Where in the Middle East Can Gay Officers Serve Their Country?" Poster created by BlueStar PR: "The Jewish Ink Tank," a San Francisco nonprofit organization that creates and distributes pro-Israel materials.

Where In The Middle East Can Gay Officers Serve Their Country?

Only in Israel

In a democracy, positions of leadership and political office are open to all citizens, no matter their race, religion, or sexual orientation.

The Israeli Declaration of Independence guarantees all citizens freedom of religion, conscience, language, education, culture, and equal access to holy sites.

Support Democracy. Support Israel.

blueStarPR
The Jewish Ink Tank
www.bluestarpr.com

But pinkwashing has many antecedents; it is one more justification of colonial rule in the long history of imperial, racial, and national violence. How has "the homosexual question" come to supplement "the woman question" of the colonial era to modulate arbitration between modernity and tradition, citizen and terrorist, homonational and queer? As elaborated by Partha Chatterjee, this question arose with some force in the decolonization movements in South Asia, whereby the capacity for an emerging postcolonial government to protect native women from oppressive patriarchal cultural practices, marked as tradition, became the barometer by which colonizers arbitrated political concessions made to the colonized.[9] Here echoes Gayatri Spivak's famous dictum regarding the colonial project: "white men saving brown women from brown men."[10] Over time the terms of the woman question have been redictated, from the nineteenth-century formulation of white women's relation to colonial women as the "white woman's burden" to present-day liberal feminist scholars who have become the arbiters of other women's modernity, or the modernity of the Other Woman. To reinvoke Spivak for the twentieth and twenty-first centuries, then: white women saving brown women from brown men. The white woman's burden from the nineteenth century is regenerated for contemporary deployment through liberal feminist frames within human rights discourses.

While the woman question has hardly disappeared as a liberal missionary narrative design, it is now accompanied by another formulation: white queers (queer men?) saving brown homosexuals from brown heterosexuals.[11] I call this the homosexual question: How well do you treat your homosexuals? A mere thirty years ago this question was of no relevance to the evaluation of a nation's capacity for sovereign governance. The homosexual question is in fact a reiteration of the woman question, insofar as it reproduces a demand for gender exceptionalism, relies on the continual reproduction of the gender binary, and as with the advertisement described above, embraces queer bodies that are cisgender and gender conforming. The homosexuals hailed by the nation-state are not gender queer or gender nonconforming—they are, rather, the ones re-creating cisgender norms through, rather than despite, homosexual identity. Obscured by pinkwashing is how trans and gender-nonconforming queers are not welcome in this new version of the proper "homonationalist" Israeli citizen. What was also known as "the Jewish question," a series of debates in the nineteenth century and early twentieth century in Europe interrogating the capacity for Jewish populations to assimilate, hinged on religious difference as the defining obstacle to Jews achieving European modernity.[12] Pivotal to my analysis, therefore, is that a quasi resolution to the Jewish question reworks the denigrated effeminate masculinity of nineteenth-century European Jewry into the elevated, rehabilitated, secular, homonationalist masculinity of the occupying and settler colonialist Israeli state.

Pinkwashing also obscures the persistent downplaying of the woman question, and attendant feminist struggles, in relation to the homosexual question. Gender segregation in some ultra-Orthodox Jewish communities in Israel is still an active practice, for one example.[13] Another is how the homosexual question might eclipse the woman question for gay and lesbian consumers. On January 11, 2011, the same day that Tel Aviv's dubious honor as the "world's best gay city" was announced, an amendment to Israel's citizenship laws that prohibits the unification of West Bank Palestinians with their spouses in Israel was upheld by the High Court of Justice.[14] As Nadera Shalhoub-Kevorkian explains, the citizenship law was approved by the Knesset in 2007 and prohibits Palestinian spouses or children of Israeli citizens from receiving permanent residency or citizenship in Israel.[15] The passage of "social suitability" laws, attempts at regulating sexual activities between foreign laborers and Israeli Jews, and the efforts of vigilante groups and social organizations that monitor and agitate against sexual liaisons between Israeli Jewish women and Palestinian men: these are forms of (hetero)sexual regulation that are submerged in the pinkwashed stories of LGBT liberation. Regulation across homo-hetero divides seeks to constrict the sexual, ethnic, reproductive, and familial activities of *all* bodies not deemed suitable for the Israeli body politic.[16]

Pinkwashing thus does more than work through an active portrayal of the Palestinian population as homophobic and thus unworthy of liberation; the biopolitical target is arguably even more so the control of heterosexual reproduction. Furthermore, we see in the advertisement described earlier that there are many forms of normativity proliferating. The fact that the opening scene suggests two heterosexual couples reflects certain versions of gender and racial normativity. Blackness in the video stands in for diversity and seeks to solicit African American and Afro-Canadian audiences, while also deflecting from the lack of presence of any notably Arab bodies.[17] This is truly notable given the efforts that the Israeli government is making to recruit African Americans into the Brand Israel project and African American Jews into birthright projects.[18] In Israel, Ethiopian Jewish women have been subjected to forced sterilization, and African populations have been protesting their labor conditions and are connecting to Black Lives Matter organizing.[19] Finally, the reclaiming of small size is worthy of mention. Tourism literature compares Israel to the state of New Jersey—"Israel is the size of New Jersey."[20] The focus on size might reflect the anxious histories of debilitation and rehabilitation in the establishment and development of the state of Israel. The notation of the "small" size of Israel is often encased in compensatory rhetoric.

In this chapter I am interested in what else pinkwashing regulates besides and alongside sexual orientation. I map out a broader biopolitical portrait of sexual regulation in the Israeli occupation of Palestine and elaborate sexuality as an assemblage not anchored through the prism of queer, lesbian, gay, bisexual, or trans identities. I am interested in this particular turn for several reasons that encompass both theoretical and pragmatic organizing issues. First, as a political response to pinkwashing in the U.S. context, I argue that it is crucial not to reiterate the fantasy of queer exceptionalism by responding to pinkwashing through an appeal to queer solidarity or queer resistance, but rather to connect the regulation of queerness to the regulation of sexuality and bodies writ large. The articulation of the specific connections between different kinds of sexualities—indeed, the sexual regulation of heterosexuality, in fact, miscegenated heterosexuality—not only provides a more nuanced understanding of how sex and biopolitics work in Palestine/Israel but also refuses to return the gaze of the exceptionalizing mandate of the Israeli state that insists on propping up homosexuals as sexual citizens par excellence.[21] This portrait of biopolitical reproductive and regenerative mechanisms necessarily implicates convergences of gender, sexuality, race, nationalism, and bodily ability and disability. Finally, what I am adding to the analysis of homonationalism is its imbrication in a nation-building project of rehabilitation, reproductive biopolitics, and the capacity and debility of bodies; how ableism and hetero and homo reproduction are entwined.

This chapter draws on the latest research from Israel 48 (a reference to the 1948 borders of Israel and a term used by those supporting the Palestinian right of return) on reproductive rights, disability organizing, and LGBTQ rights. The analysis offered in this chapter does not seek to approximate or replicate an ethnographic or area studies analysis of the quotidian aspects of living with disability, with queerness, or with the facets of reproductive duress that drive the biopolitical logic of the occupation. Rather, I hope to offer a diagram of sorts that enables researchers to take up these issues in more detail. I also wish, however, neither to reify the method of ethnography nor to prioritize any one version of area studies. The territorial project of Israeli occupation itself already lays bare the paradox of territory, wherein a deep historical connection to the land must be claimed but any genetic connection to the inhabitants of that land must be disavowed.

Rehabilitating the Diaspora

The establishment of the Israeli state itself rests on a model of rehabilitation from two debilitating conditions: the statelessness of the diasporic Jewish people and the genocide of the Holocaust. As early as 1830, the terms "civil disabilities" and "Jewish disabilities" were employed to describe the political disenfranchisement of the Jewish population in England.[22] Well before its advent, the mandate for the new Israeli state was one of an uncompromising "it has to get better" from the fate of the "sickly Jew" existing in the stateless diaspora. Max Nordau, cofounder of the World Zionist Organization, famously declared in 1898 that the image of the muscular Jew was to replace the meek or sickly Jew. From him we have the saying "Zionism is Judaism with muscles."[23] Sandy Sufian writes, "Zionism—a Jewish nationalist movement that sought to create a homeland in historic Palestine—tried to change or rehabilitate the Jewish people from their seemingly disabled state in the Diaspora to a new healthy and 'normal' nation in Palestine. Given Zionism's emphasis upon redeeming the pathological state of Diaspora Jews, the concept of disability figures as a prominent cultural signifier that underscores many facets of the Zionist nationalist project."[24] In this regard, as Noam Ostrander and Eynat Shevil write, "The image of a strong Jewish body became a symbol for a strong Jewish state."[25] Theological influences concurred. The "handicapped" body is not only shunned by halachic (traditional Judaic) convention; it also is "a reminder of the Jew's 'crippled' condition in pre-Israel times, undermining the dreams, the exaggerated visions of naïve Israeli ideology, and is therefore rejected as counterproductive to the enterprise of rebirth."[26]

This new Jewish body and the new state were also gendered masculine and became "the necessary site for healthy, heterosexual transformation," as the degenerate diaspora was understood as feminine and effeminate: a rehabilitation, then, from homosexuality.[27] Daniel Boyarin notes that "European cultures represented male Jews as 'female'; the new Hebrew culture relentlessly worked to overturn this representation, and part of how it did so was by turning its back on old Jewish intellectual traditions and replacing them with a worship of virility, productivization, and war."[28] This heteronormativization was hailed in the cultivation of the land and earth, a representation of which is the El Al advertisement of a young muscular man holding a pitchfork and narrating the imbricated regeneration of nation, land, and body.

Sherene Seikaly and Max Ajl thus argue that "Zionism erased a history of learning, reading, and intellectualism."[29] This rehabilitation project was also from the onset racialized.[30] Claiming that the racial and eugenic vision of the new state has been "sidestepped," Nadia Abu El-Haj explains: "Even though scholars have written extensively about physical regeneration, the literature has sidestepped the role of racial theory and eugenic thought in helping to frame that vision and desire. . . . there was also another source of inspiration for the commitment to Hebrew labor . . . the assessment by

My name is Israel. I am 20.

Good people died that I might be born in a land called home.

I have heard the stories and seen the graves.

But now we are here, and the land is ours. Not all milk and honey, but ours.

We share a name, the land and I—Israel. And we share a birthday.

Twenty years. For me, a long time. For my people, who waited thousands of years, almost nothing.

But we have made something of that nothing.

Now the hills of rock are hills of trees. Fifty million trees, Jerusalem pines, planted one at a time.

Cities thrive where nothing thrived. Orange trees bloom where nothing bloomed.

An almost dead language is alive again. We read the Dead Sea Scrolls as easily as you read this magazine.

We mine copper where King Solomon mined copper.

We make fresh water from the sea,

and we share what we have learned with other nations.

We build airports and schools in Asia, sell baby chickens and farm equipment in Europe, and exchange our students with even younger countries in Africa.

How do we go to so many places? Easy. We have our own airline. El Al Israel Airlines.

You don't know what El Al means?. It means "to the skies" in that almost dead language.

It also means that our jets are welcome in 17 different nations.

Yes, we have everything now: Universities, symphony orchestras, great museums, politicians, dropouts, traffic jams, a little air pollution—everything.

We are of this century, with all of the strengths and weaknesses and problems of people everywhere.

We will survive.

Because, above all, we are here. Alive. In a land called home.

The Airline of the People of Israel EL AL

FIG. 3.2. In an undated advertisement for El Al, an Israeli airline is the face of Israeli new Jewish masculinity typified by a robust, muscular man holding a pitchfork in preparation for a hard day's work.

Jewish physicians and social sciences of 'the Jews' as a degenerate race and their eugenic framework for imagining a 'solution' to the problem, that is, a revived and reborn Hebrew nation in Palestine."[31] The paradox that Abu El-Haj details is that the creation of a revived Jewish race is one both distinct from Arabs and simultaneously scientifically connected to the land of Palestine and thus to its claims to statehood.

Rehabilitation also involved three other facets: first, banishing the Oriental in the European Jew; second, re-creating Europe, in Palestine, for the Jew who was forced to leave it. Seikaly and Ajl aver, "To become fully European, the Jew had to leave Europe."[32] And finally, this process could not be complete without severing the Jew from the Arab. As Ella Shohat has so persistently and precisely shown us, Arab Jews, the linchpin figure of this rehabilitation endeavor, occupy the site of ambivalence in this racializing and sexualizing assemblage: "Mizrahi [are] ambivalent[ly] position[ed] as occupying the actantial slot of both dominated and dominators; simultaneously disempowered as 'Orientals' or 'blacks' vis-à-vis 'white' Euro-Israelis and empowered as Jews in a Jewish state vis-à-vis Palestinians."[33] As Shohat notes, then, what was rendered as a Zionist healing and return was actually a cultural "dismemberment" of the Arab from the Jew.[34] Seikaly and Ajl succinctly explain: "Certainly, the Zionists had (and continue) to struggle with the persistent reality of building a Jewish state on a land whose natives were not Jewish. But the specter of the Oriental threat did not merely hover in what Zionists understood as the inferior Palestinian. Nor did it lie only in the Oriental residue still remaining within the Jew from Europe. . . . It was the Jew from the East, in his irreducible singularity, that would pose one of the greatest threats to the rehabilitated, and now supposedly European, Jewish body."[35]

Disability Strikes

In May 2013, the renowned physicist and cosmologist Stephen Hawking decided to honor the Boycott, Divestment, and Sanctions (BDS) call and refused to attend a conference hosted by then-Israeli president Shimon Peres.[36] While BDS activists worldwide lauded this decision, others who were upset by it could not help but point out what they claimed to be an irony of the position of Hawking. Early and slow onset of amyotrophic lateral sclerosis has left Hawking paralyzed, a user of prosthetic technologies that aid in sensory and motor skills. Detractors jeered that the chip embedded in his computer that allows him to communicate via his cheeks is made in Israel.[37] Hailing the exceptional state of Israeli technology, especially for people with disabilities, does not, however, translate into similar attitudes in Israel.[38] Disability rights have a much shorter life history in Israel 48 than do gay rights, with major legislation for disability discrimination not happening until the late 1990s and more forcefully in the last decade. There are pockets of disability rights organizing, but up until rather recently, disability has been understood through paternalism and guardianship rather than empowerment provisions.[39] To be clear, I am not claiming that disability is not being attended to by the state, numerous organizations, and activist initiatives. Nor am I discussing the private spaces within which disability might be incorporated into kin networks, informal communities of care, and alternative labor circuits. What I am most interested in here is whether and how disability functions in a positive (i.e., on the side of life) rhetorical biopolitical positioning and how disability signifies and is located in public domains. Citing the work of Sagit Mor, Neta Ziv, and Ariela Ophir and Dan Orenstein, Hila Ramon-Greenspan summarizes: "Until the late 1990s, disability legislation in Israel has focused primarily on issues of disability allowances and benefits, and was founded upon a discourse of need and charity rather than of human rights and equality. . . . In contrast to Israel's extensive welfare legislation, disability rights legislation has been very much neglected and was scarce, scattered, incoherent, and under complied with or unenforced."[40] Sagit Mor writes that while Israel understands itself as being a very generous welfare state to people with disabilities, the welfare system has reinforced the divisions between three different groups of disabled, as those injured in the roles of defense and labor are less stigmatized: "IDF disabled veterans (*Nechei Tzahal*) were located at the top, work-injured (*Nechei Avoda*) were situated in the middle, and the majority of people with disabilities were positioned at the bottom."[41]

In an incisive piece that traces the kind of discursive and logistical work needed to keep disability as somehow an issue separate from the occupation, Liat Ben-Moshe describes the second occurrence of what are now known as "disability strikes" (named as such to indicate their relation to labor disputes), which began in 1999 and marked the onset of large, ongoing public protests by people with disabilities. The majority of strikers were wheelchair users at first, but the strikes increasingly gathered others; protests lasted from thirty-seven to seventy-seven days and attempted to change benefit allowances as well as draw attention to the lack of employment opportunities for people with disabilities.[42] As the second intifada began, some involved in both the disability protests and anti-occupation organizing became hesitant about appeals to the Israeli state for "rights" that essentially signaled and reinforced a "continuation and legitimization of the occupation" and, more trenchantly, settler colonialism. Ben-Moshe explains that the "disabled community" at that time was a "divided" one, avowing that "nationality based on Zionist ideology is at the basis of such disjunctures and splits within 'the movement,' not a by-product of unsuccessful organizing." Securing rights for disabled people was naturalized under the guise of liberal democracy as separate from the "ethnic-colonial mechanisms on which the state of Israel was founded and currently operates."[43]

The Israeli government used the mounting economic costs of the second intifada as one excuse for the downsizing of state welfare benefits, according to Shlomo Swirski, who notes that "the intifada may be regarded as an opportunity that presented itself for the implementation of a plan long in waiting."[44] Ben-Moshe writes: "It is in fact not at all surprising that the disability protests happened at the same time as the second Intifada, as the economic costs of suppressing the uprising of the Palestinian struggle for self-determination were beginning to accumulate and as a result of the 'zero sum game' of neoliberalism, the direct result was the decrease in benefits, health care, direct payments, etc."[45] This temporal conjunction between the strikes and the second intifada also prompts questions about how disability (activism) deals with the issue of land dispossession at the crux of Palestinian struggles, and the relationship of mobility and access to the land grab and settlement activities of the occupation.

This is already interesting in relation to the gay rights record in Israel: the state recognizes gay difference and, in theory, a certain kind of bodily difference—the robust gay male Israeli body, but not "disability" difference—worthy of fostering and folding into the biopolitics of regenerative futurism. This variable establishment of certain kinds of rights platforms may contribute to this relation: the 1998 disability legislation reform was comprehensive and was enacted through legislative governmental means, while acquiring LGBT rights has been a more patchwork, issue-by-issue type of process, often initiated by appeals to religious law by same-sex couples.[46] (This comparison might matter more within the U.S. context, where queerness and disability have a deeper entwined history. To be disabled was to be a certain queer, and to be queer was understood as a deficit, indeed, a medical deficit, of sorts.) While I will not go into further depth into the history of disability rights in Israel here, what I want to extrapolate from it in brief is that there appears scant evidence of any aspirational drive to support forms of exceptional disability that the "multicultural state" is willing to claim in its production of itself as a liberal democracy that embraces diversity. That is the case in part because Israel, while claiming to be a multicultural state, still articulates itself in relation to its ethnonationalist foundation; multiculturalism acts as a vehicle for the regrounding of ethnonationalist ideals.[47] The exception to this would be, as Sagit Mor elaborates, IDF disabled veterans, who have "a most privileged position in terms of social glory, extensive benefits, a powerful organization, and a strong political lobby."[48] The technology industry to which Hawking is unforgivably indebted also produces prosthetics in partial response to injured IDF soldiers.[49] Ben-Moshe adds that "the disability community in Israel is divided by whether one was injured during military service or not." Historically, the Association of Disabled Veterans, "the most powerful disability organization in Israel," "never fully endorsed the disability protests," worked on behalf of veterans only, did not see veterans as part of a larger disabled community, and even worked against extending the vast benefits received by disabled veterans to others.[50] As an example of this fissure, she notes: "Most mobility impaired veterans receive cars, and stipends to maintain them, from the ministry of defense, so the disabled veteran association never addressed the issue of inaccessibility of public transportation."[51]

Disability due to war injury also functions as a permanently looming specter: the disability to come from the bombings that might but mostly do not happen functions to continually justify the occupation. Noting that the Israeli media instrumentalizes disability in the service of the occupation, Ben-Moshe writes:

> The Israeli media is inundated with photos of people maimed by terror attacks in military combat. Much like the public display of funerals, which happens almost daily in Israeli news, physically disabled people remind the nation of the cost of war and increased aggression. Paradoxically this imagery and rhetoric can easily translate by the government to legitimization of more aggression, as measures of prevention and defense of future bodily casualties. The self-defense mechanism cannot operate from a position of superiority, especially when Israel is seen in the world as a military superpower. Therefore, the use of Israelis maimed in terror attacks is an important strategy to defer any criticism on the complete lack of balance between oppressor and occupied in these acts.[52]

The disability to come, then, in this context works as a specular imperial tool, projecting the fear of maiming by Palestinians onto Palestinians through the debilitating effects of the occupation; this mechanism is the displacement necessary to secure able-bodied citizenry of Israel. Another manifestation of the instrumentalization of disability as a part of the occupation machine is the discourse of trauma, in particular the post-Holocaust trauma that takes hold from 1967 onward and disavows trauma for the Palestinians through the centering of Jewish suffering.[53]

It is possible that a disability rights project in Israel is not necessarily needed by the biopolitical state because the disabled veteran (not to mention the specter of potentially debilitated citizenry) secures the logic of visibility and legitimation of injury that justifies the occupation. Israeli crip nationalism is secured through the disabled IDF veteran. So, instead of fostering a rights discourse that embraces disability as a valuable difference, the Israeli state relies on the spectacle of disability as trauma and victimhood. And yet, given Ben-Moshe's conviction that "disability is always inherent in anti-occupation and antiwar movements (for instance in relation to militarization, budgetary priorities, and the remaking of the New Israeli Jew)," the emergence of a liberal disability rights movement may only be possible if forcibly delinked from the occupation as a prime war machine that produces disability. It may also be the case that a rights-based project based on disability as an identity makes less sense in the Israeli context given that identity politics has a different history.[54] Finally, it seems the case that while the ideology of the muscular Jew drove the rehabilitation project of earlier times, the current period is marked by increasing recourse to neoliberal alibis reducing or denying support for people with disabilities. Israel's previously strong welfare state continues to decline; hence, the dispossession of the occupation is increasingly privatized.[55]

Disability in the West Bank

Palestinians are the debilitated bodies in contrast to the rehabilitated bodies protected by the Israeli state. Israel reasserts the project of rehabilitation through the disavowal of disability onto Palestine. Couched within a narrative about the liability of disability that is worse than death itself, the occupation, indeed, has created intense forms of disability through war, suicide bombings, shootings, drones, border skirmishes, and missile attacks. Equally important, it produces and sustains endemic forms of debility, for example, through food and medicine rationing to Gaza and restrictions on the access to medical care. It is unsurprising, then, that Gaza and the West Bank have some of the highest rates of disability in the world. For many on both sides of the occupation, it is better to "die for your country"—in Palestine you become a martyr—than to face a life with a body that is deemed disabled. The consequence of believing that disability is worse than death is simple: "not killing" Palestinians while rendering them systematically and utterly debilitated is not humanitarian sparing of death. It is instead a biopolitical usage and articulation of the right to maim.

Further, this debilitation happens through a concomitant deployment of maiming as a central tactic of settler colonialism in order to occupy, combined with the understanding that the Palestinian body is inherently deficient and thus carries with it the potential to be disabled. The resulting debilitation of Palestinians dehumanizes them in order to (further) ratify occupation. Laura Jordan Jaffee's work on Israeli settler colonialism and disability calls attention to the need for greater theorization of disability and settler colonialism and also to the centrality of debilitation to the maintenance of the dehumanization of Palestinian bodies, thus feeding the rationale for occupation. She argues that the growth of disability studies in Israel 48 is composed of scholarship that remains largely disconnected from the production of debilitation by the Israeli state through the occupation and lacks acknowledgment of Israel as a settler colonial state.[56] Jaffee writes: "The hopeful tone of disability studies scholarship emanating from Israel renders particularly evident the foibles of a widespread inattention to settler-coloniality and the shortfalls of Eurocentric disability studies for addressing disability-related issues in the region."[57] The maintenance of a population as precarious occurs *through* the active debilitating of that population. Israeli settler subjectivity therefore coheres through rehabilitation from disability through the systemic debilitation of Palestinians.

Disability visibility and empowerment might also be problematic for state recuperation and the management of difference in Israel because issues of access and mobility are central to the disability rights platforms increasingly embedded in global human rights agendas. The containment of mobility is one of the prime logics of the occupation. Celeste Langan notes that "mobility disability" can consider "how the built environment—social practices and material infrastructures—can create mobility disabilities that diminish the difference between the 'cripple' and the ambulatory person who may well wish to move."[58] Numerous health issues, debilitations, and deaths due to "movement restrictions" in the West Bank and Gaza attest to this slipperiness between mobility impairment and impairing mobility.[59]

Disability services in Palestine predominantly responded to blindness and deafness until the 1970s. In the aftermath of the first intifada, the number of people with permanent disabilities increased, as did a sudden interest in physical disability. Palestinian society started reclaiming its wounded and elevated the war-disabled, having acquired "honorific disabilities," to a vaulted status.[60] The NGO sector working with disability grew exponentially once the Palestinian Authority was established, and a slow move from the medical model of disability to the social model got under way. Rita Giacaman explains: "With the disabled having been much neglected until that time, they were suddenly catapulted to fame because of these devastating events. Disability and infirmity assumed political and social status in the eyes of the public, and those disabled were deemed national heroes with the full endorsement of the national political movement."[61] This created and sustained negative attitudes toward other kinds of disabilities, especially toward people with mental and intellectual disabilities, who were and continue to be the most marginalized of people with disabilities, and also not infrequently the targets of violence by the IDF.[62] Giacaman, one of the most prominent advocates for global health initiatives in Palestine, continues: "This disability movement was propelled to the forefront of national politics because of the specific circumstances of the Uprising period of the late 1980s and early 1990s, where thousands of young people were either killed or permanently injured during fighting with Israel."[63]

During this time, fewer than 10 percent of people with disabilities were able to afford services. Many services were unavailable or were unknown of because of stigma or negligence.[64] In 1999, a broad-based coalition movement led by the Palestinian General Union of People with Disability (GUPWD), a grassroots movement founded in 1991 that has been since folded into NGO networks, proposed a rights-based disability equality platform that was signed into law that same year.[65] The Palestinian Disability Law, also known as Law Number Four for the Year 1999 Concerning the Rights of the Disabled (frequently referenced as "Number Four"), was called "the most progressive legislation bill on disability compared with other countries in the region."[66] The GUPWD currently has a membership of more than 35,000 and receives funding from international, regional, and local donors and some money from the Palestinian Authority.

The transition from stigmatization—"objects of charity" and "religious obligation"—to a rights-based, empowerment approach has been tricky at best given the lack of resources to implement the law. Allam Jarar, director of the Palestinian Medical Relief Society's rehabilitation program in the West Bank and Gaza, writes that "the question remains whether this change can genuinely affect peoples' lives and whether the rights-based approach to disability can be translated from slogans and articles to hard facts and realities that can make a difference in the lives of people with disabilities."[67] Issues regarding the implementation of Number Four continue to be addressed, especially as it pertains to the inadequate distribution of resources by the Palestinian Authority.[68] According to the Palestinian Central Bureau of Statistics (PCBS) and the Palestinian Ministry of Social Affairs, in 2011, there were at least 113,000 Palestinians in the West Bank, Gaza, and occupied East Jerusalem (2.7 percent of the population) with a disability. In 2007, the PCBS recorded the disability rate as 5.3 percent, with almost 80 percent of these individuals having no jobs and 55 percent having no education. In 2011, the PCBS reported a slight decline in the percentage of people with disabilities who do not have access to education, at 37 percent; yet 84 percent still cannot find jobs and 76 percent cannot use public transportation.[69]

Numerous NGOs work on integration and empowerment programs—job skills and employment creation, access to education, and tackling stigma and discrimination—for people with disabilities in Palestine: the East Jerusalem YMCA (supported by Y Care International); Handicap International, present in Gaza since 1996; Maysoon's Kids (wellness for Palestinian children with disabilities); the Maximizing Potential Program (begun in 2015, focusing on Down syndrome, autistic spectrum disorder, visual impairment, deafness, cerebral palsy, and learning difficulties); Irada, at the Islamic University of Gaza (begun in 2008 to support the massive increase in the numbers of young people with disabilities during Operation Cast Lead). Disability in this context may well be instrumentalized as a form of economic pragmatism to secure funding for bodies through international NGO networks. These funding flows also may provide a way for international actors to offer humanitarian aid and simultaneously deflect from addressing the larger concerns of the occupation. The definition of disability in Palestine also is constantly evolving. The difference between abled bodies and disabled bodies may not be as thoroughly delineated in a context where a population experiences collective punishment largely meted out through the obstruction of mobility. The occupation itself can be understood as disabling the entire Palestinian West Bank population through the restriction of mobility, what Langan refers to as "mobility disability."

Israel's Political Economy of Fertility

Israel has produced a complex pronatalist agenda, typically ascribed to "Biblical prescription, the trauma of the Holocaust, and present day demographic politics."[70] My intent in this section is to give a brief sketch of a situation that is very complex; rife with internal contradictions; constantly changing due to legislative, economic, and corporate shifts; and explored by a vast literature debating issues beyond the scope of this analysis. Describing the "demographic threat" as "a set of tensions," Tsipy Ivry argues that there is a tendency to "translate birthrates into Israel's chances of surviving a military conflict."[71] Reproduction is also encouraged as rehabilitation from the Holocaust. While in theological terms "the barren woman is an archetype of suffering," there is more pointedly a history of state policies encouraging motherhood (for example, awards by David Ben-Gurion for "Heroine Mothers," women who had ten or more children).[72]

The population anxieties that are implicated in pronatalist policies are usually accorded to two factors. First, a one-state solution will mean Palestinians will have the demographic advantage and Jewish Israelis will be the minority. Second, there is concern that Palestinians are reproducing at a higher rate than Israeli Jews, a phenomenon usually attributed to demographic resistance on the part of Palestinians.[73] Further, as Ivry expounds, "That the two populations generally considered uncommitted to the Jewish nation-state—the ultra-orthodox and the Palestinian Arabs—have the highest fertility rates within the overall population has only worked to exacerbate the notion of the demographic threat."[74] Writing of the history of pronatalism in Israel, she continues: "Although birth has been encouraged in general, it was always 'the wrong' populations that were fruitful and multiplied, either Mizrahi Jews or ultra-Orthodox communities. The 'Zionist' population was never as enthusiastic as the state might have wanted."[75] Concerns about global assimilation and intermarriage add fuel to this anxiety.[76]

This celebrated but eugenic pronatalism takes the material force of what has been deemed the most developed assisted reproductive technology (ART) industry in the world. There is extensive literature on new reproductive technologies, and research on this field is constantly emerging and evolving. It is notable as well that much of this work, while contextualizing pronatalism within the fear of the "demographic threat," does not address the occupation specifically from an anti-Zionist stance or any approach critical of the Israeli government except as it might relate to reproduction.[77] What follows is subject to amendment as technologies proliferate, access is reorganized, and legality established and revoked. Israel is known as the world capital of in vitro fertilization (IVF) and is "often represented as having the highest number of fertility clinics per capita in the world."[78] Israeli national insurance subsidizes (for Palestinian citizens of Israel as well, depending on access) if not covers artificial insemination, ovum donation, and at one point unlimited but now seven IVF attempts.[79] Israel has the world's highest IVF rates.[80] It was the first country in the world to legalize surrogate mother agreements. A set of "guidelines" on "posthumous reproduction" was endorsed by the attorney general of the Government of Israel in October 2003.[81] This term refers to "post-mortem sperm aspiration at a widow's request, which has become standard practice in Israel since 2003 . . . even at the parents' request."[82] The "biological will" is the prime mechanism through which Israeli posthumous reproduction has been outlined and actualized.[83] New Family claims to be the only organization in the world that drafts and stores biological wills, which specifies the use of gametes and ova in case of premature death or loss of reproductive capacity. According to the founder of New Family, Irit Rosenblum, the impetus behind the biological will came from the proposal to form a sperm bank for IDF soldiers.[84] Rosenblum avers that Israel is the "world's pioneer" in posthumous reproduction and also boasts the only case in the world of "posthumous maternity."[85] While the guidelines focus on the autonomous right of the deceased to posthumous reproduction, there is no discussion of posthumous parenthood or consideration for the child, according to critics such as R. Landau, who calls the new provisions "exploitation of the dead."[86] Israel is also part of the global interest in formalizing rights for "grandparenthood."[87] This would be the right for the parents of a dead son to harvest his sperm and hire a surrogate to provide grandchildren. In June 2014 the courts approved a request from the parents of a dead son to use his sperm to father children with a woman of their choice.[88]

Susan Martha Kahn writes, "Israeli legislators have drafted regulations to provide broad-based, and in many cases unprecedented, access to these technologies . . . contemporary orthodox rabbis have spared no effort to determine appropriate uses of these technologies that are commensurate with traditional rabbinic understandings of relatedness."[89] Ellen Waldman concurs: "Despite the conservative pull Jewish scripture exerts over Israeli law, the fertility industry in Israel services married couples, lesbians, and single women alike, and religious authorities appear complicit with providers in a 'don't ask–don't tell' partnership of mutual avoidance. Fertility clinics do not keep statistics on the numbers of non-traditional families they help create and religious authorities have chosen not to agitate against the possible *Halachic* violations implicit in ART activities."[90]

The excelling of ART in Israel has a biopolitics of population racism intrinsic to its logic. Starting with an unapologetically eugenic approach to imperfect fetuses, selective abortions (which includes the legality of late-term, postdiagnostic abortions) are advocated through loose legal strictures and genetic counseling for the screening and aborting of fetuses with any kind of "malformation." (Per a 1977 law, late-term abortion is granted through a committee.)[91] This proclivity toward encouraging selective abortion may seem at odds with the pronatalism of the Israeli state.[92] (The same might be true of the targeting of Palestinian and Mizrahi women for abortions and the selective use of the contraceptive implant Depo-Provera for Ethiopian Jewish women.)[93] While Sarah Franklin has commented that in such a context, disability can be seen as a "genetic sacrifice" undertaken to bolster the nation and reproduce at any cost, these "neo-eugenic technologies" exist in tension with "inclusive discourses of disability" in many locations.[94] Some sources claim "no criticism has been voiced by disability movements in Israel against the social meaning of prenatal diagnosis," or to the "legal status of post-diagnostic abortions."[95] This may well be an overly complicit reading in support of prenatal testing stemming from lack of knowledge of different forms of disability organizing.[96] Yet another consideration is Judaic theological understandings of when life begins that posit that fetuses do not have rights; rabbinic law considers fetal life tentative until birth; and the mother's life and health take precedence over the fetus.[97]

In *A Life (Un)Worthy of Living: Reproductive Genetics in Israel and Germany*, Yael Hashiloni-Dolev undertakes a comprehensive study of genetic counseling in the two countries. Motivated by her family lineage in Germany, the historical weight of its relation to Israel, and a prior study that claims that, globally speaking, Israel and Germany inhabit diametrically opposed attitudes toward selective abortion, she writes:

> Whereas all German counselors paid respect to the idea of human genetic diversity, either for the sake of a humanistic ethos, or for the sake of biological diversity, Israelis completely mocked those ideas. Likewise, whereas German counselors felt their society had to be reminded of the fact that life is not all about money and fun, Israeli counselors did not share this feeling. For example, an Israeli women genetic counselor said: "Do people with severe disabilities make society more rich and varied? Maybe on the philosophical level. But in reality, I want to see you spend one day with a child with cerebral palsy or mental retardation, and then you will see what it really means. Then I will ask you again what you think of the high minded who say it's nice. There are enough things that make our lives diversified without suffering. One should not have disabled children in order to enrich the world or to make his neighbor more sensitive."[98]

In another comparative study, this one of pregnancy in Israel and Japan, Ivry argues that disaffected approaches to congenital disabilities are conditioned by several combining factors. They include a specific limited "economy of nurturance" from Israeli women who are expected to work outside the home and also have numerous children; destiny as embodied and unchangeable; and "continuous generation of fear of reproductive catastrophes" driven by Israeli Jewish existential threat, terror, risk, and genetic fatalism that fuels intense prenatal diagnostic testing.[99]

Pausing for a moment, I want to stress that I am not making a normative argument about the value of disabilities; rather, I am interested in how and why and which disabilities come to signify what they do. It is also worth flagging a basic point here that obviously "internal" differences among Israeli Jews are also being managed through ART and disability.[100] For example, the Egg Donation Law of 2010 prevents cross-religion egg donation within Israel; it does not legislate imported eggs.[101] Hashiloni-Dolev concurs that there is a lenient policy on abortion for eugenic reasons and as such minor "defects" that are not even necessarily probable but likely are sufficient reason for an abortion.[102] Birenbaum-Carmeli and Carmeli also aver that "the vast majority of Israelis choose to terminate . . . pregnancy" when there is an anomaly.

In earlier work, Ivry makes explicit the linkages between Israeli practices of settler colonial occupation and how these practices impact the thinking around abortions. Meira Weiss summarizes Ivry's assessment by stating that "the worldview of Israeli gynecologists is based on military terminology; abortion is justified by military thinking that killing is necessary for goals."[103] So there is some assessment here that the medical-industrial complex is coextensive with the military-industrial complex, conditioned in no small part by the fact that in most cases medical personnel once served as military medical personnel as well. Ivry concludes: "Israeli pro-natalism, with its emphasis on genetic selections and catastrophic scripts, produces a paradoxical situation in which a woman may spend much of her pregnancy—a state so desired from a pro-natalist perspective—in anxiety."[104]

Along with this, an intricate social and legal apparatus regulates and restricts Israeli Jews and Palestinians getting married, living together, and having joint resident rights.[105] The legal apparatus includes contracts signed by Chinese foreign laborers saying they will not have sex with Israeli Jews; laws that discriminate and disallow unification for Palestinian heterosexual couples to reside together and coordinate residency status (for example, Palestinians living in Israel and those in occupied East Jerusalem or the West Bank); "rape by deception" cases that criminalize "interracial" sex; and "social suitability" laws that permit communities to veto residents of the neighborhood.[106] The social apparatus includes numerous groups that police young Israeli women's relationships with Palestinian men, most notably through informal community groups and also vigilante groups such as Fire for Judaism and Youth of Love.[107]

Finally, the pronatalist population runoff may also be reflected in investment in the reproductive capacities of (some) gay and lesbian couples—and, most recently, (some) trans couples. Some aspects of ART are available to LGBT people in Israel, which is highly unusual elsewhere in the world.[108] While this investment is touted as part of the progressive status of gay rights in Israel, it also affirms the same racial-religious-ethnic logics of heterosexual reproduction and the exceptional status of queerness that is devoid of Arabness or Palestinianness. Natalie Hamou, in an article titled "Israel, a Paradise for Gay Families," wonders, "How is it that Israel became a nation so advanced in this area?" She notes that the right to adopt children, biological or nonbiological, was recognized for same-sex couples between 2005 and 2008 with, in both cases, the possibility for the spouse to adopt the children of his or her partner. Since 2009, gay couples can also benefit from paternity leave. Irit Rozenblum claims that "Israeli society is particularly family friendly, whatever the sex of the parents. One can even say that the perception towards gays is changing in their favor when they choose to grow and multiply."[109] Susan Martha Kahn also suggests that the lesbian mothers in her research sample perhaps received unexpected social support from family and friends because they "foregrounded their identities as mothers, rather than as lesbians."[110] While there is dissent from religious quarters regarding the validity of the Jewish gay family, negative commentary is often responded to quite vociferously, as with an incident in June 2014 when education minister Shai Piron, an Orthodox rabbi, stated that same-sex couples and their children are "not a family."[111]

Legalizing surrogacy for gay and lesbian families has become the rights equality issue of the LGBTQ movement in Israel, far surpassing interest in same-sex marriage. Marriage equality as an activist agenda has taken hold in many locations globally but faces difficulty in Israel because there is no civil marriage code, only religious marriage code. In an article titled "Forget Marriage Equality; Israeli Gays Want Surrogacy Rights," Zvika Krieger explains that even many heterosexual couples might have a wedding but do not actually get married because of the restrictions of the religious courts. Seventy-five percent of Israeli gay couples have children, according to a Central Bureau of Statistics report. As quoted by Krieger, Doron Mamet, who runs a gay surrogacy consultancy group, claims that "in Israel, if you don't have your family, you don't exist." Krieger also interviews legal advocate Fredrick Hertz, who reports: "In my conversations, I hear having children described as the queer contribution to building the Jewish state." Legal studies professor Aeyal Gross proclaims: "You're a good gay, you brought us nice, new children, many children—this is the ticket to normalization, much more than marriage."[112] Because domestic surrogacy is not legal in Israel, LGBT Israelis have been heavy users of overseas surrogacy markets, such as that in India.[113]

In other words, then, to be gay in Israel is not only to be Jewish (and not Palestinian and in many cases not even Arab), not only to be able-bodied (and not disabled), but also to be parents, to reproduce the national body politic along racial and rehabilitated lines. Thus, I would argue that the most pernicious thing that the discourse of pinkwashing accomplishes, along with keeping activated a discourse about Palestinian homophobia, is effacing the fact that the state's interest in homosexuality is superseded by its interest in reproductive capacities of bodies engaged in Israeli pronatalism. This capacitation of reproduction services the goals of the occupation in a much more endemic manner, through the biopolitics of population reproduction and the cultivation of a racially elevated Israeli body politic—not quite as simple as the "demographic" issue might initially seem. Pinkwashing, and the subsequent attention to the sexual regulation of homosexuality whereby the field of sexuality is completely taken up by the question of orientation, obscures intense forms of control being enacted at the level of reproduction across homo-hetero divides.

INHUMANIST POLITICS OF OCCUPATION: SEX, AFFECT, AND PALESTINE/ISRAEL

These are broadly sketched parameters of the biopolitical regulation of sex that complicates the binary discourse of sexual freedom versus sexual regulation and repression driving pinkwashing rhetoric, but also complicates the kinds of queer exceptionalism reproduced in anti-pinkwashing organizing. Here I lay out the stakes of understanding homonationalism-as-assemblage: as a structure of modernity, a convergence of geopolitical and historical forces, neoliberal interests in capitalist accumulation both cultural and material, biopolitical state practices of population control, and affective investments in discourses of freedom, liberation, and rights. I provisionally sketch how homonationalism-as-assemblage creates a global field within which the discourse of pinkwashing takes hold. The point is not merely to position Israel as a homonationalist state against which anti-pinkwashers must resist, but to further demonstrate the complex global and historical apparatus that creates the appearance of the activities of the Israeli state as legitimate and progressive. The control of the production of bodily capacity at multiple vectors—national discourse, disability, ART, pronatalist ideologies—entails that pinkwashing is part of a larger assemblage, the goal of which is to modulate debility and capacity across manifold populations.

In this final section I want to elaborate homonationalism-as-assemblage in terms of thinking about these multilayered and multiscalar nodes of control. The stakes of the kind of "queer" activism that is happening in Palestine are not necessarily in the name of queer or relegated to the dominance of the national.[114] Rather, this activism toggles tensions between the "queer Palestinian" and the "Palestinian queer." The rearranging of both terms reflects a necessarily ambivalent relation to the identity reification possible in each. Palestinian Queers for BDS, for example, was an organizing project—the most visible in the region as well as globally—that is deeply attuned to the spatial triumvirate of (1) colonization, (2) apartheid, and (3) occupation that informs the quotidian movements of Palestinians both inside and on the side of Israel today. Palestinian Queers for BDS claimed that anti-occupation activism is queer activism. Their resistance to dominant global LGBT activist agendas such as the legalization of gay marriage maintains sexuality as a contingent assemblage and network, with an axis of signification and an axis of forces that do not neatly align with the material compartmentalizing of populations.

As an affective assemblage, sexuality entails an axis of signification and an axis of forces that defy configurations that produce monoliths such as "the Israeli (and his/her modernist sexuality)" and "the Palestinian (and his/her pathological sexuality)" as supplements of a liberal and yet brutal humanism. Thinking of both homonationalism and sexuality through assemblages opens up a different trajectory or plane of territorialization. Even as the staidness of the politics of recognition gets mobilized by Israeli and global gay discourses through pinkwashing, the materiality of sexual practice and sexuality itself is so much more complex, mediated, and contingent than the stagnating politics of control and resistance can grasp. Further, sexuality is a contingent assemblage that, in the context of some U.S. academic, left, and liberal discourses, gets reterritorialized at the level of the molar in the form of "queer solidarity."

This theoretical framework does not set the "subject" against the assemblage—the subject remains within the assemblage, but positioned and signifying differently—or the molar against the molecular. Rather, the framework highlights the differential interplay among these levels or registers of the political. A molecular politics is recaptured by a molar schema in the liberal context that can only conceive of an investment in anti-occupation work insofar as it is in the name of consolidating a "queer international" or subject-bound political formation that structurally reiterates the Islamophobia of pinkwashing even in a pinkwatching setting.[115] This does not mean that the molar and the molecular exist in a binary opposition, though they may perhaps be nonaligned. This understanding of sexuality entails theorizing not only specific disciplinary sites but also broader techniques of social control, given that "feminism" and "queer" and the death or lively potential of their subjects have already been made to be productive for governance. In this oscillation between disciplinary societies and control societies, sexuality is not only contained within bodies but also dispersed across spaces. Control societies as a geopolitics of racial ontologies, as mechanisms of not just highly regulated but also deeply saturated space, and life, are important to apprehend here in terms of how the positive rhetorical function of queer operates. What is this saturation of space doing to struggles for sexual rights trans/nationally—how are these struggles being compromised but also coproduced?

Achille Mbembe writes that the contemporary colonial occupation of Palestine is the "most accomplished form of necropower," listing the territorial fragmentation of a "splintering occupation," a proliferation of sites of violence (through what Eyal Weizman describes as the triplication of space), and infrastructural warfare—a "concatenation of disciplinary, biopolitical, and necropolitical" powers.[116] The occupation thus operates less through Agamben's "state of exception," though this legal frame is certainly still applicable, and more so through this saturation of space and life with increasingly baroque modalities of control. This saturation of space impedes forms of molar queer organizing. The discourse of pinkwashing only makes sense through an erasure of the spatial logics of control of the occupation and the intricate and even intimate system of apartheid replete with a dizzying array of locational obstacles to Palestinian mobility. That queer Palestinians in Ramallah cannot travel to Haifa, Jerusalem, or Gaza to meet fellow Palestinian activists seems to be one of the most obvious ways the Israeli occupation delimits—prohibits, in fact—the possibilities for the flourishing of queer communities and organizing that Israelis have enjoyed without mobility restrictions.

Instead of understanding congregation as constitutive of queer identity and community, pinkwashing reinforces ideologies of the clash of cultures and the "cultural difference" of Palestinian homophobia rather than recognizing the constraining and suffocating spatial and economic effects of apartheid. Antagonist accusations about the (mis)treatment of homosexuals in the West Bank and the Gaza Strip fail to take into account the constant and omnipresent restrictions on mobility, contact, and organizing, necessary elements for building queer presence and politics. What becomes clear is that the purported concern for the status of homosexuals in the West Bank and the Gaza Strip is being used to shield the occupation from direct culpability in suppressing, indeed endangering, those very homosexuals. Further, the LGBT rights project itself relies on the impossibility/absence/nonrecognition of a proper Palestinian queer subject *except* within the purview of the Israeli state itself, as a rescued subject. And it presents the "gay haven" of Tel Aviv as representative of the entire country, effacing its Arab cleansing, and as a zone free of war and bombings—in effect, a disability-free zone—while also maintaining Jerusalem as the religious safeguard.

Sexuality as an affective modality is by definition nonrepresentationalist, a distinct version of what Davide Panagia calls "the ways in which sensation interrupts common sense."[117] The toggling between discipline and control moves between normal/abnormal (homo/hetero and disabled/abled binaries) to variegation, modulation, and tweaking (sexuality as sensation). Discrete sites of punishment (the prison, the mental hospital, the school) in Palestine—the checkpoints that rotate and dis/appear randomly—are "intended to encourage Palestinians to slowly evacuate their land," to coerce Palestinians to "embrace their own ethnic transfer." "Bypass roads" carve up the land and converge at "kissing points," while the "security" wall prevents Palestinians from getting to their villages, their farmland, and other Palestinians.[118] Preemptive regimes of securitization include pinkwashing; Brand Israel functions as a form of soft security. Gaza is the world's largest "open-air prison," a form of quarantine and enclosure, but then there is also the algorithmic geometry of calorie intake. Contrary to claims that insist that the Israeli state project is solely about ethnic cleansing and dispossession of land, there are subtle yet insistent forms of folding in and inclusion at work here.

The "Palestinian debt trap," for example, is a simultaneous strategy of repression and liberation, enclosure and inclusion. The Palestinian Authority carries public debt of nearly $5 billion, 70 percent of GDP, $1 billion of that being external debt, while new bank lending programs have spurred the growth of household debt. Personal income and government revenue are, as in many places, being "swallowed up by debt service." State readiness is about grooming Palestine for "sovereign debt worthiness." As such, "Israel not only profits lavishly from supplying Palestine but also wields direct discipline through its automatic powers of debt extraction. It can turn the spigot of fiscal pain on or off at will." Further beneficiaries are the Palestinian elite and business sectors, many fueling the "cappuccino lifestyle" of Ramallah for those who perpetuate the occupation through their complacent privilege, as well as international actors. For the few who can afford debt, it functions as a "self-disciplining asset, arguably more effective than any instrument of military pacification."[119]

As another example, there are at least one hundred different types of ID cards that a Palestinian might have, each delineating a microvariation from each other, performing what Helga Tawil-Souri describes as "low-tech, visible, tactile means of power that simultaneously include and exclude Palestinians from the Israeli state."[120] The fracturing of populations moves from self/other subject/object construction to microstates of differentiation and modulation of capacities and debilities. Gil Z. Hochberg makes a similar point about low-tech control, explaining: "Israel relies on the visual presence of the most primitive and unsophisticated modes of surveillance and control (namely, watchtowers, aiming guns, and checkpoints)," entailing that Palestinians are simultaneously subjected to the gaze of surveillance and the "sight of this gaze as a spectacle of its power."[121]

Disciplining the individual is enjoined with massifying populations, a form of power "directed not at man-as-body but man-as-species."[122] The annihilation of space by time, theorized by Karl Marx, David Harvey, and Neil Smith to describe markets expanding across space through (neo)colonization while compressing the time and costs of circulation to enable speedy return of accumulation, is complimented with what Jord/ana Rosenberg and Britt Rusert argue is the "disinterring of time from space." This disinterring refers to, for example, the verticalization that Weizman describes, a three-dimensional spatial expansion involving in some part the subterranean and "salvaging [of] fictive origins from within the earth" so as to order linear continuity of time.[123] A last (but not least) set of seesawing forms of discipline and control moves from the public/private binary to diffuse forms of regulation that transgress these distinctions; from state/economy to the disorganization of national capital; from enclosed institutions of civil society to the disbursement of collective care across disparate and discontinuous locations; and from the policing of profile to the patrolling of affect.

This last point about affect is crucial because while discipline works at the level of identity, control works at the level of affective intensification. Here I am prompted by Amit Rai's reformulation of sexuality as "ecologies of sensation"—as affective energies rather than identity—that transcend the humanist designations of straight and gay, queer and nonqueer, modern and pathological. On this sexuality Rai writes: "Ecologies of sensation modulate and potentialize the body's pleasures and distribute them as contagions across segmented populations not as master scripts that normalize but as self-organizing modes that modulate and tinker."[124] We can think of (sexual) identity, and identification itself, as a process involving an intensification of habituation. That is to say, identity is the intensification of bodily habit, a "returning forward" of the body's quotidian affective sensorial rhythms and vibrations to a disciplinary model of the subject, whereby sexuality is just *one* form of bodily capacity being harnessed by neoliberal capital. Similarly, the Brand Israel campaign now being equated with pinkwashing is only one form of an array of "washing" that composes this campaign. This habituation of affective intensity to the frame of identity—a relation of discipline to control, or in actuality, *disciplining control*—entails a certain stoppage of where the body once was to reconcile where the body must go. It is also a habituation that demands certain politics and forecloses an inhabitation of others.

Sensations are thus always under duress, to use Panagia's terms, to "make sense," to submit to these master scripts either as a backformation responding to multiplicity or as a demand to submit to the master script and foreclose that multiplicity. Taking up further sexuality as assemblage, a strand invested in viral replication rather than reproductive futurism, this strand might stress the import of moving away from the call-and-response relay that continues to dominate the "mainstream/global queer" versus "queer of color/non-Western queer" argumentation. Contemporary efforts to resist Israeli pinkwashing play out this relay by insisting on the authenticity and legitimacy of the "Palestinian queer," thus reproducing the terms of debate valorized by the Israeli state and the "queer international." This relay often fails to interrogate the complex social field within which "queer" is being produced as a privileged signifier *across* these boundaries.[125] One reason for this import could indeed be found in the "viral" travels of the *concept* of homonationalism—by which I mean simply the use of LGBT rights as a barometer by which civilizational aptitude and capacities for sovereign governance of a population are measured. At some moments homonationalism has been reduced to a political critique of racism and nationalism in queer communities, or used as an applied analytic to assess the level or quality of the "homonationalist" state. To reiterate, instead of theorizing homonationalism as an identity positioning or as an adjective that denounces a state or other entity, I conceive of homonationalism as an analytic to apprehend state formation and a structure of modernity—in other words, the historical changes that have produced the homosexual question in the imperative tense.

Discipline and control are mutually entwined, disjunctive from each other yet cynically compatible. This conviviality is produced through feedback loops and not through the teleological progression assumed by Michael Hardt and also most forcefully in the work of Hardt and Antonio Negri.[126] I am not claiming that Palestine is an exemplary site of this collaboration. However, the convergence of settler colonialism within a "post-colony" neoliberal accommodationist market suggests that a linear trajectory and periodization may not be complex enough to illuminate the anachronistic operations of power in Palestine.[127] At this historical juncture, the particular spatial coordinates of the occupation—this triumvirate of settler colonization (reference to 1948), occupation (1967), and apartheid (1992; post–Oslo Accords) positions Palestine/Israel as a singular site whereby these co-constitutive forms of power operate, a site where, as Weizman writes, there is "the preference for ever-flexible internal frontiers." This is an intricate and intimate territorial project that defies the neoliberal logic of queer accommodationism and therefore also must challenge any easy configuration of queer solidarity.[128] Taking on the broader biopolitical control of sexual reproduction complicates a narrative about the purported specific and exceptional interest in homosexuality by the Israeli state and the purported "co-optation" of LGBT rights. In the era of decolonization the nationalist resolution to the woman question was mediated through relegating the domestic to the feminine and the worldly to the masculine. In the context of the increasing right-wing conservatism of the Israeli state, the nationalist resolution of the homosexual question (and the unresolved tension between the woman question and the homosexual question) is mediated through the differing spatial registers of the secular "gay haven" of Tel Aviv and the religious epicenter of Jerusalem. This bifurcation of national ethos thus reinscribes the pernicious binary of queer secularism versus homophobic religiosity; those who cannot or will not accede to the relevance of the homosexual question are thus re-racialized through the fulcrum of religion.[129] Here it is important to note that gay rights in Israel began not only as a racializing project vis-à-vis the Palestinians but also as a secularizing project vis-à-vis ultra-Orthodox Israeli Jews.[130] This is a really important point because some of the most prominent Islamophobic figures in this pinkwashing debate, such as filmmaker Michael Lucas, are not only anti-Muslim but also vociferously antireligion: that is to say, they are secularist queers.

Pinkwashing is thus not a queer issue per se, or even one that instrumentalizes queers in specific for biopolitical ends. It is not about sexual identity in this regard but rather a powerful manifestation of the regulation of identity in an increasingly homonationalist world—a world that evaluates nationhood on the basis of the treatment of its homosexuals. Pinkwashing, then, works not only to obfuscate the occupation, to marginalize and pathologize and temporally quarantine Palestinian queers beholden to a reification of Palestinian homophobia. More trenchantly, I would argue, it actually works as a foil to the pronatalist, eugenically oriented practices of sexual reproduction—both homo and hetero—mapping certain ableist prototypes of homosexuality as a form of capacity that can potentiate, on the side of life. Disability, with the exception of veterans disabled through war injuries, remains firmly on the side of debility and death, limited state recognition notwithstanding. Again, thinking about nonrepresentationalist understandings of sexuality as assemblage is crucial here, as one population "suffers" at the hands of the state through its representational success, the other through its representational absence/erasure/foreclosure. Given these interconnected and multiple rubrics, enacted in the name of sex, sexual freedom, and stellar technological achievement (as with ART), any anti-pinkwashing stance that does not address the biopolitics of reproduction and regeneration may come dangerously close to reiterating the ableism not only of the Israeli state but also of (secular) queerness itself. Whereas the effeminate Jew was antithetical to the project of Zionism, and homosexuality was considered an Orientalist (and therefore, Arab) vice, the rehabilitation project of the Israeli state now embraces the potential for the new muscular Judaism to be the muscular homosexual Jew.[131] The rehabilitation of the effeminate sickly Jew of the diaspora realizes its apex in the child-rearing gay Israeli man. Building social movements through disability is a valuable way of countering the sexual exceptionalism of queerness— homonationalism—pretty much anywhere, but perhaps especially so in the context of Israel, where the subject positionings of the "queer disabled" and the "disabled queer" are thoroughly foreclosed. Given the territorial logics of saturation and control of space, land, and the underground, "disability access" in this context must be redefined not only as enabling the mobility of those with physical disabilities but also as challenging the restricted mobilities of those living under occupation. The political question, then, remains how to enliven, literally enliven, the figuration of disability without rehabilitating it into a form of capacitation that functions to the detriment of so many others, as in the case of the Israeli state itself.

[4]

"Will Not Let Die"

Debilitation and Inhuman Biopolitics in Palestine

> All this gnawing at the existence of the colonized tends
> to make of life something resembling an incomplete death.
> —FRANTZ FANON, *A Dying Colonialism*

A CATALOG OF SUFFERING

It is as yet unclear what the carnage in Gaza from the summer of 2014 will be known as, remembered as, or named. And it may remain unclear for quite some time.

The tally is in (though ever-evolving) after fifty-one days of Operation Protective Edge.

The United Nations reported that 2,131 Palestinians were killed during Israel's offensive, including 501 children; 70 percent were under the age of twelve. A total of 244 schools were shelled, and another was used as a military base by Israeli soldiers.[1]

The Ministry of Health in Gaza recorded 10,918 people injured, including 3,312 children and 2,120 women.[2]

The Palestinian human rights organization Al Mezan documented at least 10,589 houses damaged or destroyed, of which 2,715 were completely flattened.[3] (Later reports state 18,000 homes were destroyed, including high-rise apartment buildings.)[4] Eight hospitals (resulting in six being taken out of service), forty-six NGOs, fifty fishing boats, 161 mosques, and 244 vehicles were also hit. In September 2014, 80 percent of Gazan families had no means to feed themselves and were completely dependent on aid.[5] Amnesty International reported that at least thirteen health facilities and eighty-four schools were forced to close.[6]

Doctors Without Borders / Médecins Sans Frontières had difficulty reaching populations that needed assistance given the severity of the bombing, fuel shortages that grounded more than half of the ambulances, and depletion of supplies.[7] A number of hospitals were damaged, contravening the Geneva Convention, which considers civilian hospitals to be protected during wartime. Gaza City's el-Wafa Rehabilitation Center in Shijaiyah was targeted at least six times and has been severely damaged; its fifteen disabled and elderly patients finally managed to be evacuated.[8]

This is what is meant by the residents of Gaza being "under siege," a commonly used refrain that obscures much of this detail. I have resorted here to a somewhat polemical deployment of empirical information in part to counter this tendency to cloak the specifics of the occupation. Gaza is also claimed to be the most densely populated place on earth, and also the world's largest "open-air prison." Belying these tidy descriptions are what Allen Feldman calls the "new forms of imagery, discourse, war, security and state rights being carved out of the bent backs of Palestinian civilians."[9] Among the biopolitical aspects I have been tracking are the permeating relations between living and dying that complicate Michel Foucault's foundational mapping, in this case, the practice of deliberate maiming. I argue that the Israeli state manifests an *implicit* claim to the "right to maim" and debilitate Palestinian bodies and environments as a form of biopolitical control and as central to a scientifically authorized humanitarian economy. I further demonstrate the limitations of the idea of "collateral damage" that disarticulates the effects of warfare from the perpetration of violence. Finally, I note that the policy of maiming is a productive one, through the profitability of what I call a speculative rehabilitative economy.[10] This final chapter takes the biopolitics of debilitation to its furthest expanse, looking at how the population available for injury is capacitated for settler colonial occupation through its explicit debilitation. It moves the argumentation about debilitation from the production of populations *available for injury* to the targeting of populations *to be injured.*

How is the practice of maiming manifested? Medical personnel in both Gaza and the West Bank report a notable "shoot to cripple" phenomenon. Dr. Rajai Abukhalil speaks of an increasing shift from "traditional means" such as tear gas and rubber-coated metal bullets used to "disperse" protests to "firing at protestors' knees, femurs, or aiming for their vital organs."[11] In Gaza, the Israeli Defense Forces used flechette shells. While these are not "expressly forbidden under international humanitarian law in all circumstances," nevertheless they are considered inappropriate for densely populated areas because they explode upon impact into thousands of tiny steel darts.[12] As a continuity and intensification of the practice of breaking the arms of stone throwers in the first intifada, shoot to cripple *attempts* to preemptively debilitate the resistant capacities of another intifada, the next intifada.

What is often claimed by the Israeli Defense Forces (IDF) as a "let live" praxis, understood in liberal terms as less violent than killing (and thus less sensational and more under the radar), shoot to cripple appears on the surface to be a humanitarian approach to warfare.[13] Another manifestation of this purported humanitarianism is the example of the "roof knock," a preliminary assault on structures to warn residents to evacuate, sometimes happening no less than sixty seconds before a full assault. Roof knocks were insufficient, however, when disabled Palestinians with mobility restrictions were unable to escape the bombardment of the Mubaret Philistine Care Home for Orphans and Handicapped in Gaza's Beit Lahiya district; three disabled residents died.[14] These were not mobile residents; the capacity of mobility circumscribes the utility of the roof knock, though the humanitarian intention of a sixty-second warning—a short, stingy temporal frame—is dubious.[15] Civilians in Gaza were also alerted to impending airstrikes through phone calls and texts, often misdirected to the wrongly targeted households. This purportedly humanitarian practice of warning Gazans of impending strikes with phone calls appears more like a "reminder of how powerless they are" given the control that Israel has over the telecommunication networks in the West Bank and Gaza.[16] As the research of Helga Tawil-Souri on "digital occupation" documents, telecommunication companies owned and operated by Palestinians are routed through servers in Israel.[17]

What happened in the summer of 2014 was preceded by much of the same during earlier periods. During the first intifada, the human rights organization Al-Haq produced a comprehensive report titled *Punishing a Nation: Human Rights Violations during the Palestinian Uprising: December 1987–December 1988.*[18] This document contains extensive evidence of both the intent and the effect of Israeli practices of injuring and maiming. Media accounts outline then defense minister Yitzhak Rabin's discussion of starting the use of plastic bullets "to increase the number of (wounded) among those who take part in violent activities but not to kill them."[19] "Violent activities" is the term most often used for political demonstrations or rock throwing. Statistics from the United Nations Relief and Works Agency (UNRWA), reported by the *Jerusalem Post* on September 27, 1988, mark sharp increases in injuries after the introduction of plastic bullets.[20] Al-Haq's report includes affidavits from individuals describing incidents of arbitrary and unprovoked beatings unlinked to protest activity; cites the West Bank Database Project report of 1987 detailing the widening of the "opening of fire" from life-threatening situations to opening fire as part of deterrence, "shooting first at an 80-degree angle in the air, and then, with intent to injure, at the legs"; notes that the Israeli army radio confirms using "special bullets intended to injure while reducing the risk of killing"; follows debates in the *Jerusalem Post* about concern regarding the illegality of using certain bullets to increase injuries among Palestinian protesters; documents further reportage in the *Jerusalem Post* regarding the illegality of breaking someone's arm even if they had violated the law; notes the inappropriateness of high-velocity bullets and assault rifles with high muzzle velocity, which, as reported by *Haaretz*, causes the bullets to "spin around inside the victim's body, damaging the internal organs."[21] Al-Haq concludes: "The Israeli government's claims that its response to the uprising is a lawful one do not fit the facts. The assertion that the cases of illegality are mere exceptions to the rule cannot stand when seen against a wealth of documented examples showing savage behavior by the army on a regular basis."[22] As further evidence, Al-Haq cites the *Jerusalem Post* of November 30, 1988, which specifically reports that during the month of November, protests in the Gaza Strip were at their lowest while casualties were at their highest, thus contesting the claim that the IDF is merely responding to violent activity.[23]

During the second intifada, there were reports that the IDF were using "high-velocity" fragmenting bullets that created a "lead snowstorm" effect in the body—scattering the bullet throughout and creating multiple internal injuries—leading to high rates of crippling injuries.[24] Dumdum bullets, which are banned under international human rights law, are difficult to extract after they have entered and exploded outward within the body and usually guarantee those hit will "suffer for life."[25] Dr. Robert Kirschner of Physicians for Human Rights stated that "the Israeli soldiers appear to be shooting to inflict harm rather than solely in self-defense," their actions amounting to "a form of torture."[26] Dimo Qato, among other global health researchers and practitioners, argues that the "pattern of injuries cannot be claimed to be accidental."[27]

In 2002, Israeli linguist Tanya Reinhart analyzed "the policy of injuries" during the second intifada.[28] Reinhart claims that the "Israelis were not even trying to conceal their shooting policy." Citing interviews with IDF soldiers from the *Jerusalem Post*, she selects a representative example from Israeli sharpshooter Sergeant Raz of the Nashon Battalion, who proclaims: "I shot two people . . . in their knees. It's supposed to break their bones and neutralize them but not kill them."[29] Reinhart notes that the newspaper explicitly details the IDF strategy of keeping Palestinian casualties low to deflect attention, sympathy, and solidarity from the Palestinian struggle. She also turns, as many do, to human rights organizations that are close up enough to document the situation. A delegation of Physicians for Human Rights concluded "that Israeli soldiers appeared to be deliberately targeting the heads and legs of Palestinian protestors, even in non-life-threatening situations."[30]

Stating that the injured do not count in the "dry statistics of tragedy," Reinhart explicates: "The reason for this strategy is clear: Massive numbers of Palestinians killed everyday cannot go unnoticed by even the most cooperative Western media and governments. [Prime Minister Ehud] Barak was explicit about this. 'The prime minister said that were there not 140 Palestinian casualties at this point, but rather 400 or 1000, this . . . would perhaps damage Israel a great deal.'"[31] Reinhart concludes that the creation of disability is a tactical military move on the part of the IDF; injuring Palestinians has remained Israeli military policy: "Specially trained Israeli units, then, shoot in a calculated manner in order to cripple [*sic*], while keeping the statistics of Palestinians killed low."[32]

Reinhart's analysis of the policy of injuries originally appeared on November 14, 2000, in the Israeli paper *Yedioth Ahronoth*, to which she was a regular contributor. It is important to note that her assessment relies predominantly (and in some instances solely) on Israeli media sources in

FIG. 4.1. Haj Abdullah, *No to Undermining [Palestinian] Refugee Rights, Yes to Comprehensive International Protection*, 2014. The image shows a wheelchair with a United Nations flag in front of Palestinian people, marking sixty-six years of ineffective international aid. The poster received second place in BADIL's annual Al Awda Award Competition in the category of Best Poster of 2014. The theme for that year's competition was "No to undermining Palestinian refugee rights. Yes to comprehensive international protection." In BADIL's opinion, while the poster reflects the ongoing plight and displacement of Palestinian refugees, it demonstrates the international community's lack of fulfillment of its obligations toward Palestinian refugees, which includes the right to live in dignity through the provision of services until which time their refugee status is resolved through the exercise of their right of return. © BADIL, Artist Daoud Haj Abdullah.

Hebrew and English such as *Haaretz* (the English version of which, Rein-hart claims, is more censored than the Hebrew version), the *Jerusalem Post*, and *Ma'ariv*.[33]

Also documented since the first intifada are various modes of obstruction of medical care. Al-Haq reports that the "obstruction of medical care, in all its various forms, is not new. However the scope of health-related human abuses has dramatically expanded during the current Palestinian upris-ing. . . . Violation of medical human rights have occurred with frightening regularity during the past year in all parts of the Occupied Territories."[34] The obstructions include blocking ambulances and cars transporting the sick and injured, raiding hospitals and clinics, denying medical teams ac-cess to areas under curfew, withholding medical treatment from prisoners, and deprioritizing the "right of the wounded to medical treatment."[35] Dur-ing the second intifada, "Israeli forces attack[ed] Palestinian healthcare providers while on duty, and . . . [damaged] Palestinian medical facilities," demonstrating a blatant disregard for the principle of medical neutrality, which Israel is bound to by Articles 18 and 20 of the Fourth Geneva Conven-tion.[36] The Palestinian Red Crescent Society (PRCS), the main provider of emergency medical care in Palestine, reported 174 documented attacks on its ambulances during a period of approximately eighteen months from September 2000 to March 2002, damaging 78 out of 100 total available ambulances. Additionally, it reported 166 attacks on emergency medical technicians and heavy machine gun fire hitting the PRCS headquarters.[37] Another health-related section of the Fourth Geneva Convention, Article 17, prohibits obstructing the "passage of patients," in other words, delaying or preventing access to medical facilities, a quotidian occurrence even in nonbombardment times due to Israel's checkpoint regime.[38] The Israeli government's disregard for international human rights laws in Gaza and the West Bank, over time, has led to the "large-scale destruction of the de-veloping health system, the inability of local and international healthcare providers to perform their duties, and a deterioration of the health condi-tions of Palestinians."[39]

INFRASTRUCTURAL WARFARE

Thus, not only bodies but also crucial infrastructures are being maimed in Gaza. In "Necropolitics," Achille Mbembe writes of the asymmetric war against infrastructure, or the "war on life support," as he calls it: the war on life itself, on the state capacity to preserve and nourish life.[40] Two further examples from the summer of 2014 should suffice. Gaza's water system collapsed, and waste treatment services were rendered nonfunctional, leaving raw sewage spewing into streets. Several water authority technicians were killed, thus also compromising maintenance and repair work.[41] Even before the summer of 2014, the deterioration of water infrastructure, according to Ala Qandil, resulted in "households receiv[ing] running water for only six to eight hours at a time: 25 percent had access on a daily basis, 40 percent every other day, 20 percent once every three days, and the remaining 15 percent only one day out of four."[42] An apparently new tactic of infrastructural warfare was employed during Operation Protective Edge, namely, the destruction of what remained of Gaza's professional class: "The targeting of the professional class, a key pillar of Palestinian society generally considered unsympathetic to the political goals of Hamas, was a new front of economic and social warfare on Gaza."[43] Targeting the assets of the middle class by focusing on high-rises was a political message to those who remained; others had migrated since the early 2000s through Egypt when the border regime allowed.

Omar Jabary Salamanca extensively details the Israeli government's resignification of Gaza's main service buildings from infrastructural networks to "terrorist infrastructures," noting that the latter designation is used to justify Israel's policy of what he calls "infrastructural violence." This form of violence has increased, not decreased, after Israeli "disengagement" from the Gaza Strip in 2005.[44] The assault on infrastructure, Salamanca argues, is an essential, even central, component of the biopolitical regulation of a malleable humanitarian collapse, whereby "the supporting infrastructure of ordinary life became both target and weapon."[45] The disengagement from Gaza facilitates the appearance of the end of Israel's colonial presence while allowing it to retain forms of "remote" infrastructural control, a continuing yet covert colonial presence. Gaza as open-air prison is crafted through a "reassembled regime of spatial control," and works through manufacturing a "regulated humanitarian collapse."[46] Exemplifying what Sari Hanafi terms "spacio-cide," the terrain is dependent on the withdrawn colonizer's infrastructural support, which modulates calories, megawatts, water, telecommunication networks, and spectrum and bandwidth allocation to provide the bare minimum for survival. The one fiber-optic cable, for example, that connects the entirety of Gaza to the outside world passes through and is controlled by Israel. "Spectrum allocation" thus becomes another tool of control, with Israel alternately withholding and releasing bandwidth. Salamanca calls this an " 'asphixatory' application of power."[47] This capacity to asphyxiate, however, is not just one of land enclosure via territorial containment. Nor is it digital enclosure that allows and regulates access to mobility via virtual worlds. Rather, as Helga Tawil-Souri argues, "Hi-tech enclosure is a multifaceted process. . . . This combination is what makes the Gazan case unique."[48] It is this interplay of territorial and virtual enclosure that complicates the Deleuzian (digital and digitizing) configuration of control societies, redescribed by Tawil-Souri as "a physical geography cancelled by networks." What she is pointing to as well is the co-existence and reinforcement of discipline and control. Topologies overlap, she argues, to the point where "it is increasingly difficult to distinguish one form of power from another in the Gazan landscape, for the Israeli space and practice of power has become one of in-distinction."[49] This interfacing of physical enclosure and virtual high-tech enclosure is what I take to be the epitome of an asphixatory regime of power.

The target here is not just life itself, but resistance itself. Salamanca quotes Israeli politician Dov Wiesglass, who states that Israel's policy would be "like an appointment with a dietician. The Palestinians will get a lot thinner, but won't die."[50] Because of this asphixatory control, Israel can create a crisis at will, having already set in place the bare minimum requisite for life that can be withheld at any moment, what he terms "an elastic humanitarian crisis."[51] There are continuities between these forms of elasticity, withholding, and suspension with the practices of "tactical government" that have historically ruled Gaza.[52] A provisional, tactical governmental structure is one devoid of vision and one that avoids legitimacy, capacity, and accountability through continual reactivity to crises.

Clearly, the capacity to asphyxiate is not a metaphor: while the West Bank is controlled largely through checkpoints, the Gaza Strip is suffocated through choke points. The intensification of policing and control thus happens through, and not despite, "disengagement" and disinvestment, not through checkpoints but through choke points. There is a temporal shift within this asphixatory control society from a Virilian narrative of increasing speed to other forms of algorithmic, parallel, distributed, and networked time, working through suspension between states and slow attenuation, in direct contrast to the always-connected ideal. In fact, slow death itself is literalized as the slowing down of Palestinian life. In the West Bank, immaculate freeways transport Israeli settlers through a landscape of dilapidated Palestinian back roads. Checkpoints ensure one is never guaranteed to reach work on time. The fear of not reaching work on time produces migration patterns that then clear the land for more settlements.[53] Time itself is held hostage; time is lived as fear. Distance is stretched and manipulated to create an entire population with mobility disabilities. And yet space is shrunken, as people are held in place, rarely able to move far. Unlike theorizations of space-time compression, the increased spatial dispersion is not remedied with temporal simultaneity. Rather, this simultaneity is withheld.[54] Hagar Kotef articulates the paradoxical relation of freedom to movement: move too much and one is unruly, too little and one is primitive.[55] The geopolitics of racial ontology is a frame that examines the regulation of affect as a racializing form of control. Accelerationist logics map speed, movement, and their withholding as an assemblage of racial ontologies. Disciplinary enclosure consorts with micromodulations of bodily becomings to ensure a population laden with affective reactivity. A politically regulated and controlled affective logic projected and interpreted as cultural and civilizational reactivity reinforces Orientalist projections of racial difference. Sensation racializes.

It is not just the capture and stripping of "life itself" that is at stake here but the attempt to capture "resistance itself."[56] How much resistance can be stripped without actually exterminating the population? Another question is, of course, what are the productive, resistant, indeed creative, effects of such attempts to squash Palestinian vitality, fortitude, and revolt?

THE BIOPOLITICS OF SETTLER COLONIALISM

These practices of bodily as well as infrastructural debilitation, loosely effaced in concerns about "disproportionate force," indicate the extension or perhaps the perversion of the "right to kill" claimed by states in warfare into what I am calling the "right to maim." "The right to maim" supplements if not replaces "the right to kill." Maiming as intentional practice expands biopolitics beyond simply the question of "right of death and power over life." Maiming becomes a primary vector through which biopolitical control is deployed in colonized space and hence not easily demarcated "necro" as it is mapped in Mbembe's reworking of biopolitics. Mbembe discusses injury as a crucial element of enslavement: "The slave is kept alive but in a *state of injury* . . . slave life, in many ways, is a form of death-in-life."[57] Sticking with the binary of life and death with his formulation of "death-in-life," he does not pursue injury and debilitation as altering living and dying as primary poles within which populations oscillate. The four quadrants remain; death is reiterated as the ultimate loss (of life). While other scholars of biopolitics have noted the centrality of disability to the deployment of biopolitical population management, these efforts generally remain wedded to the poles of living and dying within which life is toggled. That is to say, while the distinctions between living and dying are often recognized through the "cuts" of race and the "folds" of overlapping population construction and management, maiming, debilitation, and stunting are relatively undertheorized components of these cuts and folds; centering these processes may potentially alter presumed relations to living and dying altogether. Maiming is a practice that escapes definition within both legal and biopolitical or necropolitical frameworks because it does not proceed through making live, making die, letting live, or letting die. My reframing adds a critical axis to the four quadrants, insisting that debilitation—indeed, deliberate maiming—is not merely another version of slow death or of death-in-life or of a modulation on the spectrum of life to death. Rather, it is a status unto itself, a status that triangulates the hierarchies of living and dying that are standardly deployed in theorizations of biopolitics.

Alongside examining how and why Foucault elided a theory of colonial occupation in his formulation of biopolitics, we might also ask, what is biopolitics in the twenty-first century, especially as informed by the ongoing structure of settler colonialism? Recent interventions by Alexander Weheliye and Mel Chen raise critical issues about the formulation of race in the theorization of biopolitics.[58] According to Weheliye, race only became important to Foucault when it entered the realms of European state management, not through the operations of colonialism. For this, Weheliye argues that the frame of biopolitics is foundationally flawed, for even as Foucault claims that the cut of race drives biopolitical distinctions, the severing of colonial occupation from a (belated) state racism relegates race to a derivative status. Weheliye's rather loose archival excavations of Foucault's work notwithstanding, what his and others' analyses lay bare is the dearth of theorization of the biopolitics of colonial regimes, especially that of settler colonialism, of colonialism as a structure and not an event.[59] Further, Scott Morgensen rightly notes that settler colonialism remains undifferentiated within theorizations of the biopolitics of colonialism, continuing the propagation of colonialism as a bygone event or within a naturalized frame of periodization.[60]

Foucault's frame of biopolitics is intrinsically dedicated to variations of bodily health and vulnerability. In *Security, Territory, Population*, he details the different regimes of power associated with distinct illnesses. Leprosy is banished through the sovereign power to exclude; the plague is isolated through disciplinary power of quarantining; and smallpox becomes managed and regularized as epidemic through what Foucault calls "apparatuses of security."[61] In *"Society Must Be Defended,"* Foucault writes: "Biopolitics will derive its knowledge from, and define its power's field of intervention in terms of, the birth rate, the mortality rate, various biological disabilities, and the effects of the environment."[62] Here, disability is understood as a biologically produced rather than a socially induced condition. In some sense Foucault is inadvertently yet presciently mapping the liberal elision between disability as an exceptional accident or circumstance and disability as intrinsic to the function of colonial war machines. "Various biological disabilities" (and later, "anomalies") fulfills the function of misfortune but does not in this case address the imbrication of racialization and bodily capacity: "Biopolitics' other field of intervention will be a set of phenomena some of which are universal, and some of which are accidental but which can never be completely eradicated, even if they are accidental. They have similar effects in that they incapacitate individuals, put them out of the circuit or neutralize them. This is the problem . . . of old age, of individuals who, because of their age, fall out of the field of capacity, of activity . . . includ[ing] accidents, infirmities, and various anomalies."[63] In this, one finds germinating a theory of debility and capacity.

Foucault also points to the durational debilitations of chronicity. Illness shifts from epidemic to endemic; the endemic modulates "the form, nature, extension, duration, and intensity of the illnesses prevalent in a population . . . as permanent factors which . . . sapped the populations' strength, shortened the work week, wasted energy, and cost money, both because they led to a fall in production and because treating them was expensive."[64] Within the context of emergent forms of social welfare that Foucault speaks of, illness needs to be reduced, contained, isolated, and in some cases, abolished, because it compromises the thriving of the "make life" vector. In contemporary biopolitics, however, economic life can grow without the flourishing of much of human life, which means precisely that illness is no longer a hindrance to, but rather is implicated in, "make live."

Foucault writes, "The [old] right of sovereignty was the right to take life or let live. And then this new right is established: the right to make live and to let die."[65] Foucault notes that sovereignty's old right was not replaced but rather was complemented by this new right, "which . . . penetrate[s] it, permeate[s] it."[66] Given the interpenetrations of sovereign and biopolitical power, mapping what forms the sovereign right to take life or let live are machinating is critical. The sovereign right to maim implicates all of the other vectors at once—make die and make live (because in some cases debilitation can be harnessed into "compliant" disability rehabilitation), as well as let live and let die, a version of slow death, a gradual decay of bodies that are both overworked and underresourced.[67]

Maiming functions as slow but simultaneously intensive death-making, as targeting to maim is an accelerated assault on both bodily and infrastructural fronts. Different temporalities of living and dying labor here, a different modulation of time and a reworking of the temporalities of biopolitics. The stretching of the horizon of life (what can bare life bear?) and the finality of death into perverted versions of life seem and feel like neither life nor death, not even attenuated death. In this complication of the temporalities and processes, the speed of biopolitics turns not through distinctions between fast and slow, quick and languorous, but rather through the intensification and amplification of "life itself" and, in fact, "resistance itself" as a target of neglect, damage, and speculative rehabilitation.[68]

If slow death is conceptualized as primarily through the vector of "let die" or "make die," maiming functions as "will not let die" and, its supposed humanitarian complement, "will not make die." Maiming masquerades as "let live" when in fact it acts as "will not let die." For example, the IDF policy of shooting to maim, not to kill, is often misperceived as a preservation of life. In this version of attenuated life, neither living nor dying is the aim. Instead, "will not let die" and "will not make die" replace altogether the coordinate "make live" or "let die." It is not only the right to kill but also the right to maim that is being exercised as the domain of sovereignty. What kind of sovereignty is being articulated when the right to kill is enacted as the right to maim, to target both bodies and infrastructure for debilitation? This element of biopolitics entails targeting for death but not killing.

Israeli state practices of occupation and settler colonialism may well be rationalized through the conventional parameters of living and dying in Foucault's four quadrants of biopolitical management. The work of Eyal Weizman, Sherene Seikaly, and others has shown that the calories allowed into Gaza, the plotting of the number of deaths of Hamas members, the transit of fuel, materials, supplies, all of these parameters are mediated by expert language, algorithmic calculations, rational science, and framed in a discourse of humanitarian war.[69] Thus what I am explicitly arguing is that from the discursive and empirical evidence offered by Palestinians, this foundational biopolitical frame is a liberal fantasy that produces "let live" as an alibi for colonial rule and thus indeed facilitates the covert destruction of "will not let/make die." It is from the vantage of the occupied, I argue, and not from state power or from the privilege of the occupier, that we must apprehend and contend with revising—challenging, in fact—the theorization of the violent mechanisms of biopolitical population creation and maintenance. How is "will not let die" expressed? How is the distinction between death and debility mined? And how does the capitalization of this distinction occur while simultaneously obscuring the practices of deliberate maiming?

The debilitation of the Gazan infrastructure is elaborated in the following statement from Maher Najjar, the deputy general of Gaza's Coastal Municipalities Water Utilities:

> There is no water reaching any of the houses right now. We're facing a real catastrophe. Sewage pumps cannot work because the power plant has been destroyed, so we have sewage flooding the streets of Gaza. We can't assess the extent of the damage as we can't even go out without risking our lives right now. We had five staff members killed while doing repair work, another two were killed at home with their families. It will take more than US$20 million to rebuild the water and sewage networks, but there's no way they can be rebuilt under blockade. We have the total collapse of all essential services and there's nothing we can do about it. Believe me, it would be better if the Israelis just dropped the nuclear bomb on Gaza and get done with it. This is the worst ever assault on the Gaza Strip.[70]

In this missive, debilitation is rendered a fate worse than death. Treating Najjar's statement as political speech more so than the "truth" of death as a form of mercy, the rhetorical strategy exposes the absolute farce of Israel's "let live" praxes. To suggest that the Gazan population is better off dead is surely to mock Israel's liberal democratic investment in humanitarian gestures of "let live." Najjar sharply contests this investment with a vision of humanitarianism that is startling. It is as if withholding death—will not let or make die—becomes an act of dehumanization: the Palestinians are not even human enough for death.

The implication in Najjar's statement that death is preferable to disability echoes with a general ethos of the nobility of dying for one's country. The preference of death over disability is also a stance that contravenes the human rights model of disability. Maiming is especially striking in this historical moment. In relation to the rise of disability as a recognized identity in need of state and global human rights protections, seeking to debilitate, or to further debilitate the disabled, contrasts heavily with the propagation of disability as a socially maligned condition that must be empowered to and through a liberal politics of recognition. Sanctioned maiming, capacitated in part through a deflection onto debates about the "collateral damage" of civilian deaths, bespeaks a profound failure in the global human rights framing of disability as a protected and supported social difference— protected and supported unless it is part of the war tactic of a settler colonial regime, one financially buttressed by the United States. Ironically but unsurprisingly, Israel is a signatory on the United Nations Convention on the Rights of Persons with Disabilities (as well as for the UN Convention on the Rights of the Child).[71] The distance between the cripple and the disabled is further exemplified by the fact that Gaza has a Paralympics team, one that is actually much more successful than the main Olympics team.[72]

COLLATERAL DAMAGE

Israel does not claim the actual "right" to maim in the way it claims a right to self-defense and a right to kill in warfare. Rather, I am arguing that by disobeying international protocol regarding medical neutrality (bombing hospitals and medical personnel, part of a larger tactic of infrastructural warfare), along with pacifying the injunction to minimize civilian deaths— otherwise known as collateral damage—Israel covertly enacts the right to maim through promoting itself as attempting to avoid civilian casualties. As the death toll of Palestinians soared during Operation Protective Edge in comparison to Israeli deaths, much less spectacular and less commented upon, yet potentially more deleterious to the future of the Palestinian people, are the numbers of injured civilians.

The shoot to maim but not kill vector meshes, indeed colludes, with the principle of "collateral damage," which states that the unintentional killing of civilians, and the killing and injuring of children, if not deliberately targeted, are collateral damage. Since the Vietnam War, highly visible and inhumane techniques of maiming and destroying a population had become unacceptable, and these aims have been achieved through more subtle, low-intensity forms of warfare.[73] Maiming evades the optic of collateral damage. Jennifer Leaning, the director of Harvard University's FXB Center for Health and Human Rights, notes that "the number of dead and the number of wounded convey the false impression that the wounded are going to be okay."[74] Further, the discourse of targeting people with disabilities as an illegitimate, inhumane, and often shock-worthy tactic (as reflected in the response of horror when the IDF bombed the Mubaret Philistine Care Home for Orphans and Handicapped, killing three disabled residents) is then available as a foil to obfuscate the tactic of targeting *to* debilitate.

Numerous debates about collateral damage and intentional versus unintentional civilian deaths proliferated during the summer of 2014. Critics avowed that Israel was using "unguided, indirect fire with high-explosive shells," weaponry widely understood to be "inappropriate for a densely populated area." Nadia Abu El-Haj writes that Israel's allies proclaim that "the Israeli army wages war with moral integrity. It doesn't target civilians. It never intends to kill them. It even warns Gazans when an attack is coming so they can get out of harm's way."[75] Abu El-Haj dissects the discourse of "unintentionality," arguing that "most civilian deaths in urban counterinsurgency warfare may be 'unintentional,' but they are also predictable."[76] Laleh Khalili takes a more pointed view, arguing that civilians are not accidental casualties but "the very object of a settler-colonial counterinsurgency."[77] This discussion on intentionality leaves yet another possibility unspoken. The purposiveness behind civilian deaths may be indiscernible, debatable, or, as Khalili avers, absolutely transparently obvious. What the debate on civilian deaths may obscure is the intentional activity of maiming: the proliferation of injuries leading to permanent debilitation that remain uncalculated within the metrics of collateral damage. As a term that emerges in 1961, and signals the "debt" of war—that which should be

FIG. 4.2. Hafez Omar, *Le peuple déterminé*, Palestine, 2014. This red and black graphic symbolizes the resistance of the Palestinian people, lining the rooftops of homes while missiles point from the sky directly down at them. Reprinted with the artist's permission.

avoided and must be paid back—why does collateral damage disarticulate debilitation from death? Such a disarticulation effectively disconnects the act of violent perpetration from the effects of violence. Official terminology follows suit; for example, the designation "explosive remnants of war" suggests that the war is over and that the remnants, ranging from dumdum bullets to armament toxicity to land mines, are benign, manageable, or negligible.[78]

Maiming thus functions not as an incomplete death or an accidental assault on life, but as the end goal in the dual production of permanent disability via the infliction of harm and the attrition of the life support systems that might allow populations to heal from this harm. Maiming is required. Not merely a by-product of war, of war's collateral damage, it is used to achieve the tactical aims of settler colonialism. This functions on two levels. The first is the maiming of humans within a context that is utterly and systematically resource-deprived, an infrastructural field that is unable to transform the cripple into the disabled. This point is crucial, for part of what gels the disabled body that is hailed by rights discourses is the availability of the process of cultural rehabilitation—that is, normalization practices that produce docile bodies.[79] The second is the maiming of infrastructure in order to stunt or decay the able-bodied into debilitation through the control of calories, water, electricity, health care supplies, and fuel.[80]

What does the sustained practice of maiming—in this case, sustained since the first intifada at least—accomplish for settler colonialism? What is the long-term value of will not let die, of withholding death? The understanding of maiming as a specific aim of biopolitics tests the framing of settler colonialism as a project of elimination of the indigenous through either genocide or assimilation. It asks us to reevaluate the frame of biopolitics in relation to the forms of maiming (and stunting, which I will discuss shortly) that have gone on for centuries in settler colonial occupations. The right to maim is therefore not an exceptional facet of any one form of sovereignty; it does not newly emanate from Israeli settler colonialism. Rather, the right to maim allows us to differently apprehend the wielding of Israeli state power while also challenging the current limits of biopolitical theorizing such that it may revise our thinking on other times and places. Accounting for Israeli settler colonialism and occupation is an encounter with the unspoken thresholds of biopolitical thought. Examining the role of maiming not only in Palestine but also in Canada, New Zealand, Australia, and the United States puts analytic pressure on the assumption that the goal of settler colonialism is necessarily elimination.[81]

Noting these different pressure points, Helga Tawil-Souri says of Gaza: "Israel is not seeking to assimilate the natives . . . nor enfold them (anymore) as a cheap labor force, but to treat them as refuse."[82] Here, settler colonialism is framed as a process of value extraction from populations that would otherwise be disposed of. The productivity of maiming—"will not let die"—is manifold. This third biopolitical vector, "will not let or make die," keeps the death toll numbers relatively low in comparison to injuries, while still thoroughly debilitating the population—depopulation through slow attrition, through maiming human forms. Because eventful killing is undesirable, the dying after the dying, perhaps years later, would not count as a war death alongside the quick administration of war deaths. Where do the numbers of "collateral damage" end and the demarcation of "slow death" begin?

Further, debilitation is extremely profitable economically and ideologically for Israel's settler colonial regime. Many sectors take on the "rehabilitation" of Gaza in the aftermath of war: Israel, Egypt, the Arab Gulf states, NGO actors who are embedded in corporate economies of humanitarianism. Crumbs of the reconstruction will be fought over through local forms of control brokered by Hamas and the Palestinian Authority. But these circuits of profit are uneven and perverse; who profits and how are extremely complex issues and not straightforward at an imperial scale.[83] However distinct some of these actors may appear, the overall assemblage works to feed back into the economic and ideological validation of Israel. The actors in play all calculate Palestinian life, death, and debilitation according to different economic, geopolitical, and domestic metrics. For the Arab Gulf States, this disjuncture between rhetoric and the outcome of financial exchanges points to certain political benefits, not simply profit in an economic sense but their favored status within an imperial order led by the United States.[84] Similarly, Egypt, under Abdel Fatah Al-Sisi, is rewarded for a disjuncture between policy and rhetoric, receiving military aid and support for its own domestic tyranny in return for shutting off the flow of vital goods to Gaza, all while condemning Israeli airstrikes publicly. As Max Blumenthal points out further, the team of consultants hired by the NGO complex to oversee Gaza's (privatized) rebuilding envisions a future of sweatshops producing zippers and buttons for Israeli fashion houses. The United States and other Western countries provide the majority of money for the UNRWA while providing the money and munitions that go into destroying UNRWA infrastructure like schools and hospitals.[85]

As a public health crisis, Gaza now represents a perversion of Foucault's management of health frame in that it feeds into models of disaster capitalism. Joseph Pugliese notes that Elbit, the company whose drones were tested during Israel's assault, recorded a 6 percent increase in profits during the first month of Operation Protective Edge.[86] Post-onslaught donor conferences raise billions of dollars for rebuilding infrastructure in Gaza—capitalist accumulation that ultimately feeds back into Israel's regime—despite the inevitability that Israel will destroy Gaza again.[87] This leads to "donor fatigue" due to the cycle of rebuilding infrastructure that will surely be razed yet again. It is most likely, however, that "donors will pay up because it is far easier than addressing the underlying causes of and possible solutions to the Israeli-Palestinian conflict."[88] Israel's commitment to allow the five million tons of construction materials needed to rebuild the strip have resulted in naught; as of January 2015, only 3.9 percent of that had entered Gaza.[89] Materials to rebuild Gaza are subjected to massive administrative oversight by Israel and the UN because of fears that cement will be used to rebuild the tunnels.[90] Maintenance of the "separation policy" of Gaza from the West Bank is part of the economic withholding that gives license to other networks.[91]

These multifaceted circuits suggest that the targeting of Palestinian bodies as a source of extractive value goes beyond the plus-minus logic of accumulation toward a broader strategic goal of regenerating the structure of occupation, both locally in Gaza and globally through the many circuits of the imperial order. Given the economic profitability of the occupation to numerous actors who are ultimately beholden to the geopolitical and economic legitimation of Israel, it becomes even more urgent that resistant strategies such as BDS focus on disrupting the circuits of capitalist accumulation. Resistant strategies must also respond to Ilana Feldman's urgent call to break open the obscuring frame of humanitarianism and disrupt the cycle of destruction and rebuilding that ultimately regenerates the colonial situation.[92] Anne Le More concurs: "The international donor community has financed not only Israel's continued occupation but also its expansionist agenda—at the expense of international law, of the well-being of the Palestinian population, of their right to self-determination, and of the international community's own stated developmental and political objectives."[93] "Will not let die" is monetized to great effect and to the detriment of Gazans. "Existence is resistance" must necessarily refer to an existence outside this logic, beyond an inhuman biopolitics that takes the right to maim as its prerogative.

Thus one interpretation here is that the debilitation of Gazans is not only capitalized upon in a neoliberal economic order that thrives on the profitability of debility, as is the case elsewhere, but that Gazans must be debilitated in order to make (their) life (lives) productive. Perhaps differing from earlier colonial and occupation regimes where deprivation was distributed in order to maim yet keep labor alive, there is less need for Palestinian labor, for Palestinian production. Rather, profit is derived from the dismemberment of reproduction, a function of capitalism without labor (in part because a massive increase in migrant labor has been used to offset the need for Palestinian labor). This inhuman biopolitics flourishes through and beside human populations—economic life growing without human life. In this regard we can say that along with the right to maim, Israel is also exercising a sovereign "right to repair," one that reaps profit through a speculative withholding and distribution of rehabilitation that is tactical, conditional, and controlled through Israel's security doctrine.

PREHENSIVE BIOPOLITICS

There are interesting disavowals of the Gazan civilian death toll that may expose the logic that undergirds the right to maim. Take, for instance, Benjamin Netanyahu's transposition of the make die vector from Israel onto Hamas, in this oft-quoted statement from the summer of 2014: "All civilian casualties are unintended by us but actually intended by Hamas. They want to pile up as many civilian dead as they can, because somebody said they use, I mean it's gruesome, they use telegenically dead Palestinians for their cause. They want the dead, the more the better."[94]

Here, there is a tentative answer to the question, why not just "make die"? The act of "make die" is transferred to Hamas as a wish to "let die." The anxiety generated by the term "collateral damage"—"the more dead the better"—is transformed into a favorable rather than damning equation. The statement, I suggest, serves as more than a ludicrous projection; rather, it might actually reveal an investment in "will not let die" that grounds the justification for the right to maim. These words hint at a speculative rehabilitative approach that modulates when to let die, when to maim, and when to "will not let die." Allen Feldman alludes to one reason why "make die" and even "let die" cannot usefully serve the mandate of the postgenocidal Israeli state: "The alleged manufacture of telegenic death by the Palestinians implies their subjugated knowledge of genocidal truth that both attracts and threatens Netanyahu—for in a Euro-American public sphere acculturated to the Holocaust, Palestinians become more attractive and rhetorically persuasive when dead than when alive, when televisually spiritualized rather than when protesting or resisting or simply enduring intractable prison-house materialities. Netanyahu attacks telegenic death because he fears the population bomb of Palestinian dead and wounded, wherein they become symbolic Jews."[95]

Given the prohibition and value of "dead Palestinians" that Feldman maps in his analysis, then, it is worth examining the repeated claim that

Gaza will be uninhabitable by the year 2020. The first question we might want to ask is, by what calculus is Gaza currently inhabitable? And then: With what metrics is this prognosis computed? Through which prehensive algorithms, via what naturalized logic does the agent of destruction that creates and sustains Gaza as uninhabitable drop from syntactical reference, as if the asphixatory control that Salamanca details reflects—but, in actuality, authorizes—the organic order of things?[96] How is this inevitability procured? The prehensive authorizes a set of predictive facts-on-the-ground sutured to the language of risk and probability that extends itself to a predicted "apocalypse"—in other words, the representation of Gaza as a "natural" disaster likely to happen. As an addition to reactive and preemptive forms of securitization, the prehensive is about making the present look exactly the way it needs to in order to guarantee a very specific and singular outcome in the future. A remark by Michael Oren, Israel's former ambassador to the United States, unwittingly unravels this grammatical elision by positing the inverse: "Life in Gaza is miserable now, but if Israel is permitted to prevail [i.e., destroy Hamas], circumstances can improve markedly."[97] That is to say, the apocalypse, the inevitable natural disaster, is a political outcome that can be avoided if a different scene of the present can be produced.

The year 2020 functions as a perverse apocalyptic timeline that is all too familiar to us now, largely through the predictive algorithms mapping for us the demise of the planet due to climate change. The prehensive is narratively produced as if this thing is happening to us, when indeed, we made it happen. (And, in fact, from Netanyahu's vantage: we wanted it to happen.) Through prehensive time, it is not only that the terms of futurity are already dictated in the present but also the terms of the present are dictated through the containment of the terms of the future, in an effort to keep the present in line with one version of the future that is desired. In seeding the fixed future into the present, data is fed forward in a retroactive manner that disallows us out of the present. That is to say, we cannot get out of the present because we are tethered to the desired future; past, present, and future feel somewhat futile as descriptors of temporal distinctions. These prehensive futurities are thoroughly resonant now: by such and such year, Caucasians will be the minority in California. X number of species will be extinct by year such and such. What this prehensive control over the present in order to create a certain future might suggest is that the "solution" to the "Israeli-Arab conflict" may well be, for Israel, neither one-state nor two-state but rather the current status quo. In other words, a terrifying implication is that Israel already has its solution: the permanent debilitation of settler colonialism.

There is another twist to these temporalities: the multiplicity of competing prehensive narratives that challenge the hermeneutic seal. The year 2020 is also predicted to be when Palestinians will outnumber the Jewish Israeli population. Palestinians in Israel and the Occupied Territories will outnumber Jews by 7.2 million to 6.9 million.[98] Palestinians inside Israel's 1948 borders are reproducing 33 percent faster than Israeli Jews.[99] If indeed Israel needs Gaza's gas resources by 2017, if indeed by 2020 Gaza will be uninhabitable, these time frames reveal as much about the contractions and acceleration of pace demanded within the parameters of life span as they do about slow death.[100]

But is 2020 only a human timeline? If temporality itself is already suffused with the biopolitical, to claim unfettered access to futurity is already predicated upon the genocide or slow death of others. The invocation of 2020 marks the limit of thinking biopolitical time in human terms, gesturing toward temporalities that are operating in nonreproductive modalities, since "natural" human reproduction no longer singularly drives the engine of biopolitics. Gaza is living not only human time and "population time" but also versions of inhuman time. Mel Chen's work on toxicity alerts us to the question of the half-life of depleted uranium, approximately 4.5 million years, and other elements deposited through weaponry and infrastructural warfare.[101] Prehensive time thus also signals a weaponized epigenetics where the outcome is not so much about winning or losing, or about a solution. As Reza Nagarestani so magnificently shows us, the limits of the nonhuman/human frame are already apparent through their precise deployment within capitalism, revealing the necessity of theorizing an inhuman biopolitics; the nonhuman, posthuman, and inhuman are thoroughly amenable to the circuits of capitalism that inform biopolitical power.[102] Maiming is also necessary for exploiting the project of verticalization that Eyal Weizman details. For Weizman, verticalization happens through the production of expanded Israeli military space through three-dimensional renderings of air, ground, and underground entities, legitimizing Israeli rule through the colonization of space and time.[103] Verticalization is the manufacturing of depth. As Steven Salaita writes in *Israel's Dead Soul*, interiority is accorded to the Jewish Israeli subject through the production of depth—of history, of archaeology, of presence.[104] Through debilitating practices of maiming and stunting, Palestinians are further literalized and lateralized as surface, as bodies without souls, as sheer biology, thus rendered nonhuman, part of creating surface economies of control, and captured in nonhuman temporal calculations.

NO FUTURE

Palestinian children in Gaza are on what the Israeli military leadership has called a starvation diet. You have almost 80 percent of Palestinian children living on less than $1 a day. They're at levels of what we would call poverty and extreme poverty, with extensive food insecurity. That's just another way of saying that most Palestinian children in Gaza go to bed hungry every day, so their caloric intake has been significantly reduced since the siege began within the last seven years. In addition to the reduced number of calories they take in, the kind of nutrients they're getting is also decreased, so what we see is this medical phenomenon called stunting, which results in lower birth weights for Palestinian children. Their average birth weight is going down. Their height and weight are below what you would consider basic international norm values for children that age. —DR. JESS GHANNAM, quoted in Said and Zahriyeh, "Gaza's Kids Affected Psychologically, Physically by Lifetime of Violence"

Finally, we turn to the question of generational time, characterized by the following statement: "Palestinian children in Gaza are exposed to more violence in their lifetime than any other people, any other children, anywhere in the world."[105] And yet, Palestinian trauma is classified into impossibility through "an assemblage of laws, policies, narratives, symbols, and practices that re-named trauma and suffering of the dispossessed with colonial terminology."[106] This terminology demeans Palestinians as "present-absentees," "security threats," and "demographic threats."[107] Numerous studies have documented the ongoing effects on Gazan children subject to arrests, assaults, home invasions, witnessing of deaths, and the loss of familial and community infrastructure.[108] The psychological impact on children has been deemed a form of "continuous PTSD" while the Israeli policy of the calorie regulation or the "starvation diet" has led to what medical practitioners call "stunting."[109] Exposure to white phosphorus in Operation Cast Lead and ground contamination from radioactive materials in Israeli bombs have led to increases in birth defects. Nadera Shalhoub-Kevorkian contends that "children are now one of the main targets of the

FIG. 4.3. Carlos Latuff, *Gaza*, 2008, Brazil. Reprinted with the artist's permission.

Israeli state," in large part because they are produced as "always already terrorists" and rendered nonhuman.[110] Efforts from human rights organizations to place the IDF on a United Nations list of serious violators of human rights because of the deaths of more than five hundred children and the injuries of at least thirty-three hundred during the siege of 2014 have been fraught and apparently stalled due to political pressure from the Israeli state.[111]

Once again, this is not a recent development. Research suggests that children became a prime target during the second year of the first intifada. Reports from UNRWA and the Jerusalem-based Palestine Human Rights Information Center (PHRIC) document that more than forty-one thousand children aged sixteen or younger had been treated for gunshot wounds, injuries from beatings, and exposure to teargas between 1987 and 1992.[112] In 1992, the Gaza Community Mental Health Program (GCMHP) reported that "89% of a random sample of 1,564 children between the ages of eight and fifteen had experienced raids by Israeli soldiers into their homes; 45% were subjected to beatings."[113] During the middle of the first intifada, UNRWA reported a decline in the number of child fatalities due to Israeli gunfire and a sharp increase in the number of injuries.[114] Studies from the second intifada start recording the somatization of trauma and other mental health issues among the young.[115] Samir Qouta and Eyad El Sarraj have observed that "Palestinian children have become laboratories for the study of the relationship between trauma and violence, conflict, and children's well-being during war."[116]

Targeting youth not for death but for stunting, for physical, psychological, and cognitive injuries, is another aspect of this biopolitical tactic that seeks to render impotent any future resistance, future capacity to sustain Palestinian life on its own terms, thereby debilitating generational time. It is especially cognitive and psychological injuries that have long-range, traumatic effects that potentially debilitate any resistant capacities of future generations. It is worth stating an obvious but perhaps unremarked-upon qualification here: this is a biopolitical fantasy, that resistance can be located, stripped, and emptied. "Resistance itself" becomes an implicit target of computational metrics: How to measure, calculate, and capture resistance? But not only is biopolitical control a fundamentally productive assemblage; the ontological irreducibility of "resistance itself" is fundamentally elusive.

Samera Esmeir, writing of Israel's "experimental wars" in Gaza, claims that "Gaza has become the literal testing ground for Israel's various experiments. . . . as an occupying power, Israel transformed Gaza into such a laboratory by imposing on it different forms of confinements culminating in the siege imposed and maintained since 2006."[117] Military technologies are tested in "real-life situations, on the ground," and marketed as such.[118] In the quest for complete air, space, and ground control, a thoroughly saturated economy of spatial and temporal control, what are the terms of Gaza-as-laboratory?[119] Is Gaza an experimental lab for the production, maintenance, and profitability of biopolitical debilitation? Is Gaza an experiment in mining the infinite potentialities of the schisms between death and debility—not a death camp but a debilitation camp—and the potentiating of nonhuman time?[120] And yet, labs and even many jails have better living conditions than those to which Palestinians in the Gaza Strip are subjected. Gaza emblematizes the profitability of a speculative rehabilitative economy where debilitated bodies are more valuable than dead ones because it keeps bodies in capital circulation, not as weakened, docile laborers, but as parts that are modulated with forms of life and their variegated temporalities. Maiming is a requirement for this economy, whereby settler colonialism is naturalized through a focus on the status and regulation of occupation.

I OFFER THIS analysis in the spirit of what Jord/ana Rosenberg has hailed an "anti-Zionist hermeneutic," one that insists on speaking the reality of debilitation as another form of biopolitical governmentality.[121] It is an anti-Zionist hermeneutic that seeks neither to exceptionalize Palestine nor to render it visible through containment in a comparative frame, but to understand intensifications of biopolitical modes of control that are continuous and resonant with historical modes and, indeed, across contemporary geopolitical spaces. Palestine in this sense provides an epistemological blueprint, one that opens up the connective tissue between regions, regimes of power, sites of knowledge production, historical excavations, and solidarity struggles for liberation. Rather than an exception, writes Michael Hardt, "we can see Palestine and the struggles of Palestinians as exemplary—a lesson and inspiration for those fighting back around the world."[122] Connecting Palestine to struggles elsewhere, Hardt argues that four rubrics of enclosure link different geopolitical sites: indebtedness, mediatization, securitization, and representation. This brief schema is perhaps one entrée into conceptualizations that neither exceptionalize Palestine nor minimize the role of the Israeli occupation in legitimating geopolitical technologies of securitization and sovereignty around the globe. An anti-Zionist hermeneutic recognizes the current shifting conditions in the U.S. academy—historically relatively foreclosed, as the writings of Edward Said remind us—for the possibility of genuine debate about what he called The Question of Palestine. The subject/object referred to in the phrase "the question of," explains Said, signals three things: a matter significant enough to be dealt with separately, an "intractable and insistent problem," and something that is unstable or uncertain.[123] That Palestine is all three simply means that its lessons cannot be put aside or ignored. My goal, however, is not to affirm an instrumentalist use of such a blueprint or to mobilize Palestine in order to foreground a corrective to Eurocentric theorizations of biopolitics. The ultimate purpose of this analysis is to labor in the service of a Free Palestine.

I close with a short comment on preliminary fieldwork conducted in January 2016 in the West Bank and Occupied East Jerusalem. I was there with a film team, working on a documentary about Palestinian life called *On This Land*, directed by Nitasha Dhillon and Amin Husain.[1] The film explores forms of quotidian and popular resistance, especially within the context of the uprisings that began in October 2015. We visited four refugee camps—Dheisheh, Qalandiya, Al-Aoub, and Aida—meeting with numerous families to discuss their experiences of occupation. There were IDF shootings of Palestinians (always accused of wielding knives) nearly every day of our visit. We attended one wake and also a funeral for four martyrs from the same village, three of them cousins, killed on the same night in two separate incidents. The funeral drew thousands of people, simultaneously functioning as a protest rally, a gathering facilitating collective mourning, and an incredible celebration of fortitude and resistance. Everywhere we went, we heard stories of debilitation: injured Palestinians dying while being transported through twisty back roads to avoid Israeli checkpoints en route to the hospital; men with shattered knees and other multiple permanently debilitating injuries, marking each intifada; ordinary families who had lost one, two, sometimes three sons to clashes with the IDF; women who had also been injured or killed; frightened parents worried that children, both boys and girls, were being targeted on playgrounds and in the streets of the camps; speculations regarding policies of shooting to kill and shooting to maim and when and why the IDF might switch between them. There was never a day without terrible news, without some kind of antagonism with IDF soldiers (teargas, shootings, harassment, surveillance), without some confirmed or soon-to-be-confirmed report of shootings of Palestinians, what were often referred to as field assassinations.

מעבר לנכים ועגלות

PASSAGE FOR DISABLED AND STROLLERS

معبر للمعاقين وعجلات

FIGS. POST.1 AND POST.2. Hebron, Shuhada Street Checkpoint, with close-up of a sign, stating "Passage for Disabled and Strollers," next to the entry turnstile, January 2016. Photos by Nitasha Dhillon. Reprinted with the artist's permission.

During this visit we met with disability service providers at the Bethlehem Arab Society for Rehabilitation (BASR), the largest and most central rehabilitation center in Palestine (others are located in Gaza and Ramallah).[2] Fifteen percent of its employees are people with disabilities. BASR runs eight community-based rehabilitation (CBR) programs in the West Bank.[3] We visited with one of these programs, the Shabab Al-Balad for the Disabled CBR self-support group in Al-Dahiriya, just south of Hebron.[4] We also spoke with the director of the disability center at the Al-Aoub refugee camp, and talked with people with varying bodily capacities and debilities at numerous checkpoints. And, again, there was not a single family or group of people among those we conversed with in the refugee camps that did not have close proximity to family and community histories of disability, or live with one themselves.[5]

Health is big business in the West Bank, among the most dominant forms of NGO humanitarian work conducted by European and North American agencies. It is not news that these otherwise valiant efforts are constitutive contradictions of the occupation, providing vital services and supplies while reproducing the dependency of colonized populations and legitimizing the structure of settler colonialism. The liberal, United Nations rights-based frames that these organizations generally champion foreground disability as an individual affliction to be accommodated and focus on educational and work integration, empowerment initiatives, and challenging stigma. Practitioners at BASR, however, put forward an "evolving" definition of disability, one that articulates all or most Palestinian populations as debilitated, enduring forms of collective punishment that restrict mobility for nearly everyone (albeit unevenly and differently). If the occupation is reducing able-bodied capacity across manifold Palestinian populations, literalizing mobility impairment through both targeting knees and creating infrastructural impediments to deliberately inhibit and prohibit movement, then this debilitation is multiscalar, occurring on individual, structural, and population levels. Both the medical and the social models of disability are needed to grasp the complexities of debilitation in Palestine. The medical model pathologizes disability as a defect to be repaired; and yet, in the case of Palestine, where such "repairs" are not only elusive but also withheld, the critique of the medical model is less pertinent. The social model understands the environment as disabling—curbs, stairs, elevators, in fact the checkpoints themselves, many of which do not have turnstiles or gates that allow wheelchairs to pass. But, as our

BASR hosts explained, this model tends to avoid addressing the debilitating infrastructure of the occupation itself: *the very fact of* checkpoints, divided highways, illegal settlements that fragment Palestinian transit, inability to get medical equipment repaired, dearth of medical supplies, deterioration of medical infrastructure. That is to say, addressing the debilitating effects of the occupation is a faux panacea that may deflect from challenging the causes of debilitation.

Numerous interviewees articulated this tension—between accommodation provisions within the occupation and the occupation itself as debilitating—in the narration of checkpoint crossing. Observing that the occupation does not distinguish between disabled and non-disabled Palestinians, several CBR group participants commented that they waited in line at the checkpoints just like everyone else, without any access accommodations. A young Palestinian woman suffering from physical and emotional trauma due to violent encounters with the IDF remarked: "If you want to go out, the occupation doesn't care if you are a person with a disability or not. We stay for long hours at the checkpoints, and sometimes we have to go back, we aren't always able to pass." The director of Shabab Al-Balad for the Disabled, Iyad Jabareen, further explained: "There are many obstacles to our work, such as the occupation, which further limits our ability to reach other Palestinian cities, even though there are international treaties that require states to ensure ease of access for the disabled. What we see today is that there are no provisions made for us as disabled people. We stand at checkpoints just like everyone else. At the same time, the occupation prevents NGOs from delivering aid or entering Palestine."

From this assessment of general debilitation, one could say the disabled are thus twice disabled, a formulation that could describe many populations, from residents of Flint, Michigan, to people with disabilities in prison. And yet, given the collective punishment model, disability is not always held up as a specific identity in Palestine. Jabareen speaks of how the group began in March 2013 with eleven members but now has a large community of previously housebound participants. He articulates a remarkable vision of disability as a nonidentity not wedded to the distinction between the disabled and non-disabled. As the inhabitants of the West Bank are suffering and resisting together the collective punishment of the occupation, no one is constituted as an idealized able body. Rather than saying Palestinians with disabilities are twice disabled, this frame posits that everyone is debilitated to some degree, or, in other words, no one is able-bodied. Does this debilitating structure of collective punishment create more acceptance and solidarity between those disabled and those able bodies debilitated by the infrastructure of the occupation? This is one of my ongoing research questions. Already the distinction between the two is muddy. No ailment, injury, disability, or illness escapes being severely and negatively impacted by the conditions of the occupation; each and every case heavily affects families and communities. The distinction between the war-disabled and those with other disabilities does not hold up well either. War heroes (and occasional heroines) are initially celebrated but quickly fade into the normalized landscape of trauma and loss, suffering from the same lack of support and resources as other people with disabilities. Illnesses and medical conditions that could be treated if health facilities were available become permanent disabilities. "Permanent disability" is a common euphemism for an injury that will never receive anywhere close to adequate medical attention.

There is no question that stigma toward people with disabilities, similar to many locations, is endemic. The nationalist version of Palestinian liberation unsurprisingly reinscribes able-bodied, masculinist norms. The Palestinian Authority stands accused of being uninterested in fully implementing the constitutional right of Palestinians with disability to full equality, what is called Law Number Four. One participant in the CBR group commented:

> The law is comprehensive, but not implemented. The PA has signed onto an international agreement for the rights of the disabled, it is a signatory to the treaty. But in reality, they aren't doing anything about it. The biggest responsibility for the implementation lies with the Ministry of Social Affairs, which does nothing. There is no support at all from the PA. If there is an event for the disabled, the most that will happen is a PA official will show up to be photographed with a person in a wheelchair.

Protests, actions, and petitions demanding accountability from the PA are common. The General Union of People with Disabilities was once part of a grassroots movement in the 1980s that helped to establish the constitutional amendment guaranteeing equal rights for people with disabilities. It is similarly viewed as inept, a bureaucratic entity responsible for administering surveys and tabulating statistics.

And yet, the promise of the articulation of disability by the members of the CBR support group, rendered not exceptional but convivial—in fact, the conviviality between disability and debility—is marked by the utopian appeal to collective struggle. Indeed, collective punishment is overturned into otherwise untenable lines of solidarity. Anti-occupation activism is a focal point of disability activism and includes supporting hunger strikes for Palestinian prisoners and using wheelchairs on the "frontlines . . . try[ing] to protect people behind them, thinking that maybe the IDF wouldn't shoot at them" during confrontations. The participants face daily the weaponization of debilitation that is maintained to deter resistance to the occupation, as one Palestinian man with a "permanent disability" explained: "They want to debilitate entire families so that their main concern becomes the disabled person and making sure their needs are met. Because disabled people are the responsibility of the entire community and not just of their families, this ensures that we are unable to fight the occupation. This is the occupation's calculus."

What is the main demand of disability activism? A common phrase we heard was "Treatment without checkpoints." In this context of the collective punishment of occupation, what constitutes "disability activism" is multifaceted and complex. Forms of radical insurgency—rock throwing, strikes, actions, housing demolition rallies, and civil disobedience—protest not only the legal and economic circumstances of the occupation but also the ongoing bodily debilitation of the Palestinian population. These acts of protest must be embraced as forms of disability activism and resistance. There is no type of resistance in Palestine that is not implicitly, if not explicitly, addressing and contesting the ongoing assaults to bodily capacity and health that are constitutive of and central to Israeli settler colonial occupation. There is a lack of grievance structures through rights discourses—and even when they exist, the world does not hold Israel accountable to even the most agreed-upon human rights violations. This means that disability justice activism takes on the very form of collectivity and dissent upon which tactics of debilitation are deployed.

Toward the end of our visit with the CBR self-support disability group at the Al-Dahiriya Youth Group center, we asked the twenty-odd people there of varying ages and genders what their dreams were for the future. Alongside hopes for the full implementation of "Number Four," a reference to the 1999 constitutional amendment, one respondent after another articulated desires for rehabilitation: "I hope to walk again someday"; "I want Palestine to be liberated, so we can have freedom of movement, we can get the treatment we need"; "I want to be able to know what it's like to walk."

These statements of desire for mobility are profound in the context of the mobility impairments and the enclosures of space that fuel the prime logics of settler colonial occupation. The stigmatization of disability as deficit justifies the right to maim; the production of widespread debilitation is key to maintaining colonial rule. But these desires on the part of Palestinians with disabilities point to something more entrenched. Becoming disabled is not a before-and-after event but an ongoing navigation with quotidian forms of blockage that draw populations in and out of debilitating and capacitating experiences. Efforts to claim disability as an empowered identity and to address ableism in Palestine will continue to be thwarted until the main source of producing debilitation—the occupation—is ended. The former simply cannot happen without the latter.

NOTES

PREFACE: HANDS UP, DON'T SHOOT!

1 With thanks to Colin Ashley for discussions on M4BL and disability justice organizing within the Peoples Power Assemblies (http://peoplespowerassembles.org). See also activist Leroy Moore on police brutality and disabled people in Kiley, "Why Leroy Moore, Jr. Has No Time for Small Talk."

2 Garza, "A Herstory of the #BlackLivesMatter Movement."

3 See the incredible statement by the Harriet Tubman Collective calling out the policy platform from the Movement for Black Lives released on August 1, 2016, for not specifically naming disability, ableism, or audism. The statement asserts: "We demand a centering of the Black Disabled/Deaf narrative as this narrative represents 60–80% of those murdered by the police—including all of those names that the Movement continues to uplift whilst erasing and dishonoring part of their humanity: Tanisha Anderson, Sandra Bland, Miriam Carey, Michelle Cusseaux, Ezell Ford, Shereese Francis, Eric Garner, Milton Hall, Korryn Gaines, Freddie Gray, Quintonio LeGrier, Kyam Livingston, Symone Marshall, Laquan McDonald, Natasha McKenna, Stephon Watts, Darnell Wicker, Mario Woods. We will not be martyrs for a movement that denies our humanity" (Harriet Tubman Collective, "The Vision for Black Lives Is Incomplete without Disability Solidarity"). See also black disabled activist Alexis Toliver talk about disability justice in relation to Black Lives Matter: Moore, "Black, Gifted and Disabled Interview Series: Alexis Toliver."

4 See the list of demands by the Movement for Black Lives at M4BL, "A Vision for Black Lives." The M4BL calls for cutting U.S. military expenditures and aid to Israel, stating that "the US justifies and advances the global war on terror via its alliance with Israel and is complicit in the genocide taking place against the Palestinian people. . . . Israel is an apartheid state with over 50 laws on the books that sanction discrimination against the Palestinian people." It further states, "The movement for Black lives must be tied to liberation movements around the world. The Black community is a global diaspora and our political demands must reflect this global reality. As it stands, funds and resources needed to realize domestic demands are currently used for wars and violence destroying communities abroad. State violence within the U.S. is intimately linked with empire and war-making

globally." See also the "2015 Black Solidarity Statement with Palestine" and also "A Letter from Gaza to Black America," where Mohammed Alhammami writes: "When I see this outrage against BDS and Kaepernick, a question arises in my consciousness: If they do not want us to protest nonviolently, if they do not want our fight to be based on international law and basic human rights, then what do they want us to do? If they denounce violence, then condemn our nonviolent protest, how do they want us to resist? The only answer I could find is this: Our oppressors do not really condemn our methods of resistance, but our resistance as a whole. . . . I do not know if my words will reach you, but I want you to know that I hear you, I see you and I feel your pain. When the night is darkest and you cannot seem to see the light at the end of the tunnel, know that there are people out there, on the other side of the planet, who are raising their fists in solidarity."

5 For important analysis on race and pain, see the work of Keith Wailoo, especially *Pain: A Political History*.

6 Rankine, *Don't Let Me Be Lonely*, 7.

7 Crosby, "Disabling Biopolitics."

8 Livingston, "Insights from an African History of Disability," 113.

9 Livingston, "Insights from an African History of Disability," 120. Her usage of "debility" is also demanded because there is a problem with the linguistic deployment of such a predicament in Setswana—there is no word that translates easily to "disability." See Livingston's *Debility and Moral Imagination in Botswana* for her ethnographic study. Her follow-up article, "Insights from an African History of Disability," is an exemplary intervention critiquing Euro-American disability studies. Her analysis of the overlaps between kinship idioms and bodily idioms is an especially fruitful discussion for queer disability studies.

10 See Stone, *The Disabled State*.

11 See Mitchell and Snyder, *The Biopolitics of Disability*.

12 See numerous works by Erevelles; Erevelles and Minear, "Unspeaking Offenses"; and Bell, *Blackness and Disability*. Regarding Bell's edited collection, he writes: "This volume is an intervention into the structuralist body politics underpinning African American studies and the whiteness at the heart of Disability Studies" (3). On the historical intersections between the Black Panther Party and disability rights organizing, see Schweik, "Lomax's Matrix."

13 For one recent example, see a Call for Papers for a collection titled "Crip Genealogies" edited by Mel Chen, Alison Kafer, Eunjung Kim, and Julie Avril Minich. They write: "How might we begin to recognize the capacious and generative possibilities of a disability studies that is less interested in 'incorporating' race—a formulation that suggests a tokenizing inclusion of whiteness—and more interested in engaging with the fields, practices, and knowledges of critical ethnic studies and related areas?"

14 Among several other pieces that address the Euro-American bias of disability studies, see McRuer, "Disability Nationalism in Crip Times." See also Million, *Therapeutic Nations*. In her trenchant monograph, Dian Million demonstrates the use of healing and rehabilitation apparatuses to further medicalize and pathologize

native bodies that refuse to assimilate—thus diagnosed as defaulting to their own extermination—into national and racial norms of corporeal laboring and symbolic productivity. Such rehabilitative assimilation demands accepting settler subjectivity, sublimating the experience of having one's land stolen, and forgoing reparative relief.

15 Livingston, "Insights from an African History of Disability."

16 Ben-Moshe, Chapman, and Carey, *Disability Incarcerated.*

17 For a defense of disability rights, see Charlton, *Nothing About Us Without Us.* For an argument against the inclusion of disability within the human rights framework, see Johnson, *Make Them Go Away.* For discussions on the pros and cons of including disability within the framework of human rights, see García Iriarte, McConkey, and Gilligan, *Disability and Human Rights*; Bickenbach, Felder, and Schmitz, *Disability and the Good Human Life*; Gill and Schlund-Vials, *Disability, Human Rights and the Limits of Humanitarianism.*

18 For a few notable examples, see Shah, *Contagious Divides*; Anderson, *Colonial Pathologies*; Ahuja, *Bioinsecurities*; Vora, *Life Support.*

19 Garland-Thomson, "Becoming Disabled."

20 Erevelles reminds us that the disability rights movement was mostly dominated by persons with physical disabilities, a fact that may still be accurate to this day. People with cognitive/severe disabilities are frequently not accounted for in disability theories of citizenship and personhood. See Erevelles, *Disability and Difference in Global Contexts,* 148.

21 Davis, *Freedom Is a Constant Struggle.*

22 Ben-Moshe et al., Forum, "Beyond 'Criminal Justice Reform.'"

INTRODUCTION: THE COST OF GETTING BETTER

1 I originally wrote this introduction as a talk to present at the October 2010 conference on affective tendencies at Rutgers University, during the aftermath of Tyler Clementi's suicide and with concern about the conversations that were not happening or foreclosed.

2 During the month of September 2010, there were at least five gay teen suicides in what many news articles called an "epidemic." On September 9, 2010, Billy Lucas, fifteen, of Greenburg, Indiana, hanged himself after harassment at school. On September 22, 2010, Tyler Clementi, eighteen, a student at Rutgers University, jumped off the George Washington Bridge after having a same-sex encounter broadcast on the Internet via his roommate's webcam. On September 23, 2010, Asher Brown, thirteen, of Harris, Texas, shot himself after coming out and having his parents' attempts to alert school officials to ongoing bullying ignored. On September 29, 2010, Seth Walsh, thirteen, of Tehachapi, California, hanged himself after being bullied. On September 30, 2010, Raymond Chase, nineteen, a student at Johnson and Wales University in Providence, Rhode Island, hanged himself for "unclear" reasons. See McKinley, "Suicides Put Light on Pressures of Gay Teenagers"; Hubbard, "Fifth Gay Teen Suicide in Three Weeks Sparks Debate";

Washington Blade, "National LGBT Community Reeling from 4th Teen Suicide in a Month." The popular gay news blog Towleroad.com published a post compiling a great number of media responses to the suicides (Pep, "The Tragedy of Gay Teen Suicide"). In the months that followed Clementi's suicide, there were more incidents: on October 9, 2010, Zach Harrington, nineteen, of Norman, Oklahoma, committed suicide a week after attending a local city council meeting where a "heated debate" over the proclamation of LGBT History Month took place (Knittle, "North Grad Took Own Life after Week of 'Toxic' Comments"); on October 19, 2010, Corey Jackson, nineteen, of Rochester, Michigan, a student at Oakland University, hanged himself (Heywood, "Gay Oakland University Student Found Dead of Suicide on Campus").

3 Berlant, "Slow Death."

4 Himmelstein et al., "Medical Bankruptcy in the United States, 2007."

5 A cursory search reveals myriad anti-Asian and Islamophobic remarks in the comments sections of many news articles about Clementi's suicide on news sites and blogs, including the *Advocate*, the *Huffington Post*, the *Trentonian*, *Queerty*, and *Towleroad*. The comments range from name-calling (e.g., "towelhead," "chink," "wog," "camel jockey," "paki") to predictions based on Ravi's name that he must be Muslim and therefore homophobic; from calls or wishes for Ravi's and Wei's execution or sexual violation (in and out of prison) to calls for "closing the border" and deporting them to "wherever they came from." Many racist comments appear to have been removed by blog moderators, and there are often several other commentators who criticize these types of remarks. See, e.g., reader comments on the following articles: Belonsky, "Tyler Clementi's Story Unfolded Online but Offers Real-Life Lessons"; *Advocate*, "Clementi's Roommate Indicted"; DeFalco, "Dharun Ravi, Tyler Clementi's Roommate, Hit with Bias Charge in Rutgers Suicide"; Martinez, "Nobody Saw Tyler Clementi Video, Say Lawyers"; and several from *Queerty.com*: J.D., "Tyler Clementi's Accused Tormentors Dharun Ravi and Molly Wei Withdraw from Rutgers"; Tedder, "Dharun Ravi's Anonymous Friends Defend Him against Lifelong Reputation of Being a Scumbag"; Villareal, "Dharun Ravi Pleads Not-Guilty to 15 Charges in Clementi Bullying Case."

6 Franke, "Queering the Air." See also Kim, "Against 'Bullying' or On Loving Queer Kids." In April 2011, Dharun Ravi was indicted on fifteen counts by a grand jury, including hate-crime charges. In May, Ravi pleaded not guilty to the charges. On May 21, 2012, he was fined $10,000 and sentenced to thirty days in jail, three years' probation, three hundred hours of community service, and counseling on cyberbullying and alternative lifestyles. Ravi served twenty days of his thirty-day jail term from May 31 to June 19, 2012, at the Middlesex County Adult Corrections Center in North Brunswick, New Jersey. Molly Wei was not formally charged and testified against Ravi as part of a plea deal. In addition to her testimony, she agreed to receive counseling and do three hundred hours of community service. See Foderaro, "Roommate Faces Hate-Crime Charges in Rutgers Case"; *Star-Ledger*, "Molly Wei to Testify against Tyler Clementi's Roommate Dharun Ravi as Part of

Plea Deal"; Mann, "Not Guilty Plea for Dharun Ravi, Suspected Tyler Clementi Harasser"; *Star-Ledger*, "Live Blog."

7   In 2010, *Newsweek* compiled a list of the top ten best college campuses for gay students (*Newsweek*, "The Best Gay-Friendly Schools"). Another website, Campus Pride, offers an index that rates each university's overall "LGBT-friendliness" (Campus Pride, "Campus Climate Index").

8   See Teeman's essay "Tyler Clementi's Mom" on Tyler Clementi's mother, Jane Clementi, five years after his suicide, which despite describing Tyler and Jane's relationship at great length only briefly mentions that Tyler had come out shortly before his death or that his mother had not reacted well.

9   Mulvihill, "Dharun Ravi Will Not Be Deported."

10 Bhabha, "Of Mimicry and Man."

11 The mobilization protesting Ravi's guilty conviction and mounting charges of anti-immigrant bias also, however, unfortunately reinforced some of the more subtle elements of the case that made Ravi seem self-aggrandizing and arrogant. A video released by Ravi's mother after the conviction and before the sentencing pleaded for leniency for her son. In her insistence that her son's life had already been ruined, the mother reinforced the hubris of a model minority familial configuration that articulates entitlement to the "It Gets Better" progressive trajectory that is typically reserved for racially normative subjects. In forcefully claiming that for Ravi it will never get better, and in essence that he is now consigned to a version of "slow death," she exposes how intrinsic "It Was Better" and, indeed, "It Gets Better" are to the expectations of certain aspirational nonwhite subjects of the U.S. state. Ravi's mother's plea was largely read as distasteful, in my estimation, because it was made on behalf of a child who was not white. Concerning potential alliances, see Sen, "Dharun Ravi, Tyler Clementi and the Hard Work of Truly Stopping Bullies"; on the wider Indian American community—an interesting post in its outrage—see Iyer, "Opinion"; on trials for noncitizens more generally, see Roy, "Dharun Ravi's Biggest Liability."

12 E-mail communication, October 5, 2010.

13 Rai, *Untimely Bollywood*.

14 Gordon Bell's archiving project is an extreme version of "lifelogging," unlikely to become the kind of project generally undertaken by most. However, his obsession appears less absurd when read in the context of a number of linked and related endeavors, such as MyLifeBits (developed by Jim Gemmell) and a Microsoft device in development called SenseCam, referencing Cathal Gurrin, who has worn a SenseCam every day since 2006 in hopes of leaving a "detailed digital trace" (Microsoft, "SenseCam"). Moreover, various forms of instantaneous data collection and dissemination apparatuses are increasingly akin to Facebook and Twitter. While Bell has been described as "self-involved," I would argue that the desires that animate his lifelogging practices are hardly that transparently simplistic or singular. Instead, a more capacious and porous rendering of the desires for lifelogging and to lifelog resonates through more generalized questions about what is at stake in the

forms of re-membering, recording, transmission, and information gathering and circulation that permeate modern living. The ambivalence about surveillance and daily monitoring activities is linked not only to fears of being exposed but also to desires to surveil others and fears generated by exposure to others (see also Puar interviewed by West, "Jasbir Puar: Regimes of Surveillance").

There is a broad range of consumer applicability and consumer desire for surveillance devices. While many serve scientific purposes and sporting activities, a 2010 article in the *New York Times* by Anne Eisenberg titled "When a Camcorder Becomes a Life Partner" describes the marketability of wearable cameras, many priced under two hundred dollars, "hands-free cameras worn on a headband" or "tucked over an ear." Their projected utility is for police officers, building inspectors, autobiographers, anyone who regularly loses their keys, and anyone else interested in "first-person documentation." These projections from seven years ago have largely come to fruition. These technologies are embedded in circuits whereby the seemingly endless capacity for digital storage, disregarding the physical infrastructure needed for this storage, loops into the production of material to be stored (the more we have, the more we store; the more we can store, the more we have).

15   To address these issues, Rutgers launched Project Civility in October 2010, days after Tyler Clementi's death, although it had been planned the year before. According to the project's mission statement, it is "a two-year, university-wide dialogue . . . focusing its attention on civility in the context of one of the most culturally and racially diverse research universities in the U.S." and includes forums on "gestures as simple as saying thank you to scholarly debate about the role of new technologies in society." The project was sponsored by the Office of Student Affairs and Office of Undergraduate Education and emphasizes both "responsible uses of technology" and "personal privacy" (Rutgers Student Affairs, "Project Civility"). In the wake of Clementi's suicide, the university was quick to emphasize Project Civility as a response to concerns over cyberbullying on campus. See President Richard McCormick's statement on the project's launch, which begins with a paragraph about Clementi (McCormick, "Project Civility"). The project was also mentioned in several national media sources reporting on the university's response to Clementi's suicide; see Foderaro, "Invasion of Privacy Charges after Tyler Clementi's Death"; Hamspon, "Suicide Shows Need for Civility, Privacy Online"; Kaufman, "Before Tyler Clementi's Suicide, Rutgers Planned 'Project Civility.'" Many of the media sources reporting on Clementi's death strongly emphasized, in some capacity, the role of new technology and cyberbullying. See, e.g., the following headlines among countless others: Freidman, "Victim of Secret Dorm Sex Tape Posts Facebook Goodbye, Jumps to His Death"; Pilkington, "Tyler Clementi, Student Outed as Gay on the Internet, Jumps to His Death"; Mulvihill, "Tyler Clementi's Suicide Illustrates Internet Dangers." In November 2010, Project Civility hosted a panel titled "Uncivil Gadgets: Changing Technologies and Civil Behavior," whose participants discussed how "new technologies have drastically altered our everyday behavior and how we interact with one another," as well as the new

forms of "civility" necessitated by these technological transformations. The event flyer can be accessed at http://projectcivility.rutgers.edu/files/documents/Uncivil _Gadget_Flyer_Final.pdf. On October 18, 2010, the Office of the Vice President for Student Affairs and the Center for Social Justice Education and LGBT Communities at Rutgers sponsored an event called "Rutgers Responds: An Evening with Dan Savage and the 'It Gets Better' Project." The Rutgers-based "queer centric social justice organization" Queering the Air criticized the university's decision to bring Savage, citing his "insensitivity toward people of color, women, and transgender people and people whose bodies do not fit the media's portrayal of the norm." The organization was also critical of the "It Gets Better" message and questioned why money was spent on Savage's visit rather than to "address LGBT concerns." See Queering the Air, "Rutgers Feels the Heat over Clementi Suicide"; Roache, "Savage Relays LGBT Survival Stories."

16 See also Luciana Parisi, *Abstract Sex*, on her formulation of "abstract sex" as a triangulation of the biodigital, biocultural, and biophysical.

17 What types of life events are logable, privileging which concepts of "life"? Lifelogging can be thought of as a command performance of archiving memory, a virtuosic response to or virtuosic defiance of a set of technocultural imperatives.

18 Memory is always revising itself, always a creation of the current moment inflected by that moment's reach toward a past. In that sense, memory can only ever really be a product of the present's relationship to multiple temporalities. The archive, or record, might intervene in such processes of memory, and/or it might actually exacerbate the skewed or overdetermined aspects of memory, such that an archive will mirror the tendency to emphasize some memories over others.

19 Much of this lifelogging technology is marketed as an antidote to "antiquated," inconvenient, or difficult archiving (see, e.g., Reddy and St. Clair, "The Million Book Digital Library Project"). If, as postcolonial theorist Anjali Arondekar has argued, the colonial archive (along with other minoritized archives such as postcolonial, queer, and feminist ones) is continually seized upon to unwittingly claim "simplistic and triumphant forms of empiricism" (Arondekar, *For the Record*, 2), what do we make of contemporary forces of "archive fever" when such fevers have been so heavily critiqued? What desires to remember, forget, keep track of, have access to, complete, share, be intimate with, disseminate, dominate, display, see and be seen animate lifelogging activities? What are the logics of accumulation driving contemporary practices of archive fever as lifelogging? How historical is the desire to record? And finally, to echo a query posed by Ursula Le Guin, can we imagine a society that doesn't seek to record? Also worth looking at is Jill Lepore on the attempt to archive the Internet, which, in some ways, makes ephemera more permanent and also requires hefty physical infrastructure (Lepore, "The Cobweb").

20 As Patricia Clough and Lucy Suchman, along with others, have argued, "action-at-a-distance" technologies, such as "remotely-controlled unmanned drones in Afghanistan that keep soldiers safe and simultaneously extend the combative capacities of these bodies" or "anti-terror cameras in airline seats which surveil mood and

detect anxiety," are designed to protect or create safe living (Suchman and Clough, "Action-at-a-Distance, or the Ideology of Safe Living Design").

21 Nyong'o, "School Daze."

22 See Young, "I'm Not Your Inspiration."

23 Thanks to Leerom Medovoi for this observation.

24 The "It Gets Better" project grew rapidly: more than 200 videos were uploaded in the first week, and the project's YouTube channel reached the 650-video limit the week after. The project then launched its own website, the "It Gets Better" Project, with fifty thousand entries from people of across the world (including many celebrities), which have received more than fifty million views. A book of essays from the project was released in March 2011, and the project was given the Governors Award of the Academy of Television Arts and Sciences. See Furlan, "The 'It Gets Better Project' Turns the Spotlight on Anti-gay Bullying"; Hartlaub, "Dan Savage Overwhelmed by Gay Outreach Response"; Emmys, "'It Gets Better' to Get Governors Award." In 2012, Dan Savage, with Terry Miller, edited a book based on the project titled *It Gets Better: Coming Out, Overcoming Bullying, and Creating a Life Worth Living*. Presenting "a life worth living" as the kicker to coming out and overcoming is really something to be thought about.

25 See Google Chrome's It Gets Better advertisement on YouTube in "Short Google Chrome 'It Gets Better' Commercial," posted by Andrea Swick.

26 Luciano, personal communication, October 2, 2010.

27 Quiet Riot Girl writes in "It Gets Better: What Does? For Whom?": "Basically the youtube project suggests support for queer youth has to stay 'on message' and 'upbeat.' Dissent and diversity does not seem to be encouraged. This is borne out by the vast numbers of videos being uploaded by white university-educated gay men, in comparison to those from women, transgender people, and working class people, and people from diverse ethnic backgrounds."

28 Cage, "It Doesn't Get Better. You Get Stronger."

29 In "Where Is the Proof That It Gets Better?," Latoya Peterson highlights the introduction of an alternative video campaign launched by the Embracing Intersectional Diversity Project, which argues that "the lack of discussion about the affect/impact of racism on how bullying and homophobia take shape is not only dismissive, it is in fact irresponsible."

30 Dykstra, "What If It Doesn't Get Better? Queer and Aboriginal Youth Suicide."

31 Webley, "It Doesn't Get Better."

32 This is not quite the vision of no future that Lee Edelman proposes as a political intervention in his polemic against "reproductive futurism" and normativizing gay rights equality agendas, with his critique of the centrality to queer politics of a child-worshiping culture (Edelman, *No Future*). For the most part his directive has been challenged in terms of the implicit whiteness of this precious child; not all children are equally valuable in the drive to "reproductive futurism." My own take on the debate between Edelman and his critics, stated in *Terrorist Assemblages*, concerns Edelman's misplaced calculation of biopower: he targets the figure of the child rather than the property of capacity and the process of capacitation. Direct-

ing a critique at biological reproduction presumes biological reproduction itself is the ultimate desired result of biopower. However, queer bodies might decide not to reproduce, but that does not mean that they do not *regenerate*. Dan Savage is certainly a testament to—if not emblematic of—this regenerative capacity. It matters less whether he crafts a family in his name; he is the spirit of a queer homonormative—if not homonational—neoliberal, coming-out, coming-of-age success story.

33 There were many touching videos, from *Project Runway*'s Tim Gunn's personal account of his suicide attempt to teen-produced videos such as "Make It Better" and "It Doesn't Always Get Better, You Get Stronger." See DeGeneres, "It Gets Better"; Griffin, "It Gets Better"; Gunn, "It Gets Better."

34 Lochlann Jain, *Injury*, 24.

35 For a critique of Berlant's discussion of obesity from a fat studies perspective, see Mollow, "Sized Up."

36 Berlant, "Slow Death," 756.

37 Foucault, *Security, Territory, Population*, 244.

38 Berlant, "Slow Death," 759.

39 Berlant, "Slow Death," 760–61n20.

40 Berlant, "Slow Death," 761.

41 Berlant, "Slow Death," 759.

42 Berlant, "Slow Death," 762.

43 Mitchell, Keynote Plenary for the Society for Disability Studies Conference.

44 Mitchell and Snyder, *Cultural Locations of Disability*, 17.

45 Berlant, "Slow Death," 765.

46 Queerness as a machine of capacity is a different rendering of the "normative/ antinormative debate," which is still ongoing in rather stark terms; see Wiegman and Wilson, "Introduction." I argue that antinorm and norm can both be modes of capacitation at different moments and in different racializing and sexual assemblages.

47 José Muñoz surveys these debates in *Cruising Utopia*; see also Berlant, *Cruel Optimism*; Duggan and Muñoz, "Hope and Hopelessness"; Edelman, *No Future*; Snediker, *Queer Optimism*.

48 See, e.g., Thacker, *The Global Genome*; Rajan, *Biocapital*.

49 Foucault, *The Birth of Biopolitics*, 219.

50 Foucault, *The Birth of Biopolitics*, 225.

51 Foucault, *The Birth of Biopolitics*, 226.

52 Foucault, *The Birth of Biopolitics*, 226.

53 Foucault, *The Birth of Biopolitics*, 228–30.

54 Shildrick, "Prosthetic Performativity," 115.

55 For a sustained examination of this phenomenon, see Mitchell and Snyder, *The Biopolitics of Disability*; Bogdan, *Picturing Disability*.

56 Interviewed in Talley, "Feminists We Love."

57 Mingus, "Moving toward the Ugly."

58 Mingus, "Changing the Framework."

59 Mingus, "Changing the Framework"; see also Mingus, "Access Intimacy."

60 Mingus, "Medical Industrial Complex Visual."

61 Berlant, "Slow Death," 761.

62 Ashman, "Editorial Introduction."

63 Berlant, "Slow Death," 770.

64 Deleuze, "Postscript on Societies of Control," 6–7.

65 Patel, "Risky Subjects."

66 For an overview of critical animal studies and its overlaps with posthumanism, see Pedersen, "Release the Moths."

67 See Barad, "Posthumanist Performativity." Barad is very useful in thinking about how performativity has come to signal a predominantly linguistic process. Her notion of "ontological realism" is an effort to destabilize linguistic essentialism. This frame, however, may privilege an essentialized truth produced through matter, a sort of ontological essentialism or materialist essentialism that uses a linguistic frame—performativity—to shore up the durational temporalities of matter. A similar conundrum appears in Jane Bennett's *Vibrant Matter*. Bennett's otherwise instructive theorization of the vitality of matter is undercut by the use of "agency" as something that can be accorded to certain forms of matter. Agency as it has historically been deployed refers to the capacities of the liberal humanist subject, an anthropocentric conceptualization of movement.

68 Kirby, *Quantum Anthropologies*.

69 Chen, *Animacies*.

70 Massumi interviewed by McKim, "Of Microperception and Micropolitics."

71 Foucault, *"Society Must Be Defended"*; Wilmut, Campbell, and Tudge, *The Second Creation*.

72 Agamben, "On Security and Terror."

73 Deleuze, "Postscript on Control Societies."

74 See the work of Hardt, "The Withering of Civil Society"; Clough, "Future Matters"; Hardt and Negri, *Empire*; Foucault, *Security, Territory, Population*; Deleuze, "Postscript on Control Societies."

75 Some important texts comprising the so-called affective turn include Clough, *The Affective Turn*; Gregg and Seigworth, *The Affect Theory Reader*; Massumi, *Parables for the Virtual*; Brennan, *The Transmission of Affect*; Sedgwick, *Touching Feeling*; and Stewart, *Ordinary Affects*, among others.

76 Foucault, *Security, Territory, Population*, 45.

77 Foucault, *Security, Territory, Population*, 57.

78 Foucault, *Security, Territory, Population*, 63.

79 McRuer, "Disability Nationalism in Crip Times."

80 Mitchell and Snyder, *The Biopolitics of Disability*.

81 See also an important collection of essays edited by Shelley Tremain, first published in 2005 and enlarged and revised for a 2015 edition, on the usefulness of Foucauldian theory to the study of disability. In the 2005 edition, Tremain writes: "A Foucauldian analysis of disability would show that the juridical conception of disability that is assumed within the terms of the social model and most existing

disability theory obscures the productive constraints of modern (bio-)power. A Foucauldian approach to disability would show that the governmental practices into which the subject is inducted or divided from others produce the *illusion* that they have a prediscursive, or natural, antecedent (impairment), which in turn provides the justification for the multiplication and expansion of the regulatory effects of these practices." I am interested in both building off these analyses and also challenging the manner in which they deploy the category of disability or people with disabilities as a discrete, definable group or population, named and/or identified as such, instead of thinking of biopolitics as a variegated process of slow death. Tremain, "Foucault, Governmentality, and Critical Disability Theory," 1–24.

82 Mitchell and Snyder, *The Biopolitics of Disability*.

83 Foucault, *Security, Territory, Population*, 12.

84 Deleuze, "Postscript on Control Societies."

85 Foucault, *"Society Must Be Defended,"* 246.

86 Foucault, *"Society Must Be Defended,"* 246–47.

87 Hardt, "The Withering of Civil Society."

88 Deleuze, "Postscript on Control Societies."

89 Feldman, *Police Encounters*, 13.

90 Franklin, *Control*.

91 Rose, "Neurochemical Selves," 53, quoting the 2001 World Health Organization report.

92 Rose, "Biopolitics in an Age of Biological Control."

93 Roberts, *Fatal Invention*; Metzl, *The Protest Psychosis*. Rose also elaborates at length on the culture and industry of diagnostic testing, which is another important element of the debility of debt. Diagnostic testing has ironically become part of, if not substituted for, a "preventative care" regime that is even more profitable than responsive care.

94 Moten, *In the Break*.

95 Kim, "Why Do Dolls Die," 94–95.

96 Kim, "Why Do Dolls Die," 105.

97 In *Animacies*, Chen argues that through the encounters with toxicity that MCS demands, "inanimate objects take on a greater, holistic importance," as the act of connectivity takes predominance over the entity to which one connects: "Anyone or anything I manage to feel any kind of connection with, whether it's my cat or a chair or a friend or a plant or a stranger or my partner, I think they are, and remember they are, all the same ontological thing." In challenging the static contours of the human body, Chen here simultaneously interrupts the fantasy of the autonomy of objects propagated by the most extreme proponents of object-oriented ontology, what they term "transobjectivity." In this transobjectivity, "enabled by the absence of attention to human sociality," Chen clarifies that humans become objects in the same manner as objects are objects.

98 Kirby, *Quantum Anthropologies*.

99 Maturana and Varela, *Autopoiesis and Cognition*.

100 See Derrida, *The Animal That Therefore I Am*; Chen, *Animacies*, 112.

101 DeLanda, *New Philosophy of Society*; Barad, "Posthumanist Performativity"; Wynter, "Unsettling the Coloniality of Being/Power/Truth/Freedom."

102 I am interested in Spivak's text not for its impelling of a politics of representing subalterneity, or diagnosing difference as a problematic within knowledge production projects—an epistemological corrective. Re-reading Spivak's text for the foreclosures it insists upon, the impossibility of representation, and the inevitability of essentialization reveals the limits of epistemological correctives. Encountering these limits is yet another defining feature of the affective turn.

103 Spivak, "Can the Subaltern Speak?," 297.

104 Spivak, "Can the Subaltern Speak?," 295.

105 Wynter, "Unsettling the Coloniality of Being/Power/Truth/Freedom."

106 In "The Human as Just an Other Animal," Licia Carson "interrogat[es] the convergence of two contemporary discourses: one which asks us to humanize our view of the 'cognitively disabled' and the other which demands that as humans we embrace our animality and rethink our relationship to the *animal other*" (127). She reviews *Madness and Civilization*, where Foucault writes most explicitly about nonhuman animality and its link to madness, arguing that "animality lies at the heart of madness itself" (120) in that "madness, in its animality, [is] in opposition to the natural order" (121).

107 Taylor, "Beasts of Burden," 197. For a less successful version of collaboration between disability rights and animal rights, see Donna Haraway's *When Species Meet*, where she discusses her father's disability in a manner that, I would argue, restabilizes human exceptionalism and undermines her otherwise compelling formulation of interspecies encounters in a slippage from companionate species to speciesism.

108 Weheliye, *Habeas Viscus*, 23.

109 Jackson, "Animal," 673.

110 Goodley, Lawthom, and Runswick Cole, "Posthuman Disability Studies."

ONE. BODIES WITH NEW ORGANS

1 Slack, "Biden Says 'Transgender Discrimination Civil Rights Issue of Our Time'";
Somerville, "Queer Loving." Biden's proclamation was met with skepticism from transgender grassroots activists asking critical questions about welfare, safety, work, economics, and health care. For some examples, see Smith, "Joe Biden Calls Transgender Discrimination 'the Civil Rights Issue of Our Time'"; Lennard, "What Took Biden So Long on Trans Discrimination?"

2 In its May 2015 "Hollywood Trans Formation" issue, *Variety*'s cover featured Laverne Cox, the trans woman who plays Sophia Burset in Netflix's hit show *Orange Is the New Black*. Cox had already been featured on the cover of *Time* magazine's May 29, 2014, issue, under the banner "The Transgender Tipping Point" (see Steinmetz, "The Transgender Tipping Point"). *Vanity Fair* made history with its June 2015 issue, featuring a transgender woman for the first time; Caitlyn Jenner, Olympic medalist and former star of *Keeping Up with the Kardashians*, appeared on

the cover of the magazine under the words "Call Me Caitlyn." On July 26, 2015, Jenner launched her new reality show on the E! network, an eight-part, one-hour series called *I Am Cait*. However, if this "transgender turn" has propelled some trans women to the center of U.S. popular culture, the acknowledgment of the recurrent murder of transgender women of color has not been brought to light. On August 18, 2015, *Democracy Now* reported that the United States is in a "state of emergency," with at least seventeen transgender women of color being murdered that year alone, an issue rarely discussed in the media (Strangio interviewed by Goodman, "A State of Emergency"). In regard to this media silence, on August 28, 2015, awQward artist Vita E Cleveland dropped a response song, "Hell Y'all Ain't Talmbout," to Janelle Monae's praised summer release, "Hell You Talmbout." Cleveland's song pays homage to some of the black trans people lost to violence and was created to raise awareness of the black victims of state violence. However, "nowhere in Monae's song is there any mention of the 19+ trans people who have been murdered so far in 2015—the majority of whom are black trans women" (Mase III, "Hell Y'all Ain't Talmbout").

3 Povinelli, lecture.

4 Haritaworn and Snorton, "Trans Necropolitics," 67.

5 See Aizura, "Of Borders and Homes"; Haritaworn and Snorton, "Trans Necropolitics"; Salah, "Notes on the Subaltern"; Wu Tsang's documentary film *Wildness*; Gossett, "We Will Not Rest in Peace"; Gossett, "Abolitionist Imaginings"; Juang, "Transgendering the Politics of Recognition."

6 Stryker and Aizura, "Introduction."

7 Aizura, "Of Borders and Homes," 295.

8 Susan Stryker (personal communication, e-mail, June 20, 2013, and August 25, 2013) has referred to this as "transnormative citizenship." As she wonders: "Is trans just an additive to the concept of homonationalism, or does it create (trans) gender trouble for the concept? My own sense is that homonationalism involves the capture of homonormativity by state/governmentality, and the capture of transnormative gender is another instance of the same process, but is not necessarily homo (sometimes it is, sometimes it isn't)."

9 Dan Irving writes that "constructions of transsexuals as viable social subjects by medical experts, transsexual individuals, researchers, and allies were, and continue to be, shaped significantly by discourses of productivity emerging from and reinforcing regimes of capitalist accumulation. To move toward achieving social recognition, the transsexual body must constitute a productive working body, that is, it must be capable of participating in capitalist production processes." Irving claims that this results in "the construction of transsexual subjectivities in ways that reinforce dominant exploitative class relations." Perhaps it is worth affirming this assessment can be made of many bodies solicited for neoliberal subjecthood. Irving goes on to exceptionalize the trans body by arguing that "appeals to mainstream society to accept transsexuals as legitimate subjects often emphasized their valuable contributions to society through their labor" ("Normalized Transgressions," 42).

10 This chapter draws on the critical interventions that Robert McRuer enacted with his conceptualization of an alliance between queer theory and critical disability studies. He notes mutual interests between the two fields in the social constructionist model; the critique of bodily norms; and the too-easy metaphorization of queerness as disability and vice versa ("As Good as It Gets," 97–98). McRuer's groundbreaking work in *Crip Theory* on the able-bodiedness of heterosexuality offers an important analysis of the complex rehabilitation of queer bodies through "compliance," a process that solicits gendered norms—sometimes as a prerequisite for access to health and homes—to regulate disabled bodies (see especially chapter 3). McRuer's discussion excavates the difficult navigations of "noncompliance" and sexuality. Much of queer theory has destabilized normative assumptions about sexual and kinship object choices, challenging who has sex or cohabitates or kins with which sex. More recently, there is growing attention to what sex is and how it becomes reified as the activity or body par excellence that defines the transgressive capacities of queerness. Queer ableism not just inhabits an aspiration to able-bodiedness that one can note in various queer body discourses and cultures, but more insidiously coheres through the normativization of sex—both the sex of the body and the sex that the body has—as a certain kind of (able) bodily attribute, pleasure, and capacity (see McRuer and Mollow, "Introduction," 1–34). My intent here is neither to mobilize trans bodies to queer queer theory nor to posit trans as paradigmatically queer, but rather to highlight that the tendencies toward normativities of queerness have produced costly exclusions, transgender nonconforming bodies among them.

11 Part of the interest in assemblages is impelled by desires to methodologically move beyond the mutual interruptions of field X by field Y and vice versa. Such mutual interruptions are themselves symptoms of the liberal deployment of intersectionality, implicitly based on the assumption of the equality of each vector to the other and absence of the other in the other.

12 At this point in time the potential alliance politics of trans disability are seemingly perceived in terms of the intersectional "trans-disabled subject" or the "disabled trans subject." Often the intersectional subject gets tokenized or instrumentalized as a foil such that the presence of this subject actually then prohibits accountability toward broader alliances. Such approaches produce these intersectional subjects from which people can disavow their responsibility and implicated interface with these subjects while maintaining that the representational mandate for diversity has been satisfied—in other words, a gestural intersectionality.

13 Nakamura, "Trans/Japan, Trans/Disability," explains the use of the DSM in Japan.

14 See Valentine, *Imagining Transgender*; Stryker, "We Who Are Sexy"; Irvine, *Disorders of Desire*.

15 Section 12221 of the 1990 Americans with Disabilities Act reads as follows:

> (a) HOMOSEXUALITY AND BISEXUALITY
> For purposes of the definition of "disability" in section 12102(2) of this title, homosexuality and bisexuality are not impairments and as such are not disabilities under this chapter.

(b) CERTAIN CONDITIONS
Under this chapter, the term "disability" shall not include
(1) transvestism, transsexualism, pedophilia, exhibitionism, voyeurism, gender identity disorders not resulting from physical impairments, or other sexual behavior disorders;
(2) compulsive gambling, kleptomania, or pyromania; or
(3) psychoactive substance use disorders resulting from current illegal use of drugs.

16 Hiegel, "Sexual Exclusions."
17 Herbert, "Transforming Transsexual and Transgender Rights."
18 Gorton, "Transgender Health Benefits," 84. Gorton continues: "Therefore, although obtaining transgender services through Medicaid is difficult but possible depending on the court, obtaining federal protections through the ADA involves convincing courts not only that gender identity disorder is a legitimate illness needing treatment but also that the exclusion within the law itself is unconstitutional—a much more formidable challenge. To date, no court has struck down the ADA's exclusion of transgender people" (84).
19 Hong, "Categorical Exclusions," 123.
20 See Colker, "Homophobia, AIDS Hysteria, and the Americans with Disabilities Act," 8.
21 Barry, "Disabilityqueer."
22 We might ask what the shift from GID to gender dysphoria entails: Will there be a shift away from the emphasis on childhood? What new populations will be impelled and curated? While the topic is beyond the scope of this discussion, the elimination of GID from the DSM might entail that successfully litigating for ADA coverage of transgender people is an even more remote possibility.
23 Hiegel, "Sexual Exclusions," 1452–53.
24 Markotic and McRuer, "Leading with Your Head."
25 Snyder and Mitchell, "Ablenationalism and the Geo-politics of Disability," 124.
26 Snyder and Mitchell, "Ablenationalism and the Geo-politics of Disability," 122.
27 Spillers, "Mama's Baby, Papa's Maybe."
28 Spillers, "Mama's Baby, Papa's Maybe," 72.
29 Spillers, "Mama's Baby, Papa's Maybe," 66.
30 See ENDAblog, "Queer Channel Media: Trans-washing the ADA."
31 Strassburger, "Disability Law and the Disability Rights Movement for Transpeople," 114. See also Stryker in Currah, "Stepping Back, Looking Outward," 96: "Transgender activism can function as a vital critique of this new homonormativity. It brings into visibility at least one incipient norm present in U.S. gay and lesbian political movements since the 1950s—that is, the extent to which these gay and lesbian social formations have predicated their minority sexual-orientation identities on the gender-normative notions of man and woman that homosexual subcultures tend to share with the heteronormative societies of Eurocentric modernity." She continues: "When this gender-normative, assimilationist brand of homosexuality

circulates internationally with the privileges of its first-world point of origin, it all too readily becomes the primary template through which human rights are secured, or resources for living are accessed, by people rooted in nonheteronormative formations of sexgender-sexuality that have developed from nonEurocentric traditions in diverse locations around the world—gay, in other words, has the power to colonize." Stryker is optimistic about transgender activism not producing such neocolonial dynamics, an optimism that I think underpins some theorizations of trans identity that remain racially unmarked: "Transgender poses a similar risk, but to the extent that transgender activism can distinguish itself from homonormative neoliberalism, it can help create a different set of openings for resisting the homogenizing forces of global capital than those that have circulated through the categories lesbian, gay, or homosexual" (96).

32 If trans has become the figure of radical alterity from a now-domesticated queer, as it is increasingly claimed, then is trans the disabled Other of a queer ableism? Is transphobia in queer organizations and communities, for example, in part a manifestation of ableism, of anxiety or phobia toward disability? This is not in any way meant to reduce transphobia to ableism, or to any other -ism, but to ask what components, including race, class, and ableism, might be fueling the assemblage that is transphobia. Is there value in conceptualizing transphobia as a variant of ableism?

33 Strassburger, "Disability Law and the Disability Rights Movement for Transpeople," 3–4.

34 Stryker, personal communication, e-mail, August 25, 2013.

35 Lee, "Trans Models in Prison," 464–65.

36 Lee, "Trans Models in Prison," 470.

37 Chung, "Identity or Condition"; Spade, "Resisting Medicine, Re/Modeling Gender," 37.

38 Stryker and Aizura, "Introduction," 1.

39 Wilkerson, "Normate Sex and Its Discontents," 184–85.

40 Clare, "Body Shame, Body Pride," 262.

41 Clare, "Body Shame, Body Pride," 262.

42 Mitchell and Snyder, *Narrative Prosthesis*; Mitchell and Snyder, "Introduction," 6.

43 Beauchamp, "Artful Concealment and Strategic Visibility," 357.

44 Beauchamp, "Artful Concealment and Strategic Visibility," 357.

45 Metzl and Kirkland, *Against Health*.

46 Clare, "Body Shame, Body Pride," 265.

47 Hayward, "Lessons from a Starfish." Hayward writes in a footnote: "Again, I risk reading the 'Cripple' as a trans-subject not to iterate the pathologization of transfolks, but to explore the imaginings of the song. For the transsexual/transgender subject, gender assignments can feel 'disabling,' even wounding. I'm speaking about this traumatic experience, not about transgressive exceptionalism" (254).

48 Kier, "Interdependent Ecological Transsex," 194, 196.

49 On amputation, see the movie *(W)hole*; on deafness, see *Make Me Deaf*, described on the front page as "The blog of a woman in her mid twenties who wishes she were moderately or severely deaf" (http://makemedeaf.blogspot.com/).

50 Lawrence, "Clinical and Theoretical Parallels between Desire for Limb Amputation and Gender Identity Disorder," quoted in Stevens, "Interrogating Transability."

51 Sullivan, "Dis-orienting Paraphilias?"

52 Another way in which people engage in body-modification practices that aim to increase gender illegibility is "neutrois." Neutrois, referred to by some as a "more florid" coinage for "agender" (White, "Neither Man nor Woman"), describes individuals who feel that they have no gender or are gender neutral (Hicks et al., "Mining Twitter as a First Step toward Assessing the Adequacy of Gender Identification Terms on Intake Forms," 7). The term was adopted by Facebook in February 2014, when the social media platform introduced a "custom gender option" that would allow users to select a gender identity beyond the traditional categories of "male" and "female," and choose between fifty-eight gender options (Zimmer and Carson, "Among the New Words," 471). The term has also been adopted in campaigns such as "Beyond the Binary," run by the Australian Gay/Straight Alliance Network to raise consciousness about issues facing gender-nonconforming youths in middle and high schools (Cleves, "Beyond the Binaries in Early America," 461–62). For the attitude of one neutrois toward genderlessness, see "What Is Neutrois?" (http://neutrois.com/what-is-neutrois/); see also "Neutrois Nonsense" (http://neutrois.me/).

53 "I learned of no one who needed a developmental disability, a traumatic brain injury, mental health disabilities, etc. What does this say about the hierarchy of disability or which disabilities have the best performance factor?" (Stevens, "Interrogating Transability").

54 Stevens, "Interrogating Transability."

55 Mitchell and Snyder, "Disability as Multitude," 190–91.

56 For an incisive critique of the ahistorical claims regarding the particularization of bodies necessary to capitalism, see Rosenberg, "The Molecularization of Sexuality," 9.

57 Foucault, The Birth of Biopolitics: "On one side it means generalizing the 'enterprise' form within the social body or social fabric; it means taking this social fabric and arranging things so that it can be broken down, subdivided, and reduced, not according to the grain of individuals, but according to the grain of enterprises. The individual's life must be lodged, not within a framework of a big enterprise like the firm or, if it comes to it, the state, but within the framework of a multiplicity of diverse enterprises connected up to and entangled with each other, enterprises which are in some-way ready to hand for the individual, sufficiently limited in their scale for the individual's actions, decisions, and choices to have meaningful and perceptible effects, and numerous enough for him not to be dependent on one alone. And finally, the individual's life itself—with his relationships to his private property, for example, with his family, household, insurance, and retirement—must make him into a sort of permanent and multiple enterprise" (241).

58 Halberstam, In a Queer Time and Place, 18.

59 See West, "PISSAR's Critically Queer and Disabled Politics."

60 Jacques, "Remembering Our Dead." On the distinctions between MTF and FTM and trans women of color, see O'Brien, "Tracing This Body."

61 For a transnational analysis of racial difference that informs the possibility of transformative experiences of surgical procedures, see Aizura, "The Romance of the Amazing Scalpel."

62 Quoted in Currah, "Stepping Back, Looking Outward," 100.

63 The Audre Lorde Project's TransJustice group, a project led by trans and gender-nonconforming people of color, distributes a list of points of unity on the annual Transgender Day of Action in New York City, reproduced here. It is available on the Audre Lorde Project website at http://alp.org/tdoa_pou.

TRANS DAY OF ACTION FOR SOCIAL
AND ECONOMIC JUSTICE—POINTS OF UNITY

Initiated by TransJustice of the Audre Lorde Project, a Lesbian, Gay, Bisexual, Two-Spirit, Trans and Gender Non-Conforming People of Color Center for Community Organizing.

We call on our Trans and Gender Non-Conforming (TGNC) community and our allies from many movements to join us for the 8th Annual Trans Day of Action for Social and Economic Justice. We as TGNC People of Color (POC) recognize the importance of working together alongside other movements to create the world we want to see. We live in a time when oppressed peoples including people of color, immigrants, youth and elders, people with disabilities, women and TGNC people, and poor people are under-served, face higher levels of discrimination, heightened surveillance and experience increased violence at the hands of the state. We must unite and work together towards dismantling the transphobia, racism, classism, sexism, ageism, ableism, homophobia and xenophobia that permeates [sic] our movements for social justice, while also celebrating the victories and strides for the rights of TGNC POC. Let's come together to let the world know that TGNC rights will not be undermined and together we will not be silenced! These are the points of unity, which hold together the purpose of this important march:

- We demand an end to profiling, harassment and brutality at the hands of the police. Like many other oppressed communities TGNC people are targeted, profiled and brutalized by the police. This violence does not occur in isolation, and is aggravated by racism, classism, ableism, xenophobia, misogyny, ageism and homophobia. We call for an end to the current NYPD Quality of Life Initiative and efforts to "clean up" Christopher St. with increased policing. We support FIERCE's campaign to counter the displacement and criminalization of LGBTQ youth of color at the Christopher Street Pier. We support legislation that would stop police and prosecutors from using possession of condoms as evidence of "criminal activity." As members of Communities United for Police Reform we demand an end to the discriminatory "Stop and Frisk" and other "Broken Windows" practices of the NYPD.

- We demand access to respectful and safe housing. Many TGNC POC face severe discrimination from landlords and housing administrators displacing us from our homes due to gender identity or expression. A disproportionate number of TGNC POC have been or are currently homeless. However, many homeless TGNC POC also face discrimination and violence when trying to access shelters and other assisted living programs. NYC law and the Department of Homeless Services (DHS) state that people will be placed in shelters according to their gender identity and that discrimination based on gender identity will not be tolerated. We support Queers for Economic Justice in their demand that all DHS shelters provide adequate Trans sensitivity trainings for all personnel and enforce clear non-discrimination policies that respect the dignity and safety of all homeless people. We celebrate that the U.S. Department of Housing and Urban Development has developed policy and procedures to prevent discrimination related to sexual orientation and gender orientation in their housing programs.

- We demand access to the NYC LGBT Center without fear of harassment, or censorship. We oppose the NYC LGBT Center's moratorium, on groups using the Center as a meeting space to organize on "the issue of the Israeli/ Palestinian divide" and we support demands for restoration of the right of pro-Palestinian groups to meet at the Center. We oppose the reduction in programming and services for the TGNC POC community at the LGBT Center. We call for community members to hold community spaces accountable by voicing discrimination.

- We demand the full legalization of all immigrants. We stand in solidarity with Indigenous-identified Two-Spirit people and the sovereignty of the First Nations, on whose land we now see the US attempt to enforce arbitrary borders. TGNC POC people deserve the right to access competent and respectful immigration services. We demand that the consulates of all countries respect and honor our identities and issue passports and other documentation that accurately reflects who we are. We oppose the Secure Communities program, the guest worker program, the Real ID Act, enforcement provisions to build more walls and give greater powers to the Department of Homeland Security, increased barriers for asylum seekers, and other anti-immigrant policies.

- We are in solidarity with all prisoners, especially the many TGNC POC people behind the walls. We call attention to the under-reported accounts of violence and rape that our community faces at the hands of correction officers and other prisoners, in psychiatric facilities, and group homes. We demand an end to the torture and discrimination TGNC POC prisoners face. We demand that all TGNC POC prisoners receive competent and respectful healthcare. We oppose the continued growth of the prison industrial complex that continues to target our communities, yet we recognize that TGNC POC people need access to services and facilities that lessen our vulnerability to violence within the present jails and prisons. We call attention to the criminal injustice system that increasingly puts POC, immigrants, people with disabilities, TGNC POC and poor people behind bars —criminalizing our communities and our lives.

- We oppose the U.S. "War on Terrorism" as an excuse to legitimize the expansion of the U.S. as an imperial super power and to justify a national security strategy that is really meant to militarize our borders and heighten surveillance and control over people living in the U.S., separating our communities by fostering feelings of hate, xenophobia, and violence. We demand the immediate removal of all U.S. troops from all countries under occupation and demand an end of use of U.S. dollars to cultivate and sponsor wars against people in the U.S. and abroad.

- We demand health care. TGNC POC people deserve the right to access health care, receive hormones and necessary surgery. We demand that health care providers and insurance providers acknowledge this right and provide this service without bias and discrimination.

- We demand safety while utilizing public transportation. We celebrate that due to a court ruling, TGNC POC are now protected while utilizing public transportation in NYC and can take action against the MTA (NYC's public transportation system) if its employees use discriminatory language. TGNC POC utilize the MTA daily and should be addressed by their preferred gender pronoun, should not be targeted by employees or harassed by other customers. We call on the MTA to insure the safety not only of TGNC POC but of women, children and all riders.

- We demand that all people receiving public assistance be treated with respect and dignity. We are in solidarity with all people living on public assistance. We celebrate that the Human Resources Administration (HRA), the NYC welfare agency, passed the procedure for serving TGNC clients and approved a community developed training curriculum, but we call for full implementation of the procedure including culturally competent trainings for all employees that does not put the burden of education on the TGNC POC community.

- We demand that TGNC POC people have equal access to employment and education opportunities. We are outraged by the high numbers of TGNC POC who are unemployed. Many TGNC POC continue to face blatant discrimination and harassment from employers due to systemic transphobia. Few TGNC POC have access to opportunities for learning in a safe school environment. TGNC POC demand that all employers and educational institutions implement non-discrimination policies that respect the rights of all workers and students and that they comply with the NYC Human Rights Law that prohibits discrimination against gender identity and expression.

- We demand justice for the many TGNC POC who have been beaten, assaulted, raped, and murdered. Yet these incidents continue to be silenced or misclassified. Instead of disrespecting the identities of TGNC POC, like the New York Times recently did with Lorena Escalera, we call for media to address individuals by their preferred names and pronouns. The police and the media continue to criminalize us even when we try to defend ourselves. Hate crime laws will not solve the problem but will give increased power to the state to put more people in jail. Instead we call for a unified effort for all of us to look deeper into the root causes of why these incidents happen. In striving for social justice we seek to find ways of holding people accountable and coming to a joint understanding of how we can make our communities safer.

  We commemorate the memory of Tracy Bumpus, Yvonne McNeil, Deoni Jones, LaShai McLean, Brandy Martell, Paige Clay, Shelly Hillard, Coko Williams and the many brave souls we have lost, who struggled and lived their lives fearlessly, being true to who they were. They keep the fire of struggle burning within all of us.

64 Stryker and Sullivan, "King's Member, Queen's Body," 51.

65 Stryker and Sullivan, "King's Member, Queen's Body," 61.

66 See Metzl and Kirkland, *Against Health*.

67 Stryker and Sullivan, "King's Member, Queen's Body," 61.

68 Deleuze and Guattari, *A Thousand Plateaus*, 147.

69 Overboe, "Affirming an Impersonal Life," 254.

70 For instance, Petra Kuppers argues for a "rhizomatic model of disability" in which the extrinsic model (social constructivism) and the medical model (biological essentialism) "mix and merge" ("Toward a Rhizomatic Model of Disability," 225). Moving through this binary, which invokes other binaries such as physical impairment versus mental disabilities, and "visible" disabilities versus "invisible" disabilities, and disability versus disease, is one of the most powerful implications of poststructuralist approaches to disability. Citing Deleuze and Guattari from *A Thousand Plateaus*, she writes: "Without knowing what specific assemblages will emerge for any one reader-operator, a rhizomatic model allows the co-existence of 'not only different regimes of signs but also states of things of different status' . . . resonates with my lived experience of disability as one that lives in simultaneity of codes, devalued and valued at the same time. The rhizomatic model of disability produces an abundance of meanings that do not juxtapose pain and pleasure or pride and shame, but allow for an immanent transformation a coming into being of a state of life in this world, one that is constantly shifting and productive of new subject/individual positions. But, like all Deleuzoguattarian concepts, this rhizomatic model of disability is only useful when used. It cannot have truth status, for it is empty of specific meaning. It is a movement rather than a definition" (226). While the arborescent reproduces lineage, roots, origins, and developmentalist trajectories, the rhizomatic "ceaselessly establishes connections between semiotic chains,

organizations of power and circumstances relative to the arts, sciences, and social struggles. A semiotic chain is like a tuber agglomerating very diverse acts, not only linguistic, but also perceptive, mimetic, gestural, cognitive; there is no language in itself, nor are there any linguistic universals, only a throng of dialects, patois, slangs and specialized languages. There is no ideal speaker-listener, any more than there is an homogenous linguistic community" (Deleuze and Guattari, *A Thousand Plateaus*, 7).

71 In a special issue of the *Journal of Literary and Cultural Disability Studies*, the editors Petra Kuppers and James Overboe begin their introduction by noting that "Deleuzoguattarian thought occupies strange and marginal spaces in Disability Studies literature. While some scholars find great depth and richness in work that de-naturalizes language and bodily experience, some find it too far removed from everyday life" (Kuppers and Overboe, "Introduction," 217). They note that the contributions focus less on "the historical relationship" between the fields of disability studies and Deleuze; rather, they write "with and in (rather than for or against)" Deleuzoguattarian thought—"what it *does* rather than what it is" (217).

72 Currah, Moore, and Stryker, "Introduction," 11.

73 See Weinstein, "Transgenres and the Plane of Gender Imperceptibility." Weinstein provides an important rereading of Nietzsche and a corrective around Judith Butler's use of "no doer behind the deed," asserting that the doer and the deed are both fictions according to Nietzsche, and imploring us in nonessentialist terms to "become what we are" (162–63).

74 Chen, *Animacies*, 155. The most transported and seized-upon Deleuzian construct that has been imported into many theories of corporeality is the now-infamous elaboration of the Body without Organs, or the BwO, as Deleuze and Guattari shorthand it. As an opposition to the territorialization of naturalized orderings of organs and set functions, the BwO is first and foremost a critique of normative notions of the organism. The body-as-organism, and its attendant regimes of coherence, individuation, and autonomy, is the enemy. Thus, the BwO is not actually in opposition to a body *with* organs but concerned with the standardization of organ ordering. Insofar as a BwO is a process rather than a product, one can never *become* a BwO, as it is a becoming that tugs at the threshold between experimentation and obsession. This deterritorialization with caution, as Deleuze and Guattari remind us, can result in failures—the reterritorialization of the body through the hypochondriac, or the junkie for whom the skin becomes overdetermined as the ur-organ. This threshold event of the BwO, whereby bodily capacities and debilities are solicited, redistributed, transmuted, is most obviously convivial with disability studies because it reimagines bodily vulnerability, deficiency, deviancy, and debility as forms of affirmative becoming that, one, unsettle bodily norms of productivity, two, open up avenues toward corporeal experimentation and the unknown of bodily sensation, and three, deconstruct the contours of the organic body such that connections to other bodies are foregrounded over the disabled body as enclosed, unitary, closed off, and defined through lack. The taking up of BwO has been prolific and fruitful, but I want to destabilize the attachment to BwO because it is too easy a rendering of nonnormative bodies, one perhaps a tad mired

in romanticized sentimentality, and it is also too often rendered as a metaphor, whereas Deleuze and Guattari insist on the radical materiality of the BwO.

75 See also Crawford, "Transgender without Organs?"

76 Deleuze and Guattari, *A Thousand Plateaus*: "This research should go from the worst to the best since it would cover precious, metaphorical, or stultifying regimes as well as cries-whispers, feverish improvisations, becomings-animal, becomings-molecular, real transsexualities, continuums of intensity, constitutions of bodies without organs" (147).

77 Deleuze and Guattari, *A Thousand Plateaus*, 147.

78 Writes Edward Mussawir on these three steps:

> The first and simplest level of this problematic is that of heterosexual loves. This level of sexuality is social, public and superficial. To function properly in a sexed society on this level is to appear to be heterosexual, and to believe in or affirm everyone else's worldly heterosexual appearances. Males and females meet, therefore, on this first level within an institution which, through its regimentation of signs and appearances, makes the sex of individuals completely "readable". . . . There may, in fact, be no such underlying truth, but the search itself which makes up the narrative, introduces the reader to the possibility of surveying another secret or hypothetical level of sexual relations. For the one who searches for the truth—which according to Deleuze, Proust develops through the character of jealousy—all the superficial signs of heterosexuality and their interpretation become deceptive and converge upon a "secret" homosexual world that excludes the member of the other sex. On this second more profound "secret" and "accursed" level, the sexes shall never meet or communicate because they each express a homosexual world, or belong to a homosexual series, that ultimately excludes the other. Belonging to separate worlds, the sexes enter into relation only indirectly and through disguise: a man who really loves other men, for example, will have to play the role of a woman in order to be an object for the woman who really loves other women, and so on. It is at this level of signs, Deleuze contends—in which there is no longer any essential coherence or correspondence between the entity and its statistically determined sex—that the reality of guilt prevails in sexual desire and the laws of love. Just as there is no true or transparent sex or sexuality of any individual, the sexes address one another only through a block of mutual deception and becoming.
>
> If the homosexual level of signs is more profound than the transparent signs of heterosexuality, Deleuze nevertheless introduces an even more complex and concealed third level which is neither homosexual nor heterosexual but which he names transsexual. The second level already hinted at a certain transsexual ethic in which one should not enter into a sexual relation other than by undergoing some kind of "change" or by a mutual "becoming" of each individual. The sexes themselves, however, remained statistical, aggregate or "molar" on this level as on the first (since each individual belongs to either

one series or the other at any given time). The "transsexual" level, however, is one which cannot sustain the form of individual sexual identities, since for Deleuze it "transcends the individual as well as the entity: it designates in the individual the coexistence of fragments of both sexes, [as] partial objects that do not communicate."

   This is why—in making sense of the previous two levels—the third is also figured as an "initial hermaphroditism" because rather than either being united in the conventional world of heterosexuality, or consigned to secret fragmented homosexual worlds, the two sexes remain disjunct and non-communicating; but disjoined on the one body. The Proustian theory of sexuality for Deleuze "will assume its entire meaning only if we consider that the two sexes are both present and separate in the same individual." (*Jurisdiction in Deleuze*, 44–45)

79 Kier, "Interdependent Ecological Transsex," 189.
80 Weinstein, "Transgenres and the Plane of Gender Imperceptibility," 156.
81 Livingston and Puar, "Introduction." In the paragraphs that follow, I paraphrase several points from our co-written introduction.
82 Foucault, *Security, Territory, Population*, 75.
83 Foucault, *The History of Sexuality*, 146.
84 On sex dimorphism, see Roughgarden, *Evolution's Rainbow*. See Hayward and King, "Toxic Sexes." Hayward and King theorize toxicity as a threat and a possibility.
85 Hird, "Animal Trans," 242.
86 Kirby, *Quantum Anthropologies*; Lynn Margulis and Dorion Sagan, quoted in Hird, "Animal Trans," 241.
87 Much of this early dialogue revolves around Temple Grandin, an autistic person known for her work on livestock animal behavior. See Wolfe, "Learning from Temple Grandin"; Weil, *Thinking Animals*.
88 See Max Hantel's review of *Queering the Non/Human*. Hantel, "Posthumanism, Landscapes of Memory, and the Materiality of AIDS in South Africa."
89 Chen, *Animacies*, 137.
90 The phrase "mutilating gender" is from Dean Spade's essay by that title.
91 Noble, "Our Bodies Are Not Ourselves," 249.
92 Foucault, *"Society Must Be Defended,"* 255.
93 Many other critical race theorists have made this point, including Kim Tallbear, Nadia Abu El-Haj, and Dorothy Roberts. See Tallbear, *Native American DNA*; Abu El-Haj, *The Genealogical Science*. Denise Ferreira da Silva has written on the passage from the biopolitics of race to nanopolitics: "That cancer cells do not indicate dark brown skin or flat noses can be conceived of as emancipatory only if one forgets, or minimizes, the political context within which lab materials will be collected and the benefits of biotechnological research will be distributed" (*Toward a Global Idea of Race*, 8–9).
94 On UK legislation that requires the acquiring of one's transgender status to be committed to "until death," see Grabham, "Governing Permanence."
95 Weinstein, "Transgenres and the Plane of Gender Imperceptibility."

96 If we follow the lines of thought that inform Deleuze and Guattari's "becoming," we see that becoming animal and becoming woman are aspirational trajectories not toward these coordinates but beyond them. A becoming manifests not as an occupation of these categories but of the dissolution of the binary frames that inform the coherence of the categories in the first instance. Becoming animal is not a reaching out of the human to the experiences of the animal but, rather, a dissolution of the human animal/nonanimal binary such that it no longer makes sense, no longer signifies as sensemaking, sensible. Becoming woman, for example, is Deleuze and Guattari's version of actual transsexualism. It is the potentiality of overwhelming—not deconstructing or transcending but, rather, overwhelming through infinite multiplicity—sexual difference into incoherence. Edward Mussawir writes, "'Becoming woman,' a figure indeed suggestive of transsexualism, links 'minor' politics with an ontology of movement" (*Jurisdiction in Deleuze*, 53).

97 Spade, "Resisting Medicine, Re/Modeling Gender."

98 Preciado, "The Pharmaco-pornographic Regime," 271.

99 Preciado, "The Pharmaco-pornographic Regime," 271.

100 Preciado, "The Pharmaco-pornographic Regime," 271.

101 Rai, "Race Racing," 67.

102 For a summation of this approach, see Nigianni and Storr: "Within this framework, difference can only be conceived of as a deviation from one, single model: a hierarchical differentiation starting and descending from the dominant signifier (the white (hu)man Face, the majoritarian, white, hetero, able bodied male) that leads to a prolific production of minoritarian others always in response to the established norms. It thus fails to conceive of difference beyond the level of the signifier, outside the Law: so that 'our' claim for a positive difference that precedes signification and pre-exists constitution is simply unimaginable, unintelligible within a linguistic framework" ("Introduction," 4).

103 For Claire Colebrook, this means a politics that is organized "according to virtual series, all the encounters that are potential or not yet actualised. Once we abandon conditions of recognition we can interrogate a practice according to the potentiality of its encounters. Rather than seeing gay marriage, trans-gendering, or gay parenting as compromised maneuvers in which the queer self repeats and distorts given norms, we need to look at the positivity of each encounter. How do bodies establish relations in each case, and what powers are opened (or closed) to further encounters and modifications?" ("On the Very Possibility of Queer Theory," 21).

104 Saldanha, "Reontologizing Race," 12, 20–21.

105 Rai, "Race Racing," 74.

106 For Rosenberg, see their essay "The Molecularization of Sexuality."

TWO. CRIP NATIONALISM

1 Jünger, *The Glass Bees*, quoted in Deleuze and Guattari, *A Thousand Plateaus*, 426.

2 On the relationship between war and the emergence of services for people with disabilities in the United States, see Switzer, *Disabled Rights*.

3 See, e.g., Lukin, "Disability and Blackness"; Metzl, *The Protest Psychosis*; Metzl and Kirkland, *Against Health*; Million, *Therapeutic Nations*.

4 Jünger, *The Glass Bees*, quoted in Deleuze and Guattari, *A Thousand Plateaus*, 426.

5 Mitchell and Snyder, *The Biopolitics of Disability*.

6 Kafer, *Feminist, Queer, Crip*, 33.

7 See in particular Kafer, *Feminist, Queer, Crip*, chap. 4.

8 Erevelles, *Disability and Difference in Global Contexts*, 130; Chow, *The Protestant Ethnic and the Spirit of Capitalism*.

9 For criticisms of inclusion models of disability, see Lane, "Construction of Deafness"; Davidson, "Universal Design"; Smith, "The Vulnerable Articulate"; Hevey, "The Enfreakment of Photography"; Gibilisco, *Politics, Disability and Social Inclusion*; Knight, "Democratizing Disability"; Minich, "Life on Wheels"; Nguyen, "Genealogies of Disability in Global Governance"; and Poon-McBrayer, "The Evolution from Integration to Inclusion."

10 See Barker and Murray, "Disabling Postcolonialism"; Bell, *Blackness and Disability*; Bell, "Introducing White Disability Studies"; Lukin, "Disability and Blackness."

11 For a very clear example of this co-constitutive relationship between the war on terror and the "war on autism," see McGuire, "'Life Worth Defending.'" McGuire writes: "The historical simultaneity of these two wars is not mere happenstance, nor are the striking resonances in their wartime rhetorics, rationalities, and technologies. . . . The war on autism and the war on terror, as well as their respective oppositional figures of terrorist and warrior, are intimately connected, and even dependent on one another, functioning continuously to define, secure, and surveil the borders of a liberal normativity" (351).

12 Meekosha, "Decolonising Disability," 668. Meekosha continues: "Following Connell . . . I argue that disability studies 'almost never cites non metropolitan thinkers and almost never builds on social theory formulated outside the metropole.' The civil wars and genocide that have swept many postcolonial countries in the twentieth and twenty-first centuries producing mutilation and impairments barely rate a mention in mainstream disability studies literature. Interestingly, this is often the terrain of medical anthropologists. . . . Medical anthropologists have studied the impact of these phenomena at a local level and have therefore paved the way for disability studies scholars" (669).

13 Garland-Thomson, *Staring*, 19; for "ontological contingency," see Turner, *Vulnerability and Human Rights*.

14 Garland-Thomson, *Staring*, 19.

15 Lukes, "The Sovereignty of Subtraction."

16 Erevelles, *Disability and Difference in Global Contexts*.

17 Chow, *The Protestant Ethnic and the Spirit of Capitalism*, 3.

18 Erevelles, "The Color of Violence," 118. See Garland-Thomson, "Disability Studies," for a succinct history of the field and recent developments.

19 Meekosha, "Decolonising Disability," 668.

20 Meekosha, "Decolonising Disability," 671.

21 See Garland-Thomson, *Extraordinary Bodies*; Lane, "Construction of Deafness"; Shakespeare, "The Social Model of Disability"; Zola, "Toward the Necessary Universalizing of a Disability Policy."

22 The first Disability Pride Day in the United States, seen as an occasion to celebrate people with disabilities, was held in Boston in 1990 and again in 1991. New York City followed the example and held the Disability Independence Day March from 1992 to 1996. Chicago picked up the tradition in 2004, inspired by the Boston-based parades of the 1990s, and in 2010, Mountain View, California; Columbia, Missouri; Logan, Utah; and Davis, California, followed suit. Colorado Springs and Philadelphia joined in 2012; and in 2015, New York City and Atlanta held their first parades.

23 Markotic and McRuer, "Leading with Your Head."

24 By noting a privileged class of disabled citizens, I mean to highlight the way the ADA encourages a responsibilization narrative of disability that relies on the individuation of disability and uses the state as the arbiter of the productivity and value of the disabled subject-citizen. Major criticism of the ADA revolves around two things: first, the misuse of a civil rights framework in constructing the ADA and, second, the failure to provide an operational definition of "reasonable accommodation." Both of these problems lead to further privatization of resources to address disability and thus create further class stratification in terms of which individuals and populations can avail themselves of benefits from the ADA or mobilize resources that the ADA does not provide for. So the designation of a privileged class of disabled citizens invokes literal class privilege along with the structural components of race and populations that intensify class stratification. For further elaboration, see Burris and Moss, "Employment Discrimination Provisions of the Americans with Disabilities Act"; Harrison, "Has the Americans with Disabilities Act Made a Difference?"; Leonard, "The Equality Trap"; Maroto and Pettinicchio, "The Limitations of Disability Antidiscrimination Legislation"; and Draper et al., "Workplace Discrimination and the Record of Disability." Another critique of the celebratory approach to the ADA comes from Nirmala Erevelles, who notes that people with cognitive/severe disabilities are not factored in notions of equality, the citizen, and personhood (Erevelles, *Disability and Difference in Global Contexts*, 149).

25 Critiques of the Convention of the Rights of Persons with Disabilities (CRPD) include difficulty in implementation in relation to states' domestic laws, lack of any constant definition of disability, and lack of visibility and knowledge of the CRPD; finally, there are no provisions for collecting data or monitoring the effectiveness of the CRPD. One of the key sites of controversy around the CRPD involves Article 12, which sets out to ensure the right to equal legal capacity. According to Gooding, "concerns include: the historical evolution of the concept of legal capacity . . . the challenges of cognitive disability to moral philosophy; the regulation of personhood in constructions of legal capacity; typologies of support in line with Article 12; supported decision-making in the context of extreme self-harm and suicide, mental health law, and elder law" ("Navigating the 'Flashing Amber Lights' of the Right to Legal Capacity in the United Nations Convention on the Rights of Persons

with Disabilities," 7). For more discussion of the CRPD, see Chan, "Challenges to Realizing the Convention on the Rights of Persons with Disabilities (CRPD) in Australia"; Dhanda, "Legal Capacity in the Disability Rights Convention"; Gooding, "Navigating the 'Flashing Amber Lights' of the Right to Legal Capacity"; Groves, "Should the Senate Ratify the Disabilities Treaty?"; Kinker, "Evaluation of the Prospects for Successful Implementation of the Convention on the Rights of Persons with Disabilities in the Islamic World"; and Mittler, "The UN Convention on the Rights of Persons with Disabilities."

26 In *Biocapital*, Kaushik Sunder Rajan details the neoliberal circuits of political economy that generate incipient forms of materiality as well as change the grammar of "life itself." New forms of currency, biological material and information, simultaneously produce the materialization of information on the one hand, and a decoupling from its material biological source on the other. He describes a constitutive contradiction informing this dialectic between bodily material and information: "Information is detached from its biological material originator to the extent that it does have a separate social life, but the 'knowledge' provided by the information is constantly relating back to the material biological sample. . . . It is knowledge that is always relating back to the biological material that is the source of the information; but it is also knowledge that can only be obtained, in the first place, through extracting information from the biological material" (42).

27 Mitchell and Snyder, *The Biopolitics of Disability*.

28 Sarah Lochlann Jain offers, but does not develop, the proposition that "living in prognosis" moves from the disabled subject to the prognostic subject, from the subject of disability to the subject of prognosis, thus changing the category of disability itself. She argues that "all of us in American risk culture live to some degree in prognosis" ("Living in Prognosis," 79). She suggests that "living in prognosis" might be a more helpful articulation of this simultaneous sense of life and death, whereby prognosis may reflect a "measure of hope." Prognosis time, for Jain, "severs the idea of a time line," puts pressure on the assumption of an expected life span—a barometer of one's modernity—and the privilege one has or does not have to presume what one's life span will be, hence troubling any common view of life phases, generational time, and longevity. When and how do we stop saying things like "He died so young" or "She was too young to die"? Jain's query is instructive in this regard: "If you are going to die at 40, should you be able to get the senior discount at the movie when you're 35? (Is the discount a reward for long life or for proximity to death?) This relation to time makes death central to life in prognosis, death as an active loss—as if there were some right to a certain lifespan—rather than just something that happens to everybody at the end of life" (81).

29 Ford and Airhihenbuwa, "Critical Race Theory, Race Equity, and Public Health."

30 Much of the work on poverty and disability is situated within development discourses and national and international government reports that focus on it as a global problem located in the "Third World." For work on disability and poverty, see Albert, "Is Disability Really on the Development Agenda?"; Singal, "Introduc-

tion"; World Bank, "The World Bank Disability Overview"; Yeo, "Disability, Poverty and the New Development Agenda."

31 Metzl and Kirkland, *Against Health*.

32 In her 2015 piece "Dead, White, and Blue," Barbara Ehrenreich writes, "There has also been a major racial gap in longevity—5.3 years between white and black men and 3.8 years between white and black women—though, hardly noticed, it has been narrowing for the last two decades. Only whites, however, are now dying off in unexpectedly large numbers in middle age, their excess deaths accounted for by suicide, alcoholism, and drug (usually opiate) addiction." According to the Centers for Disease Control and Prevention (CDC), the life expectancy gap between black and white men in the United States is narrowing; between 1999 and 2013, the comparative life expectancy of white men and black men in the United States shrunk from 6.8 years' difference to 4.4. Moreover, the CDC reports that life expectancy at birth on the whole has risen for both populations. See http://www.cdc .gov/nchs/data/databriefs/db218.htm. While the CDC outlines the major causes of death for each group, it does not include a broader systemic analysis of structural impediments of racism. Ehrenreich's piece generated debates around privilege, race and labor, the prison-industrial complex, Black Lives Matter, and the rise of Donald Trump as a presidential candidate. See Schulman and Lui, "Dialogue with Barbara Ehrenreich—Connecting White Privilege and White Death."

33 In David A. Gerber's article "Disabled Veterans, the State, and the Experience of Disability in Western Societies, 1914–1950," he argues, "Indeed in the twentieth century, veterans, and especially disabled veterans, whose numbers greatly increased because of a combination of the lethal violence of modern warfare and the progress of military and civilian medicine in saving lives, became both a project of the modern Western welfare state and pioneers on the frontiers of social welfare policy" (899). Gerber explores the relationship between veterans, the state, and group identity formation. Though it is not explicitly mentioned in this piece, one can infer a relationship between group identity formation for disabled veterans and the occlusion of warfare as a project of biopolitical debilitation. Moreover, the article suggests that disabled veterans' fight for recognition by the state was predicated on disabled subjects making themselves available as a disabled population. This disabled population in need of rescue was thus leveraged in opposition to discourses around independence and self-reliance. Also see O'Brien, *Crippled Justice*.

34 For work on activism leading up to the passage of the ADA, see Shapiro, *No Pity*. A summary of key moments in the disability rights movement since the 1960s, Shapiro's book addresses the key figures in the disability rights movement and their involvement in initiating and organizing activist movements around disability rights in the 1970s, particularly the Independent Living Movement. It also details the campaign to pass the ADA in 1990. See also Davis, *Enabling Acts*, which details the events that led up to the passage of the ADA, covering the history of activist organizing around disability legislature and the political negotiation in DC to push through the ADA. Finally, Sharon N. Barnartt and Richard K. Scotch write in

Disability Protests about the history of protests around disability rights between 1970 and 1999 and examine the causes and ramifications of the protests.

35 The ADA has been a touchstone for other countries in the process of enacting disability rights legislation, as well as in the development of the United Nations Convention on the Rights of Persons with Disabilities. Much of the comparative analysis has focused on the changes necessary to localize tenets of the ADA to the resources and needs of other countries, the extraterritorial applications of the ADA in a transnational economy, the educational and employment opportunities for persons with disabilities, and the ADA in colonial and settler colonial contexts. Most of the literature fits within policy review, human rights frameworks, and development discourse. See the following: Eskay et al. "Disability within the African Culture"; Harris, "Americans with Disabilities Act and Australia's Disability Discrimination Act"; Jandura, "Rural Cherokee Children with Disabilities"; Kanter, "The Americans with Disabilities Act at 25 Years"; Koehler, "Using Disability Law to Protect Persons Living with HIV/AIDS"; Kubo, "Extraterritorial Application of the Americans with Disabilities Act"; Mackey, "Educational Administration in Indian Country"; National Council on Disability, "Finding the Gaps"; Shender, "Claims by Non-citizens under the Americans with Disabilities Act"; Umeasiegbu, Bishop, and Mpofu, "The Conventional and Unconventional about Disability Conventions"; Walker, "Comparing American Disability Laws to the Convention on the Rights of Persons with Disabilities."

36 Stewart and Russell, "Disablement, Prison, and Historical Segregation," 66.

37 The majority of these sources report limited improvement in employment rates for persons with disabilities since the passing of the ADA. See Burkhauser, "Post-ADA"; PR Newswire, "U.S. Census Bureau Facts for Features"; Harrison, "Has the Americans with Disabilities Act Made a Difference?"; Karger and Rose, "Revisiting the Americans with Disabilities Act after Two Decades"; Siperstein, Heyman, and Stokes, "Pathways to Employment."

38 Stewart and Russell, "Disablement, Prison, and Historical Segregation," 65. See also Liat Ben-Moshe and Jean Stewart's tribute piece to Marta Russell titled "Disablement, Prison, and Historical Segregation: 15 Years Later," in which they include these updates:

> In 2013 only 14 percent of working-age Americans with a work-limiting disability were employed, compared with 29 percent in 1990 (Thomson-DeVeaux, 2015).
>
> Given the recent recession and rise in unemployment nationwide, we should perhaps not be surprised by these figures, as marginalized populations are always harder hit by economic downturns. Stewart and Russell explain the ADA's failings by reminding us that unemployment, underemployment and the forging of disability into a defining characteristic of a surplus population (along with race, gender/sexuality, and nationality/citizenship) are necessary for the maintenance of capitalism. Under the capitalist mode of production, disability becomes a social class, an administrative category, an abject population, and a commodity for a whole category of professionals.

> Why have laws failed to move people with disabilities into employment? Because that is not their function. Litigation and rights discourse appeals to the state to remedy social ills of its own creation. (92–93)

39 One argument is that rather than working to implement the ADA, courts and employers have actively worked to restrict and nullify provisions that would enable persons with disabilities to enter the workforce. Most ADA-related lawsuits are ruled in favor of employers over employees. It is easier for persons already in the workforce to acquire accommodations than it is for those who are trying to enter the workforce. Another argument claims that the ADA outlines an "ethic of care" that could potentially "soften" capitalism and liberalism—first, because "reasonable accommodation" focuses on the completion of specific tasks not inherently linked to a particular disability/condition and, second, because ideally the ADA could be a tool for employees to combat the standardization of the workplace to satisfy their needs. This argument, which posits the ADA as a model of resistance, is unconvincing, for two reasons. First, a civil rights–based framework of inclusion in a disability environment is inadequate. Second, the neoliberal focus is on work and responsibility fueled in part to cut social welfare programs. The legislation foregrounds employment in a manner that does little to question what a worker is or does, what work means, who is expected to work, and the ideology of work in general. Finally, the ADA contributes to the juridical mobilization of protected class categories, further minoritizing disabled individuals by "protecting" them not only from the marketplace but also from other "protected class categories." See Burkhauser, "Post-ADA"; Burris, Scott, and Moss, "Employment Discrimination Provisions of the Americans with Disabilities Act"; Karger and Rose, "Revisiting the Americans with Disabilities Act after Two Decades"; McMahon et al., "Workplace Discrimination and the Record of Disability"; O'Brien, "Subversive Act"; Turner, "Americans with Disabilities Act and the Workplace." On the ideology of work, see Weeks, *The Problem with Work*.

40 I have not been able to find any literature, analysis, or activist or organizational materials connecting the ADA to the first Gulf War.

41 Russell and Malhotra, "Capitalism and Disability," 211–12.

42 Marx speaks of the central contradiction of capitalism thus:

> But in its blind unrestrainable passion, its were-wolf hunger for surplus-labour, capital oversteps not only the moral, but even the merely physical maximum bounds of the working-day. It usurps the time for growth, development, and healthy maintenance of the body. It steals the time required for the consumption of fresh air and sunlight. It higgles over a meal-time, incorporating it where possible with the process of production itself, so that food is given to the labourer as to a mere means of production, as coal is supplied to the boiler, grease and oil to the machinery. It reduces the sound sleep needed for the restoration, reparation, refreshment of the bodily powers to just so many hours of torpor as the revival of an organism, absolutely exhausted, renders essential. It is not the normal maintenance of the labour-power which

is to determine the limits of the working-day; it is the greatest possible daily expenditure of labour-power, no matter how diseased, compulsory, and painful it may be, which is to determine the limits of the labourers' period of repose. Capital cares nothing for the length of life of labour-power. All that concerns it is simply and solely the maximum of labour-power, that can be rendered fluent in a working-day. It attains this end by shortening the extent of the labourer's life, as a greedy farmer snatches increased produce from the soil by robbing it of its fertility.

The capitalistic mode of production (essentially the production of surplus-value, the absorption of surplus-labour), produces thus, with the extension of the working-day, not only the deterioration of human labour-power by robbing it of its normal, moral and physical, conditions of development and function. *It produces also the premature exhaustion and death of this labour-power itself. It extends the labourer's time of production during a given period by shortening his actual life-time.* (*Capital*, 1:375–76; emphasis added)

43 Marx, *Capital*, chap. 10, "The Working Day." See also an important dissection of Marx, labor, and productivity in Guéry and Deleule, *The Productive Body*.
44 On this point, see Russell and Malhotra, "Capitalism and Disability."
45 Mitchell and Snyder, "Disability as Multitude," 179. Also in Mitchell and Snyder, *The Biopolitics of Disability*, 204–5.
46 Mitchell and Snyder, *The Biopolitics of Disability*, 205.
47 Mitchell and Snyder, *The Biopolitics of Disability*, 180.
48 Erevelles, "The Color of Violence," 127.
49 Mitchell and Snyder, "Disability as Multitude," 186.
50 Mitchell and Snyder, "Disability as Multitude," 184.
51 Mitchell and Snyder, "Disability as Multitude," 188. "Disabled persons are made, willingly or not, into the legitimate 'non-workers'—those who refuse to participate not in productivity but in the productive net of capitalism that ensnares all in the seemingly infinite practice of consumption as synonymous with life" (188–89).
52 Mitchell and Snyder, "Disability as Multitude," 188–89. Snyder and Mitchell write: "And here we will make our claim: within this formulation of resistant 'bodies' Hardt and Negri essentially recognize forms of incapacity as the new galvanizing agent of postmodern resistance . . . 'non-productive bodies' represent those who belong to populations designated as 'unfit' by capitalism. Thus, whereas traditional theories of political economy tend to stop at the borders of the laboring subjects (including potential laborers), the concept of non-productive bodies expansively rearranges the potentially revolutionary subject of leftist theory" ("Disability as Multitude," 186).
53 See Spivak, "Scattered Speculations on the Question of Value," for her prescient critique of Negri and the notion of immaterial labor that ultimately, as Spivak demonstrates, relies on the elision of the intensification of production in the global south.

54 See Spivak, "Can the Subaltern Speak?"; and also Spivak, "Scattered Speculations on the Question of Value."

55 Mitchell and Snyder, "Disability as Multitude," 189.

56 For work linking care work, precarity, and debilitation, see Boris and Parreñas, *Intimate Labors*; Padilla et al., *Love and Globalization*; Kolářová, " 'Grandpa Lives in Paradise Now' "; and McCormack and Salmenniemi, "The Biopolitics of Precarity and the Self."

57 For discussion of disability and care economies, see especially the special issue of *Scholar & Feminist Online* titled "Valuing Domestic Work," guest edited by Gisela Fosado and Janet R. Jakobsen.

58 Rembis, "The New Asylums," 146. Rembis elaborates on the rise of mass incarceration and who was funneled into it as "mad": black men. For a complication of this story about the transfer of populations from asylums to prisons, Liat Ben-Moshe argues that the populations that were deinstitutionalized are not the same as those that have been mass incarcerated ("Are Prisons the New Asylums?," lecture presented at New York University, September 16, 2016).

59 Stewart and Russell, "Disablement, Prison, and Historical Segregation."

60 See Ben-Moshe, Chapman, and Carey, *Disability Incarcerated*, in particular Nirmala Erevelles's essay "Crippin' Jim Crow."

61 See Rembis, "The New Asylums"; see also Jonathan Metzl on blackness and the deinstitutionalization of schizophrenia in *The Protest Psychosis*.

62 For one history of this entwinement, see Schweik, *The Ugly Laws*.

63 See Ben-Moshe, Chapman, and Carey, *Disability Incarcerated*; Davis, *Freedom Is a Constant Struggle*.

64 Erevelles, "Crippin' Jim Crow"; Alexander, *The New Jim Crow*.

65 Erevelles, "Disability as 'Becoming,'" in *Disability and Difference in Global Contexts*.

66 Erevelles, *Disability and Difference in Global Contexts*, 40.

67 For a remarkable study of corporeal distress and debilitation during the Middle Passage, including toxicity, disease, psychological trauma, impairment, sexual violence, and torture, see Mustakeem, *Slavery at Sea*. Like Spillers, Mustakeem does not employ the language of ableism or disability that Erevelles seeks to infuse into Spillers's analysis. I believe, again, that this non-usage bespeaks a biopolitics of debilitation, wherein to call these bodies disabled would be to exceptionalize what was an endemic state by rehearsing a redundancy: in the context of slavery in the Americas, the black body was the disabled body.

68 Ervelles, *Disability and Difference in Global Contexts*, 6.

69 For recent statistics on disabled prisoners, see Ben-Moshe, "Disabling Incarceration."

70 For case studies of U.S. tort law in relation to product design injury, see Jain, *Injury*.

71 For some representative literature on these exploitative extractive economies, see the work of Dorothy Roberts, Alondra Nelson, Kaushik Sunder Rajan, and Nadia Abu El-Haj.

72 Sunder Rajan, *Biocapital*.

73 Connell, "Southern Bodies and Disability," 1376.

74 Sunder Rajan, *Biocapital.*

75 Waldby and Mitchell, *Tissue Economies,* 187.

76 Snyder and Mitchell, "Introduction," 117.

77 Snyder and Mitchell, "Introduction," 125.

78 Sunder Rajan, *Biocapital,* 144.

79 See Lane, *Shyness,* for a recent accounting of this process.

80 Neurologist Anjan Chatterjee coined the term in 2004, intending to link what he thinks is the eventual normalization of neuroenhancers to the normalization of cosmetic surgery. See Talbot, "Brain Gain," 35. "Smart drugs" in fact are easier to obtain and cheaper than cosmetic surgery and are part of a growing "lifestyle improvement market" promoted by ventures like NeuroInsights and concepts such as the "neuro-society" and "enabling" people to use these drugs not only therapeutically but also for "competitive advantage" (36).

81 Connell, "Southern Bodies and Disability," 1375–76.

82 Mitchell and Snyder, "Re-engaging the Body," 368.

83 On "inspiration porn," see Hamilton, "Working Out Some Issues"; on "rehabilitated futurism," see McRuer and Mollow, *Sex and Disability.*

84 Ralph, "'Flirt[ing] with Death' but 'Still Alive.'"

85 Smith, "Queer Theory and Native Studies"; Morgensen, *Spaces between Us.*

86 Afro-pessimists who have argued that blackness remains ontologically incongruent with emphases on futurity, or that ontology itself is built on the exclusion of blackness, include Wilderson, "Biko and the Problematic of Presence"; Wilderson, *Red, White, and Black*; Sexton, "Unbearable Blackness"; Sexton, "Ante-Anti-Blackness."

87 See Kafer's discussion of Edelman and Halberstam in *Feminist, Queer, Crip.*

88 Gilmore, *Golden Gulag.*

89 Gilmore, *Golden Gulag,* 247.

90 Ford and Airhihenbuwa, "Critical Race Theory, Race Equity, and Public Health."

91 Klein, *The Shock Doctrine.*

92 Klein, *The Shock Doctrine.*

93 McRuer, roundtable discussion.

94 Meekosha, "Decolonizing Disability," 677.

95 Meekosha, "Decolonizing Disability," 677.

96 Jaffee, "Disrupting Global Disability Frameworks," 118.

97 In regard to slow death and forms of durational death, the insights of postcolonial, transnational, critical race studies, and area studies scholars provide pivotal interventions into the field of disability studies. Julie Livingston's research suggests a relation to the necropolitics of debility that foregrounds colonial and postcolonial violence, labor migrations, economic exploitation, and the interventions of Western biomedicine, such that impaired miners are termed "lucky," in local discourses, because of access to "the most clear cut system for processing newly impaired persons and providing them with tools [wheelchairs, leg braces, and prosthetic limbs] for managing their newly uneven and often arbitrary bodily states" ("Insights from an African History of Disability," 111). Livingston's work prompts an investigation

into a disarticulation of "disability" from "disabled subjects" by asking, what does it mean to have a disability but not identify as disabled?

98 Breckenridge and Vogler, "The Critical Limits of Embodiment," 355.

99 Dawson, *Extinction*, 112.

100 Chen, *Animacies*, 218. Unlike environmental justice frames where toxicity is distinctly tied to geographies of race- and class-bound populations and are in some sense locatable, though the travels of toxicity may not be, MCS does not discriminate through environment and in a sense changes what we mean when we invoke the term: it is not something we can leave or distance ourselves from (if we actually have the means to do so) should it prove uninhabitable. Stacy Alaimo explains, "Most environmental justice struggles must demonstrate that particular places have exposed particular people to particular toxins. For those with MCS, however, nearly every human environment, even domestic space, is harmful" (*Bodily Natures*, 118).

101 Chen writes: "We can, in a sense, claim toxicity as already 'here,' already a truth of nearly every body, and also as a biopolitically interested distribution (the deferral of toxic work to deprivileged or already 'toxic subjects'). Such a distribution, in its failures to effectively segregate, leaks outside of its bounds to 'return,' and it might allow a queer theoretical move that readily embraces, rather than refuses in advance, heretofore unknown reflexes of raciality, gender, sexuality, (dis-)ability. In assuming both individual and collective vulnerability, it suggests an ulterior ethical stance. . . . It has the possibility to intervene into the binary between the segregated fields of 'life' and 'death,' vitality and morbidity. Toxicity straddles boundaries of 'life' and 'nonlife' . . . in ways that introduce a certain complexity to the presumption of integrity of either lively or deathly subjects" (*Animacies*, 218).

102 Chen, *Animacies*, 195–97.

103 On the higher rates of post-traumatic stress disorder and suicide, see especially Wool, *After War*.

104 Crawford, "War-Related Death, Injury, and Displacement in Afghanistan and Pakistan," 6.

105 Fineman, "10-Year War Disfigures a Nation and Its People." See also *Al Arabiya News*, "Scattered Landmines Turn Afghans into Amputees"; Gardner, "Afghan War Amputees Turn Prosthesis Pros"; International Committee of the Red Cross, "Afghanistan: Facts and Figures for 2014"; United Nations Assistance Mission in Afghanistan and United Nations Office of the High Commissioner for Human Rights, "Afghanistan: Annual Report 2014 Protection of Civilians in Armed Conflict"; Walsh and Walsh, "Rehabilitation of Landmine Victims."

106 Crawford, "War-Related Death, Injury, and Displacement in Afghanistan and Pakistan," 1.

107 Trani and Bakhshi, "Understanding the Challenge Ahead," 7.

108 Nordland, "Maimed Defending Afghanistan, Then Neglected."

109 Walsh, quoted in Erevelles, *Disability and Difference in Global Contexts*, 20.

110 Dewachi, "The Toxicity of Everyday Survival in Iraq."

111 Cockburn, "Toxic Legacy of US Assault in Fallujah Worse than Hiroshima."

112 Dewachi, "The Toxicity of Everyday Survival in Iraq."
113 Dewachi, "Blurred Lines."
114 Dewachi, "Blurred Lines."
115 Dewachi, "Blurred Lines."
116 See Ackerman, "Doctors Without Borders Airstrikes"; Mirkinson, "The American Atrocities We Refuse to See"; Gottesdiener, "What's the Real Story Behind the American Attack on Doctors Without Borders?"; Goldstein and Schmitt, "Human Error Cited in U.S. Strike on Kunduz Hospital."
117 Erevelles, "The Color of Violence," 131.
118 Dewachi, "Blurred Lines."

THREE. DISABLED DIASPORA, REHABILITATING STATE

1 See Size Doesn't Matter, "Videos."
2 "Pinkwashing!" has become a rallying cry to mobilize queer activists globally to stand in solidarity with Palestine by resisting the so-called co-optation of LGBTQ identity by the state of Israel. As its shorthand use proliferates in anti-occupation organizing forums internationally, pinkwashing must be situated within the wider homonationalizing geopolitical context. While it is crucial to challenge the Israeli state, it must be done in a manner that acknowledges the assemblage of homonationalism goes beyond the explicit activities of any one nation-state, even Israel. I have been unconvinced that pinkwashing is a practice singular to the Israeli state, though the specific manifestations of this practice on the part of the Israeli state are singular and noteworthy. Building on theoretical points first articulated in my book *Terrorist Assemblages*, I contend that pinkwashing appears to be an effective strategy not necessarily because of any exceptional activities on the part of the Israeli state but because of the history of settler colonial violence, the international LGBT tourism industry, the gay and lesbian human rights industry, and, finally, the role of the United States.
3 Maikey, "Sexual Liberation and Decolonization in Occupied Palestine."
4 Most nations that aspire to forms of Western or European modernity now have gay and lesbian tourism marketing campaigns. In that sense, Israel is doing what other states do and what is solicited by the gay and lesbian tourism industry—promoting itself. The effects of this promotion are deeply detrimental in the case of the occupation. But we might want to pose questions about the specifics of the Brand Israel campaign, which has been located as the wellspring of Israel's pinkwashing. In what ways does the Brand Israel campaign differ from a conventional state-sponsored advertising campaign targeting gay and lesbian tourists? See Sarah Schulman's detailing of Brand Israel at prettyqueer.com.
5 This is an important tactic within the context of a gay and lesbian human rights industry that proliferates Euro-American constructs of identity (not to mention the assumption of a universal attachment to sexual identity itself), that privilege identity politics, "coming out," public visibility, legislative measures as the dominant barometers of social progress, and a flat invocation of "homophobia" as an

automatic unifying experiential frame. Palestinian queer organizers assert that it is irrelevant whether Palestinian society is homophobic or not, and that the question of homophobia within Palestinian society has nothing to do with the fact that the occupation must end. For the political platform of the Palestinian Queers for BDS and Al-Qaws for Sexual and Gender Diversity in Palestinian Society queer organizing is anti-occupation organizing; likewise, anti-occupation work is queer organizing. Palestinian Queers for BDS is not a liberal project that is demanding acceptance, tolerance, or inclusion within a "nationalist" movement. Rather, through foregrounding the occupation as its primary site of struggle, Palestinian Queers for BDS is slowly, strategically, and carefully insisting upon and creating systemic and thorough changes in the terms of Palestinian society itself. Al-Qaws claims that its primary work is about ending the occupation, not about reifying a homosexual identity that mirrors an "Israeli" or "Western" self-serving form of sexual freedom.

6 See Puar, "Citation and Censorship."

7 See Bhandar, "Acts and Omissions," on whether the use of the concept/frame of "settler colonialism" imports the language of indigeneity into a context where it might not resonate/operate.

8 Pinkwashing has become an important flash point for queer organizing in Europe and North America, but we should also ask why, and why now? Are the linkages between the United States and Israel, and in particular their roles in the naturalization of settler colonialism, always explicit? Is there a concerted effort to link the violence of the U.S. war on terror to the U.S. support of Israel?

9 Chatterjee, The Nation and Its Fragments.

10 Spivak, "Can the Subaltern Speak?" This particular triangulation has thus set the stage for an enduring drama between feminists protesting colonial and neocolonial regimes, and nationalists, who discount the presence and politics of these feminists in their own quests for decolonization.

11 This trajectory from the woman question to the homosexual question has multiple prongs, subject to contextualization in various divergent locations. The supplementing of homosexuality to women is the result of the merging of the postcolonial hangover (where, vis-à-vis Jacqui Alexander's work, the postcolonial state shores up its respectability and legitimacy to prove its right to sovereignty to the colonial father) with the folding in or acknowledging of homosexual subjects into legal and consumer legitimacy via neoliberal economies. Some homosexuals, once on the side of death (AIDS), are now on the side of life, or productive for nation building.

12 See Bauer, Die Judenfrage; "Die Fähigkeit der heutigen Juden und Christen, frei zu warden"; Marx, "On the Jewish Question."

13 For background on debates about gender segregation in ultra-Orthodox communities in Israel, see Triger, "The Self-Defeating Nature of 'Modesty'-Based Gender Segregation," which describes current popular and legal debates about private gender-segregated bus lines that operate for ultra-Orthodox communities. See also Prince-Gibson, "Ultra-Orthodox Request Gender-Segregated University Study."

14   See Hartman, "Tel Aviv Named 'World's Best Gay City' for 2011."

15   See full discussion in Shalhoub-Kevorkian, *Security Theology, Surveillance and the Politics of Fear*, 50–56. The author details the history of the legislation, including various amendments and provisions and the manner in which the law is used to produce Palestinians married to Israeli citizens as terrorists and national threats, and how the discourse of unification is perverted into fears of actualizing Palestinian right of return.

16   In "'We Are All Israelis,'" Alex Lubin writes: "Hence, in 2002, Israel amended its citizenship law to prevent 'family unification' among married Israeli and non-Israeli Palestinians when it passed the Citizenship and Entry into Israel Law. The amendment denied Israeli citizenship through marriage only for Palestinians. In defending and upholding the amendment in 2006, Israeli judge Michael Chechin argued that the amendment merely reproduced a form of security practiced by Western governments: 'The Palestinian Authority is an enemy government, a government that wants to destroy the state and is not prepared to recognize Israel. . . . Why should we take chances during wartime? Did England and America take chances with Germans seeking their destruction during the Second World War? No one is preventing them from building a family but they should live in Jenin instead of in [the Israeli Arab city of] Umm al-Fahm' (Donald Macintyre, "'Racist' Marriage Law Upheld by Israel," *Independent*, May 15, 2006). Those opposed to the amendment drew a different kind of comparison, claiming that the antifamily law mirrors U.S. anti-miscegenation laws in order to preclude increasing numbers of Palestinian citizens in Israel. The Israeli amendment to its citizenship law relies on a comparative imaginary that links U.S. and Israeli forms of colonial rule" (685).

17   Yityish Aynam, an Ethiopian-born Israeli model and former IDF lieutenant, was the first black woman to be crowned Miss Israel in 2013. In the face of protests against racism toward black Jews in Israel, she has been leveraged as proof that Israel does not have a race problem and has herself repeated the Israeli right-wing argument that questions the validity of allowing African migrants to enter or stay in Israel due to their supposed violent nature. See *The Stream*, "Black and Jewish in Israel"; Gray, "First Black Miss Israel."

18   See Wessler, "The Israel Lobby Finds a New Face." To counteract the rhetoric from Palestinian solidarity activists that Israel is a racist state that practices apartheid, the American Israel Public Affairs Committee (AIPAC), the largest pro-Israel lobby in the United States, maintains a presence on and recruits students from historically black campuses. AIPAC lures students by offering career-building opportunities to visit Capitol Hill, meet political figures of the highest level such as President Obama and Prime Minister Netanyahu, and participate in lobbying and campaigning on behalf of AIPAC's agenda. AIPAC educates these students in a Zionist version of Middle Eastern politics and deploys them to argue that it is a mischaracterization and offensive to black Americans to use terms like "racist" or "apartheid" to describe Israel. See also "'Blackwashing' and the Israeli Lobby," a roundtable hosted by *Al Jazeera*'s *The Stream*. That AIPAC places an emphasis on

leveraging African American support of Israel is especially clear in an April 2012 story published in AIPAC's biweekly *Near East Report*, "Student Leaders across America Oppose Nuclear Iran," which states that 122 universities and colleges across the United States had signed a statement that "opposes the development of an Iranian nuclear weapons capability" and supports a "strong U.S.-Israel alliance and Israel's right to defend itself." The story specifies that "17 Historically Black Colleges and Universities (HBCUS) are represented, including Morehouse College in Georgia, Grambling State University in Louisiana, and Oakwood University in Alabama."

19   Ben-eliezer, "Becoming a Black Jew." Despite being allowed to settle in Israel as many other immigrant Jews have done, Ethiopian Jews and their descendants continue to face antiblack racism in Israel. For a history of Ethiopian Jewish migration to Israel and subsequent racial discrimination, see Chehata, "Israel: Promised Land for Jews . . . as Long as They're Not Black?," 67–77. Israeli officials have also admitted to forcibly or nonconsensually sterilizing Ethiopian Jewish women during and after the settlement process. Some of these women have testified that they were not allowed inside the country without being administered a long-lasting sterilization shot. See Gordts, "Ethiopian Women Claim Israel Forced Them to Accept Birth Control Shots." Israel also employs a policy of ethnic cleansing through deportation and detainment on African migrants. As the *New Yorker* reported in January 2014 in Margalit, "Israel's African Asylum Seekers Go on Strike," undocumented African migrants protested across Tel Aviv new laws that further criminalized their presence and allowed for the indefinite detainment of migrant workers, who are primarily from Sudan and Eritrea, in an open-air prison in the Negev Desert. The Israeli government currently gives undocumented migrants whom they seize a choice: leave Israel or face indefinite detainment.

20   In a speech to AIPAC in 2010, Prime Minister Netanyahu compared the size of Israel to that of the state of New Jersey in an effort to impress on his audience the "security predicament" Israel finds itself in, describing Israel as a tiny nation besieged on all sides by terrorist groups that fire "6,000 rockets into that small state" and "amass another 60,000 more missiles to fire at you" (*Haaretz* Service, "Prime Minister Benjamin Netanyahu's Speech to AIPAC Conference").

21   The challenge, then, is to not allow the liberal or establishment gays in Euro-America (who are the primary target of pinkwashing) to redirect the script of anti-pinkwashing activism away from this radical approach. Failing this, as Maya Mikdashi has so brilliantly articulated in "Gay Rights as Human Rights," the rewriting of a radical Palestinian queer politics by a liberal Euro-American queer politics would indeed be a further entrenchment of homonationalism. Organizing against pinkwashing through a "queer international" platform can potentially unwittingly produce an affirmation of the terms within which the discourse of pinkwashing articulates its claims, namely, that queer identity emboldened through rights is the predominant manner through which sexual subjectivities should be lived. While one may agree with Joseph Massad's damning critique of the "gay international" in *Desiring Arabs*, it is also important to ask exactly how the "queer international"

proposed by Sarah Schulman, in *Israel/Palestine and the Queer International*, is an alternative or antidote to the gay international. Is it the case that simply by virtue of being articulated through "queer" rather than "gay," and through a global solidarity movement, the pitfalls of the gay international are really avoided? How is such a positioning of queer one that purports to be transgressive, morally and politically untainted, and outside of power? That is to say, "queer solidarity" cannot be contingent on "them" producing a model of sexuality that is acceptable to "us."

22 Macaulay, "On the Civil Disabilities of the Jews."

23 Nordau, *Degeneration*, 10–11.

24 Sufian and LeVine, *Reapproaching Borders*.

25 Ostrander and Shevil, "The Social Value of Death versus Disability in Israel." See the work of Mary Douglas, who has produced extensive literature on the theological rendering of the rehabilitated Jewish body: "The threatened boundaries of their body politic would be well mirrored in their care for the integrity, unity, and purity of the physical body" (*Purity and Danger*, 164). Thus, as the national body's borders become threatened, there is an increased scrutiny of the physical body. The symbolic pairing of the physical body of the Jews with the national body of Israel is avowed by Max Nordau, who was a cofounder of the World Zionist Organization. See Weiss, *The Chosen Body*; Yosef, *Beyond Flesh*; Vital, *The Origins of Zionism*.

26 Weiss, *The Chosen Body*, 91.

27 Quotation from Weiss, *The Chosen Body*, 15.

28 Boyarin, *Unheroic Conduct*, 34.

29 Seikaly and Ajl, "Of Europe," 128. Thanks to Paul Amar for bringing to my attention the differences between homosocial colonial administration and what could be seen as Israel's current homonational colonial administration.

30 In their chapter, "Of Europe: Zionism and the Jewish Other," in *Europe after Derrida*, Sherene Seikaly and Max Ajl write: "Zionists, like many Europeans, saw Jewish males as effeminate, and so subjected them to a misogynistic contempt. The need to reinstate the Jewish man as a figure of courage, honor, and masculinity was one of the driving forces behind Herzl's early proposal for Jewish assimilation. . . . [One] early proposal was dueling matches, which Herzl hoped would both bring about and evidence a transformed Jewish masculinity. . . . Even as Herzl moved away from his earlier commitment to assimilation, he retained European understandings of a deformed Jewish masculinity. . . . The vision of the 'new Hebrew man' internalized and nourished notions of a stained and corrupt Jew who required geographic displacement to become truly rehabilitated" (126).

31 Abu El-Haj, *The Genealogical Science*, 80.

32 In "Of Europe: Zionism and the Jewish Other," Seikaly and Ajl write: "Zionism promised Jews, who lived in Europe, full and emancipated membership in the category of the Western, the European, and the enlightened. But that membership was to be conditional. To become fully European, the Jew had to leave Europe. . . . Becoming fully European required a hierarchical understanding of humanity—

the 'clash' between the enlightened and benighted. The Zionist thus 'othered' and 'inferiorised' the other to become European, just as the European had done to him. Zionism did not merely constitute Jews as being outside Europe. In accepting that Europe, geographically, could only hold certain kinds of political communities, it constituted Europe. And in embracing the task of molding a territorially displaced European society, dependent on the continual displacement of native Palestinians, it has continued constituting that Europe, culturally and politically" (131). They continue: "Zionism, its proponents argued, would propel Jews' entry into history by becoming almost but never quite fully European. But by geographically displacing the Jewish Question instead of resolving it politically, Zionism ended up keeping that question alive. It maintained 'Jews' as a distinct entity from Europeans, perhaps provisionally members of the metropolitan race but also with an air of difference, as liminal to modernity. . . . Zionism's reclamation of Jewish pride and honor was premised on understanding the Jewish past just as Europeans did, deformed and Oriental. In this discourse, becoming European depended on leaving Europe and the history of penury, supposed effeminacy, intellectualism, and all else that was linked with exile. The historical erasure was nearly total" (128).

33 Shohat, "Rupture and Return," 50. See also pages 65–66 for a discussion of the kidnapping of babies from newly migrated Yemeni Jews, who were seen as inferior because they were from Arab and Muslim countries and were considered "careless breeders." The parents of these babies were told they had died when in actuality they were adopted by Ashkenazi Jews.

34 Shohat, "Rupture and Return," 62.

35 Seikaly and Ajl, "Of Europe."

36 See Sherwood and Kalman, "Stephen Hawking Joins Academic Boycott of Israel."

37 Siskind, "Stephen Hawking, BDS, and Why Geniuses Can Be Dumb."

38 Sinai, "The Economic Situation of People with Disabilities in Israel."

39 Here I want to flag the work of Liat Ben-Moshe, who is a cofounder of the Israeli Disability Studies Network.

40 Ramon-Greenspan, "Disability Politics in Israel."

41 Mor, "Between Charity, Welfare, and Warfare."

42 Ben-Moshe, "Movements at War?," 1.

43 Ben-Moshe, "Movements at War?," 4.

44 Swirski, "The Price of Occupation."

45 Ben-Moshe, "Movements at War?," 11.

46 Thanks to Aeyal Gross for bringing this to my attention.

47 See Tzfadia, "Abusing Multiculturalism," 1115–30.

48 Mor, "Between Charity, Welfare, and Warfare," 65. For further details on these benefits and the differences between IDF and non-IDF disabled persons, see also Ivry, *Embodying Culture*, 265–66n3.

49 Shamah, "Advanced Prosthetic Knees Will Turn Disabled IDF Vets into 'Bionic Men'": "The state-of-the-art knees are manufactured by Germany's Otto Block, and imported to Israel by Chemitec. 'It's not a prosthetic, but a bionic knee,' said

Chemitec CEO Yossi Levin. 'We are very proud to be bringing this technology to Israel, providing IDF soldiers injured in the line of duty with the opportunity to live normal lives once again.'" See also Leichman, "The Men Who Make New Limbs." Worth viewing as well is a video of the Acrobat system developed by the Israeli firm Softwheel: Reuters, "Israeli Company Invents the Wheel." Softwheel product specialist Dror Cohen, an Israeli who uses a wheelchair, says, "Where I want to go I just go."

50 Ben-Moshe, "Movements at War?," 5–7.

51 Ben-Moshe, "Movements at War?," 6–7, explains the history of the 1949 Invalids' Law (Benefits and Rehabilitation), which provided and provides numerous services not available to nonveteran disabled people (see Gal and Bar, "The Needed and the Needy"). These benefits are better than those distributed by the Social Security Administration.

52 Ben-Moshe, "Movements at War?," 14. See also a study arguing that deaths and debilitation due to war are more valued in terms of journalistic coverage: Ostrander and Shevil, "The Social Value of Death versus Disability in Israel."

53 See Massad, "Jewish Suffering, Palestinian Suffering," on resisting the effacement of Palestinian suffering through invocations of Holocaust suffering. Massad writes that invocations of the Holocaust always already contain within them the erasure of Israeli crimes against Palestinians. See also Finkelstein, "The Holocaust Industry," on the exploitation of the Holocaust as a political tool in the service of Israel and its supporters and its development as a rallying point after the 1967 war.

54 There is much discussion of the way in which identity politics function or have functioned in the Israeli state management of difference within Israeli and queer cinema studies. See, e.g., Talmon, "Discursive Identities in the (R)evolution of the New Israeli Queer Cinema." Additionally, see Yiftachel's book *Ethnocracy: Land and Identity Politics in Israel/Palestine*; and Avishai's article in the *New Yorker*, "Is Liberal Zionism Impossible?"

55 See Hanieh, "The Oslo Illusion," and Lubin, "Peace Dividends," on Oslo and neoliberalism.

56 For an early assessment of disability studies in Israel, see the introduction to "The State of Disability in Israel/Palestine," a special issue of *Disability Studies Quarterly* edited by Liat Ben-Moshe and Sumi Colligan.

57 Jaffee, "Disrupting Global Disability Frameworks," 5.

58 Langan, "Mobility Disability," 459.

59 Jamjoum, "The Effects of Israeli Violations during the Second Uprising 'Intifada' on Palestinian Health Conditions," 53–72.

60 See Salem, "Stigma and the Origin of Disability," unpublished master's thesis, cited in Epstein, "Esau's Mission, or Trauma as Propaganda."

61 Giacaman, in "A Community of Citizens," writes: "In Palestine, the rise of the disability movement emanated out of the inception and development of a relatively strong social action movement which took root in the Israeli Occupied West Bank and Gaza Strip in the late 1970s and 1980s focusing on: women's rights, the rights to health and other services—combined with the imperative of the national ques-

tion and resistance to military rule. This disability movement was propelled to the forefront of national politics because of the specific circumstances of the Uprising period of the late 1980s and early 1990s, where thousands of young people were either killed or permanently injured during fighting with Israel. Written less than 2 years after the beginning of the Uprising, a study found that at least 4000 persons had been injured during this period. In one year alone, 2600 children were injured by army or settler gun fire; 11000 were beaten to the degree of requiring medical treatment, and 4000 were injured by rubber bullets in the West Bank" (640). Giacaman et al., *Towards the Formulation of a Rehabilitation Policy*. See also Nassar and Heacock, *Intifada*: "This is precisely the realization that prompted the Palestinian disability movement—led by the Union of Disabled People, CBR workers and Support Team, community volunteers, and upheld by the local democratic movement—to work intensively on the development of a draft disability law that is rights based during the past few years. Vigorous lobbying, defended by a holistic, strong and effective CBR programme and a strategy with citizen's rights as a fundamental principle, eventually led to the promulgation of this Law in the latter part of 1999 by the Palestinian Legislative Council" (643).

62 For some of the many reported instances of the IDF targeting Palestinians with disabilities, see Al Qadi, "Disabled Palestinians Struggling for Their Rights." See also Hardigan, "Palestinians with Disabilities Are Not Immune from Israeli Violence"; *Al Jazeera*, "Israel Bomb Hits Disabled Centre in Gaza"; Henderson, "Israel Air Strike 'Hits Charitable Association for Disabled' in Gaza."

63 Giacaman, "A Community of Citizens," 643.

64 Abu Nahleh, "Gender and Disabilities." "According to a study conducted by the Institute of Community Health at Birzeit University in the early nineties, fewer than 10 percent of people with disability in Palestine had access to rehabilitation services either due to the unavailability or prohibitive cost of those services or out of negligence and ignorance as a result of the existing social stigma." For stories of individuals, see also McIntyre, "From Isolation to Disability Union Leadership"; McIntyre, "Interview."

65 The Chairman of the Executive Committee of the Palestine Liberation Organization and the President of the Palestinian National Authority, *Palestinian Disability Law*.

66 Abu Nahleh, "Gender and Disabilities": "The recent census has revealed some striking figures amongst the population of the disabled according to the Palestinian Central Bureau of Statistics (PCBS). The disability rate as appears in 2007 is 5.3 percent of the total population based on the classification of disability that has been agreed upon by the technical committee of the census, whereas the PCBS revealed that the percentage of disability in the census conducted for families in 2006 was around 2.7 percent in the Palestinian territories. This discrepancy is probably due to the different classification system used by PCBS for disability in the two censuses. The census of 2007 shows that less than 20 percent of working-age disabled (according to ILO criteria) are employed, whereas almost 80 percent of them have no jobs; 55 percent have had no education whatsoever; and more than

70 percent of the disabled have had access to rehabilitation and other types of services."

67 Jarar, "Disability in Palestine."

68 See "On 19th International Day of Disabled Persons, Conditions of Palestinian Disabled Persons Continue to Deteriorate" on the *Occupied Palestine* blog. "Internally, disabled persons have continued to suffer from severe deterioration in the level of enjoyment of their rights in view of the ongoing political division, the existence of two Palestinian governments in the Gaza Strip and the West Bank, and non-application—for more than 11 years—of the provisions of the Rights of Disabled Palestinians' Law No. 4 of 1999 which ascribes them health, educational, rehabilitation, employment, recreational, sports and social rights. The irregular payment of the aid provided by the Ministry of Social Affairs to disabled persons has resulted in the deterioration of their economic and social conditions. They and their families are suffering poverty and lack of rehabilitation services, including the provision of necessary equipment. Disabled persons are still waiting for the implementation of the Rights of Disabled Palestinians Law that includes the issuance of a 'Disabled' card entitling the disabled to a variety of services."

69 For a survey of disability in the West Bank, types, rates of occurrence, problems faced by people with disabilities, and available services as of 2006, see Hamdan and Al-Akhrass, *A Survey of People with Special Needs at 27 Palestinian Villages in Tulkarm and Qalqilia Districts*; Palestinian Central Bureau of Statistics and Ministry of Social Affairs, press conference report, Disability Survey 2011; Nordic Consulting Group, Feb 2012. *Mainstreaming Disability in the New Development Paradigm*. For a gendered analysis, see Abu Nahleh, "Gender and Disabilities."

70 For a full deconstruction of this trifecta, see Birenbaum-Carmeli and Carmeli, "Introduction: Reproductive Technologies among Jewish Israelis," 1–50 (quote from p. 6). In this introduction to their edited collection, they note different matriarchal traditions favoring the egg, the womb, or the mother as defining Jewish lineage; the state history of pronatalist measures and "mother-friendly taxation"; an examination of (dropping) fertility rates across different Israeli populations, challenging a monolithic pronatalist assessment; and antinatalist attitudes toward Mizrahi Jews.

71 Ivry, "Ultrasonic Challenges to Pro-natalism," 197; for further discussion, see Ivry, *Embodying Culture*, 37.

72 Kahn, *Reproducing Jews*, 3–4.

73 For discussion of these tactics, see Kanaaneh, *Birthing the Nation*.

74 Ivry, *Embodying Culture*, 37.

75 Ivry, *Embodying Culture*, 271–72n6.

76 Waldman, "Cultural Priorities Revealed": "Concerns that intermarriage and assimilation are diluting Jewish identity also figure into supportive attitudes toward Jewish reproduction. A 1990 survey sponsored by the United Jewish Communities and the Jewish Federation system reported that over half of all 'born Jews' were married to non-Jews" (72).

77 For early feminist analysis of the demographic threat, see Yuval-Davis, "National Reproduction and 'the Demographic Race' in Israel," 92–109. Michal Rachel Nahman's study of IVF and egg donations, *Extractions: An Ethnography of Reproductive Tourism*, is an important exception to the Zionist-inflected scholarship. Nahman writes that IVF practices in Israel cannot be "examined outside the history and contemporary discursive practices of state Zionism" and connects the first Israeli egg donation in 1984 to the beginning of the first intifada three years later (*Extractions*, 17). Specifically attending to the reproduction of race and racism through IVF, and the privileging of Ashkenazi Jewishness as the most legitimate lineage of Israeli citizenship, she discusses the Egg Donation Law of 2010, which bans cross-religious donation, arguing that the genetic/religious/racial makeup of egg donations have become increasingly important to the Israeli state. There is a particularly interesting discussion about whether Israeli Jewish women would accept an Arab or Palestinian egg. This is not, however, exceptional to the Israeli state, as egg donation markets reproduce racial stratification in many nation-states. Nahman's focus on ethnicity rather than religion allows for a de-exceptionalizing of racial reinscription through assisted reproductive technologies. Nahman also gathers reportage from B'Tselem, the Israeli Information Center for Human Rights in the Occupied Territories, Jerusalem, of IDF shootings of pregnant Palestinian women en route to the hospital.

78 Nahman, *Extractions*, 12.

79 The state subsidizes unlimited egg donation within Israel for women aged forty-five through fifty-one until the birth of two children. Nahman, *Extractions*, 13.

80 Susan Martha Kahn, in her formative study *Reproducing Jews*, provides comprehensive ethnographic details on the uses of new reproductive technologies by varying sectors of Israeli society, even those groups that might seem disinclined. Her text is scrupulously attentive to the differences among Sephardic and Ashkenazi groups, as well as Orthodox and secular groups. Although it was published in 2000 and therefore is not current on recent developments, her text is useful for understanding discursive, secular, rabbinical, and state attitudes toward fertility, maternity, paternity, marriage, lineage, uses of technology, and the reproduction of "Jewishness." In this book the history of state subsidization of fertility treatments and the creation and growth of legal apparatuses and religious textual interpretations and practices to integrate technological conception are carefully attended to.

81 The guidelines are for female partners of deceased male partners who had indicated they wanted offspring after their death; in other words, "presumed consent" must be discernible. For discussion of these guidelines, see Ravitsky, "Posthumous Reproduction Guidelines in Israel," 6–7.

82 Birenbaum-Carmeli and Carmeli, "Reproductive Technologies among Jewish Israelis," 19. See also Siegel-Itzkovich, "Israel Allows Removal of Sperm from Dead Men at Wives' Request," 1187; Landau, "Posthumous Sperm Retrieval for the Purpose of Later Insemination or IVF in Israel," 1952–56; Hasson, "For the First Time."

83 *New Family*, "Creating New Life from the Dead by Biological Will™."

84 Irit Rosenblum, "Respect the Dead by Creating New Life."

85 For a comparative look at posthumous reproduction laws around the world, see Rosenblum, "The Biological Will," 89–95. On posthumous reproduction in the United States, see Kindregan, "Dead Dads," 9–36. On Danish and Australian cases, see Kroløkke and Adrian, "Sperm on Ice."

86 Landau, "Posthumous Sperm Retrieval for the Purpose of Later Insemination or IVF in Israel."

87 Goldberg, "Made in Heaven."

88 Efrati, "Israeli Court Decides Dead Man's Sperm Can Be Used after All"; see also Abramov, "Woman Gives Birth Using Dead Man's Frozen Sperm"; *Haaretz* Service, "Court: Israeli Woman Can Use Deceased Man's Sperm to Get Pregnant."

89 Kahn, *Reproducing Jews*, 1.

90 Waldman, "Cultural Priorities Revealed," 69.

91 Levush, *Israel: Reproduction and Abortion*. According to a 1977 law, women seeking abortions in Israel must obtain approval from a Committee for Interruption of Pregnancy (CIP), a number of which operate in public and private hospitals across the country. The committee must consist of three members—a social worker, an obstetrician and gynecologist, and another physician who specializes in obstetrics and gynecology, internal medicine, family medicine, public health, or psychiatry. At least one committee member must be a woman. The CIP may grant permission for an abortion if the person is under seventeen or over forty years of age; if the child will be born with a mental or physical disability; if the pregnancy is a result of rape or incest or is out of wedlock; or if the pregnant woman's life or health is endangered.

92 In her comparative analysis, Ivry complicates the presumption of Israeli state pronatalism considerably. She notes that the detection rates of fetal anomalies and the rate of abortion may appear high because screening is done until the end of term. She thus asks, "Why would a state so burdened with security expenses provide so many prenatal tests? Why would a state so preoccupied with birthrates and so threatened demographically be (relatively) liberal about abortions?" (*Embodying Culture*, 40–41).

93 See Kanaaneh, *Birthing the Nation*, on the use of abortions for Palestinian women; see Amir and Benjamin, "Sexuality and the Female National Subject," for discussion of abortions and Mizrahi women.

94 Sarah Franklin, personal communication, May 2014; Ginsberg and Rapp, "Enabling Disability," 538.

95 Ivry, *Embodying Culture*, 39, 250. Most sources, including Ivry, cite one article on this topic, Aviad Raz's "'Important to Test, Important to Support.'" In this article, Raz argues that support for prenatal diagnosis and eugenic improvement of health came even from representatives of Israeli disability organizations, who advocated prenatal testing while still advocating for the needs of those already born with disabilities. Nitzan Rimon-Zarfary and Aviad Raz further argue that "media reports . . . revealed a similar pro-eugenics approach by stating that the wide

variety of prenatal diagnoses available in Israel enables the reduction of the number of births of children with embroyopathies" ("Abortion Committees as Agents of Eugenics," 218–19). The authors note that the definition of genetic defect is very porous, and 15 to 20 percent of applications for abortion are due to genetic defects of varying severity. Their overall analysis suggests that genetic counselors and abortion committees are proponents of selective abortion, and this is in contrast to disability rights advocacy in the United States and the United Kingdom. They write: "The majority of respondents and all the print media reports subscribed to and supported the eugenic goal of prenatal diagnosis. This study thus complements a growing number of studies which characterize Israel as a pro-eugenic society" (217). They conclude, "Comparative evidence suggests that the Israeli case is exceptional" (217).

96 Liat Ben-Moshe, personal communication, November 2015.

97 Ivry, *Embodying Culture*, 248.

98 Hashiloni-Dolev, *A Life (Un)Worthy of Living*.

99 See Ivry's discussion in *Embodying Culture*, 249–52. Ivry writes: "As one pregnant Israeli woman explained to me when discussing the idea of giving birth to a Down's syndrome baby, 'Why should I invest my energies, and you know how much it takes to raise a little baby into a child. . . . Why should I invest in a child that might not even smile back at me in the end? Why?' The description that the same woman gave of her relationship with her healthy son was one of absolute dedication" (250). Ivry, *Embodying Culture*, 75–76. For an explanation of the "terrorization of pregnancy itself" and the construction of catastrophe in relation to prenatal diagnosis, selective abortion, and disability, see Ivry, "Ultrasonic Challenges to Pro-natalism," 174–201.

100 Meira Weiss argues that Israel is number one in the world in its rate of child rejection due to visible impairments. See *The Chosen Body* and also Weiss's 1998 study "Parents' Rejection of Their Appearance-Impaired Newborns" on "appearance-impaired" children with conditions such as spina bifida, cleft palate, bone malformations, and Down syndrome, which reports that 50.8 percent of children born with a major medical or physical defect were abandoned at the hospital; of these, 68.4 percent were appearance impaired.

101 For discussion, see Nahman, *Extractions*, 15.

102 See also Weiss, *Conditional Love*, in which she explores the ways in which the myth of unconditional love between parents and their children is troubled when children are born with disabilities.

103 Weiss, *The Chosen Body*, 32.

104 Ivry, *Embodying Culture*, 255. Also: "The kind of genetic selectivity found in Israel, I argue, depends heavily on a continuous generation of fear of reproductive catastrophes (as well as doctors' fears of lawsuits), whether through technological illustrations of reproduction gone awry or folk practices to combat the evil eye. The imminence of catastrophe is a multilayered idea in contemporary Israeli society. Fear of a potential catastrophe is an ideal substrate for militarism but cannot be reduced to it" (266).

105 See Shalhoub-Kevorkian, *Security Theology, Surveillance and the Politics of Fear.*

106 See Urquhart, "Chinese Workers in Israel Sign No-Sex Contract"; Shalhoub-Kevorkian, *Security Theology, Surveillance and the Politics of Fear*, 50; Rubenfeld, "The Riddle of Rape-by-Deception and the Myth of Sexual Autonomy."

107 Frenkel, "Vigilantes Patrol for Jewish Women Dating Arab Men."

108 Kraft, "Where Families Are Prized, Help Is Free." In vitro fertilization is provided at no cost to all women under the age of forty-five in Israel, including lesbians and bisexual women, for however long it takes until they have two surviving children to take home. This is relatively unusual. According to the International Federation of Fertility Societies report *IFFS Surveillance 2013*, fourteen of sixty-two countries surveyed, or around 22 percent, allow lesbians to use assisted reproductive technology in some form. Unlike Israel, however, few of these countries cover all or any of the costs of ART for LGBT women. See Ben Porat, "Outrage in Jewish Home as 'Surrogacy Bill' Passes." An amendment to alter surrogacy laws to allow gay couples to have children through surrogate mothers passed its first reading in the Knessett in 2014. However, at the time of writing, surrogacy for gay parents is not available in Israel. See also Twine, *Outsourcing the Womb*, 29–30, for more on surrogacy and the gay Israeli market for reproductive tourism abroad.

109 The courts have also recognized children born abroad via surrogacy (since 2008); this method of reproduction is presently available in the country only for heterosexual couples, a situation that the Israeli Ministry of Social Affairs is committed to change. Rozenblum quoted in Hamou, "Israel, a Paradise for Gay Families."

110 Kahn, *Reproducing Jews*, 54–55.

111 Sommer, "Offended Gay Israelis Blast Apologetic Education Minister."

112 Krieger, "Forget Marriage Equality."

113 Ghert-Zand, "If Daddy Says No, Ask Abba."

114 Puar, "The Center Cannot Hold."

115 Schulman, *Israel/Palestine and the Queer International.*

116 Mbembe, "Necropolitics," 27, 29.

117 Panagia, *The Political Life of Sensation*, 2.

118 On verticality, see Weizman, "The Politics of Verticality"; on the separation wall, see Lubin et al., "The Israel/Palestine Field School," 87, and also Lubin, "'We Are All Israelis'": "Although the Israeli security fence operates like a militarized international border, the Israeli state continues to call it a 'security wall' and not a border. In this way, the wall can be justified in the context of a global war on terror while also performing the dispossessive act of carving up Palestinian territory in order to minimize the geography of a future Palestinian state. The 730-kilometer wall is, among other things, a tool of land dispossession and forced expulsion of Palestinians. Its design takes it deep into the West Bank and does not observe the 1967 border. In doing so, the wall confiscates nearly 47 percent of the West Bank. The territory between the wall and the Green Line has been designated a 'seam zone,' and Palestinians living in these areas will need to carry special permits in order to remain in their homes and use their land. The wall consists of thirty-four checkpoints with three main terminals that regulate passage between Israel and

the West Bank" (686–87). See also Anti-Apartheid Wall Campaign, fact sheet at www.stop thewall.org/factsheets/883.shtml. For an incisive reading of the politics of graffiti on the wall, see Gould, "The Materiality of Resistance," 1–21.

119 Strike Debt and Occupy Wall Street, "Colonizer as Lender," 16–17. As a solidarity manifesto, this document seeks to link these various movements to the liberation of Palestine by marking debt as a form of virtual and territorial enclosure that is crucial to the global capitalist expansion of financial control. The authors also note the limits of anti-austerity movements that do not engage with the liberation of Palestine as part of their platform, observing that the 2011 protests against austerity in Israel did not address the forms of Israeli settler colonial control rendered through debt extraction.

120 On Palestinian ID cards, see Tawil-Souri, "Colored Identity," 69. Tawil-Souri writes: "The Israeli state is accused of trying to eradicate Palestinians, and yet the state institutes an impressive infrastructure of control based on Palestinians' continued presence in Palestine/Israel. Against the background of transfer, fragmentation, and erasure exists a bureaucratic system of keeping Palestinians where they are: subjects of sustained, if changing, forms of colonialism, occupation, and oppression. . . . There may very well be a practice of fragmenting, isolating, transferring, and erasing Palestinians, but they need to be counted, documented, monitored, and controlled first" (68).

121 Hochberg, *Visual Occupations*, 26.

122 Foucault, *"Society Must Be Defended,"* 243.

123 Rosenberg and Rusert write: "The settler colonial project in Palestine produced a narrative of salvaging fictive origins from within the earth: this narrative then functioned as a supporting ideology for the annihilation or enclosure of spaces of subsistence in the name of the resuscitation of these origins. . . . The politicization of the subterranean that takes place through verticalization is a politics not only of space but also of time and of their complex relation. For if verticialization is a form of enclosure, it is not only an enclosure of spaces and landscapes but a temporal and narrative kind of enclosure as well. Verticalization, in other words, spatially manifests a fantasy about time. This fantasy is that a Jewish past is incarnated with the earth and thus can be unburied and produced as a set of enclosures that function at a political level as a claim to statehood" ("Framing Finance," 79). What Rosenberg and Rusert are describing is the function of discipline (as enclosure) within the control practices of the virtualization of space inherent in Weizman's schema.

124 Rai, *Untimely Bollywood*, 9.

125 See Nidhal, "The Burden of Queer Palestine."

126 Hardt, "The Withering of Civil Society." See also Hardt and Negri, *Empire*.

127 The most incisive resource I have come across demonstrating the porosity of discipline and control in Palestine is Ophir, Givoni, and Ḥanafi, *The Power of Inclusive Exclusion*. The volume situates the Israeli occupation as a completely rational rather than absurd or extreme form of governmentality, elaborated through a carapace of contradictory laws, the oppressive use of architecture and geography, and the intricate relations between disciplinary and control forms of power.

128 Weizman, "The Politics of Verticality."

129 See also Adi Kuntsman's important work on Russian Israeli queers and ethnic difference within Israeli Jewish queer communities. Kuntsman, *Figurations of Violence.*

130 Solomon, "Viva La Diva Citizenship."

131 See Boyarin, *Unheroic Conduct*; also Gross, "Disabled Diaspora."

FOUR. "WILL NOT LET DIE"

1 United Nations Office for the Coordination of Humanitarian Affairs, "Occupied Palestinian Territory"; Kasrils, "Gaza and the 'Crime of Crimes.'"

2 Al Mezan Center for Human Rights, "Al Mezan Calls for Accountability for War Crimes and an End to Israel's Occupation of the Occupied Palestinian Territory."

3 Al Mezan Center for Human Rights, "IOF Declare Intentions to Commit Further Violations of International Law in Gaza under International Silence."

4 Avni, "Plans to Rebuild Gaza Keep Getting Undermined."

5 Kasrils, "Gaza and the 'Crime of Crimes.'"

6 Amnesty International, "Israel/Gaza"; Taylor, "In the Fight between Israel and Hamas, Gaza's Hospitals Are in the Middle."

7 Doctors Without Borders, "Gaza."

8 Amnesty International, "Israel/Gaza"; Alashi, interview with Goodman and González, "Israel Bombs Gaza's Only Rehab Hospital."

9 Feldman, "Genocidal Desistance in Gaza."

10 Epigenetics, part of this economy, refers to developing research on how external factors such as environment and social factors can affect how genes are expressed by switching them on or off, particularly during fetal development and early childhood. These gene de/activations may also be inherited by offspring. Racism and other structural inequalities have been shown to have strong epigenetic effects (Kuzawa and Sweet, "Epigenetics and the Embodiment of Race"). In a 2013 talk, "Abnormality, Race, and the New Epigenetic Biopolitics of Environmental Health," Becky Mansfield argued that the U.S. government has tried to manage the population effects of methyl mercury pollution, exposure to which produces epigenetic changes during fetal and childhood development, by placing responsibility on the individual to make proper choices about health and consumption. Without resources to "protect" themselves, vulnerable communities are made responsible for the effects of large-scale environmental pollution on their bodies and futures. See also Dupras and Ravitsky, "Epigenetics in the Neoliberal 'Regime of Truth,'" which argues that the new epigenetic turn is more likely to produce a push toward individual biomedicalized interventions rather than policy-level changes to address social and environmental sources of epigenetic changes.

11 Quoted in Blumenthal, "Evidence Emerges of Israeli 'Shoot to Cripple' Policy in the Occupied West Bank."

12 Sherwood, "Israel Using Flechette Shells in Gaza"; Withnall, "Israel-Gaza Conflict."

13 Neda Atanasoski has argued that contemporary U.S. military intervention is authorized through an appeal to humanitarian ethics, deploying rhetoric of doing battle against illiberal forms of intolerance. As such, positioning other locations as intolerant and illiberal "elicit[s] Euro-America's humanitarian gaze and calls for the military and juridical humanization of barbarous geographies," which are posed against the humanitarian West (*Humanitarian Violence*, 2). Religious and ideological difference becomes a mode of racialization, positioning the target as profoundly inhumane and in a state of permanent need for reform, thus justifying disciplinary intervention in the form of humanitarian militarism. See also Lopez, Bhungalia, and Newhouse, "Geographies of Humanitarian Violence," on "moral technologies" and humanitarianism as a means of perpetuating conditions of violence.

14 Henderson, "Israel Air Strike 'Hits Charitable Association for Disabled' in Gaza."

15 Beaumont, "Disabled Palestinians Unable to Escape Israeli Air Strike."

16 Taylor, "Israel Hopes Phone Calls to Palestinians Will Save Lives."

17 Tawil-Souri, interview by Dawes, "Digital Occupation"; Tawil-Souri, "Hacking Palestine." The Oslo Accords allowed Palestinians to build their own telecommunications network, but everything about its infrastructure would ultimately remain under Israeli control. There has been much enthusiasm about apps to monitor road conditions in the West Bank. One can use Ezma (which means "traffic jam" in Arabic) or Wasselni ("give me a ride" in Arabic), an Uber-like service recently launched in the Gaza Strip or else text "Q" on a Jawwal mobile phone to get access updates on "traffic conditions" at the Qalandia Checkpoint, the busiest checkpoint in the West Bank. One can follow discussions about these technological platforms on a Facebook group called Qalandia Conditions (https://www .facebook.com/groups/247012432000459/). Posted articles have cheery headlines that announce, for example, "Facebook Makes the Wait at the Qalandia Checkpoint Easier." The harnessing of "innovation," or "work-arounds," what Amit Rai describes as *jugaad* in the Indian context, entails lauding the creative and entrepreneurial spirit, the merging of the scales of the macropolitical and the experience of daily living, the diffusion and reappropriation of mobile technologies, and concomitantly an extension in and of the occupation. Tawil-Souri's work on digital occupation demonstrates West Bank technological fragmentation, rendering a digital map of the occupation that amends the geographic mapping. Zones A, B, and C—fragmented and separated from each other—are being morphed into quasi Gazas. Despite the hype, there is deep skepticism about "a text message service created by Palestine's largest telecommunications provider in order to profit from the need to pass through an Israeli military checkpoint inside the West Bank" (Tawil-Souri, "Occupation Apps"). Tawil-Souri continues, "There is nothing revolutionary about services that help you gauge traffic through a checkpoint . . . nor profits [that] are made on aspects of life dependent on and made desperate by the occupation."

18 Al-Haq, *Punishing a Nation*.

19 Al-Haq, *Punishing a Nation*, 16.

20 Al-Haq, *Punishing a Nation*, 16.

21 Al-Haq, *Punishing a Nation*, 21–26, 46, 47, 49, 53.

22 Al-Haq, *Punishing a Nation*, 43.

23 Al-Haq, *Punishing a Nation*, 44.

24 Andoni and Tolan, "Shoot to Maim."

25 Blumenthal, "Evidence Emerges of Israeli 'Shoot to Cripple' Policy in the Occupied West Bank." See also Giacaman, "A Population at Risk of Risks" Giacaman reports that from "28 September 2000 until March 28th [2002], on the eve of this invasion, not less than 1300 Palestinians had died and around 27,000 were injured by Israeli army violence, adding serious burdens on the existing medical and health care system."

26 Kirschner quoted in Qato, "The Politics of Deteriorating Health," 351.

27 Qato, "The Politics of Deteriorating Health," 351. See also Helweg-Larsen et al., "Systematic Medical Data Collection of Intentional Injuries during Armed Conflicts," 17–23.

28 Reinhart, *Israel/Palestine*, 112

29 Reinhart, *Israel/Palestine*, 113.

30 Ephron, *Boston Globe*, November 4, 2000, cited in Reinhart, *Israel/Palestine*, 113.

31 *Jerusalem Post*, October 30, 2000, cited in Reinhart, *Israel/Palestine*, 115.

32 Reinhart, *Israel/Palestine*, 114.

33 Reinhart, *Israel/Palestine*, 11

34 Al-Haq, *Punishing a Nation*, 70.

35 Al-Haq, *Punishing a Nation*, 69–75.

36 Jamjoum, "The Effects of Israeli Violations during the Second Uprising on Palestinian Health Conditions," 56.

37 Jamjoum, "The Effects of Israeli Violations during the Second Uprising on Palestinian Health Conditions," 56.

38 Beste, "The Reason Why Israel Killed So Many Pregnant Women in Gaza."

39 Jamjoum, "The Effects of Israeli Violations during the Second Uprising 'Intifada' on Palestinian Health Conditions," 72.

40 Mbembe, "Necropolitics."

41 Hass and Efrati, "Gaza's Water System Collapsing Due to IDF Strikes, Says Red Cross"; Chick, "Under Fire in Gaza and Not a Drop to Drink."

42 Qandil, "Gaza Faces Imminent Water Crisis."

43 Cohen, "In the Last Days of 'Operation Protective Edge' Israel Focused on Its Final Goal."

44 Salamanca, "Unplug and Play."

45 Salamanca, "Unplug and Play," 25

46 Salamanca, "Unplug and Play," 26.

47 Salamanca, "Unplug and Play," 30.

48 Tawil-Souri, "The Hi-Tech Enclosure of Gaza," 6.

49 Tawil-Souri, "The Hi-Tech Enclosure of Gaza," 12.

50 Salamanca, "Unplug and Play," 30.

51 Salamanca, "Unplug and Play," 32.

52 See Feldman, *Governing Gaza*, on the history of governmentality in Gaza and an elaboration of technologies of tactical government.

53 There is an interesting ongoing Palestinian settlement project in the West Bank. In Rawabi, just outside of Ramallah, a Palestinian millionaire named Bashar Masri is building the first ever Palestinian gated community, a completely new city built from scratch. Most aspects of this project are unprecedented: the scale of wealth being deployed as well as consolidated in the West Bank, the autonomy of the structure from anything that preceded it, the perverse circuits of capital that both enable and block the process of construction, the emblazoning of the post-Oslo consolidation of a class society in the West Bank. It will have upscale housing for twenty-five thousand residents, an amphitheater, a football stadium, cinemas, shops, and parks. The project is funded in part by the government of Qatar; in return, the Qatar Investment Authority expects a very large mosque to be built. Of course, all permission to build is controlled and cleared by Israel. Rawabi also, at this point in time, has no water. Challenged by solidarity activists with being complicit with the occupation, Masri responds by claiming that Rawabi is a "countersettlement" strategy that resists the occupation by mimicking the logic of land grab that sustains the occupation. But not only mimicking but also aggrandizing, exaggerating the scale and practice of illegal settlement—this is a huge volley of countersettlement. Part of "defying the occupation," claims Masri, is his desire to turn Ateret, an Israeli settlement, into a suburban satellite of Rawabi, so in a sense, an attempt not just to outshadow but to outrun the settlement by its copy. This is a parallel strategy of building on hilltops to create "facts on the ground," what Steven Salaita has called the "Israeli settlement as a form of geostrategic gentrification." This example functions as a kind of retort to Eyal's Weizman's project *Forensic Architecture*, where he situates architecture as a tactical tool, and, as he says "we just need to know how to decode it." There is no decoding at work here; rather, like meets like and attempts to override. The illegal settlements—perhaps we should call them colonies, says Kendall Thomas—are part of what Elias Khoury claims is the second Nakba already in progress, the displacement of Palestinians from the West Bank.

54 For more discussion, see the fantastic special issue of *Middle East Report* titled "Waiting: The Politics of Time in Palestine."

55 Kotef, *Movement and the Ordering of Freedom*.

56 Rose, *The Politics of Life Itself*.

57 Mbembe, "Necropolitics," 21.

58 Weheliye, *Habeas Viscus*; Chen, *Animacies*.

59 See especially Wolfe, *Settler Colonialism and the Transformation of Anthropology*; Wolfe, "Settler Colonialism and the Elimination of the Native."

60 Morgensen, "The Biopolitics of Settler Colonialism."

61 Foucault, *Security, Territory, Population*, 34, 37.

62 Foucault, *"Society Must Be Defended,"* 245.

63 Foucault, *"Society Must Be Defended,"* 244.

64 Foucault, *"Society Must Be Defended,"* 243–44.

65 Foucault, *"Society Must Be Defended,"* 241.

66 Foucault continues in *"Society Must Be Defended"*: "What does the right of life and death actually mean? Obviously not that the sovereign can grant life in the same way that he can inflict death. The right of life and death is always exercised in an unbalanced way: the balance is always tipped in favor of death. Sovereign power's effect on life is exercised only when the sovereign can kill. The very essence of the right of life and death is actually the right to kill: it is the moment when the sovereign can kill that he exercises his right over life" (240–41).

67 Berlant, "Slow Death."

68 This analysis of the role of maiming of course also begs the visage of the opening passages of Foucault's *Discipline and Punish*. Foucault traces the "the disappearance of torture as a public spectacle": the transition of the spectacle of the punishment of torture, and specifically of severing limbs, from the purview of the public to the routinization of punishment in the prison. Torture thus remains a transgressive ritual but no longer a spectacle. In both the spectacle of maiming and its domestication in the prison, maiming is a disciplinary mode of punishment. But through its endemic and intrinsic incorporation into the "largest open-air prison" in the world (as Gaza is so often referred to), the banality of maiming becomes a form of torture that is crucial to how control functions. It is returned to the public sphere but still removed from its specularization, and thus normalized as a facet of life rather than an act of torture. In Gaza torture is not disappeared into the private, nor is there a return to the spectacle of torture. Rather more insidiously, torture is regularized as integral to settler colonialism (*Discipline and Punish*, 7).

69 In *The Least of All Possible Evils*, Eyal Weizman details Israel's tactic of calculating the minimum number of calories necessary for Palestinians living in Gaza to remain at just above the UN definition of hunger in order to determine the exact amount of food allowed inside Gaza. Israeli officials calculated 2,100 daily calories for men, 1,700 for women, and varying amounts for children; however, even these numbers were not met as Israel found reasons to more than halve the amount of food trucks going into Gaza necessary to meet even this basic caloric intake. Sherene Seikaly traces the racial and economic history of the calorie, expanding on Israel's policy of calorie counting, in "Counting Calories and Making Lemonade." Seikaly writes that in Israel we see the deployment of the calorie as a racialized tool of political containment in order to contain Gazans and incite anger against Hamas. For a history of the development of "nutritional economy" in Mandate Palestine, see Seikaly, *Men of Capital*, chap. 3.

70 Quotation provided by Karl Schembri in a Facebook post on July 30, 2014; partially quoted in Al-Helou and Waters, "Lack of Power Keeps Gazans in Dark during War."

71 Schulze, "Understanding the UN Convention on the Rights of Persons with Disabilities."

72 Al-Mughrabi, "Gaza Paralympians Confident of Success in London"; Degun, "Palestinian Paralympic Committee Headquarters Destroyed in Gaza Bombings."

73 Graff, "Crippling a People."

74 Quoted in Said and Zahriyeh, "Gaza's Kids Affected Psychologically, Physically by Lifetime of Violence."

75 Abu El-Haj, "Nothing Unintentional."

76 Abu El-Haj, "Nothing Unintentional."

77 Khalili, "A Habit of Destruction."

78 See Khatib and Kasozi, "Disability and Explosive Remnants of War in Gaza"; McFann, "Violent Waste."

79 Here I am following Mitchell and Snyder's definition of cultural rehabilitation described in *The Biopolitics of Disability*, 205.

80 Seikaly, "Counting Calories and Making Lemonade in Gaza"; Weizman, *The Least of All Possible Evils*.

81 See Stevenson, "The Psychic Life of Biopolitics."

82 Tawil-Souri, "The Digital Occupation of Gaza," 3.

83 Foreign countries and international organizations, especially on the part of the United States, have strong financial investments in the occupation. The United States signed a Free Trade Agreement with Israel in 1985, increasing exports to Israel by more than 500 percent and imports from Israel by more than 1200 percent. Since then, the occupation has shifted increasingly toward market-driven decisions. The privatization of the occupation that resulted from the Oslo peace process netted large sums of international aid money for Israel and has generated an industry for private military investments between the United States and Israel (see also Klein, *The Shock Doctrine*, chap. 21). The United States began offering "peace dividends" to countries that would enter into trade agreements with Israel (and, indirectly, the United States) and later created the Regional Business Council to establish trade relations between Israel and other Middle Eastern countries while explicitly excluding the West Bank and Gaza, implying a tacit approval of the occupation in favor of opened trade between Israel and countries such as Egypt and Jordan (Lubin, "Peace Dividends"). Grassroots organizations have called neoliberal financial institutions such as the IMF and the World Bank the "shadow government" in the West Bank, dictating the development program and expenditure of the Palestinian Authority. Under the guidance of the United States, the European Union, Israel, and these international financial institutions, the PA adopted a brutally economically stunting policy of reform and development in 2007, eliminating an enormous percentage of the jobs in the West Bank. This policy also called for the development of industrial zones in the West Bank where labor laws would not apply and relocating to these zones Turkish businesses that would produce cheap goods for the United States, the European Union, and the Gulf States. The wealthiest Palestinian business groups, foreign businesses (such as Coca-Cola and Marriott), and U.S. and European aid organizations (such as USAID) convened at a conference in 2008 to confirm the reform policies. The conference also highlighted a multinational plan to turn Palestinian farmers into day laborers and subcontractors for big agricultural industry in the Jordan Valley, producing exports to Israel and the Gulf States (Hanieh, "Palestine in the Middle East"). See also Lubin,

"The Disappearing Frontiers of US Homeland Security"; the Who Profits website, www.whoprofits.org.

84 Hamid, "Why Are the Arab Gulf Countries Silent on Gaza?"

85 Blumenthal, "International Community Promises to Rebuild Gaza."

86 Pugliese, "Forensic Ecologies of Occupied Zones and Geographies of Dispossession," 3.

87 Cohen, "In the Last Days of 'Operation Protective Edge' Israel Focused on Its Final Goal."

88 Dyke, "Analysis."

89 Gisha-Legal Center for Freedom of Movement, "The Gaza Cheat Sheet."

90 Beaumont, "Corruption Hampers Effort to Rebuild Gaza after Summer Conflict."

91 Gisha-Legal Center for Freedom of Movement, "A Costly Divide."

92 Feldman, "Gaza's Humanitarianism Problem," 33–34.

93 Le More, "Killing with Kindness," 983.

94 Netanyahu, interview with Blitzer, "Netanyahu."

95 Feldman, "Genocidal Desistance in Gaza."

96 Luciana Parisi draws on Whitehead's notion of the prehensive as a capacity to grasp and transform, suggesting that "the new function of algorithms within the programming of spatiotemporal forms and relations reveals how the degree of prehension proper to algorithms has come to characterize computational culture. Algorithms are no longer seen as tools to accomplish a task: they are the constructive material or abstract 'stuff' that enables the automated design of buildings, infrastructures, and objects. Algorithms are thus actualities, defined by an automated prehension of data in the computational processing of probabilities. From this standpoint, digital algorithms are not simply representations of data, but are occasions of experience insofar as they prehend information in their own way, which neither strictly coincides with the binary or fuzzy logic of computation nor with the agency of external physical inputs. Instead, as actual occasions, algorithms prehend the formal system into which they are scripted, and also the external data inputs that they retrieve" (Parisi, *Contagious Architecture*, xii).

97 Oren, "Israel Must Be Permitted to Crush Hamas."

98 Palestinian Central Bureau of Statistics, "On the 65th Anniversary of the Palestinian Nakba"; Deutsche Presse-Agenteur, "Palestinians to Outnumber Jewish Population by 2020, Report Says."

99 Chamie, "By 2035, Jewish Population in Israel/Palestine Is Projected at 46 Percent."

100 Ahmed, "Armed Robbery in Gaza"; Ahmed, "IDF's Gaza Assault Is to Control Palestinian Gas, Avert Israeli Energy Crisis"; United Nations Relief and Work Agency for Palestine Refugees in the Near East, "Gaza in 2020."

101 Chen, *Animacies*. A number of toxic materials have been detected at elevated levels in Gaza. Phosphorous, which is potentially destructive to the environment and to the health of local populations, has been detected at high levels in Gazan soil samples. While phosphorous is a common agricultural soil additive, these samples included urban and other nonagricultural areas that have specifically been hit by white phosphorous bombs (Hamada, Aish, and Shahwan, "Potential of Phospho-

rous Pollution in the Soil of the Northern Gaza Strip, Palestine," 295). A study of wound tissue from victims of Israel's 2007 and 2009 military operations in Gaza detected the presence of several toxic heavy metals and other known carcinogens, including mercury, arsenic, titanium, barium, and cesium (Skaik et al., "Metals Detected by ICP/MS in Wound Tissue of War Injuries without Fragments in Gaza"). An additional study on levels of toxic heavy metals in newborns with birth defects in Gaza examined children with birth defects born to parents directly exposed to military operations or their immediate aftermath during Operation Cast Lead. The study found that these newborns had significantly elevated levels of mercury, tin, and selenium compared with children born to parents not exposed directly to military operations during the same period (Manduca, Naim, and Signoriello, "Specific Association of Teratogen and Toxicant Metals in Hair of Newborns with Congenital Birth Defects or Developmentally Premature Birth in a Cohort of Couples with Documented Parental Exposure to Military Attacks"). See also Weir, "Conflict Rubble"; www.toxicremnantsofwar.info.

102 Negarestani, "Drafting the Inhuman."

103 Weizman, *The Least of All Possible Evils.*

104 Salaita, *Israel's Dead Soul.*

105 Ghannam quoted in Said and Zahriyeh, "Gaza's Kids Affected Psychologically, Physically by Lifetime of Violence." See also Thabet, Abed, and Vostanis, "Effect of Trauma on the Mental Health of Palestinian Children and Mothers in the Gaza Strip," 413–21.

106 Shalhoub-Kevorkian, "Criminality in Spaces of Death." For research on the relationship of trauma to the occupation, see Al-Krenawi, Graham, and Sehwail. "Mental Health and Violence/Trauma in Palestine," 185–209; Zaqout, "Psychological Support in Palestine," 94–106; Abu-Mourad et al., "Self-Reported Health Complaints in a Primary Care Population Living under Stressful Conditions in the Gaza Strip, Palestine," 68–79. On life expectancy, see Qlalweh, Duraidi, and Bronnum-Hansen, "Health Expectancy in the Occupied Palestinian Territory." On rising suicide rates in Gaza, see Abou Jalal, "Gaza Suicides Rise as Living Conditions Deteriorate"; Kamel, "Gaza's Youth Lose Hope"; Shakra, "No Exit but Suicide in Gaza."

107 Shalhoub-Kevorkian, "Criminality in Spaces of Death."

108 A further reference: "It would be safe to assume that most Palestinian children sixteen years or younger have either been hit by Israeli gunfire, beaten up by Israeli troops or colonists, or asphyxiated, burned, or nauseated by US-manufactured, highly concentrated CS or CN gases. The statistics and projections of child injuries from IDF gunfire and beating show that Palestinian children were massively targeted by the IDF, and that the scope of those assaults went far beyond what might have been required to contain demonstrations and cope with stone-throwing" (Graff, "Crippling a People," 53).

109 The current medical definition of stunting was introduced in 1973 as a deficit in height as a result of prolonged malnutrition that produces "a retardation in linear growth." Children are considered stunted when they are two standard

deviations below the determined average for their age and sex (Schmidt, "Beyond Malnutrition").

110 Shalhoub-Kevorkian, "Palestinian Children as Tools for 'Legalized' State Violence."

111 Sherwood, "UN Officials Accused of Bowing to Israeli Pressure over Children's Rights List."

112 Graff, "Crippling a People," 47.

113 Graff, "Crippling a People," 47–48.

114 Graff, "Crippling a People," 50.

115 Thabet and Vostanis, "Impact of Political Violence and Trauma in Gaza on Children's Mental Health and Types of Interventions"; Thabet and Vostanis, "Child Mental Health Problems in the Gaza Strip"; Thabet et al., "Comorbidity of Post Traumatic Stress Disorder, Attention Deficit with Hyperactivity, Conduct, and Oppositional Defiant Disorder in Palestinian Children Affected by War on Gaza."

116 Qouta and El Sarraj, "Prevalence of PTSD among Palestinian Children in Gaza Strip," 11.

117 Esmeir, "Colonial Experiments in Gaza."

118 Tawil-Souri, "The Digital Occupation of Gaza," 5. Tawil-Souri further states: "Gaza demonstrates what urban warfare looks like and how this model can be exported and/or emulated elsewhere . . . the drone wars over Afghanistan, Pakistan and Yemen; the forms of aerial and urban warfare being waged in Iraq and Syria; the electrified fences and remote-controlled sensors along various international borders; aerial surveillance over São Paolo" (5).

119 See an important collection, Tawil-Souri and Matar, Gaza as Metaphor, for a discussion of various descriptors used to delineate Gaza in ways that deny its historical and political specificity: Gaza as an open-air prison, Gaza as archive, Gaza as zoo, Gaza as a humanitarian crisis, Gaza as a torture chamber, Gaza as an object of humanitarian concern, Gaza as/is disaster capitalism.

120 Many thanks to Ittai Orr for this specific formulation and for his comments in response to an early version of this chapter presented at Yale University on February 4, 2015.

121 Rosenberg, lecture presented at the Reflection on Dispossession symposium.

122 See Hardt, preface to "Palestine: Cartography of an Occupation." See also MTL Collective, "The Slow, Sure Death of Palestine."

123 Said, The Question of Palestine, 4.

POSTSCRIPT: TREATMENT WITHOUT CHECKPOINTS

1 For more information on the film project, see MTL Collective, On This Land.

2 For more information about BASR's history and work, see Bethlehem Arab Society for Rehabilitation, Annual Report 2010.

3 For research on the growth and impact of CBRs in Palestine, see Eide, "Impact of Community-Based Rehabilitation Programmes," 199–210.

4 All interview material is from meetings that took place on January 5 and January 7, 2016. Simultaneous translation conducted on-site by Baraah Awad Owdeh. Written transcriptions and translations by Rasha Moumneh.

5 In the summer of 2016, reports released from BADIL Resource Center for Palestinian Residency and Refugee Rights and *Haaretz* documented the targeting of Palestinian youth for injuries and kneecapping, particularly in the refugee camps in the West Bank. The majority of injured Palestinians (since the beginning of 2016) have been shot with live ammunition in the legs and knees. BADIL has collected testimonies regarding an Israeli commander in Area A known as Captain Nidal making statements such as "I will make all the youth of the camp disabled"; "I will have all of you walking with crutches and in wheelchairs"; "I will make half of you disabled, and let the other half push the wheelchairs"; and "I will make all of you stand in line at the ATM waiting for your disability subsides and assistance." BADIL, "Israeli Forces Targeting Palestinian Youth in the West Bank." See also Barrows-Friedman, "Israeli Captain." Israeli journalist Amira Hass provides testimony from numerous injured Palestinian young men; the accounts are published in *Haaretz*. She reports that Nidal "tells young people there will be no martyrs in the camp, but 'all of you will end up on crutches.'" In the village of Tekoa there is a "Captain Imad" who threatens to cripple anyone who confronts the IDF soldiers. Hass writes: "In many places there's a growing realization that the army is intensifying its use of live fire in confrontations with unarmed stone throwers, and that the wounds inflicted are deliberately more severe. There must be more than 100 people across the West Bank, including many minors, who have been crippled by the IDF over the last year. But there is still no exchange of information or collation of data to confirm the seeming trend" ("Is the IDF Conducting a Kneecapping Campaign in the West Bank?").

BIBLIOGRAPHY

Abou Jalal, Rasha. "Gaza Suicides Rise as Living Conditions Deteriorate." *Al-Monitor*, July 3, 2013. Accessed November 5, 2016. http://www.al- monitor.com/pulse /originals/2013/07/gaza-suicide-hamas-blockade.html#ixzz2Zdpjkh9O.

Abramov, Eti. "Woman Gives Birth Using Dead Man's Frozen Sperm." *Ynetnews*, October 2, 2015.

Abu El-Haj, Nadia A. *The Genealogical Science: Genetics, the Origins of the Jews, and the Politics of Epistemology*. Chicago: University of Chicago Press, 2012.

———. "Nothing Unintentional." *London Review of Books*, July 29, 2014. Accessed February 1, 2015. http://www.lrb.co.uk/blog/2014/07/29/nadia-abu-el-haj/nothing -unintentional/.

Abu-Mourad, Tayser, Anotonis Koutis, Athanasios Alegakis, Adelais Markaki, Christine Jildeh, Christos Lionis, and Anastas Philalithis. "Self-Reported Health Complaints in a Primary Care Population Living under Stressful Conditions in the Gaza Strip, Palestine." *Medicine, Conflict and Survival* 26, no. 1 (2010): 68–79.

Abu Nahleh, Lamis. "Gender and Disabilities: Marginal Issues in Palestinian Development and Rights Initiatives." *This Week in Palestine*, no. 137 (September 2009). http://archive.thisweekinpalestine.com/details.php?id=2869&ed=173&edid=173.

Ackerman, Spencer. "Doctors Without Borders Airstrikes: US Alters Story for Fourth Time in Four Days." *Guardian*, October 6, 2015.

The Advocate Online. "Clementi's Roommate Indicted." April 20, 2011. Accessed February 1, 2011. http://www.advocate.com/News/Daily_News/2011/04/20/ Clementi_Roommate_Indicted.

Agamben, Giorgio. "On Security and Terror." Translated by Carolin Emcke. *Theory and Event* 5, no. 4 (2001): 30–53.

Ahmed, Nafeez. "Armed Robbery in Gaza—Israel, US, UK Carve Up the Spoils of Palestine's Stolen Gas." *Ecologist*, July 24, 2014. Accessed February 1, 2015. http://www .theecologist.org/News/news_analysis/2489992/armed_robbery_in_gaza_israel_us _uk_carve_up_the_spoils_of_palestines_stolen_gas.html.

———. "IDF's Gaza Assault Is to Control Palestinian Gas, Avert Israeli Energy Crisis." *Guardian*, July 9, 2014. Accessed February 1, 2015. http://www.theguardian.com /environment/earth-insight/2014/jul/09/israel-war-gaza-palestine-natural-gas-energy -crisis.

Ahuja, Neel. *Bioinsecurities: Disease Interventions, Empire, and the Government of Species.* Durham, NC: Duke University Press, 2016.

Aizura, Aren Z. "Of Borders and Homes: The Imaginary Community of (Trans)sexual Citizenship." *Inter-Asia Cultural Studies* 7 (2006): 289–309.

———. "The Romance of the Amazing Scalpel." *Transgender Studies Reader 2*, edited by Susan Stryker and Aren Z. Aizura, 496–511. New York: Routledge, 2013.

Alaimo, Stacy. *Bodily Natures: Science, Environment, and the Material Self.* Bloomington: Indiana University Press, 2010.

———. "MCS Matters: Material Agency in the Science and Practices of Environmental Illness." *TOPIA: Canadian Journal of Cultural Studies* 21 (2009): 8–27.

Al Arabiya News. "Scattered Landmines Turn Afghans into Amputees." November 28, 2009. Accessed March 25, 2016. http://english.alarabiya.net/articles/2009/11/28/92607.html.

Alashi, Basman, interview with Amy Goodman and Juan González. "Israel Bombs Gaza's Only Rehab Hospital: Staff Forced to Evacuate Paralyzed Patients after Shelling." *Democracy Now,* July 18, 2014. Accessed February 1, 2015. http://www.democracynow.org/2014/7/18/israel_bombs_gazas_only_rehab_hospital.

Albert, Bill. "Is Disability Really on the Development Agenda? A Review of Official Disability Policies of the Major Governmental and International Development Agencies." London: Disability Knowledge and Research Programme, 2004.

Alexander, Michelle. *The New Jim Crow: Mass Incarceration in the Age of Colorblindness.* New York: New Press, 2012.

Alhammami, Mohammed. "A Letter from Gaza to Black America." *Mondoweiss,* October 3, 2016. Accessed November 5, 2016. http://mondoweiss.net/2016/10/letter-black-america/.

Al-Haq, Law in the Service of Man (Ramallah). *Punishing a Nation: Human Rights Violations during the Palestinian Uprising: December 1987–December 1988.* 1988. Accessed September 30, 2016. http://www.alhaq.org/publications/publications-index/item/punishing-a-nation-human-rights-violations-during-the-palestinian-uprising-december-1987-1988.

Al-Helou, Yousef, and Angela Waters. "Lack of Power Keeps Gazans in Dark during War." *USA Today,* July 30, 2014. Accessed February 1, 2015. http://archive.thetimesherald.com/usatoday/article/13364225.

Al Jazeera. "Israel Bomb Hits Disabled Centre in Gaza." July 13, 2014. Accessed November 5, 2016. http://www.aljazeera.com/news/middleeast/2014/07/israel-bombs-hit-centre-disabled-gaza-201471274035753506.html.

Al-Krenawi, Alean, John R. Graham, and Mahmud A. Sehwail. "Mental Health and Violence/Trauma in Palestine: Implications for Helping Professional Practice." *Journal of Comparative Family Studies* 35, no. 2 (2004): 185–209.

Al Mezan Center for Human Rights. "Al Mezan Calls for Accountability for War Crimes and an End to Israel's Occupation of the Occupied Palestinian Territory." Accessed March 12, 2017. http://www.mezan.org/en/post/19514.

———. "IOF Declare Intentions to Commit Further Violations of International Law in Gaza under International Silence." August 25, 2014. Accessed February 1, 2015. http://www.mezan.org/en/post/19396.

Al-Mughrabi, Nidal. "Gaza Paralympians Confident of Success in London." Reuters, August 15, 2012. Accessed February 1, 2015. http://www.reuters.com/article/2012/08 /15/us-olympics-paralympics-palestine-idUSBRE87E0LD20120815.

Al Qadi, Muthanna. "Disabled Palestinians Struggling for Their Rights." *Palestine Report* 10, no. 23 (December 10, 2003). Accessed November 5, 2016. http://www .palestinereport.ps/article.php?article=190.

American Israel Public Affairs Committee (AIPAC). "Student Leaders across America Oppose Nuclear Iran." *Near East Report*, April 24, 2012.

Americans with Disabilities Act of 1990, Pub. L. No. 101–336, 104 Stat. 328 (1990).

Amir, Delilva, and Orly Benjamin. "Sexuality and the Female National Subject: Contraception and Abortion Policy in Israel." In *Politics of Sexuality: Identity, Gender, Citizenship*, edited by Terrel Caver and Véronique Mottier, 158–68. New York: Routledge, 1998.

Amnesty International. "Israel/Gaza: Prevent Further War Crimes after Israeli Ground Assault." July 18, 2014. Accessed February 1, 2015. http://www.amnesty .org/en/news/israelgaza-prevent-further-war-crimes-after-israeli-ground-assault -2014-07-18.

Anderson, John. "Festival in Oslo Rejects Film by Roy Zafrani, Citing Cultural Boycott of Israel." *New York Times*, August 18, 2015.

Anderson, Warwick. *Colonial Pathologies: American Tropical Medicine, Race, and Hygiene in the Philippines*. Durham, NC: Duke University Press, 2006.

Andoni, Lamis, and Sandy Tolan. "Shoot to Maim." *Village Voice*, February 20, 2001. Accessed February 1, 2015. http://www.villagevoice.com/2001-02-20/news/shoot-to -maim/.

Arondekar, Anjali. *For the Record: On Sexuality and the Colonial Archive in India*. Durham, NC: Duke University Press, 2009.

Ashman, Sam. "Editorial Introduction to the Symposium on the Global Financial Crisis." *Historical Materialism* 17, no. 2 (2009): 103–8.

Atanasoski, Neda. *Humanitarian Violence: The U.S. Deployment of Diversity*. Minneapolis: University of Minnesota Press, 2013.

Audre Lorde Project. "Trans Day of Action for Social and Economic Justice—Points of Unity." N.d. Accessed November 5, 2016. http://alp.org/tdoa_pou.

Avishai, Bernard. "Is Liberal Zionism Impossible?" *New Yorker*, September 5, 2014.

Avni, Benny. "Plans to Rebuild Gaza Keep Getting Undermined." *Newsweek*, November 3, 2014. Accessed February 1, 2015. http://www.newsweek.com/plans-rebuild -gaza-keep-getting-undermined-281694.

BADIL: Resource Center for Palestinian Residency and Refugee Rights. "Israeli Forces Targeting Palestinian Youth in the West Bank." August 23, 2016. Accessed November 5, 2016. http://www.badil.org/en/publication/press-releases/77-2016/4629-pr-en -230816-37.htm.

Banks, Martha E., and Ellyn Kaschak, eds. *Women with Visible and Invisible Disabilities: Multiple Intersections, Multiple Issues, Multiple Therapies*. New York: Haworth Press, 2003.

Barad, Karen. "Posthumanist Performativity: Toward an Understanding of How Matter Comes to Matter." *Signs: Journal of Women in Culture and Society* 28, no. 3 (2003): 801–31.

Barker, Clare, and Stuart Murray. "Disabling Postcolonialism: Global Disability Cultures and Democratic Criticism." *Journal of Literary and Cultural Disability Studies* 3 (2010): 219.

Barnartt, Sharon N., and Richard K. Scotch. *Disability Protests: Contentious Politics 1970–1999*. Washington, DC: Gallaudet University Press, 2001.

Barrows-Friedman, Nora. "Israeli Captain: 'I Will Make You All Disabled.'" *Electronic Intifada*. September 1, 2016. Accessed November 5, 2016. https://electronicintifada .net/content/israeli-captain-i-will-make-you-all-disabled/17821.

Barry, Kevin M. "Disabilityqueer: Federal Disability Rights Protection for Transgender People." *Yale Human Rights and Development Journal* 16, no. 1 (2013): 1–50.

Bauer, Bruno. "Die Fähigkeit der heutigen Juden und Christen, frei zu werden" [The capacity of present-day Jews and Christians to become free]. In *Einundzwanzig Bogen aus der Schweiz*, edited by Georg Herwegh, 56–71. Zurich and Winterthur: Literarische Comptoir Zürich und Winterthur, 1843.

———. *Die Judenfrage* [The Jewish question]. Braunschweig: Druck und Verlag von Friedrich Otto, 1843.

Beauchamp, Toby. "Artful Concealment and Strategic Visibility: Transgender Bodies and US State Surveillance after 9/11." *Surveillance and Society* 6, no. 4 (2009): 356–66.

Beaumont, Peter. "Corruption Hampers Effort to Rebuild Gaza after Summer Conflict." *Guardian*, December 25, 2014. Accessed February 1, 2015. http://www.theguardian .com/world/2014/dec/25/corruption-hampers-effort-to-rebuild-gaza.

———. "Disabled Palestinians Unable to Escape Israeli Air Strike." *Guardian*, July 12, 2014. Accessed February 1, 2015. http://www.theguardian.com/world/2014/jul/12 /disabled-palestinians-unable-escape-israeli-air-strike.

Bell, Christopher M., ed. *Blackness and Disability: Critical Examinations and Cultural Interventions*. East Lansing: Michigan State University Press, 2011.

———. "Introducing White Disability Studies: A Modest Proposal." In *Disability Studies Reader*, 2nd ed., edited by Lennard J. Davis, 275–83. New York: Routledge, 2006.

Belonsky, Andrew. "Tyler Clementi's Story Unfolded Online but Offers Real-Life Lessons." *Towleroad*, September 30, 2010. Accessed February 1, 2011. http://www .towleroad.com/2010/09/tyler-clementis-story-unfolded-online-but-offers-real-life -lessons.html.

Ben-eliezer, Uri. "Becoming a Black Jew: Cultural Racism and Anti-racism in Contemporary Israel." *Social Identities* 10, no. 2 (2004): 245–66.

Ben-Moshe, Liat. "Disabling Incarceration: Connecting Disability to Divergent Confinements in the USA." *Critical Sociology* 39, no. 3 (2013): 385–403.

———. "Movements at War? Disability and Anti-occupation Activism in Israel." In *Occupying Disability: Critical Approaches to Community, Justice, and Decolonizing Disability*, edited by Pamela Block, Devva Kasnitz, Akemi Nishida, and Nick Pollard, 47–62. New York: Springer, 2016.

Ben-Moshe, Liat, Chris Chapman, and Allison C. Carey, eds. *Disability Incarcerated: Imprisonment and Disability in the United States and Canada*. New York: Palgrave Macmillan, 2014.

Ben-Moshe, Liat, and Sumi Colligan. "The State of Disability in Israel/Palestine: An Introduction." *Disability Studies Quarterly* 27, no. 4 (2007).

Ben-Moshe, Liat, and Jean Stewart. "Disablement, Prison and Historical Segregation: 15 Years Later." In *Disability Politics in a Global Economy: Essays in Honour of Marta Russell*, edited by Ravi Malhotra, 87–104. Abingdon, Oxon: Routledge, 2017.

Ben-Moshe, Liat, et al. Forum, "Beyond 'Criminal Justice Reform': Conversations on Police and Prison Abolition." NYU Law School, New York, October 14, 2016.

Ben Porat, Ido. "Outrage in Jewish Home as 'Surrogacy Bill' Passes." *Arutz Sheva: Israel National News*, October 28, 2014.

Bennett, Jane. *Vibrant Matter: A Political Ecology of Things*. Durham, NC: Duke University Press, 2010.

Berlant, Lauren. *Cruel Optimism*. Durham, NC: Duke University Press, 2011.

———. "Slow Death (Sovereignty, Obesity, Lateral Agency)." *Critical Inquiry* 33 (2007): 754–80.

Best Colleges. "Overview of College Resources for Students with Disabilities." N.d. Accessed April 21, 2017. http://www.bestcolleges.com/resources/disabled-students/.

Beste, Robin. "The Reason Why Israel Killed So Many Pregnant Women in Gaza." *Stop the War Coalition*, August 16, 2014. Accessed February 1, 2015. http://stopwar.org.uk /news/the-reason-why-israel-is-killing-so-many-pregnant-women-in-gaza#.U9CG7 -MaZZT.

Bethlehem Arab Society for Rehabilitation. *Annual Report 2010*. Accessed November 5, 2016. http://www.basr.org/en/images/reports/annualreport2010.pdf.

Bhabha, Homi. "Of Mimicry and Man: The Ambivalence of Colonial Discourse." *October* 28 (1984): 125–33.

Bhandar, Brenna. "Acts and Omissions: Framing Settler Colonialism in Palestine Studies." *Jadaliyya*, January 14, 2016.

Bickenbach, Jerome, Franziska Felder, and Barbara Schmitz, eds. *Disability and the Good Human Life*. Cambridge: Cambridge University Press, 2015.

Birenbaum-Carmeli, Daphna, and Yoram S. Carmeli. "Introduction: Reproductive Technologies among Jewish Israelis: Setting the Ground." In *Kin, Gene, Community: Reproductive Technologies among Jewish Israelis*, edited by Daphna Birenbaum-Carmeli and Yoram S. Careli, 1–48. New York: Berghahn, 2010.

Black Solidarity with Palestine. "2015 Black Solidarity Statement with Palestine." N.d. Accessed November 5, 2016. http://www.blackforpalestine.com/read-the-statement .html.

Block, Pamela, Devva Kasnitz, Akemi Nishida, and Nick Pollard, eds. *Disability*. New York: Springer, 2016.

Blumenthal, Max. "Evidence Emerges of Israeli 'Shoot to Cripple' Policy in the Occupied West Bank." *Alternet*, August 8, 2014. Accessed February 1, 2015. http://www.alternet .org/world/evidence-emerges-israeli-shoot-cripple-policy-occupied-west-bank.

———. "International Community Promises to Rebuild Gaza . . . with Sweat Shops to Exploit Palestinian Workers." *Alternet*, October 16, 2014. Accessed February 1, 2015. http://www.alternet.org/world/international-community-promises-rebuild-gaza -sweat-shops-exploit-palestinian-workers.

Bogdan, Robert. *Picturing Disability: Beggar, Freak, Citizen, and Other Photographic Rhetoric*. Syracuse, NY: Syracuse University Press, 2012.

Boris, Eileen, and Rhacel Salazar Parreñas, eds. *Intimate Labors: Cultures, Technologies, and the Politics of Care*. Stanford, CA: Stanford Social Sciences, 2010.

Boyarin, Daniel. *Unheroic Conduct: The Rise of Heterosexuality and the Invention of the Jewish Man*. Berkeley: University of California Press, 1997.

Breckenridge, Carol Appadurai, and Candace A. Vogler. "The Critical Limits of Embodiment: Disability's Criticism." *Public Culture* 13, no. 3 (2001): 349–57.

Brennan, Teresa. *The Transmission of Affect*. Ithaca, NY: Cornell University Press, 2004.

Burkhauser, Richard V. "Post-ADA: Are People with Disabilities Expected to Work?" *Annals of the American Academy of Political and Social Science* 549 (1997): 71–83.

Burris, Scott, and Kathryn Moss. "The Employment Discrimination Provisions of the Americans with Disabilities Act: Implementation and Impact." *Hofstra Labor and Employment Law Journal* 1 (2007): 1–32.

Butler, Ruth, and Sophia Bowlby. "Bodies and Spaces: An Exploration of Disabled People's Experiences of Public Space." *Environment and Planning D: Society and Space* 15, no. 4 (1997): 411–33.

Cage, Diana. "It Doesn't Get Better. You Get Stronger." *Velvetpark*, October 2, 2010. Accessed February 1, 2011. http://velvetparkmedia.com/blogs/it-doesnt-get-better -you-get-stronger.

Campus Pride. "Campus Climate Index." 2015. Accessed July 1, 2015. http://www .campusclimateindex.org.

Carlson, Licia. "The Human as Just an Other Animal: Madness, Disability, and Foucault's Bestiary." In *Phenomenology and the Non-human Animal*, edited by Corrine Painter and Christian Lotz, 117–33. Dordrecht: Springer, 2007.

Cavanagh, Sheila. "Touching Gender: Abjection and the Hygienic Imagination." In *Transgender Studies Reader 2*, edited by Susan Stryker and Aren Z. Aizura, 426–42. New York: Routledge, 2013.

The Chairman of the Executive Committee of the Palestine Liberation Organization and the President of the Palestinian National Authority. *Palestinian Disability Law: Law Number 4 for the Year 1999 Concerning the Rights of the Disabled*. Gaza City, 1999. http://siteresources.worldbank.org/DISABILITY/Resources/Regions/MENA /PalestinianDisLaw.pdf.

Chamie, Joseph. "By 2035, Jewish Population in Israel/Palestine Is Projected at 46 Percent." *Mondoweiss*, February 21, 2014. Accessed February 1, 2015. http:// mondoweiss.net/2014/02/population-israelpalestine-projected#sthash.n5jmabrE .dpuf.

Chan, Jeffrey. "Challenges to Realizing the Convention on the Rights of Persons with Disabilities (CRPD) in Australia for People with Intellectual Disability and Behaviours of Concern." *Psychiatry, Psychology and Law* 23, no. 2 (2015): 207–14.

Charlton, James. *Nothing about Us without Us: Disability Oppression and Empowerment*. Berkeley: University of California Press, 1998.

Chatterjee, Partha. *The Nation and Its Fragments: Colonial and Postcolonial Histories*. Princeton, NJ: Princeton University Press, 1993.

Chehata, Hanan. "Israel: Promised Land for Jews . . . as Long as They're Not Black?" *Race and Class* 53, no. 4 (2012): 67–77.

Chen, Mel. *Animacies: Biopolitics, Racial Mattering, and Queer Affect*. Durham, NC: Duke University Press, 2012.

Chick, Kristen. "Under Fire in Gaza, and Not a Drop to Drink." *Christian Science Monitor*, July 24, 2014. Accessed February 1, 2015. http://www.csmonitor.com /World/Middle-East/2014/0724/Under-fire-in-Gaza-and-not-a-drop-to-drink -video.

Chow, Rey. *The Protestant Ethnic and the Spirit of Capitalism*. New York: Columbia University Press, 2002.

Chung, Jeannie J. "Identity or Condition: The Theory and Practice of Applying State Disability Laws to Transgender Individuals." *Columbia Journal of Gender and Law* 21, no. 1 (2011): 1–45.

Clare, Eli. "Body Shame, Body Pride: Lessons from the Disability Rights Movement." In *Transgender Studies Reader 2*, edited by Susan Stryker and Aren Z. Aizura, 261–65. New York: Routledge, 2013.

Cleves, Rachel H. "Beyond the Binaries in Early America: Special Issue Introduction." *Early American Studies: An Interdisciplinary Journal* 12, no. 3 (2014): 459–68.

Clough, Patricia, ed. *The Affective Turn: Theorizing the Social*. Durham, NC: Duke University Press, 2007.

———. "Future Matters: Technoscience, Global Politics, and Cultural Criticism." *Social Text* 22, no. 3 80 (2004): 1–23.

CNN wire staff. "Document: Israel Calculated Calorie Needs for Embargoed Gazans." CNN, October 18, 2012. Accessed April 21, 2017. http://www.cnn.com/2012/10/17 /world/meast/israel-calorie-count-gaza/.

Cockburn, Patrick. "Toxic Legacy of US Assault on Fallujah 'Worse Than Hiroshima.' " *Independent*, July 24, 2010.

Cohen, Dan. "In the Last Days of 'Operation Protective Edge' Israel Focused on Its Final Goal—the Destruction of Gaza's Professional Class." *Mondoweiss*, October 13, 2014. Accessed February 1, 2015. http://mondoweiss.net/2014/10/protective -destruction-professional.

Colebrook, Claire. "On the Very Possibility of Queer Theory." In *Deleuze and Queer Theory*, edited by Chrysanthi Nigianni and Merl Storr, 11–23. Edinburgh: Edinburgh University Press, 2009.

Colker, Ruth. "Homophobia, AIDS Hysteria, and the Americans with Disabilities Act." *Journal of Gender, Race and Justice* 8, no. 1 (2004): 1–20.

Connell, Raewyn. "Southern Bodies and Disability: Re-thinking Concepts." *Third World Quarterly* 32, no. 8 (2011): 1369–81.

Craggs, Ryan. "Stephen Hawking Boycotts Israel Academic Conference." *Huffington Post*, May 7, 2013. http://www.huffingtonpost.com/2013/05/08/stephen-hawking -israel-boycott-pulls-out-of-israel-conference_n_3235337.html.

Crawford, Lucas Cassidy. "Transgender without Organs? Mobilizing a Geo-affective Theory of Gender Modification." *Women's Studies Quarterly* 36, nos. 3/4 (2008): 127–43.

Crawford, Neta C. "War-Related Death, Injury, and Displacement in Afghanistan and Pakistan." http://reliefweb.int/report/afghanistan/war-related-death-injury-and-displacement-afghanistan-and-pakistan-2001–2014.

Crosby, Christina. "Disabling Biopolitics: Optimal Capacity, Optimal Debility Panel." Panel discussion at the annual meeting of the American Studies Association, San Juan, Puerto Rico, November 17, 2012.

Currah, Paisley. "Stepping Back, Looking Outward: Situating Transgender Activism and Transgender Studies—Kris Hayashi, Matt Richardson, and Susan Stryker Frame the Movement." *Sexuality Research and Social Policy* 5, no. 1 (2008): 93–105.

Currah, Paisley, Lisa Jean Moore, and Susan Stryker. "Introduction: Trans-, Trans, or Transgender?" *wsq: Women's Studies Quarterly* 36, nos. 3–4 (2008): 11–22.

Da Silva, Denise Ferreira. *Toward a Global Idea of Race*. Minneapolis: University of Minnesota Press, 2007.

Davidson, Michael. "Universal Design: The Work of Disability in an Age of Globalization." In *The Disability Studies Reader*, 2nd ed., edited by Lennard J. Davis, 117–31. New York: Routledge, 2006.

Davis, Angela Y. *Freedom Is a Constant Struggle: Ferguson, Palestine, and the Foundations of a Movement*. Chicago: Haymarket Books, 2016.

Davis, Lennard J. *Enabling Acts: The Hidden Story of How the Americans with Disabilities Act Gave the Largest US Minority Its Rights*. Boston: Beacon, 2015.

Dawes, Simon. "The Digital Occupation of Gaza: An Interview with Helga Tawil-Souri." *Networking Knowledge: Journal of the MeCCSA Postgraduate Network* 8, no. 2 (2015).

Dawson, Ashley. *Extinction: A Radical History*. New York: OR Books, 2016.

Dawson, Ashley, and Bill V. Mullen, eds. *Against Apartheid: The Case for Boycotting Israeli Universities*. Chicago: Haymarket Books, 2015.

DeFalco, Beth. "Dharun Ravi, Tyler Clementi's Roommate, Hit with Bias Charge in Rutgers Suicide." *Huffington Post*, April 20, 2011. Accessed February 1, 2015. http://www.huffingtonpost.com/2011/04/20/dharun-ravi-tylerclement_n_851497.html.

DeGeneres, Ellen. "It Gets Better." YouTube, September 30, 2010. Accessed August 1, 2015. https://www.youtube.com/watch?v=_B-hVWQnjjM.

Degun, Tom. "Palestinian Paralympic Committee Headquarters Destroyed in Gaza Bombings." *Inside the Games*, November 22, 2012. Accessed February 1, 2015. http://www.insidethegames.biz/paralympics/1011785-palestinian-paralympic-committee-headquarters-destroyed-in-gaza-bombings.

DeLanda, Manuel. *New Philosophy of Society: Assemblage Theory and Social Complexity*. Continuum: London, 2006.

Deleuze, Gilles. *Negotiations, 1972–1990*. New York: Columbia University Press, 1995.

———. "Postscript on Control Societies." In *Negotiations 1972–1990*. New York: Columbia University Press, 1995.

Deleuze, Gilles, and Félix Guattari. *A Thousand Plateaus: Capitalism and Schizophrenia*. Translated by Brian Massumi. Minneapolis: University of Minnesota Press, 1987.

Deleuze, Gilles, and Timothy S. Murphy. "The Grandeur of Yasser Arafat." *Discourse* 20, no. 3 (1998): 30–33.

Derrida, Jacques. *The Animal That Therefore I Am*. Translated by David Wills. New York: Fordham University Press, 2008.

Deutsche Presse-Agenteur. "Palestinians to Outnumber Jewish Population by 2020, Report Says." *Seattle Times*, December 31, 2012. Accessed February 1, 2015. http://seattletimes.com/html/nationworld/2020031415_palestinianpopulationxml.html.

Dewachi, Omar. "Blurred Lines: Warfare and Health Care." *Medicine Anthropology Theory*, July 8, 2015.

———. "The Toxicity of Everyday Survival in Iraq." *Jadaliyya*, August 13, 2013.

Dhanda, Amita. "Legal Capacity in the Disability Rights Convention: Stranglehold of the Past or Lodestar for the Future." *Syracuse Journal of International Law and Commerce* 2 (2006): 429–62.

Disabled World. "Invisible Disabilities: List and Information." April 13, 2015.

Doctors Without Borders. "Gaza: A Population under Siege." July 14, 2014. Accessed February 1, 2015. http://www.doctorswithoutborders.org/news-stories/gaza-population-under-siege.

Douglas, Mary. *Purity and Danger: An Analysis of Concepts of Pollution and Taboo*. London: Routledge, 2002.

Draper, William, Carolyn Hawley, Brian T. McMahon, and Christina A. Reid. "Workplace Discrimination and the Record of Disability." *Journal of Vocational Rehabilitation* 36, no. 3 (2012): 199–206.

Duggan, Lisa, and José E. Muñoz. "Hope and Hopelessness: A Dialogue." *Women and Performance: A Journal of Feminist Theory* 19, no. 2 (2009): 275–93.

Dupras, Charles, and Vardit Ravitsky. "Epigenetics in the Neoliberal 'Regime of Truth': A Biopolitical Perspective on Knowledge Translation." *Hastings Center Report* 46, no. 1 (2016): 26–35.

Dyke, Joe. "Analysis: Donors Threaten to Withhold Gaza Aid." IRIN: *Humanitarian News and Analysis*, October 7, 2014. Accessed March 1, 2015. http://www.irinnews.org/report/100690/analysis-donors-threaten-to-withhold-gaza-aid.

Dykstra, Laurel. "What If It Doesn't Get Better? Queer and Aboriginal Youth Suicide." *CommonDreams*, October 9, 2010. Accessed February 1, 2011. http://www.commondreams.org/views/2010/10/09/what-if-it-doesn't-get-better-queer-and-aboriginal-youth-suicide.

Edelman, Lee. *No Future: Queer Theory and the Death Drive*. Durham, NC: Duke University Press, 2004.

Efrati, Ido. "Israeli Court Decides Dead Man's Sperm Can Be Used after All." *Haaretz*, June 16, 2014.

Ehrenreich, Barbara. "Dead, White, and Blue: The Great Die-Off of America's Blue Collar Whites." *TomDispatch*, December 1, 2015.

Eide, Arne H. "Impact of Community-Based Rehabilitation Programmes: The Case of Palestine." *Scandinavian Journal of Disability Research* 8, no. 4 (2006): 199–210.

Eisenberg, Anne. "When a Camcorder Becomes a Life Partner." *New York Times*, November 6, 2010. Accessed February 1, 2011. http://www.nytimes.com/2010/11/07/business/07novel.html?_r=0.

Emmys. "'It Gets Better' to Get Governors Award." Emmys.com, August 29, 2012. Accessed August 1, 2015. http://www.emmys.com/news/awards-news/it-gets-better-get-governors-award.

ENDAblog. "Queer Channel Media: Trans-washing the ADA." July 28, 2011. Accessed April 21, 2017. https://endablog.wordpress.com/2011/07/28/queer-channel-media-trans-washing-the-ada/.

Epstein, Mary. "Esau's Mission, or Trauma as Propaganda: Disability after the Intifada." *Review of Disability Studies: An International Journal* 2, no. 3 (2006): 12–23.

Erevelles, Nirmala. "The Color of Violence: Reflecting on Gender, Race, and Disability in Wartime." In *Feminist Disability Studies*, edited by Kim Q. Hall, 117–35. Bloomington: Indiana University Press, 2011.

———. "Crippin' Jim Crow: Disability, Dis-location, and the School-to-Prison Pipeline." In *Disability Incarcerated: Imprisonment and Disability in the United States and Canada*, edited by Liat Ben-Moshe, Chris Chapman, and Allison C. Carey, 81–99. New York: Palgrave Macmillan, 2014.

———. *Disability and Difference in Global Contexts: Enabling a Transformative Body Politic.* New York: Palgrave Macmillan, 2011.

Erevelles, Nirmala, and Andrea Minear. "Unspeakable Offenses: Untangling Race and Disability in Discourses of Intersectionality." *Journal of Literary and Cultural Disability Studies* 4, no. 2 (2010): 127–45.

Eskay, M., V. C. Onu, J. N. Igbo, N. Obiyo, and L. Ugwuanyi. "Disability within the African Culture." *US-China Education Review* 2, no. 4b (2012): 473–84.

Esmeir, Samera. "Colonial Experiments in Gaza." *Jadaliyya*, July 14, 2014. Accessed February 1, 2015. http://www.jadaliyya.com/pages/index/8482/colonial-experiments-in-gaza.

Fanon, Frantz. *A Dying Colonialism.* Translated by Haakon Chevalier. New York: Grove Press, 1994.

Feldman, Allen. "Genocidal Desistance in Gaza." *Social Text Online*, August 27, 2014. Accessed February 1, 2015. http://socialtextjournal.org/genocidal-desistance-in-gaza/.

Feldman, Ilana. "Gaza's Humanitarianism Problem." *Journal of Palestine Studies* 38, no. 3 (2009): 22–37.

———. *Governing Gaza: Bureaucracy, Authority, and the Work of Rule, 1917–1967.* Durham, NC: Duke University Press, 2008.

———. *Police Encounters: Security and Surveillance in Gaza under Egyptian Rule.* Stanford, CA: Stanford University Press, 2015.

Femmephane. "Why I Don't Like Dan Savage's It Gets Better." Blog entry. September 30, 2010. Accessed February 1, 2011. http://tempcontretemps.wordpress.com/2010/09/30/why-i-dont-like-dan-savages-it-gets-better-project-as-a-response-to-bullying/.

Fineman, Mark. "10 Year War Disfigures a Nation and Its People: Afghanistan: Amputees Flood Daily into Kabul for Help. Many Must Wait Months for Artificial Limbs." *Los Angeles Times*, April 2, 1990.

Finkelstein, Norman G. *The Holocaust Industry: Reflections on the Exploitation of Jewish Suffering.* London: Verso, 2000.

Foderaro, Lisa. "Invasion of Privacy Charges after Tyler Clementi's Death." *New York Times*, September 20, 2010. Accessed February 1, 2011. http://www.nytimes.com /2010/09/30/nyregion/30suicide.html.

———. "Roommate Faces Hate-Crime Charges in Rutgers Case." *New York Times*, April 20, 2011. Accessed July 1, 2011. http://www.nytimes.com/2011/04/21/nyregion /rutgers-roommate-faces-hate-crime-charges-in-spying-suicide.html.

Ford, Chandra L., and Collins O. Airhihenbuwa. "Critical Race Theory, Race Equity, and Public Health: Toward Antiracism Praxis." *American Journal of Public Health* 100, suppl. 1 (2010): s30–s35.

Fosado, Gisela, and Janet R. Jakobsen, eds. "Valuing Domestic Work." Special issue, *Scholar & Feminist Online* 8, no. 1, 2009.

Foucault, Michel. *The Birth of Biopolitics: Lectures at the College de France, 1978–1979*. Translated by Graham Burchell. New York: Picador, 2010.

———. *Discipline and Punish: The Birth of the Prison*. Translated by Alan Sheridan. New York: Random House, 1977.

———. *The History of Sexuality*. Vol. 1, *An Introduction*. Translated by Robert Hurley. New York: Vintage, 1990.

———. *Security, Territory, Population: Lectures at the Collège de France 1977–1978*. Translated by Graham Burchell. New York: Picador, 2009.

———. *"Society Must Be Defended": Lectures at the College de France, 1975–1976*. Translated by David Macey. New York: Picador, 2003.

Franke, Katherine. "Queering the Air: Rutgers Queer Community Responds Thoughtfully to Clementi's Suicide." *Columbia Gender and Sexuality Law Blog*, October 21, 2010. Accessed February 1, 2011. http://blogs.law.columbia.edu /genderandsexualitylawblog/2010/10/21/queering-the-air-rutgers-queer-community -responds-thoughtfully-to-clementis-suicide/comment-page-13/.

Franklin, Seb. *Control: Digitality as Cultural Logic*. Cambridge, MA: MIT Press, 2015.

Freidman, Emily. "Victim of Secret Dorm Sex Tape Posts Facebook Goodbye, Jumps to His Death." ABC News, September 29, 2010. Accessed February 1, 2011. http:// abcnews.go.com/US/victim-secret-dorm-sex-tape-commits-suicide/story?id =11758716.

Frenkel, Sheera. "Vigilantes Patrol for Jewish Women Dating Arab Men." Interview by Renee Montagne. NPR, October 12, 2009.

Furlan, Julia. "The 'It Gets Better Project' Turns the Spotlight on Anti-gay Bullying." WNYC, March 22, 2011. Accessed March 30, 2011. http://www.wnyc.org/story/119356 -it-gets-better-project-page-and-nyc/.

Gal, John, and Michael Bar. "The Needed and the Needy: The Policy Legacies of Benefits for Disabled War Veterans in Israel." *Journal of Social Policy* 29, no. 4 (2000): 577–98.

García Iriarte, Edurne, Roy McConkey, and Robert Gilligan, eds. *Disability and Human Rights: Global Perspectives*. London: Palgrave Macmillan, 2015.

Gardner, Simon. "Afghan War Amputees Turn Prosthesis Pros." *Relief Web*, September 10, 2007. Accessed March 25, 2016. http://reliefweb.int/report/afghanistan /afghan-war-amputees-turn-prosthesis-pros.

Garland-Thomson, Rosemarie. "Becoming Disabled." *New York Times*, August 18, 2016. Accessed November 5, 2016. http://www.nytimes.com/2016/08/21/opinion/sunday/becoming-disabled.html.

———. "Disability Studies: A Field Emerged." *American Quarterly* 65, no. 4 (2013): 915–26.

———. *Extraordinary Bodies: Figuring Physical Disability in American Culture and Literature*. New York: Columbia University Press, 1997.

———. *Staring: How We Look*. Oxford: Oxford University Press, 2009.

Garza, Alicia. "A Herstory of the #BlackLivesMatter Movement." *Feminist Wire*, October 7, 2014. Accessed November 6, 2016. http://www.thefeministwire.com/2014/10/blacklivesmatter-2/.

Gerber, David A. "Disabled Veterans, the State, and the Experience of Disability in Western Societies, 1914–1950." *Journal of Social History* 35, no. 4 (2003): 899–916.

Ghert-Zand, Renee. "If Daddy Says No, Ask Abba." *Jerusalem Post*, December 26, 2011.

Giacaman, Rita. "A Community of Citizens: Disability Rehabilitation in the Palestinian Transition to Statehood." *Disability and Rehabilitation* 23, no. 14 (2001): 639–44.

———. "A Population at Risk of Risks: No One Is in a Healthy State in Palestine." Ramallah: Institute of Community and Public Health, Birzeit University, 2002.

Giacaman, Rita, Ibrahim Deibes, Atieh H. Salem, and Rustum Nammari. *Towards the Formulation of a Rehabilitation Policy: Disability in the West Bank*. West Bank, Palestine: Birzeit University, 1989.

Gibilisco, Peter. *Politics, Disability and Social Inclusion: People with Different Abilities in the 21st Century*. Beau Bassin, Mauritius: VDM, 2011.

Gilbert, Melody. *(W)hole*. IMDBPro. 2003.

Gill, Michael, and Cathy J. Schlund-Vials, eds. *Disability, Human Rights and the Limits of Humanitarianism*. Farnham, UK: Ashgate, 2014.

Gilmore, Ruth Wilson. *Golden Gulag: Prisons, Surplus, Crisis, and Opposition in Globalizing California*. Berkeley: University of California Press, 2007.

Gisha–Legal Center for Freedom of Movement. "A Costly Divide: Economic Repercussions of Separating Gaza and the West Bank." February 2015. Accessed August 16, 2015. http://gisha.org/UserFiles/File/publications/a_costly_divide/a_costly_divide_en-web.pdf.

———. "The Gaza Cheat Sheet: Real Data on the Gaza Closure." July 9, 2015. Accessed August 16, 2015. http://www.gisha.org/UserFiles/File/publications/Info_Gaza_Eng.pdf.

Goldberg, Michelle. "Made in Heaven." *Tablet Magazine*, March 17, 2011.

Goldstein, Joseph, and Eric Schmitt. "Human Error Cited in U.S. Strike on Kunduz Hospital." *New York Times*, November 24, 2015.

Gooding, Piers. "Navigating the 'Flashing Amber Lights' of the Right to Legal Capacity in the United Nations Convention on the Rights of Persons with Disabilities: Responding to Major Concerns." *Human Rights Law Review* 15, no. 1 (2015): 45–71.

Goodley, Dan, Rebecca Lawthom, and Katherine Runswick Cole. "Posthuman Disability Studies." *Subjectivity* 7 (2014): 342–61.

Gordts, Eline. "Ethiopian Women Claim Israel Forced Them to Accept Birth Control Shots." *Huffington Post*, January 28, 2013. Accessed April 21, 2017. http://www.huffingtonpost.com/2013/01/28/ethiopian-women-israel-birth-control-shots_n_2567016.html.

Gorton, R. Nick. "Transgender Health Benefits: Collateral Damage in the Resolution of the National Health Care Financing Dilemma." *Sexuality Research and Social Policy Journal of NSRC* 4, no. 4 (2007): 81–91.

Gossett, Che. "Abolitionist Imaginings: Interview with Bo Brown, Reina Gossett and Dylan Rodriguez." In *Captive Genders: Trans Embodiment and the Prison Industrial Complex*, edited by Eric A. Stanley and Nat Smith, 323–42. Oakland, CA: AK Press, 2011.

———. "We Will Not Rest in Peace: AIDS Activism, Black Radicalism, Queer and/or Trans Resistance." In *Queer Necropolitics*, edited by Adi Kuntsman, Jin Haritaworn, and Silvia Posocco, 31–50. New York: Routledge, 2014.

Gottesdiener, Laura. "What's the Real Story behind the American Attack on Doctors Without Borders?" *Nation*, November 16, 2015.

Gould, Rebecca. "The Materiality of Resistance: Israel's Apartheid Wall in an Age of Globalization." *Social Text* 32, no. 1 118 (2014): 1–21.

Grabham, Emily. "Governing Permanence: Trans Subjects, Time, and the Gender Recognition Act." *Social and Legal Studies* 19, no. 1 (2010): 107–26.

Graff, James A. "Crippling a People: Palestinian Children and Israeli State Violence." *Alif: Journal of Comparative Poetics* 13 (1993): 46–63.

Gray, Rosie. "First Black Miss Israel: 'I'm Not Ashamed to Say There Is Racism in Israel.'" *BuzzFeed*, February 20, 2015.

Gregg, Melissa, and Gregory J. Seigworth, eds. *The Affect Theory Reader*. Durham, NC: Duke University Press, 2010.

Griffin, Kathy. "It Gets Better." YouTube, October 4, 2010. Accessed August 1, 2015. https://www.youtube.com/watch?v=Vu2JeZn1Uwo.

Gross, Aeyal. "Disabled Diaspora, Rehabilitating State: The Queer Politics of Reproduction in Israel/Palestine." Roundtable discussion, University of London School of Oriental and African Studies, May 2014.

Groves, Steven. "Should the Senate Ratify the Disabilities Treaty?" *U.S. News Digital Weekly* 6, no. 2 (2014): 15.

Guéry, François, and Didier Deleule. *The Productive Body*. Translated by Philip Barnard and Stephen Shapiro. Winchester, UK: Zero Books, 2014.

Gunn, Tim. "It Gets Better." YouTube, October 5, 2010. Accessed August 1, 2015. https://www.youtube.com/watch?v=9GGAgtq_rQc.

Haaretz Service. "Court: Israeli Woman Can Use Deceased Man's Sperm to Get Pregnant." *Haaretz*, June 12, 2012.

———. "Prime Minister Benjamin Netanyahu's Speech to AIPAC Conference." *Haaretz*, April 23, 2010.

Halberstam, J. [Jack]. *In a Queer Time and Place: Transgender Bodies, Subcultural Lives*. New York: NYU Press, 2005.

Hamada, Mazen Solaiman, Adnan Aish, and Mai Shahwan. "Potential of Phosphorous Pollution in the Soil of the Northern Gaza Strip, Palestine." *Agrivita* 33, no. 3 (2011): 291–99.

Hamdan, Motasem, and Nihad Al-Akhras. *A Survey of People with Special Needs at 27 Palestinian Villages in Tulkarm and Qalqilia Districts.* Nablus: Union of Health Care Committees, 2006. Accessed April 21, 2017. http://www.ochaopt.org/documents/opt_health_uhcc_disabled_needs_nwb_july_2008.pdf.

Hamid, Habiba. "Why Are the Arab Gulf Countries Silent on Gaza?" *Guardian*, August 8, 2014. Accessed March 1, 2015. http://www.theguardian.com/commentisfree/2014/aug/08/arab-gulf-states-silent-on-gaza.

Hamilton, Anna. "Working Out Some Issues: The Latest in 'Inspirational' Ableism." *Bitch* 62 (2014): 5.

Hamou, Nathalie. "Israel, a Paradise for Gay Families." *New Family*, January 13, 2011.

Hamspon, Rich. "Suicide Shows Need for Civility, Privacy Online." *USAToday*, October 4, 2010. Accessed February 1, 2011. http://www.usatoday.com/news/nation/2010-09-30-rutgers-suicide-sex-video_N.htm.

Hancock, Ange-Marie. "Intersectionality as a Normative and Empirical Paradigm." *Politics and Gender* 3, no. 2 (2007): 248–54.

Hanieh, Adam. "The Oslo Illusion." *Jacobin* 10 (2013): 68–74.

———. "Palestine in the Middle East: Opposing Neoliberalism and US Power: Part 1." *Monthly Review Zine*, July 19, 2008.

Hantel, Max. "Posthumanism, Landscapes of Memory, and the Materiality of AIDS in South Africa." *Women's Studies Quarterly* 40, no. 1 (2012): 251–56.

Haraway, Donna. *When Species Meet.* Minneapolis: University of Minnesota Press, 2007.

Hardigan, Richard. "Palestinians with Disabilities Are Not Immune from Israeli Violence." *Mondoweiss*, September 12, 2016. Accessed November 6, 2016. http://mondoweiss.net/2016/09/palestinians-disabilities-violence/.

Hardt, Michael. Preface to "Palestine: Cartography of an Occupation." *Creative Time Reports*, September 16, 2013. Accessed November 6, 2016. http://creativetimereports.org/2013/09/16/palestine-mtl-cartography-occupation/.

———. "The Withering of Civil Society." *Social Text* 14, no. 4 45 (1995): 27–44.

Hardt, Michael, and Antonio Negri. *Empire.* Cambridge, MA: Harvard University Press, 2001.

Haritaworn, Jin, and C. Riley Snorton. "Trans Necropolitics: A Transnational Reflection on Violence, Death, and the Trans of Color Afterlife." In *Transgender Studies Reader 2*, edited by Susan Stryker and Aren Z. Aizura, 66–76. New York: Routledge, 2013.

Harriet Tubman Collective. "The Vision for Black Lives Is Incomplete without Disability Solidarity." *For Harriet*, September 2016. Accessed November 4, 2016. http://www.forharriet.com/2016/09/the-vision-for-black-lives-is.html.

Harris, Lynn J. "The Americans with Disabilities Act and Australia's Disability Discrimination Act: Overcoming the Inadequacies." *Loyola of Los Angeles International and Comparative Law Review* 1 (1999): 51–98.

Harrison, Tracie Culp. "Has the Americans with Disabilities Act Made a Difference? A Policy Analysis of Quality of Life in the Post–Americans with Disabilities Act Era." *Policy, Politics and Nursing Practice* 3, no. 4 (2002): 333–47.

Hartlaub, Peter. "Dan Savage Overwhelmed by Gay Outreach's Response." *San Francisco Chronicle*, October 8, 2010. Accessed August 1, 2015. http://www.sfgate.com/news/article/Dan-Savage-overwhelmed-by-gay-outreach-s-response-3171312.php.

Hartman, Ben. "Tel Aviv Named 'World's Best Gay City' for 2011." *Jerusalem Post*, January 11, 2012.

Hashiloni-Dolev, Yael. *A Life (Un)Worthy of Living: Reproductive Genetics in Israel and Germany*. Dordrecht: Springer, 2007.

Hass, Amira. "Is the IDF Conducting a Kneecapping Campaign in the West Bank?" *Haaretz*, August 27, 2016. Accessed November 5, 2016. http://www.haaretz.com/israel-news/1.738889.

Hass, Amira, and Ido Efrati. "Gaza's Water System Collapsing Due to IDF Strikes, Says Red Cross." *Haaretz*, July 16, 2014. Accessed February 1, 2015. http://www.haaretz.com/news/middle-east/.premium-1.605332.

Hasson, Nir. "For the First Time: Parents of a Deceased Soldier Are Allowed to Use His Sperm to Fertilize a Woman He Has Not Known" [Hebrew]. *Haaretz*, January 15, 2007.

Hayward, Eva. "Lessons from a Starfish." In *Queering the Non/Human*, edited by Noreen Giffney and Myra J. Hird, 249–64. Burlington, VT: Ashgate, 2008.

Hayward, Eva, and Malin Ah King. "Toxic Sexes: Perverting Pollution and Queering Hormone Disruption." *O-Zone: A Journal of Object Oriented Studies* 1 (2013): 1–12.

Helweg-Larsen, Karin, Ashraf Hasan Abdel-Jabbar Al-Qadi, Jalal Al-Jabriri, and Henrik Bronnum-Hansen. "Systematic Medical Data Collection of Intentional Injuries during Armed Conflicts: A Pilot Study Conducted in West Bank, Palestine." *Scandinavian Journal of Public Health* 32, no. 1 (2004): 17–23.

Henderson, Barney. "Israel Air Strike 'Hits Charitable Association for Disabled' in Gaza." *Telegraph*, July 12, 2014. Accessed February 1, 2015. http://www.telegraph.co.uk/news/worldnews/middleeast/israel/10963427/Israel-air-strike-hits-charitable-association-for-disabled-in-Gaza.html.

Herbert, L. Camille. "Transforming Transsexual and Transgender Rights." *William and Mary Journal of Women and the Law* 15, no. 3 (2009): 535–90.

Hevey, David. "The Enfreakment of Photography." In *The Disability Studies Reader*, 2nd ed., edited by Lennard J. Davis, 367–79. New York: Routledge, 2006.

Heywood, Todd A. "Gay Oakland University Student Found Dead of Suicide on Campus." *Michigan Messenger*, October 20, 2010. Accessed February 1, 2011. http://michiganmessenger.com/42754/gay-oakland-university-student-found-dead-of-suicide-on-campus.

Hicks, Amanda, William R. Hogan, Michael Rutherford, Bradley Malin, Mengjun Xie, Christiane Fellbaum, Zhijun Yin, Daniel Fabbri, Josh Hanna, and Jiang Bian. "Mining Twitter as a First Step toward Assessing the Adequacy of Gender Identification Terms on Intake Forms." Paper. 2015. Accessed September 1, 2015. http://jiangbian.me/papers/2015/GenderIdentificationOnTwitter_AMIA2015.pdf.

Hiegel, Adrienne L. "Sexual Exclusions: The Americans with Disabilities Act as a Moral Code." *Columbia Law Review* 94, no. 4 (1994): 1451–94.

Himmelstein, David, Deborah Throne, Elizabeth Warren, and Steffie Woolhandler. "Medical Bankruptcy in the United States, 2007: Results of a National Study." *American Journal of Medicine* 122, no. 8 (2009): 741–46.

Hird, Myra. "Animal Trans." In *Queering the Non/Human*, edited by Noreen Giffney and Myra J. Hird, 227–48. Burlington, VT: Ashgate, 2008.

Hochberg, Gil Z. *Visual Occupations: Violence and Visibility in a Conflict Zone*. Durham, NC: Duke University Press, 2015.

Hong, Kari. "Categorical Exclusions: Exploring Legal Responses to Health Care Discrimination against Transsexuals." *Columbia Journal of Gender and Law* 11 (2002): 88–126.

Horwitz, Allan V., and Jerome C. Wakefield. *The Loss of Sadness: How Psychiatry Transformed Normal Sorrow into Depressive Disorder*. Oxford: Oxford University Press, 2007.

Hubbard, Jeremy. "Fifth Gay Teen Suicide in Three Weeks Sparks Debate." abc News, October 3, 2010. Accessed February 1, 2011. http://abcnews.go.com/US/gay-teen-suicide-sparks-debate/story?id=11788128.

International Committee of the Red Cross. "Afghanistan: Facts and Figures for 2014." February 9, 2016. Accessed March 25, 2016. https://www.icrc.org/en/document/afghanistan-facts-and-figures-between-january-and-december-2014.

International Federation of Fertility Societies. *iffs Surveillance 2013*. Report.

Invisible Disabilities Association. "What Is an Invisible Disability?" N.d. Accessed April 21, 2017. https://invisibledisabilities.org/what-is-an-invisible-disability/.

Irvine, Janice M. *Disorders of Desire: Sexuality and Gender in Modern American Sexology*. Philadelphia: Temple University Press, 1990.

Irving, Dan. "Normalized Transgressions: Legitimizing the Transsexual Body as Productive." *Radical History Review* 100 (2008): 38–59.

Ivry, Tsipy. *Embodying Culture: Pregnancy in Japan and Israel*. New Brunswick, NJ: Rutgers University Press, 2010.

———. "Ultrasonic Challenges to Pro-natalism." In *Kin, Gene, Community: Reproductive Technologies among Jewish Israelis*, edited by Daphna Birenbaum-Carmeli and Yoram S. Carmeli, 174–201. New York: Berghahn, 2010.

Iyer, Ravi. "Opinion: The Dharun Ravi Case Reveals Our Collective Passivity." *Khabar*, May 2012. Accessed August 1, 2012. http://www.khabar.com/magazine/features/opinion_the_dharun_ravi_case_reveals_our_collective_passivity.

Jabareen, Iyad (director of Shabab Al-Balad for the Disabled). Interviewed by author. Al-Dahiriya, Hebron, Palestine. January 7, 2016.

Jackson, Zakiyyah Iman. "Animal: New Directions in the Theorization of Race and Posthumanism." *Feminist Studies* 39, no. 3 (2013): 669–85.

Jacques, Juliet. "Remembering Our Dead: Global Violence against Trans People." *OpenDemocracy* (digital commons), November 26, 2013. Accessed June 13, 2015. http://www.opendemocracy.net/5050/juliet-jacques/remembering-our-dead-global-violence-against-trans-people.

Jaffee, Laura Jordan. "Disrupting Global Disability Frameworks: Settler-Colonialism and the Geopolitics of Disability in Palestine/Israel." *Disability & Society* 31, no. 1 (2016): 116–30.

J.D. "Tyler Clementi's Accused Tormentors Dharun Ravi and Molly Wei Withdraw from Rutgers." *Queerty*, October 29, 2010. Accessed February 1, 2011. http://www.queerty.com/tyler-clementis-accused-tormentors-dharun-ravi-and-molly-wei-withdraw-from-rutgers-20101029.

Jain, Sarah Lochlann. *Injury: The Politics of Product Design and Safety Law in the United States*. Princeton, NJ: Princeton University Press, 2006.

———. "Living in Prognosis: Toward an Elegiac Politics." *Representations* 98, no. 1 (2007): 77–92.

———. *Malignant: How Cancer Becomes Us*. Berkeley: University of California Press, 2013.

Jamjoum, Lama. "The Effects of Israeli Violations during the Second Uprising 'Intifada' on Palestinian Health Conditions." *Social Justice* 29, no. 3 (2002): 53–72.

Jandura, Collette. "Rural Cherokee Children with Disabilities: Parental Stories of Special Education." PhD diss., University of the Incarnate Word, 2013. *ProQuest* (3571024).

Jarar, Allam. "Disability in Palestine: Realities and Perspectives." *This Week in Palestine*, no. 137 (September 2009).

Johnson, Mary. *Make Them Go Away: Clint Eastwood, Christopher Reeve and the Case against Disability Rights*. Louisville, KY: Advocado Press, 2003.

Juang, Richard. "Transgendering the Politics of Recognition." In *The Transgender Studies Reader*, edited by Susan Stryker and Stephen Whittle, 706–14. New York: Taylor and Francis, 2006.

Jünger, Ernst. *The Glass Bees*. New York: Noonday Press, 1961.

Kafer, Alison. *Feminist, Queer, Crip*. Bloomington: Indiana University Press, 2013.

Kahn, Susan Martha. *Reproducing Jews: A Cultural Account of Assisted Conception in Israel*. Durham, NC: Duke University Press, 2000.

Kamel, Sanaa. "Gaza's Youth Lose Hope." *Al Akhbar English*, September 25, 2012. Accessed November 7, 2016. http://english.al-akhbar.com/node/12624.

Kanaaneh, Rhoda Ann. *Birthing the Nation: Strategies of Palestinian Women in Israel*. Berkeley: University of California Press, 2002.

Kanter, Arlene S. "The Americans with Disabilities Act at 25 Years: Lessons to Learn from the Convention on the Rights of People with Disabilities." *Drake Law Review* 63, no. 3 (2015): 819–83.

Karger, H., and S. R. Rose. "Revisiting the Americans with Disabilities Act after Two Decades." *Journal of Social Work in Disability and Rehabilitation* 9, nos. 2/3 (2010): 73–86.

Kasrils, Ronnie. "Gaza and the 'Crime of Crimes.'" *Al Jazeera*, September 26, 2014. Accessed February 1, 2015. http://www.aljazeera.com/indepth/opinion/2014/09/gaza-crime-crimes-20149266404355756.html.

Kaufman, Gil. "Before Tyler Clementi's Suicide, Rutgers Planned 'Project Civility.'" MTV, October 1, 2010. Accessed February 1, 2011. http://www.mtv.com/news/articles/1649193/before-tyler-clementis-suicide-rutgers-planned-project-civility.jhtml.

Khalili, Laleh. "A Habit of Destruction." *Society and Space*, August 25, 2014. Accessed February 1, 2015. http://societyandspace.com/material/commentaries/laleh-khalili-a-habit-of-destruction/.

Khatib, Alaa, and Silvester Kasozi. "Disability and Explosive Remnants of War in Gaza." *This Week in Palestine*, no. 223 (November 2016).

Kier, Bailey. "Interdependent Ecological Transsex: Notes on Re/production." In *Transgender Studies Reader 2*, edited by Susan Stryker and Aren Z. Aizura, 189–98. New York: Routledge, 2013.

Kiley, Kathleen. "Why Leroy Moore, Jr. Has No Time for Small Talk." *Huffington Post*, September 30, 2016. Accessed November 6, 2016. http://www.huffingtonpost.com /kathleen-kiley/why-leroy-moore-jr-has-no_b_8215840.html.

Kim, Eunjung. "Why Do Dolls Die: The Power of Passivity and the Embodied Interplay between Disability and Sex Dolls." *Review of Education, Pedagogy, and Cultural Studies* 34 (2012): 94–106.

Kim, Richard. "Against 'Bullying' or On Loving Queer Kids." *Nation*, October 6, 2010. Accessed February 1, 2011. http://www.thenation.com/blog/155219/against-bullying -or-loving-queer-kids.

Kindregan, Charles P., Jr. "Dead Dads: Thawing an Heir from the Freezer." *William Mitchell Law Review* 35, no. 2 (2009): 433–48.

Kinker, Brenton. "An Evaluation of the Prospects for Successful Implementation of the Convention on the Rights of Persons with Disabilities in the Islamic World." *Michigan Journal of International Law* 2 (2013): 443–83.

Kirby, Vicki. *Quantum Anthropologies: Life at Large*. Durham, NC: Duke University Press, 2011.

Klein, Naomi. *The Shock Doctrine: The Rise of Disaster Capitalism*. Toronto: Alfred A. Knopf Canada, 2007.

Knight, Amber. "Democratizing Disability: Achieving Inclusion (without Assimilation) through 'Participatory Parity.'" *Hypatia: A Journal of Feminist Philosophy* 30, no. 1 (2015): 97–114.

Knittle, Andrew. "North Grad Took Own Life after Week of 'Toxic' Comments." *Norman Transcript*, October 10, 2010. Accessed February 1, 2011. http://normantranscript .com/headlines/x1477594493/-I-m-sure-he-took-it-personally.

Kochanek, Kenneth D., Elizabeth Arias, and Robert N. Anderson. "Leading Causes of Death Contributing to Decrease in Life Expectancy Gap between Black and White Populations: United States, 1999–2013." Centers for Disease Control and Prevention, November 2015.

Koehler, Pamela. "Using Disability Law to Protect Persons Living with HIV/AIDS: The Indian and American Approach." *Journal of Transnational Law and Policy* 19, no. 2 (2010): 401–27.

Kolářová, Kateřina. "'Grandpa Lives in Paradise Now': Biological Precarity and the Global Economy of Debility." *Feminist Review* 111, no. 1 (2015): 75–87.

Kotef, Hagar. *Movement and the Ordering of Freedom: On Liberal Governances of Modernity*. Durham, NC: Duke University Press, 2015.

Kraft, Dina. "Where Families Are Prized, Help Is Free." *New York Times*, July 17, 2011.

Krieger, Zvika. "Forget Marriage Equality; Israeli Gays Want Surrogacy Rights." *Atlantic*, April 4, 2014.

Kroløkke, Charlotte, and Stine Adrian. "Sperm on Ice: Fatherhood and Life after Death." *Australian Feminist Studies* 28, no. 77 (2013): 263–78.

Kubo, Melody. "Extraterritorial Application of the Americans with Disabilities Act." *Asian-Pacific Law and Policy Journal* 1 (2001): 259–90.

Kuntsman, Adi. *Figurations of Violence and Belonging: Queerness, Migranthood and Nationalism in Cyberspace and Beyond.* Oxford: Peter Lang, 2009.

Kuntsman, Adi, and Rebecca L. Stein. *Digital Militarism: Israel's Occupation in the Social Media Age.* Stanford, CA: Stanford University Press, 2015.

Kuppers, Petra. "Toward a Rhizomatic Model of Disability: Poetry, Performance and Touch." *Journal of Literary and Cultural Disability Studies* 3, no. 3 (2009): 221–40.

Kuppers, Petra, and James Overboe. "Introduction: Deleuze, Disability, and Difference." *Journal of Literary and Cultural Disability Studies* 3, no. 3 (2009): 217–20.

Kuzawa, C. W., and E. Sweet. "Epigenetics and the Embodiment of Race: Developmental Origins of US Racial Disparities in Cardiovascular Health." *American Journal of Human Biology* 21, no. 1 (2009): 2–15.

Landau, Ruth. "Posthumous Sperm Retrieval for the Purpose of Later Insemination or IVF in Israel: An Ethical and Psychosocial Critique." *Human Reproduction* 19, no. 9 (2004): 1952–56.

Lane, Christopher. *Shyness: How Normal Behavior Became a Sickness.* New Haven, CT: Yale University Press, 2007.

Lane, Harlan. "Construction of Deafness." In *The Disability Studies Reader*, 2nd ed., edited by Lennard J. Davis, 79–93. New York: Routledge, 2006.

Langan, Celeste. "Mobility Disability." *Public Culture* 3 (2001): 459–84.

Lawrence, Anne A. "Clinical and Theoretical Parallels between Desire for Limb Amputation and Gender Identity Disorder." *Archives of Sexual Behavior* 35, no. 3 (2006): 263–78.

Lee, Alvin. "Trans Models in Prison: The Medicalization of Gender Identity and the Eighth Amendment Right to Sex Reassignment Therapy." *Harvard Journal of Law and Gender* 31 (2008): 447–71.

Leichman, Abigail Klein. "The Men Who Make New Limbs." *Times of Israel*, November 11, 2011. Accessed November 5, 2016. http://www.israel21c.org/the-men-who-make-new-limbs/.

Le More, Anne. "Killing with Kindness: Funding the Demise of a Palestinian State." *International Affairs* 81, no. 5 (2005): 981–99.

Lennard, Natasha. "What Took Biden So Long on Trans Discrimination?" *Salon*, October 31, 2012. Accessed November 30, 2012. http://www.salon.com/2012/10/31/if_trans_discrimination_is_the_civil_rights_issue_of_our_time_why_is_biden_just_mentioning_it_now/.

Leonard, James. "The Equality Trap: How Reliance on Traditional Civil Rights Concepts Has Rendered Title I of the ADA Ineffective." *Case Western Reserve Law Review* 56, no. 1 (2005): 1–63.

Lepore, Jill. "The Cobweb: Can the Internet Be Archived?" *New Yorker*, January 26, 2015. Accessed August 1, 2015. http://www.newyorker.com/magazine/2015/01/26/cobweb.

Levush, Ruth. *Israel: Reproduction and Abortion: Law and Policy*. Legal Report. Law Library of Congress. February 2012.

Livingston, Julie. *Debility and Moral Imagination in Botswana*. Bloomington: Indiana University Press, 2005.

———. "Insights from an African History of Disability." *Radical History Review* 94 (2006): 111–26.

Livingston, Julie, and Jasbir Puar. "Introduction: Interspecies." *Social Text* 29, no. 1 106 (2011): 3–14.

Lopez, Patricia J., Lisa Bhungalia, and Léonie S. Newhouse. "Geographies of Humanitarian Violence." *Environment and Planning A* 47, no. 11 (2015): 2232–39.

Lubin, Alex. "The Disappearing Frontiers of US Homeland Security: Mapping the Transit of Security across the US and Israel." *Jadaliyya*, February 26, 2013.

———. "Peace Dividends." *Social Text Online—Periscope*, June 5, 2014.

———. " 'We Are All Israelis': The Politics of Colonial Comparisons." *South Atlantic Quarterly* 107, no. 4 (2008): 671–90.

Lubin, Alex, Les W. Field, Melanie K. Yazzie, and Jakob Schiller. "The Israel/Palestine Field School Decoloniality and the Geopolitics of Knowledge." *Social Text* 31, no. 4 117 (2013): 79–97.

Lukes, Heather N. "Causalgia of the Heart: Phantom Limb Syndrome, Disability and Queer Feeling." *Women and Performance: A Journal of Feminist Theory* 19, no. 2 (2009): 227–46.

———. "The Sovereignty of Subtraction: Hypo/Hyperhabilitation and the Cultural Politics of Amputation in America." *Social Text* 33, no. 2 123 (2015): 1–27.

Lukin, Josh. "Disability and Blackness." In *The Disability Studies Reader*, 4th ed. edited by Lennard J. Davis, 308–16. New York: Routledge, 2013.

Macaulay, Thomas. "On the Civil Disabilities of the Jews." *Edinburgh Review* 104 (1831): 363–74.

Mackey, Hollie J. "Educational Administration in Indian Country: The Peculiar Position of Indigenous Languages, Tribal Self-Determination, and Federal Policy." *Advances in Educational Administration* 24 (2015): 165–80.

Maikey, Haneen. "Sexual Liberation and Decolonization in Occupied Palestine." Talk presented at Cornell University, October 2013.

Manduca, P., A. Naim, and S. Signoriello. "Specific Association of Teratogen and Toxicant Metals in Hair of Newborns with Congenital Birth Defects or Developmentally Premature Birth in a Cohort of Couples with Documented Parental Exposure to Military Attacks: Observational Study at Al Shifa Hospital, Gaza, Palestine." *International Journal of Environmental Research and Public Health* 11, no. 5 (2014): 5208–23.

Mann, Camille. "Not Guilty Plea for Dharun Ravi, Suspected Tyler Clementi Harasser." CBS News, May 23, 2011. Accessed July 1, 2011. http://www.cbsnews.com/8301 -504083_162-20065341-504083.html.

Mansfield, Becky. "Abnormality, Race, and the New Epigenetic Biopolitics of Environmental Health." Dimensions of Political Ecology. Talk presented at Political Ecology conference, University of Kentucky, Lexington, May 8, 2013.

Margalit, Ruth. "Israel's African Asylum Seekers Go on Strike." *New Yorker*, January 8, 2014.

Markotic, Nicole, and Robert McRuer. "Leading with Your Head: On the Borders of Disability, Sexuality, and the Nation." In *Sex and Disability*, edited by Robert McRuer and Anna Mollow, 165–82. Durham, NC: Duke University Press, 2012.

Maroto, Michelle, and David Pettinicchio. "The Limitations of Disability Antidiscrimination Legislation: Policymaking and the Economic Well-Being of People with Disabilities." *Law and Policy* 36, no. 4 (2014): 370–407.

Martin, Roger H. "ABC's of Accommodation." *New York Times*, October 30, 2012.

Martinez, Edecio. "Nobody Saw Tyler Clementi Video, Say Lawyers." CBS News, November 1, 2010. Accessed February 1, 2011. http://www.cbsnews.com/news/tyler-clementi-suicide-no-one-saw-rutgers-sex-broadcast-say-lawyers/.

Marx, Karl. *Capital*. Vol. 1, *A Critique of Political Economy*. Translated by Ben Fowkes. London: Penguin, 1992.

———. "On the Jewish Question." In *The Marx-Engels Reader*, edited by Robert Tucker, 26–46. New York: Norton, 1978.

Mase, J., III "Hell Y'all Ain't Talmbout: An Epic Response to Trans Erasure." *Huffington Post*, August 28, 2015. Accessed September 1, 2015. http://www.huffingtonpost.com/j-mase-iii/hell-yall-aint-talmbout-a_b_8038996.html.

Massad, Joseph. *Desiring Arabs*. Chicago: University of Chicago Press, 2007.

———. "Jewish Suffering, Palestinian Suffering." *Al-Jazeera*, December 3, 2013.

Massad, Joseph, interviewed by Félix Boggio Éwanjé-Épée and Stella Magliani-Belkacem. "The Empire of Sexuality: An Interview with Joseph Massad." *Jadaliyya*, March 5, 2013. Accessed August 1, 2015. http://www.jadaliyya.com/pages/index/10461/the-empire-of-sexuality_an-interview-with-joseph-m.

Massumi, Brian. *Parables for the Virtual: Movement, Affect, Sensation*. Durham, NC: Duke University Press, 2002.

Massumi, Brian, interviewed by Joel McKim. "Of Microperception and Micropolitics: An Interview with Brian Massumi." *Inflections* 3 (2009): 1–20.

Maturana, Humberto, and Francisco Varela. *Autopoiesis and Cognition: The Realization of the Living*. Dordrecht: Reidel, 1979.

Mbembe, Achille. "Necropolitics." Translated by Libby Meintjes. *Public Culture* 15, no. 1 (2003): 11–40.

McCormack, Donna, and Suvi Salmenniemi. "The Biopolitics of Precarity and the Self." *European Journal of Cultural Studies* 19, no. 1 (2016): 3–15.

McCormick, Richard. "Project Civility." Rutgers Student Affairs website, 2010. Accessed February 1, 2011. http://projectcivility.rutgers.edu/president-mccormicks-words.

McFann, Hudson. "Violent Waste." 2014. Accessed February 1, 2015. http://www.geographiesofwaste.com/projects.html.

McGuire, Anne. "'Life Worth Defending': Biopolitical Frames of Terror in the War on Autism." In *Foucault and the Government of Disability*, edited by Shelley Tremain, 350–71. Ann Arbor: University of Michigan Press, 2015.

McIntyre, Jody. "From Isolation to Disability Union Leadership." *Electronic Intifada*, August 23, 2010. Accessed November 7, 2016. https://electronicintifada.net/content/isolation-disability-union-leadership/8994.

———. "Interview: Disabled Activist Continues Struggle in Bilin." *Electronic Intifada*, January 11, 2010. Accessed November 6, 2016. https://electronicintifada.net/content /interview-disabled-activist-continues-struggle-bilin/8617.

McKinley, Jessie. "Suicides Put Light on Pressures of Gay Teenagers." *New York Times*, October 3, 2010. Accessed February 1, 2011. http://www.nytimes.com/2010/10/04/us /04suicide.html.

McRuer, Robert. "American Studies Meets Disability Studies," Roundtable Presentation, American Studies Association, Toronto, 2015.

———. "As Good as It Gets: Queer Theory and Critical Disability." GLQ: *A Journal of Lesbian and Gay Studies* 9, nos. 1–2 (2003): 79–105

———. *Crip Theory: Cultural Signs of Queerness and Disability*. New York: NYU Press, 2006.

———. "Disability Nationalism in Crip Times." *Journal of Literary and Cultural Disability Studies* 4, no. 2 (2010): 163–78.

McRuer, Robert, and Anna Mollow, eds. *Sex and Disability*. Durham, NC: Duke University Press, 2012.

Meekosha, Helen. "Decolonising Disability: Thinking and Acting Globally." *Disability and Society* 26, no. 6 (2011): 667–82.

Metzl, Jonathan. *The Protest Psychosis: How Schizophrenia Became a Black Disease*. Boston: Beacon, 2009.

Metzl, Jonathan M., and Anna Kirkland, eds. *Against Health: How Health Became the New Morality*. New York: NYU Press, 2010.

Microsoft. "SenseCam." N.d. Accessed August 1, 2015. http://research.microsoft.com /en-us/um/cambridge/projects/sensecam/.

Mikdashi, Maya. "Gay Rights as Human Rights: Pinkwashing Homonationalism." *Jadaliyya*, August 9, 2012.

Million, Dian. *Therapeutic Nations: Healing in an Age of Indigenous Human Rights*. Tucson: University of Arizona Press, 2013.

Mingus, Mia. "Access Intimacy: The Missing Link." *Leaving Evidence*, May 5, 2011. Accessed August 1, 2015. https://leavingevidence.wordpress.com/2011/05/05/access -intimacy-the-missing-link/.

———. "Changing the Framework: Disability Justice, How Our Communities Can Move beyond Access to Wholeness." *Leaving Evidence*, February 12, 2011. Accessed August 1, 2015. https://leavingevidence.wordpress.com/2011/02/12/changing-the -framework-disability-justice/.

———. "Medical Industrial Complex Visual." *Leaving Evidence*, February 6, 2015. Accessed August 1, 2015. https://leavingevidence.wordpress.com/2015/02/06/medical -industrial-complex-visual/.

———. "Moving toward the Ugly: A Politic beyond Desirability." *Leaving Evidence*, August 22, 2011. Accessed August 1, 2012. https://leavingevidence.wordpress.com/2011 /08/22/moving-toward-the-ugly-a-politic-beyond-desirability/.

Minich, Julie A. "Life on Wheels: Disability, Democracy, and Political Inclusion in *Live Flesh* and *The Sea Inside*." *Journal of Literary and Cultural Disability Studies* 1 (2010): 17.

Mirkinson, Jack. "The American Atrocities We Refuse to See: Doctors Without Borders, Fumbling Officials and Our Blindness to Civilian Deaths." *Salon*, October 6, 2015.

Mitchell, David. Keynote Plenary for the Society for Disability Studies Conference, Temple University, June 12, 2010.

Mitchell, David, and Sharon Snyder. *The Biopolitics of Disability: Neoliberalism, Ablenationalism, and Peripheral Embodiment*. Ann Arbor: University of Michigan Press, 2015.

———. *Cultural Locations of Disability*. Chicago: University of Chicago Press, 2006.

———. "Disability as Multitude: Re-working Non-productive Labor Power." *Journal of Literary and Cultural Disability Studies* 4, no. 2 (2010): 179–93.

———. "Introduction: Disability Studies and the Double Bind of Representation." In *The Body and Physical Difference: Discourses of Disability*, edited by David Mitchell and Sharon Snyder, 1–34. Ann Arbor: University of Michigan Press, 1997.

———. *Narrative Prosthesis: Disability and the Dependencies of Discourse*. Ann Arbor: University of Michigan Press, 2000.

———. "Re-engaging the Body: Disability Studies and the Resistance to Embodiment." *Public Culture* 13, no. 3 (2001): 367–89.

Mittler, Peter. "The UN Convention on the Rights of Persons with Disabilities: Implementing a Paradigm Shift." *Journal of Policy and Practice in Intellectual Disabilities* 12, no. 2 (2015): 79–89.

Moore, Leroy. "Black, Gifted and Disabled Interview Series: Alexis Toliver." National Black Disability Coalition. Accessed November 7, 2016. http://blackdisability.org /content/black-gifted-disabled-interview-series-alexis-toliver.

Mor, Sagit. "Between Charity, Welfare, and Warfare: A Disability Legal Studies Analysis of Privilege and Neglect in Israeli Disability Policy." *Yale Journal of Law and the Humanities* 1 (2006): 63–76.

Morgensen, Scott L. "The Biopolitics of Settler Colonialism: Right Here, Right Now." *Settler Colonial Studies* 1, no. 1 (2011): 52–76.

———. *Spaces between Us: Queer Settler Colonialism and Indigenous Decolonization*. Minneapolis: University of Minnesota Press, 2011.

Moten, Fred. *In the Break: The Aesthetics of the Black Radical Tradition*. Minneapolis: University of Minnesota Press, 2003.

Movement for Black Lives. "A Vision for Black Lives: Policy Demands for Black Power, Freedom, and Justice." N.d. Accessed November 7, 2016. https://policy.m4bl.org/.

MTL Collective. *On This Land*, June 16, 2016. Accessed November 1, 2016. https:// onthislandfilm.wordpress.com/.

———. "The Slow, Sure Death of Palestine." *Creative Time Reports*, September 3, 2013. Accessed November 6, 2016. http://creativetimereports.org/2013/09/03/the-slow -sure-death-of-palestine/.

Mulvihill, Geof. "Dharun Ravi Will Not Be Deported, Immigration and Customs Enforcement Official Says." *Huffington Post*, June 18, 2012. Accessed August 1, 2012. http://www.huffingtonpost.com/2012/06/18/dharun-ravi-not-deported-ice_n _1606817.html.

———. "Tyler Clementi's Suicide Illustrates Internet Dangers." *Huffington Post*, October 1, 2010. Accessed February 1, 2011. http://www.huffingtonpost.com/2010/10/01 /tyler-clementis-suicide-i_n_746624.html.

Muñoz, José E. *Cruising Utopia: The Then and There of Queer Futurity*. New York: NYU Press, 2009.

Mussawir, Edward. *Jurisdiction in Deleuze: The Expression and Representation of Law*. New York: Routledge, 2011.

Mustakeem, Sowande M. *Slavery at Sea: Terror, Sex, and Sickness in the Middle Passage*. Urbana: University of Illinois Press, 2016.

Nahman, Michal Rachel. *Extractions: An Ethnography of Reproductive Tourism*. New York: Palgrave Macmillan, 2013.

Nakamura, Karen. "Trans/Japan, Trans/Disability." Lecture presented at the "Debilitating Queerness" conference, University of Maryland, April 5, 2013.

Nassar, Jamal R., and Roger Heacock, eds. *Intifada: Palestine at the Crossroads*. New York: Praeger, 1990.

National Center for Education Statistics. "Fast Facts: Students with Disabilities." 2015. Accessed April 21, 2017. https://nces.ed.gov/fastfacts/display.asp?id=64.

National Council on Disability. "Finding the Gaps: A Comparative Analysis of Disability Laws in the United States to the United Nations Convention on the Rights of Persons with Disabilities (CRPD)." 2008.

Negarestani, Reza. "Drafting the Inhuman: Conjectures on Capitalism and Organic Necrocracy." In *The Speculative Turn: Continental Materialism and Realism*, edited by Levi Bryant, Nick Srnicek, and Graham Harman, 182–201. Melbourne: re.press, 2011.

Nelson, Alondra. *The Social Life of DNA: Race, Reparations, and Reconciliation after the Genome*. Boston: Beacon, 2016.

Netanyahu, Benjamin. Address presented at the American Israel Public Affairs Committee Conference, Washington, DC, March 22, 2010.

Netanyahu, Benjamin, interview with Wolf Blitzer. "Netanyahu: Israel Seeks 'Sustainable Quiet' with Gaza." *CNN*, July 21, 2014. Accessed February 1, 2015. http://www.cnn.com/2014/07/20/world/meast/mideast-crisis-blitzer-netanyahu-interview/.

New Family. "Creating New Life from the Dead by Biological Will™." December 30, 2013.

Newsweek. "The Best Gay-Friendly Schools." September 12, 2010. Accessed July 1, 2011. http://education.newsweek.com/2010/09/12/the-best-gay-friendly-schools.all.html.

Nguyen, Xuan-Thuy. "Genealogies of Disability in Global Governance: A Foucauldian Critique of Disability and Development." *Foucault Studies* 19 (2015): 67–83.

Nidhal. "The Burden of Queer Palestine." *Aswat Group*, July 9, 2013. Accessed July 9, 2013. http://www.aswatgroup.org/en/article/burden-queer-palestine.

Nigianni, Chrysanthi, and Merl Storr. "Introduction." In *Deleuze and Queer Theory*, edited by Chrysanthi Nigianni and Merl Storr, 1–10. Edinburgh: Edinburgh University Press, 2009.

Noble, Bobby Jean. "Our Bodies Are Not Ourselves: Tranny Guys and the Racialized Class Politics of Incoherence." In *Transgender Studies Reader 2*, edited by Susan Stryker and Aren Z. Aizura, 248–58. New York: Routledge, 2013.

Nordau, Max Simon. *Degeneration*. 7th ed. New York: D. Appleton and Company, 1895.

———. "Stenographisches Protokoll der Verhandlungen des II." Zionisten-Congresses (Basel, August 28–31, 1898), 14–27. Vienna: Verlag des Vereines "Erez Israel," 1898.

Nordic Consulting Group. *Mainstreaming Disability in the New Development Paradigm: Evaluation of Norwegian Support to Promote the Rights of Persons with Disabilities: The Palestinian Territory Country Report*. Oslo: Norwegian Agency for Development Cooperation, 2012. Accessed April 21, 2017. https://www.norad.no/om -bistand/publikasjon/2012/mainstreaming-disability-in-the-new-development -paradigm-evaluation-of-norwegian-support-to-promote-the-rights-of-persons-with -disabilities/.

Nordland, Rod. "Maimed Defending Afghanistan, Then Neglected." *New York Times*, May 2, 2015.

Nyong'o, Tavia. "School Daze." *Bully Bloggers*, September 30, 2010. Accessed February 1, 2011. http://bullybloggers.wordpress.com/2010/09/30/school-daze/.

O'Brien, Michelle. "Tracing This Body: Transsexuality, Pharmaceuticals, and Capitalism." In *Transgender Studies Reader 2*, edited by Susan Stryker and Aren Z. Aizura, 56–65. New York: Routledge, 2013.

O'Brien, Ruth. *Crippled Justice: The History of Modern Disability Policy in the Workplace*. Chicago: University of Chicago Press, 2001.

———. "A Subversive Act: The Americans with Disabilities Act, Foucault, and an Alternative Ethic of Care at the Global Workplace." *Texas Journal of Women and the Law* 1 (2003): 55–89.

Occupied Palestine. "On 19th International Day of Disabled Persons, Conditions of Palestinian Disabled Persons Continue to Deteriorate." November 30, 2011. Accessed April 21, 2017. https://occupiedpalestine.wordpress.com/2011/11/30/on-19th -international-day-of-disabled-persons-conditions-of-palestinian-disabled-persons -continue-to-deteriorate/.

Ophir, Adi, Michal Givoni, and Sārī Ḥanafī. *The Power of Inclusive Exclusion: Anatomy of Israeli Rule in the Occupied Palestinian Territories*. New York: Zone Books, 2009.

Oren, Michael. "Israel Must Be Permitted to Crush Hamas." *Washington Post*, July 24, 2014. Accessed February 1, 2015. http://www.washingtonpost.com/opinions /michael-oren-israel-must-be-permitted-to-crush-hamas/2014/07/24/bd9967fc -1350-11e4-9285-4243a40ddc97_story.html.

Ostrander, Noam, and Eynat Shevil. "The Social Value of Death versus Disability in Israel: Why It Is Better to Die for Your Country." *Disability Studies Quarterly* 27, no. 4 (2007).

Overboe, James. "Affirming an Impersonal Life: A Different Register for Disability Studies." *Journal of Literary and Cultural Disability Studies* 3, no. 3 (2009): 241–56.

Padilla, Mark, et al., eds. *Love and Globalization: Transformations of Intimacy in the Contemporary World*. Nashville: Vanderbilt University Press, 2007.

Palestinian Central Bureau of Statistics. "On the 65th Anniversary of the Palestinian Nakba." May 14, 2013. Accessed February 1, 2015. http://www.pcbs.gov.ps/site/512 /default.aspx?tabID=512&lang=en&ItemID=788&mid=3171&wversion=Staging.

Palestinian Central Bureau of Statistics and Ministry of Social Affairs. Press conference report, Disability Survey, 2011. Ramallah, Palestine. Accessed April 21, 2017. http:// www.pcbs.gov.ps/portals/_pcbs/pressrelease/disability_e2011.pdf.

Panagia, Davide. *The Political Life of Sensation*. Durham, NC: Duke University Press, 2009.

Parisi, Luciana. *Abstract Sex: Philosophy, Biotechnology and the Mutations of Desire*. London: Bloomsbury Academic, 2004.

———. *Contagious Architecture: Computation, Aesthetics, and Space*. Cambridge, MA: MIT Press, 2013.

Patel, Geeta. "Risky Subjects: Insurance, Sexuality, and Capital." *Social Text* 24, no. 4 89 (2006): 25–65.

Pedersen, Helena. "Release the Moths: Critical Animal Studies and the Posthumanist Impulse." *Culture, Theory and Critique* 52, no. 1 (2011): 65–81.

Peoples Power Assemblies. "Fight Police Terror." N.d. Accessed November 5, 2016. http://peoplespowerassemblies.org/fight-police-terror/.

Pep, Steve. "The Tragedy of Gay Teen Suicide—A Roundup." *Towleroad*, October 3, 2010. Accessed February 1, 2011. http://www.towleroad.com/2010/10/suicide.html.

Peterson, Latoya. "Where Is the Proof That It Gets Better? Queer POC and the Solidarity Gap." *Racialicious*, October 19, 2010. Accessed February 1, 2011. http://www.racialicious.com/2010/10/19/where-is-the-proof-that-it-gets-better-queer-poc-and-the-solidarity-gap/.

Phillips, Adam. *On Flirtation*. Cambridge, MA: Harvard University Press, 1996.

Pilkington, Ed. "Tyler Clementi, Student Outed as Gay on the Internet, Jumps to His Death." *Guardian*, September 30, 2010. Accessed February 1, 2011. http://www.guardian.co.uk/world/2010/sep/30/tyler-clementi-gay-student-suicide.

Poon-McBrayer, Kim Fong. "The Evolution from Integration to Inclusion: The Hong Kong Tale." *International Journal of Inclusive Education* 18, no. 10 (2014): 1004–13.

Povinelli, Elizabeth. Lecture. American University of Beirut, March 14, 2013.

Preciado, Beatriz [Paul]. "The Pharmaco-pornographic Regime: Sex, Gender, and Subjectivity in the Age of Punk Capitalism." *Transgender Studies Reader 2*, edited by Susan Stryker and Aren Z. Aizura, 266–77. New York: Routledge, 2013.

Prince-Gibson, Eeta. "Ultra-Orthodox Request Gender-Segregated University Study." *Al-Monitor*, April 11, 2014.

PR Newswire. "U.S. Census Bureau Facts for Features: 25th Anniversary of Americans with Disabilities Act: July 26." July 22, 2015.

Puar, Jasbir K. "The Center Cannot Hold: The Flourishing of Queer Anti-occupation Activism." *Huffington Post*, October 3, 2011. Accessed March 12, 2017. http://www.huffingtonpost.com/jasbir-k-puar/the-center-cannot-hold-th_b_991572.html.

———. "Citation and Censorship: The Politics of Talking about the Sexual Politics of Israel." *Feminist Legal Studies* 19 (2011): 133–42.

———. "The Cost of Getting Better: Suicide, Sensation, Switchpoints." GLQ: *Journal of Lesbian and Gay Studies* 18, no. 1 (2011): 149–58.

———. "Ecologies of Sex, Sensation, and Slow Death." *Social Text Online—Periscope*, November 27, 2010. Accessed February 1, 2011. http://socialtextjournal.org/periscope_article/ecologies_of_sex_sensation_and_slow_death/.

———. *Terrorist Assemblages: Homonationalism in Queer Times*. Durham, NC: Duke University Press, 2007.

Puar, Jasbir K., interviewed by Lewis West. "Jasbir Puar: Regimes of Surveillance." *Cosmologics: Magazine of Science, Religion, and Culture*, December 14, 2014. Accessed August 1, 2015. http://cosmologicsmagazine.com/jasbir-puar-regimes-of-surveillance/.

Pugliese, Joseph. "Forensic Ecologies of Occupied Zones and Geographies of Dispossession: Gaza and Occupied East Jerusalem." *Borderlands e-journal* 14, no. 1 (2015): 1–37.

Qandil, Ala. "Gaza Faces Imminent Water Crisis." *Al Jazeera*, July 17, 2014. Accessed February 1, 2015. http://www.aljazeera.com/news/middleeast/2014/07/gaza-faces -imminent-water-crisis-201471755035576420.html.

Qato, Dima. "The Politics of Deteriorating Health: The Case of Palestine." *International Journal of Health Services* 34, no. 2 (2004): 341–64.

Qlalweh, Kahled, Mohammed Duraidi, and Henrik Bronnum-Hansen. "Health Expectancy in the Occupied Palestinian Territory: Estimates from the Gaza Strip and the West Bank: Based on Surveys from 2006 to 2010." *BMJ Open* 2, no. 6 (2012): 1–6.

Qouta, Samir, and Eyad El Sarraj. "Prevalence of PTSD among Palestinian Children in Gaza Strip." *Arabpsynet Journal* 2 (2004): 8–13.

Queering the Air. "Rutgers Feels the Heat over Clementi Suicide." Press release, October 18, 2010. Accessed July 1, 2011. http://campuspride.besstaging.com/map/release -rutgers-feels-the-heat-over-clementi-suicide/.

Quiet Riot Girl. "It Gets Better: What Does? For Whom?" Blog entry. October 10, 2010. Accessed February 1, 2011. http://quietgirlriot.wordpress.com/2010/10/06/it -gets-better-what-does-for-whom/.

Rada, Ester. "SDM Presents: Israeli-Ethiopian Artist Ester Rada (Benefiting the Regent Park School of Music)." Online video clip. *Size Doesn't Matter*. http://www .sizedoesntmatter.com/media/videos/.

Rai, Amit. "Race Racing: Four Theses on Race and Intensity." *WSQ: Women's Studies Quarterly* 40, nos. 1–2 (2012): 64–75.

———. *Untimely Bollywood: Globalization and India's New Media Assemblage*. Durham, NC: Duke University Press, 2009.

Ralph, Michael. "'Flirt[ing] with Death' but 'Still Alive': The Sexual Dimension of Surplus Time in Hip Hop Fantasy." *Cultural Dynamics* 18, no. 1 (2006): 61–88.

Rankine, Claudia. *Don't Let Me Be Lonely: An American Lyric*. Saint Paul, MN: Graywolf Press, 2004.

Rapp, Rayna, and Faye D. Ginsburg. "Enabling Disability: Rewriting Kinship, Reimagining Citizenship." *Public Culture* 3 (2001): 533–56.

Ravitsky, Vardit. "Posthumous Reproduction Guidelines in Israel." *Hastings Center Report* 34, no. 2 (2004): 6–7.

Raz, Aviad. "'Important to Test, Important to Support': Attitudes toward Disability Rights and Prenatal Diagnosis among Leaders of Support Groups for Genetic Disorders in Israel." *Social Science and Medicine* 59, no. 9 (2004): 1857–66.

Reddy, Raj, and Gloriana St. Clair. "The Million Book Digital Library Project." Carnegie Mellon University, December 1, 2001. Accessed February 1, 2011. http://www.rr.cs .cmu.edu/mbdl.htm.

Reinhart, Tanya. *Israel/Palestine: How to End the War of 1948*. New York: Seven Stories, 2002.

Rembis, Michael. "The New Asylums: Madness and Mass Incarceration in the Neoliberal Era." In *Disability Incarcerated: Imprisonment and Disability in the United States and Canada*, edited by Liat Ben-Moshe, Chris Chapman, and Allison C. Carey, 139–59. New York: Palgrave Macmillan, 2014.

Reuters. "Israeli Company Reinvents the Wheel." April 23, 2014. Accessed November 5, 2016. http://www.reuters.com/video/2014/04/23/israeli-company-reinvents-the -wheel?videoId=312698474.

Rimon-Greenspan, Hila. "Disability Politics in Israel: Civil Society, Advocacy, and Contentious Politics." *Disability Studies Quarterly* 27, no. 4 (2007).

Rimon-Zarfaty, Nitzan, and Aviad E. Raz. "Abortion Committees as Agents of Eugenics: Medical and Public Views on Selective Abortion Following Mild or Likely Fetal Pathology." In *Kin, Gene, Community: Reproductive Technologies among Jewish Israelis*, edited by Daphna Birenbaum-Carmeli and Yoram S. Carmeli, 202–25. New York: Berghahn Books, 2009.

Roache, Colleen. "Savage Relays LGBT Survival Stories." *Daily Targum*, October 19, 2010. Accessed February 1, 2011. http://www.dailytargum.com/news/savage-relays -lgbt-survival-stories-1.2373623.

Roberts, Dorothy. *Fatal Invention: How Science, Politics, and Big Business Re-create Race in the Twenty-First Century*. New York: New Press, 2011.

Rose, Nikolas. "Biopolitics in an Age of Biological Control." Lecture presented at New York University, October 15, 2009.

———. "Neurochemical Selves." *Society* 3 (2003): 46–59.

———. *The Politics of Life Itself: Biomedicine, Power, and Subjectivity in the Twenty-First Century*. Princeton, NJ: Princeton University Press, 2007.

Rosenberg, Jord/ana. Lecture presented at "Reflection on Dispossession" symposium, School of Oriental and African Studies, University of London, October 24, 2014.

———. "The Molecularization of Sexuality: On Some Primitivisms of the Present." *Theory and Event* 17, no. 2 (2014): 1–19.

Rosenberg, Jord/ana, and Brit Rusert. "Framing Finance: Rebellion, Dispossession, and the Geopolitics of Enclosure in Samuel Delany's *Nevèrÿon* Series." *Radical History Review* 118 (2014): 64–92.

Rosenblum, Irit. "The Biological Will: A New Paradigm in ART?" In *17th World Congress on Controversies in Obstetrics Gynecology and Infertility*, edited by Z. Ben-Rafael, 89–95. Milan: Monduzzi Editoriale, 2013.

———. "Respect the Dead by Creating New Life." *Haaretz*, April 23, 2012.

Roughgarden, Joan. *Evolution's Rainbow: Diversity, Gender, and Sexuality in Nature and People*. Berkeley: University of California Press, 2004.

Roy, Sandip. "Dharun Ravi's Biggest Liability: He Was Indian." *New America Media*, March 17, 2012. Accessed August 1, 2012. http://newamericamedia.org/2012/03 /dharun-ravis-biggest-liability-he-was-indian.php.

Rubenfeld, Jed. "The Riddle of Rape-by-Deception and the Myth of Sexual Autonomy." *Yale Law Journal* 6 (2012): 1372–669.

Russell, Marta, and Ravi Malhotra. "Capitalism and Disability." *Socialist Register* 38 (2002): 211–28.

Rutgers Student Affairs. "Project Civility." Website, 2010. Accessed February 1, 2011. http://projectcivility.rutgers.edu/about-project-civility.

Said, Edward W. *The Question of Palestine*. New York: Times Books, 1979.

Said, Hashem, and Ehab Zahriyeh. "Gaza's Kids Affected Psychologically, Physically by Lifetime of Violence." *Al Jazeera*, July 31, 2014. Accessed February 1, 2015. http://america.aljazeera.com/articles/2014/8/1/health-gaza-children.html.

Salah, Trish. "Notes on the Subaltern." TSQ: *Transgender Studies Quarterly* 1, nos. 1–2 (2014): 297–305.

Salaita, Steven. *Israel's Dead Soul*. Philadelphia: Temple University Press, 2011.

Salamanca, Omar Jabary. "Unplug and Play: Manufacturing Collapse in Gaza." *Human Geography* 4, no. 1 (2011): 22–37.

Saldanha, Arun. "Reontologizing Race: The Machinic Geography of Phenotype." *Environment and Planning: Society and Space* 24, no. 1 (2006): 9–24.

Salem, Moura Odeh. "Stigma and the Origin of Disability: The Case of the Palestinians." Master's thesis, University of Manchester, 1990.

Savage, Dan, and Terry Miller, eds. *It Gets Better: Coming Out, Overcoming Bullying, and Creating a Life Worth Living*. New York: Dutton, 2011.

Schmidt, Charles W. "Beyond Malnutrition." *Environmental Health Perspectives* 122, no. 11 (2014): A298–A303.

Schulman, Joy, and Meizhu Lui. "Dialogue with Barbara Ehrenreich—Connecting White Privilege and White Death." *Freedom Road Socialist Organization*, January 5, 2016.

Schulman, Sarah. *Israel/Palestine and the Queer International*. Durham, NC: Duke University Press, 2012.

Schulze, Marianne. "Understanding the UN Convention on the Rights of Persons with Disabilities." *Handicap International*, July 2010. Accessed February 1, 2015. http://www.hiproweb.org/uploads/tx_hidrtdocs/HICRPDManual2010.pdf.

Schweik, Susan. "Lomax's Matrix: Disability, Solidarity, and the Black Power of 504." In *Foundations of Disability Studies*, edited by Matthew Wappet and Katrina Arendt, 105–23. New York: Palgrave Macmillan, 2013.

———. *The Ugly Laws: Disability in Public*. New York: NYU Press, 2009.

Sedgwick, Eve Kosofsky. *Touching Feeling: Affect, Pedagogy, Performativity*. Durham, NC: Duke University Press, 2003.

Seikaly, Sherene. "Counting Calories and Making Lemonade in Gaza." *Jadaliyaa*, November 12, 2012. Accessed February 1, 2015. http://www.jadaliyya.com/pages/index/8339/counting-calories-and-making-lemonade-in-gaza.

———. *Men of Capital: Scarcity and Economy in Mandate Palestine*. Stanford, CA: Stanford University Press, 2016.

Seikaly, Sherene, and Max Ajl. "Of Europe: Zionism and the Jewish Other." In *Europe after Derrida: Crisis and Potentiality*, edited by Agnes Czajka and Bora Isyar, 120–33. Edinburgh: Edinburgh University Press, 2014.

Sen, Rinku. "Dharun Ravi, Tyler Clementi and the Hard Work of Truly Stopping Bullies." *Colorlines*, March 21, 2012. Accessed August 1, 2012. http://www.colorlines.com/articles/dharun-ravi-tyler-clementi-and-hard-work-truly-stopping-bullies.

Sexton, Jared. "Ante-anti-blackness: Afterthoughts." *Lateral: Journal of the Cultural Studies Association* 1.

———. "Unbearable Blackness." *Cultural Critique* 90 (2015): 159–78.

Shah, Nayan. *Contagious Divides: Epidemics and Race in San Francisco's Chinatown.* Berkeley: University of California Press, 2011.

Shakespeare, Tom. "The Social Model of Disability." In *The Disability Studies Reader*, 2nd ed., edited by Lennard J. Davis, 197–205. New York: Routledge, 2006.

Shakra, Natalie Abou. "No Exit but Suicide in Gaza." *Ghazzawiyya* (blog), July 11, 2013. Accessed November 6, 2016. http://gaza08.blogspot.com/2013/07/no-exit-but -suicide-in-gaza.html.

Shalhoub-Kevorkian, Nadera. "Criminality in Spaces of Death: The Palestinian Case Study." *British Journal of Criminology* 54, no. 1 (2014): 38–52.

———. "Palestinian Children as Tools for 'Legalized' State Violence." *Borderlands* 13, no. 1 (2014). Accessed April 21, 2017. http://www.borderlands.net.au/Vol13No1 _2014/shalhoub-kevorkian_children.htm.

———. *Security Theology, Surveillance and the Politics of Fear.* Cambridge: Cambridge University Press, 2015.

Shamah, David. "Advanced Prosthetic Knees Will Turn Disabled IDF Vets into 'Bionic Men.'" *Times of Israel*, July 11, 2012. Accessed November 6, 2016. http://www .timesofisrael.com/advanced-prosthetic-knees-turn-disabled-idf-vets-into-bionic-men/.

Shapiro, Joseph P. *No Pity: People with Disabilities Forging a New Civil Rights Movement.* New York: Times Books, 1993.

Shender, Michelle. "Claims by Non-citizens under the Americans with Disabilities Act: Proper Extraterritorial Application in *Torrico v. International Business Machines*." *Pace International Law Review* 1 (2005): 131–59.

Sherwood, Harriet. "Israel Using Flechette Shells in Gaza." *Guardian*, July 20, 2014. Accessed February 1, 2015. https://www.theguardian.com/world/2014/jul/20/israel -using-flechette-shells-in-gaza.

———. "UN Officials Accused of Bowing to Israeli Pressure over Children's Rights List." *Guardian*, March 17, 2015. Accessed March 28, 2015. http://www.theguardian.com /world/2015/mar/17/un-officials-accused-buckling-israeli-pressure-childrens-rights -list.

Sherwood, Harriet, and Matthew Kalman. "Stephen Hawking Joins Academic Boycott of Israel." *Guardian*, May 7, 2013. Accessed March 30, 2017. https://www.theguardian .com/world/2013/may/08/stephen-hawking-israel-academic-boycott.

Shildrick, Margrit. "Prosthetic Performativity: Deleuzian Connections and Queer Corporealities." In *Deleuze and Queer Theory*, edited by Chrysanthi Nigianni and Merl Storr, 115–33. Edinburgh: Edinburgh University Press, 2009.

Shohat, Ella. "Rupture and Return: Zionist Discourse and the Study of Arab Jews." *Social Text* 21, no. 2 75 (2003): 49–74.

Siegel-Itzkovich, Judy. "Israel Allows Removal of Sperm from Dead Men at Wives' Request." *British Medical Journal* 327, no. 7425 (2003): 1187.

Sinai, Ruth. "The Economic Situation of People with Disabilities in Israel: The Most Difficult in the Western World." *Haaretz*, December 3, 2007.

Singal, Nidhi. "Introduction." In *Disability, Poverty and Education*, edited by Nidhi Singal, 1–6. New York: Routledge, 2013.

Siperstein, Gary N., Miriam Heyman, and Jeffrey E. Stokes. "Pathways to Employment: A National Survey of Adults with Intellectual Disabilities." *Journal of Vocational Rehabilitation* 41, no. 3 (2014): 165–78.

Siskind, Lawrence. "Stephen Hawking, BDS, and Why Geniuses Can Be Dumb." *Algemeiner*, February 19, 2015.

Size Doesn't Matter. "Videos." N.d. Accessed March 12, 2017. http://www .sizedoesntmatter.com/media/videos/.

Skaik, S., Nafiz Abu-Shaban, Nasser Abu-Shaban, Mario Barbieri, Maurizio Barbieri, Umberto Giani, and Paola Manduca. "Metals Detected by ICP/MS in Wound Tissue of War Injuries without Fragments in Gaza." *BMC International Health and Human Rights* 10 (2010). Accessed April 21, 2017. https://bmcinthealthhumrights .biomedcentral.com/articles/10.1186/1472-698X-10-17.

Slack, Donovan. "Biden Says 'Transgender Discrimination Civil Rights Issue of Our Time.'" *Politico*, October 30, 2012. Accessed April 21, 2017. http://www.politico.com /blogs/politico44/2012/10/biden-says-transgender-discrimination-civil-rights-issue -of-our-time-147761.

Smith, Andrea. "Queer Theory and Native Studies: The Heteronormativity of Settler Colonialism." *GLQ: A Journal of Lesbian and Gay Studies* 16, nos. 1–2 (2010): 42–68.

Smith, Marquard. "The Vulnerable Articulate: James Gillingham, Aimee Mullins, and Matther Barney." In *The Disability Studies Reader*, 2nd ed., edited by Lennard J. Davis, 309–21. New York: Routledge, 2006.

Smith, S. E. "Joe Biden Calls Transgender Discrimination 'the Civil Rights Issue of Our Time.'" *xo Jane*, October 31, 2012. Accessed November 1, 2012. www.xojane.com /issues/joe-biden-calls-transgender-discrimination-the-civil-rights-issue-of-our-time.

Snediker, Michael. *Queer Optimism: Lyric Personhood and Other Felicitous Persuasions*. Minneapolis: University of Minnesota Press, 2008.

Snyder, Sharon L., and David T. Mitchell. "Ablenationalism and the Geo-politics of Disability." *Journal of Literary and Cultural Disability Studies* 4, no. 2 (2010): 113–25.

Solomon, Alisa. "Viva La Diva Citizenship: Post-Zionism and Gay Rights." In *Queer Theory and the Jewish Question*, edited by Daniel Boyarin, Daniel Itzkovitz, and Ann Pellegrini, 149–65. New York: Columbia University Press, 2003.

Somerville, Siobhan B. "Queer Loving." *GLQ: A Journal of Lesbian and Gay Studies* 11, no. 3 (2005): 335–70.

Sommer, Allison Kaplan. "Offended Gay Israelis Blast Apologetic Education Minister: We Are Family!" *Haaretz*, June 29, 2014.

Spade, Dean. "Mutilating Gender." In *Transgender Studies Reader*, edited by Susan Stryker and Stephen Whittle, 315–32. New York: Routledge, 2006.

———. "Resisting Medicine, Re/Modeling Gender." *Berkeley Women's Law Journal* 18, no. 1 (2003): 14–37.

Spillers, Hortense J. "Mama's Baby, Papa's Maybe: An American Grammar Book." *Diacritics* 17, no. 2 (1987): 64–81.

Spivak, Gayatri. "Can the Subaltern Speak?" In *Marxism and the Interpretation of Culture*, edited by Cary Nelson and Larry Grossberg, 271–313. Basingstoke: Macmillan Education, 1988.

———. "Scattered Speculations on the Question of Value." *Diacritics* 15, no. 4 (1985): 73–93.

Star-Ledger Staff. "Dharun Ravi Sentencing: Impact Statements from Ravi's Parents." *Star-Ledger*, May 21, 2012. Accessed August 1, 2012. http://www.nj.com/news/index .ssf/2012/05/dharun_ravi_sentencing_impact.htm.

———. "Live Blog: Dharun Ravi Sentenced to 30 Days in Jail." *Star-Ledger*, May 21, 2012. Accessed July 1, 2012. http://www.nj.com/news/index.ssf/2012/05/dharun_ravi _sentenced_for_bias.htm.

———. "Molly Wei to Testify against Tyler Clementi's Roommate Dharun Ravi as Part of Plea Deal." *Star-Ledger*, May 7, 2011. Accessed July 1, 2011. http://www.nj.com /news/index.ssf/2011/05/molly_wei_defendant_in_tyler_c_1.html.

Steinmetz, Katy. "The Transgender Tipping Point." *Time*, May 29, 2014.

Stevens, Bethany. "Interrogating Transability: A Catalyst to View Disability as Body Art." *Disability Studies Quarterly* 31, no. 4 (2011). Accessed October 7, 2013. http://dsq -sds.org/article/view/1705/1755.

Stevenson, Lisa. "The Psychic Life of Biopolitics: Survival, Cooperation, and Inuit Community." *American Ethnologist* 39, no. 3 (2012): 592–613.

Stewart, Jean, and Marta Russell. "Disablement, Prison, and Historical Segregation." *Monthly Review* 53, no. 3 (2001): 61–75.

Stewart, Kathleen. *Ordinary Affects*. Durham, NC: Duke University Press, 2007.

Stone, Deborah. *The Disabled State*. Philadelphia: Temple University Press, 1984.

Strangio, Chase, interviewed by Amy Goodman. "'A State of Emergency': At Least 17 Transgender Women Have Been Murdered This Year." *Democracy Now*, August 18, 2015. Accessed September 1, 2015. http://www.democracynow.org/2015/8/18/a_state _of_emergency_at_least.

Strassburger, Zach. "Disability Law and the Disability Rights Movement for Transpeople." *Yale Journal of Law and Feminism* 24, no. 2 (2012): 101–37.

The Stream, Al Jazeera. "Black and Jewish in Israel." Online video broadcast, May 7, 2015.

———. "'Blackwashing' and the Israeli Lobby." Online video broadcast, March 5, 2012.

Strike Debt and Occupy Wall St. "Colonizer as Lender: Free Palestine, Occupy Wall Street, Strike Debt." *Tidal*, February 2013. Accessed November 7, 2016. http:// tidalmag.org/issue4/colonizer-as-lender/.

Stryker, Susan. "We Who Are Sexy: Christine Jorgensen's Transsexual Whiteness in the Postcolonial Philippines." *Social Semiotics* 19, no. 1 (2009): 79–91.

Stryker, Susan, and Aren Z. Aizura. "Introduction: Transgender Studies 2.0." In *Transgender Studies Reader 2*, edited by Susan Stryker and Aren Z. Aizura, 1–12. New York: Routledge, 2013.

Stryker, Susan, and Nikki Sullivan, "King's Member, Queen's Body." In *Somatechnics: Queering the Technologisation of Bodies*, edited by Nikki Sullivan and Samantha Murray, 49–63. Farnham, UK: Ashgate, 2009.

Suchman, Lucy, and Patricia Clough. "Action-at-a-Distance,' or the Ideology of Safe Living Design." New Sciences of Protection Conference: Second Plenary, July 16, 2008.

Sufian, Sandra M., and Mark LeVine. *Reapproaching Borders: New Perspectives on the Study of Israel-Palestine.* Lanham, MD: Rowman and Littlefield, 2007.

Sullivan, Nikki. "Dis-orienting Paraphilias? Disability Desire and the Question of (Bio) Ethics." *Bioethical Inquiry* 5 (2008): 183–92.

Sunder Rajan, Kaushik. *Biocapital: The Constitution of Postgenomic Life.* Durham, NC: Duke University Press, 2006.

Swick, Andrea. "Short Google Chrome 'It Gets Better' Commercial." YouTube, February 27, 2012. Accessed April 21, 2017. https://www.youtube.com/watch?v =a6LDc_Ro9YA.

Swirski, Shlomo. "The Price of Occupation: The Cost of the Occupation to Israeli Society." *Palestine-Israel Journal* 12, no. 1 (2005): 110–20.

Switzer, Jacqueline Vaughn. *Disabled Rights: American Disability Policy and the Fight for Equality.* Washington, DC: Georgetown University Press, 2003.

Talbot, Margaret. "Brain Gain: The Underground World of 'Neuroenhancing' Drugs." *New Yorker*, April 2009.

Tallbear, Kim. *Native American DNA: Tribal Belonging and the False Promise of Genetic Science.* Minneapolis: University of Minnesota Press, 2013.

Talley, Heather Laine. "Feminists We Love: Mia Mingus." *Feminist Wire*, November 22, 2013. Accessed August 1, 2015. http://www.thefeministwire.com/2013/11/feminists -we-love-mia-mingus/.

Talmon, Miri, and Yaron Peleg. "Discursive Identities in the (R)evolution of the New Israeli Queer Cinema." In *Israeli Cinema: Identities in Motion,* edited by Miri Talmon and Yaron Peleg, 313–25. Austin: University of Texas Press, 2011.

Tawil-Souri, Helga. "Colored Identity: The Politics and Materiality of ID Cards in Palestine/Israel." *Social Text* 29, no. 2 107 (2011): 67–97.

———. "Digital Occupation: Gaza's High-Tech Enclosure." *Journal of Palestine Studies* 41, no. 2 (2012): 27–43.

———. "Hacking Palestine: A Digital Occupation." *Al Jazeera*, November 9, 2011. Accessed February 1, 2015. http://www.aljazeera.com/indepth/opinion/2011/11 /201111715155960195 7.html.

———. "The Hi-Tech Enclosure of Gaza." Birzeit University Working Paper No. 2011/18 (ENG)—CPE Module. February 1, 2011.

Tawil-Souri, Helga, and Dina Matar, eds. *Gaza as Metaphor.* London: Hurst and Company, 2016.

Taylor, Adam. "In the Fight between Israel and Hamas, Gaza's Hospitals Are in the Middle." *Washington Post*, July 22, 2014. Accessed February 1, 2015. http://www .washingtonpost.com/blogs/worldviews/wp/2014/07/22/in-the-fight-between-israel -and-hamas-gazas-hospitals-are-in-the-middle/.

———. "Israel Hopes Phone Calls to Palestinians Will Save Lives. It Ends Up Looking Orwellian." *Washington Post*, July 17, 2014. Accessed February 1, 2015. http://www .washingtonpost.com/blogs/worldviews/wp/2014/07/17/israel-hopes-phone-calls-to -palestinians-will-save-lives-it-ends-up-looking-orwellian/.

Taylor, Sunaura. "Beasts of Burden: Disability Studies and Animal Rights." *Qui Parle: Critical Humanities and Social Sciences* 19, no. 2 (2011): 191–222.

Tedder, Ryan. "Dharun Ravi's Anonymous Friends Defend Him against Lifelong Reputation of Being a Scumbag." *Queerty*, September 30, 2010. Accessed February 1, 2011. http://www.queerty.com/dharun-ravis-anonymous-friends-defend-him-against-lifelong-reputation-of-being-a-scumbag-20100930/.

Teeman, Tim. "Tyler Clementi's Mom: How I Survived My Gay Son's Suicide." *Daily Beast*, November 4, 2015. Accessed November 6, 2016. http://www.thedailybeast.com/articles/2015/11/04/jane-clementi-i-almost-killed-myself-after-tyler-s-suicide-this-is-how-i-survived.html.

Terzi, Lorella. "The Social Model of Disability: A Philosophical Critique." *Journal of Applied Philosophy* 21, no. 2 (2004): 141–57.

Thabet, Abdelazis, Y. Abed, and P. Vostanis. "Effect of Trauma on the Mental Health of Palestinian Children and Mothers in the Gaza Strip." *Eastern Mediterranean Health Journal* 7, no. 3 (2001): 413–21.

Thabet, Abdelazis, Ahmad Abu Tawahina, Eyad El Sarraj, David Henely, Henrick Pelleick, and Panos Vostanis. "Comorbidity of Post Traumatic Stress Disorder, Attention Deficit with Hyperactivity, Conduct, and Oppositional Defiant Disorder in Palestinian Children Affected by War on Gaza." *Health* 5 (2013): 994–1002.

Thabet, Abdelazis, and Panos Vostanis. "Child Mental Health Problems in the Gaza Strip." *Israel Journal of Psychiatry and Related Sciences* 42, no. 2 (2005): 84–87.

———. "Impact of Political Violence and Trauma in Gaza on Children's Mental Health and Types of Interventions: A Review of Research Evidence in a Historical Context." *International Journal of Peace and Development Studies* 2, no. 8 (2011): 214–18.

Thacker, Eugene. *The Global Genome*. Cambridge, MA: MIT Press, 2006.

Times of Israel staff. "Cabinet Approves 'Surrogacy Equality' Bill for Gay Couples." *Times of Israel*, June 1, 2014.

Tough, Paul. "Can a Stressful Childhood Make You a Sick Adult?" *New Yorker*, March 21, 2011. Accessed July 1, 2011. http://www.newyorker.com/magazine/2011/03/21/the-poverty-clinic.

Trani, Jean-Francois, and Parul Bakhshi. "Understanding the Challenge Ahead: National Disability Survey in Afghanistan, 2005." Accessed March 12, 2017. http://www.cbm.org/article/downloads/82788/National_Disability_Survey_in_Afghanistan.pdf.

Tremain, Shelley. "Foucault, Governmentality, and Critical Disability Theory: An Introduction." In *Foucault and the Government of Disability*, edited by Shelley Tremain, 1–24. Ann Arbor: University of Michigan Press, 2005.

Triger, Zvi. "The Self-Defeating Nature of 'Modesty'-Based Gender Segregation." *Israel Studies* 18, no. 3 (2013): 19–28.

Turner, Bryan S. *Vulnerability and Human Rights*. University Park: Pennsylvania State University Press, 2006.

Turner, Ronald. "The Americans with Disabilities Act and the Workplace: A Study of the Supreme Court's Disabling Choices and Decisions." *New York University Annual Survey of American Law* 2 (2004): 379–452.

Twine, France Winddance. *Outsourcing the Womb: Race, Class, and Gestational Surrogacy in a Global Market*. New York: Routledge, 2011.

Tzfadia, Erez. "Abusing Multiculturalism: The Politics of Recognition and Land Allocation in Israel." *Environment and Planning D: Society and Space* 26, no. 6 (2008): 1115–30.

Umeasiegbu, Veronica I., Malachy Bishop, and Elias Mpofu. "The Conventional and Unconventional about Disability Conventions: A Reflective Analysis of United Nations Convention on the Rights of Persons with Disabilities." *Rehabilitation Research, Policy and Education* 27, no. 1 (2013): 58–72.

United Nations Assistance Mission in Afghanistan and United Nations Office of the High Commissioner for Human Rights. "Afghanistan: Annual Report 2014: Protection of Civilians in Armed Conflict." February 2015. Accessed March 25, 2016. https://unama.unmissions.org/sites/default/files/2014-annual-report-on-protection -of-civilians-final.pdf.

United Nations Office for the Coordination of Humanitarian Affairs. "Occupied Palestinian Territory: Gaza Emergency—Situation Report (as of 4 September 2014, 08:00 hrs)." September 4, 2014. Accessed February 1, 2015. http://www.ochaopt.org /documents/ocha_opt_sitrep_04_09_2014.pdf.

United Nations Relief and Work Agency for Palestine Refugees in the Near East. "Gaza in 2020: A Liveable Place?" August 27, 2012. Accessed February 1, 2015. http://www .unrwa.org/newsroom/press-releases/gaza-2020-liveable-place.

Unreported World. "Going for Gold in Gaza." Channel 4, UK, September 8, 2000.

Urquhart, Conal. "Chinese Workers in Israel Sign No-Sex Contract." *Guardian*, December 24, 2003.

Valentine, David. *Imagining Transgender: An Ethnography of a Category*. Durham, NC: Duke University Press, 2007.

Villareal, Daniel. "Dharun Ravi Pleads Not-Guilty to 15 Charges in Clementi Bullying Case." *Queerty*, May 23, 2011. Accessed July 1, 2011. http://www.queerty.com/dharun -ravi-pleads-not-guilty-to-15-charges-in-clementi-bullying-case-20110523/.

Vital, David. *The Origins of Zionism*. Oxford: Clarendon, 1975.

Vora, Kalindi. *Life Support Biocapital and the New History of Outsourced Labor*. Minneapolis: University of Minnesota Press, 2015.

Wailoo, Keith. *Pain: A Political History*. Baltimore: Johns Hopkins University Press, 2014.

"Waiting: The Politics of Time in Palestine." Special issue, *Middle East Report* 248, no. 38 (2008).

Waldby, Catherine, and Robert Mitchell. *Tissue Economies: Blood, Organs, and Cell Lines in Late Capitalism*. Durham, NC: Duke University Press, 2006.

Waldman, Ellen. "Cultural Priorities Revealed: The Development and Regulation of Assisted Reproduction in the United States and Israel." *Health Matrix* 16, no. 1 (2006): 65–106.

Walker, Kevin. "Comparing American Disability Laws to the Convention on the Rights of Persons with Disabilities with Respect to Postsecondary Education for Persons with Intellectual Disabilities." *Journal of International Human Rights* 12, no. 1 (2014): 115–31.

Walsh, Nicolas E., and Wendy S. Walsh. "Rehabilitation of Landmine Victims: The Ultimate Challenge." *Bulletin of the World Health Organization* 81, no. 9 (2003): 665–70.

Washington Blade. "National LGBT Community Reeling from 4th Teen Suicide in a Month." October 1, 2010. Accessed February 1, 2011. http://www.washingtonblade.com/2010/10/01/national-lgbt-community-reeling-from-4th-teen-suicide-in-a-month/.

Webley, Alec. "It Doesn't Get Better." *Daily Pennsylvanian*, November 28, 2010. Accessed February 1, 2011. http://www.thedp.com/article/2010/10/smart_alec_it_doesnt_get_better.

Weeks, Kathi. *The Problem with Work: Feminism, Marxism, Antiwork Politics, and Postwork Imaginaries*. Durham, NC: Duke University Press, 2011.

Weheliye, Alexander. *Habeas Viscus: Racializing Assemblages, Biopolitics, and Black Feminist Theories of the Human*. Durham, NC: Duke University Press, 2014.

Weil, Kari. *Thinking Animals: Why Animal Studies Now*. New York: Columbia University Press, 2012.

Weinstein, Jami. "Transgenres and the Plane of Gender Imperceptibility." In *Undutiful Daughters: New Directions in Feminist Thought and Practice*, edited by Henriette Gunkel, Chrysanthi Nigianni, and Fanny Söderbäck, 155–68. New York: Palgrave Macmillan, 2012.

Weir, Doug. "Conflict Rubble: A Ubiquitous and Under-Studied Toxic Remnant of War." *Toxic Remnants of War*, July 10, 2014. Accessed April 21, 2017. http://www.toxicremnantsofwar.info/conflict-rubble-a-ubiquitous-toxic-remnant-of-war/.

Weiss, Meira. *The Chosen Body: The Politics of the Body in Israeli Society*. Stanford, CA: Stanford University Press, 2002.

———. *Conditional Love: Parents' Attitudes toward Handicapped Children*. Westport, CT: Bergin and Garvey, 1994.

———. "Parents' Rejection of their Appearance-Impaired Newborns: Some Critical Observations Regarding the Social Myth of Bonding." *Marriage & Family Review* 27, no. 2/4 (1998): 191–209.

Weizman, Eyal. *Hollow Land: Israel's Architecture of Occupation*. London: Verso, 2007.

———. *The Least of All Possible Evils: Humanitarian Violence from Arendt to Gaza*. New York: Verso, 2012.

———. "The Politics of Verticality." *OpenDemocracy*, April 24, 2002. Accessed April 21, 2017. https://www.opendemocracy.net/ecology-politicsverticality/article_801.jsp.

Wessler, Seth Freed. "The Israel Lobby Finds a New Face: Black College Students." *Colorlines*, January 18, 2012. Accessed April 21, 2017. http://www.colorlines.com/articles/israel-lobby-finds-new-face-black-college-students.

West, Issac. "PISSAR's Critically Queer and Disabled Politics." *Communication and Critical/Cultural Studies* 7, no. 2 (2010): 156–75.

White, Rachel. "Neither Man nor Woman: Meet the Agender." *New York Magazine*, August 20, 2012. Accessed September 1, 2015. http://nymag.com/thecut/2012/08/neither-man-nor-woman-meet-the-agender.html.

Wiegman, Robyn, and Elizabeth A. Wilson. "Introduction: Antinormativity's Queer Conventions." *differences* 26, no. 1 (2015): 1–25.

Wilderson, Frank B., III. "Biko and the Problematic of Presence." *Biko Lives! Contesting the Legacies of Steve Biko*, edited by Andile Mngxitama, Amanda Alexander, and Nigel C. Gibson, 95–114. New York: Palgrave Macmillan, 2008.

———. *Red, White, and Black: Cinema and the Structure of U.S. Antagonisms.* Durham, NC: Duke University Press, 2010.

Wildness. Directed by Wu Tsang. 2012. DVD.

Wilkerson, Abby L. "Normate Sex and Its Discontents." In *Sex and Disability*, edited by Robert McRuer and Anna Mollow, 183–207. Durham, NC: Duke University Press, 2012.

Wilmut, Ian, Keith Campbell, and Colin Tudge. *The Second Creation: Dolly and the Age of Biological Control.* Cambridge, MA: Harvard University Press, 2001.

Withnall, Adam. "Israel-Gaza Conflict: Deadly Flechette Shells 'Used by Israeli Military in Gaza Strip.'" *Independent*, July 20, 2014. Accessed February 1, 2015. http://www.independent.co.uk/news/world/middle-east/israelgaza-conflict-israeli-military-using-flechette-rounds-in-gaza-strip-9617480.html.

Wolfe, Cary. "On Service Dogs: Learning from Temple Grandin, or, Animal Studies, Disability Studies, and Who Comes after the Subject." *New Formations* 64 (2008): 110–23.

Wolfe, Patrick. "Settler Colonialism and the Elimination of the Native." *Journal of Genocide Research* 8, no. 4 (2006): 387–409.

———. *Settler Colonialism and the Transformation of Anthropology: The Politics and Poetics of an Ethnographic Event.* London: Bloomsbury Academic, 1999.

Wool, Zoë H. *After War: The Weight of Life at Walter Reed.* Durham, NC: Duke University Press, 2015.

World Bank. "The World Bank Disability Overview." September 29, 2015. Accessed April 21, 2017. http://www.worldbank.org/en/topic/disability/overview.

Wynter, Sylvia. "Unsettling the Coloniality of Being/Power/Truth/Freedom: Towards the Human, after Man, Its Overrepresentation—An Argument." *New Centennial Review* 3, no. 3 (2003): 257–337.

Yeo, Rebecca. "Disability, Poverty and the New Development Agenda." London: Disability Knowledge and Research Programme, 2005.

Yiftachel, Oren. *Ethnocracy: Land and Identity Politics in Israel/Palestine.* Philadelphia: University of Pennsylvania Press, 2006.

Yosef, Raz. *Beyond Flesh: Queer Masculinities and Nationalism in Israeli Cinema.* New Brunswick, NJ: Rutgers University Press, 2004.

Young, Stella. "I'm Not Your Inspiration, Thank You Very Much." TED (video blog), April 2014. Accessed November 6, 2016. https://www.ted.com/talks/stella_young_i_m_not_your_inspiration_thank_you_very_much.

Yuval-Davis, Nira. "National Reproduction and 'the Demographic Race' in Israel." In *Woman-Nation-State*, edited by Floya Anthias and Nira Yuval Davis, 92–109. New York: Palgrave Macmillan, 1989.

Zaqout, Iyad. "Psychological Support in Palestine: Review of Palestinian Mental Health in Gaza Strip during Al-Aqsa Intifada." In *Advances in Disaster Mental Health and Psychological Support*, edited by J. Prewitt Diaz, 94–106. New Delhi: Voluntary Health Association of India Press, 2006.

Zimmer, Benjamin, and Charles E. Carson. "Among the New Words." *American Speech* 89, no. 4 (2014): 470–96.

Zola, Irving Kenneth. "Toward the Necessary Universalizing of a Disability Policy." *Milbank Quarterly* 83, no. 4 (2005): 1–27.

INDEX

Boycott, Divestment, and Sanction (BDS), 104

Brown, Michael, ix

campus pride, 2–3, 167n7

capacity, xv, 18–19, 50, 77–78, 81–83, 118; fiscal, 73; machine of, xviii, 13, 171n46; resistance as, 79

capitalism, 13–14, 18, 30, 56; biocapital, 82; debilitation and, xvi, xx, 64, 72–74, 81, 84, 153; disability and, 22, 45–46, 65, 76–79; disaster, 87, 145–46; racial capitalism, xviii, xxiii, 49

care, 78–80, 82, 84

Chatterjee, Partha, 98

Chen, Mel, 19, 26–27, 52, 54, 137; animacies, 20, 173n97; toxicity, 89–90, 149

Chow, Rey, 66, 69

citizenship: Israeli, 100; sexual citizens, 101

Clare, Eli, 42–43

Clementi, Tyler, 2–6, 165–66n2, 166n5, 167n8

Clough, Patricia, 21, 169–70n20

Colebrook, Claire, 187n103

collateral damage, 128, 141–43, 145, 147

colonialism, xix–xx, 79, 67, 92, 98–99, 118–19, 137–38. See also settler colonialism; woman question

control societies, 18, 22, 24, 49, 51, 57, 135; affect and, 2, 20–21; geopolitics of racial ontology and, 55, 119. See also biopolitics; disciplinary power; discipline and control; security

Cox, Laverne, 33, 174–75n2

crip nationalism, 14, 38–39, 70–71, 93, 107

Crosby, Christina, xv

Davis, Angela, xxii, 191–92n34

debilitation, xxi, 72–73, 78, 84, 124, 142; capitalism and, 87; definition of, xiii–xiv, xvi–xviii; displacement of, 92; global inequality and, 65–67, 69–70, 81; of infrastructure, 140; occupation

of Palestine and, 109, 128; as product of war, 89; settler colonialism and, xiii–xiv, 108–9

debility, x, 17, 20; biopolitics of, xviii, 71–72; capitalism and, 73–75, 87–88; control societies and, 22–22; definition of, xiv–xvii, 1–2, 19; imperialism and, 88–90; neoliberal exceptionalism and, 42–43; slow death and, 11–13, 15–16. See also capacity

debt, 73; debt trap, 121

DeLanda, Manuel, 19, 27

Deleuze, Gilles, 18, 21–24, 51–52, 64; becoming, 56, 187n96; Body without Organs, 184–85n74; disability and, 183–84n70

Dewachi, Omar, 91–92

Diagnostic and Statistical Manual of Mental Disorders, 25, 37, 177n22

disability, xv, 65–68, 70, 74–75, 124, 141–42; intersection with transgender, 42, 46; labor and, 77–79; medicine and, 83; narrative prosthesis and, 84–87; in Palestine, 157–61; physical vs. cognitive, 165n20; rights in Israel, 104–7; transability, 43–45. See also eugenics; Palestinians: restriction of mobility

disability justice, xiii, 15–16, 160; Black Lives Matter, xxiv; debilitation and, 67, 89

Disability Pride March, xi–xii

disability rights, x, xvii, xxi, 12, 15, 25, 42–43, 66; and black activism, xxii, xxiv; and colonialism, xix, 79, 89; in Israel, 104–9, 204n51

disability studies, 29–30, 41–24, 89, 109; coloniality, 66–67; Euro-American, xix–xx; in Israel, 204n56; whiteness, xix

disciplinary power, 20–24, 56–57, 120–23, 211n123. See also biopolitics; control societies; discipline and control

discipline and control, xx–xxi, 21, 23–24, 51, 119–20, 123. See also biopolitics;